AMERICAN IMPRESSIONISM

A NEW VISION
1880-1900

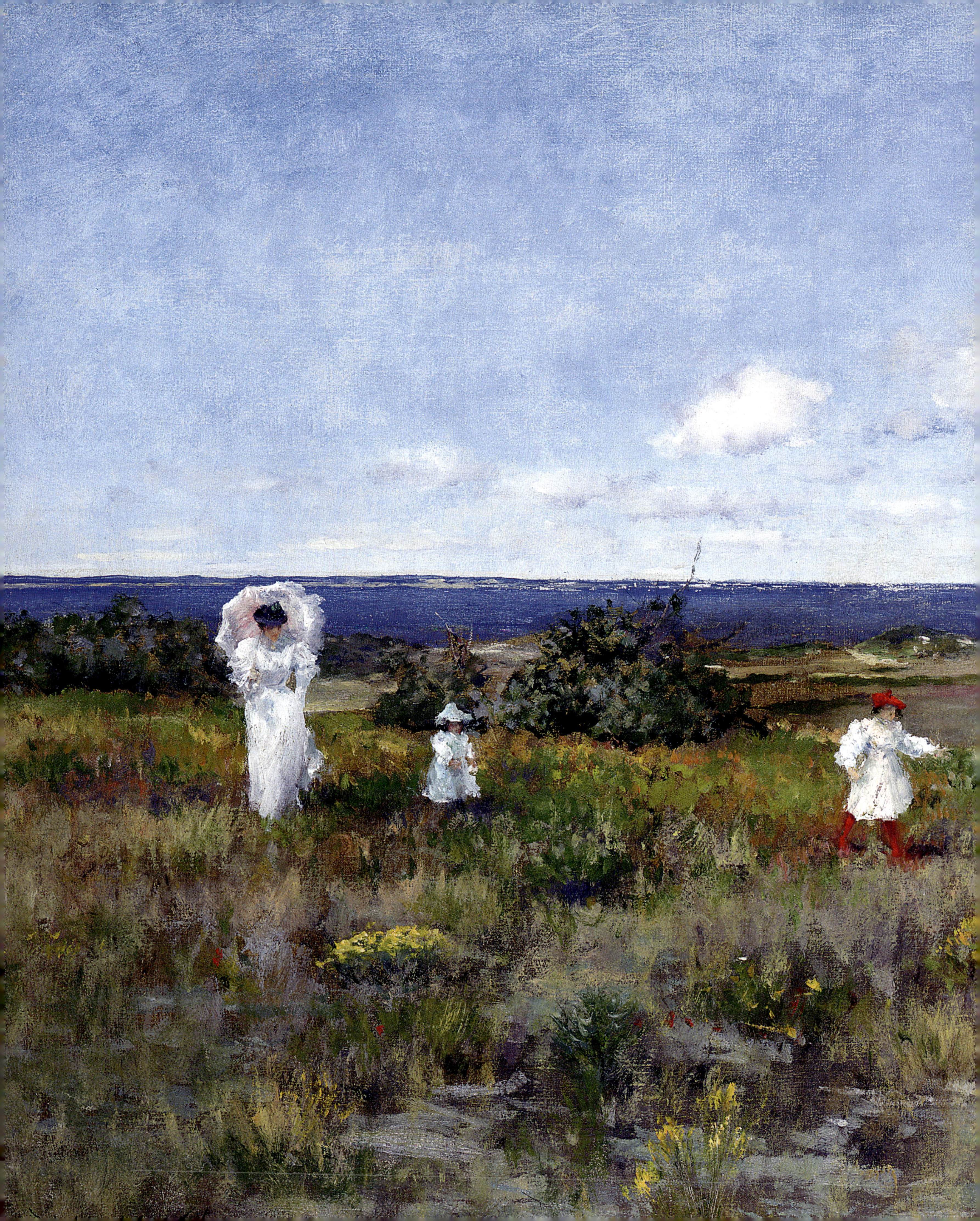

AMERICAN IMPRESSIONISM

A NEW VISION 1880–1900

Edited by Katherine M. Bourguignon

Essays by Richard Brettell, Frances Fowle and Katherine M. Bourguignon

Distributed by Yale University Press, New Haven and London

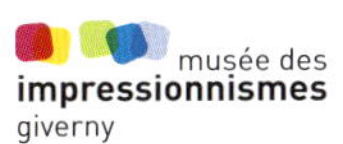

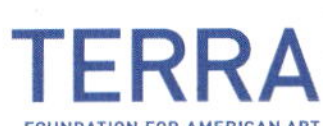

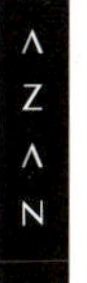

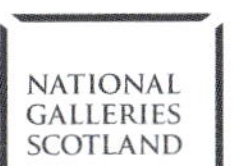

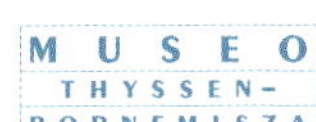

Catalogue published by the musée des impressionnismes Giverny, the National Galleries of Scotland, the Museo Thyssen-Bornemisza, and Éditions Hazan, in partnership with the Terra Foundation for American Art

99, rue Claude Monet, 27620 Giverny, France
www.mdig.fr

73 Belford Road, Edinburgh EH4 3DS, Scotland, United Kingdom
www.nationalgalleries.org

Paseo del Prado 8, 28014 Madrid, Spain
www.museothyssen.org

www.editions-hazan.com
Published in France by Éditions Hazan
11, rue Paul Bert, 92247 Malakoff Cedex

Printed and bound by Pollina, Luçon, France-L67716
ISBN: 978 0 300 206104
National Galleries of Scotland ISBN: 978-1-906270-70-4
Library of Congress Cataloging-in-Publication Data Number: 2013047895
A catalogue record for this book is available from The British Library

This exhibition is organized by the musée des impressionnismes Giverny and the Terra Foundation for American Art in collaboration with the National Galleries of Scotland and the Museo Thyssen-Bornemisza.

With the generous support of the Terra Foundation for American Art.

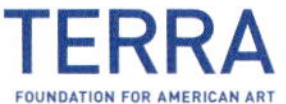

Musée des impressionnismes Giverny
L'Impressionnisme et les Américains
28 March to 29 June 2014

National Galleries of Scotland
American Impressionism: A New Vision, 1880-1900
19 July to 19 October 2014

Museo Thyssen-Bornemisza
Impresionismo americano
4 November 2014 to 1 February 2015

In France, the exhibition has received the patronage of Madame Aurélie Filippetti, Ministry of Culture and Communication

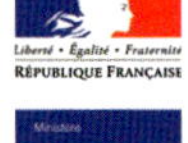

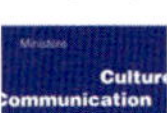

and of the Embassy of The United States of America in France.

Caisse d'Epargne Normandie is a local sponsor

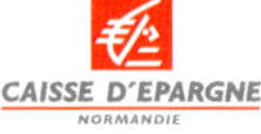

Founding members of the musée des impressionnismes Giverny

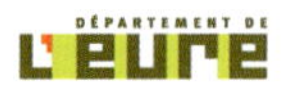

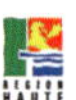
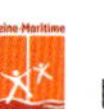
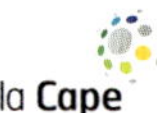

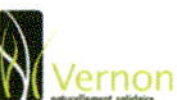

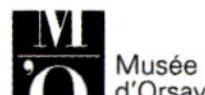

TERRA

In Spain, this exhibition has been made possible with the assistance of the Government Indemnity Scheme provided by Spanish Government.

In Scotland, this exhibition has been made possible with the assistance of the Government Indemnity Scheme provided by Scottish Government.

EXHIBITION

TERRA FOUNDATION FOR AMERICAN ART

Curator
Katherine M. Bourguignon

Registrar
Cathy Ricciardelli

MUSÉE DES IMPRESSIONNISMES GIVERNY

Curatorial Department
Marina Ferretti, Camille Larroumet, Vanessa Lecomte

Registrars
Céline Mittelette, Élodie Perrault

NATIONAL GALLERIES OF SCOTLAND

Curatorial Department, Scottish National Gallery
Frances Fowle

Registrar
Rosalyn Clancey

MUSEO THYSSEN-BORNEMISZA

Modern Painting Department
Paloma Alarcó, Clara Marcellán

Registrar
Lucia Cassol

CATALOGUE

Editor
Katherine M. Bourguignon, Associate Curator, Terra Foundation for American Art

MUSÉE DES IMPRESSIONNISMES GIVERNY

Exhibition Coordinator
Camille Larroumet

French Translation
Anne-Laure Guichard

French copy-editing
Anne Chapoutot

NATIONAL GALLERIES OF SCOTLAND

Publishing Department
Christine Thompson

Copy-editing
Kate Bell

MUSEO THYSSEN-BORNEMISZA

Publishing Department
Ana Cela, Catali Garrigues, Ángela Villaverde

Spanish Translation
Fernando Villaverde

ÉDITIONS HAZAN

Design
Sylvie Milliet

Cover design
Jean-Marc Barrier

Editorial coordination
Anne-Isabelle Vannier

Production
Claire Hostalier and Marie Dubourg

Colour Reproduction
Litho Art, Turín, Italy

Cover: *Summertime*, 1894 (detail, see p.63)
Page 2: *Near the Beach, Shinnecock*, 1895 (detail, see p.109)
Page 12: *Lady Agnew of Lochnaw*, 1892 (detail, see p.112)

LENDERS

We would like to extend our heartfelt thanks to all the collectors whose generous loans have made this exhibition possible:

Spain
Bilbao, Museo de Bellas Artes
Madrid, Museo Thyssen-Bornemisza
Madrid, Carmen Thyssen-Bornemisza Collection, on loan at the Museo Thyssen-Bornemisza

United States
Atlanta, Georgia, High Museum of Art
Boston, Massachusetts, Museum of Fine Arts
Brooklyn, New York, Brooklyn Museum
Chicago, Illinois, Terra Foundation for American Art
Philadelphia, Pennsylvania, Pennsylvania Academy of the Fine Arts
Philadelphia, Pennsylvania, Philadelphia Museum of Art
Hartford, Connecticut, Wadsworth Atheneum Museum of Art
Indianapolis, Indiana, Indianapolis Museum of Art
Milwaukee, Wisconsin, Milwaukee Art Museum
Minneapolis, Minnesota, Minneapolis Institute of Arts
New Britain, Connecticut, New Britain Museum of American Art
Northampton, Massachusetts, Smith College Museum of Art
New York, New York, The Metropolitan Museum of Art
Providence, Rhode Island, Museum of Art, Rhode Island School of Design
Rochester, New York, Memorial Art Gallery, University of Rochester
Toledo, Ohio, Toledo Museum of Art
Tulsa, Oklahoma, Gilcrease Museum
Washington D. C., Corcoran Gallery of Art
Washington D. C., House Collection, Dumbarton Oaks
Washington D. C., National Gallery of Art
Washington D. C., Smithsonian American Art Museum
Water Mill, New York, Parrish Art Museum
Waterville, Maine, Colby College Museum of Art

France
Montpellier Agglomération, Musée Fabre
París, Musée d'Orsay
París, Petit Palais, Musée des Beaux-Arts de la ville de Paris

Portugal
Lisbon, Museu Calouste Gulbenkian

United Kingdom
Edinburgh, National Galleries of Scotland
London, Tate

ACKNOWLEDGEMENTS FROM THE CURATOR

American Impressionism: a New Vision, 1880-1900 is the result of an extraordinary collaboration among institutions and individuals in four countries, on both sides of the Atlantic. Diego Candil, Director of the musée des impressionnismes Giverny and Elizabeth Glassman, President of the Terra Foundation for American Art conceived of this project almost four years ago as a way to fulfill multiple goals: to continue to showcase American art in Giverny; to maintain and develop the historic links that exist between their two institutions; and to build networks with major museums across Europe. I am grateful for their vision and support throughout the development of the exhibition. I extend a special word of thanks to the Conseil d'Administration of the musée des impressionnismes Giverny for their dedication and to the Board of Directors of the Terra Foundation for American Art for their sponsorship and encouragement.

The opportunity to work in close collaboration with the National Galleries of Scotland, the Museo Thyssen-Bornemisza, and the musée des impressionnismes Giverny has been a rich, fulfilling experience, and I am grateful to colleagues at these institutions for their enthusiasm, suggestions and assistance at every phase. The project received early support from directors John Leighton and Michael Clarke in Edinburgh and Guillermo Solana in Madrid. I am especially grateful to Frances Fowle, Senior Curator of French Art at the Scottish National Gallery who helped shape the exhibition over the years and who has written an excellent, thoughtful text for the catalogue. I have also benefited from the expertise of curators Paloma Alarcó, Clara Marcellán, Marina Ferretti, Vanessa Lecomte, and Elizabeth Turner in what has been an inspiring cross-cultural dialogue about American art and Impressionism. Thanks also to Richard Brettell for his advice on the checklist and for his clever introduction.

I wish to extend my gratitude to the many lenders, both public and private, whose generosity has made the exhibition possible. By agreeing to share their masterpieces, they have allowed this unprecedented exhibition of American art to inspire visitors. These loans involve endless emails, phone calls and travel, and I am grateful to the registrars at our partner institutions: Lucia Cassol, Rosalyn Clancey, Celine Mittelette, Élodie Perrault, and Catherine Ricciardelli.

Research Assistants and interns at the Terra Foundation office in Paris have propelled the exhibition forward at critical moments: Lisa Chezerkian, Laura Valette, Hadrien Viraben, and, especially Emily Burns. Colleagues in Paris, Chicago, and Giverny have contributed critical insight and assistance, especially Camille Larroumet at the musée des impressionnismes, Francesca Rose and Veerle Thielemans at the Terra Foundation. Every department at each of the participating museums has contributed to the successful realization of the exhibition, and Hazan has worked closely with us to produce this beautiful catalogue.

Special thanks go to the following colleagues throughout the world:

Stephane Bayard, Kate Bell, Barbara Bertucio, Fred Bollerer, Véronique Bossard, Mary Bourguignon, David Brenneman, Géraldine Brilhault, Charles Brock, Phillip Brookman, Elisabeth Broun, Gudrun Buehl, Mary Busick, Thomas Campbell, Terry Carbone, James Carder, Sarah Cash, Joao Castel-Branco Pereira, Hubert Cavaniol, Ana Cela, Anne Chapoutot, Erin Coe, Isabelle Collet, Caroline Collier, Sharon Corwin, John Davis, Lorraine DeLaney, Jennifer Donnelly, Charles Eldredge, Kaywin Feldman, Alison Fenn, Ruth Fine, Kathleen Foster, Catali Garrigues, Tracee Glab, Anne-Laure Guichard, Amy Gunderson, George Gurney, Paula Haymon, John Henry, Stephanie Heydt, Erica Hirshler, Douglas Hyland, Kimberly Jones, Daniel Keegan, Brian Kennedy, Elizabeth Kornhauser, Louise Laplante, Nancy Leeman, Arnold Lehman, Christophe Leribault, Alicia Longwell, Lisa MacDougall, Miguel Magalhaes, Andrea Mall, Anna Marley, Caroline Mathieu, Mark Mitchell, Linda Muehlig, Sophie Nadeau, Larry Nichols, Jessica Nicoll, Alexander Noelle, Patrick Noon, Maureen O'Brien, Peter Ott, Michael Owen, Kim Pashko, Sylvie Patry, Sherry Peglow, Harry Philbrick, Colleen Piccone, Isolde Pludermacher, Earl A. Powell III, Joseph Rishel, Malcolm Rogers, Timothy Rub, William Rudolph, Luisa Sampaio, Sir Nicholas Serota, Michael Shapiro, Monica Simpson, John W. Smith, Terrie Sultan, Susan L. Talbott, Christine Thompson, Baronness Thyssen-Bornemisza, John Urgo, Anne-Isabelle Vannier, Javier Viar, Barbara Weinberg, Katie Welty, Amy Zinck, Jan Ziolkowski, Marta Zlotnick.

And to Régis, Guillaume and Gabrielle Bailly

Katherine M. Bourguignon

Edmund Tarbell's 1891 painting *In the Orchard* exemplifies the transatlantic narrative of American Impressionism. Tarbell painted the landscape while working in France in 1886, populating the canvas with a thoughtfully arranged group of family and friends only after his return to Boston. The picture echoes French impressionist masterpieces such as Claude Monet's monumental *Le Déjeuner sur l'herbe*, 1865–6, and Pierre-Auguste Renoir's *Luncheon of the Boating Party*, 1880–1, in its size, bold colours, and sun-dappled rendering of an outdoor scene. Yet when Tarbell's painting appeared at the Chicago World's Columbian Exposition in 1893, critics hailed it as uniquely American.

Impressionism did not take hold in America in a linear fashion. While expatriates such as Mary Cassatt and John Singer Sargent worked alongside their French colleagues and helped shape the avant-garde trends of their time, younger Americans artists learned of Impressionism through the paintings they saw in Paris, as well as on their home turf in Boston and New York. They appropriated certain aspects of impressionist art and invented others, adapting their individual styles for an American audience. These artists were highly trained, widely travelled, cosmopolitan painters who sought inspiration and praise both at home and abroad—they would have been pleased to know their paintings are being shared with audiences in Giverny, Edinburgh, and Madrid.

Our founder, Daniel Terra, believed that engagement with original works of art could be a transformative experience, and throughout his lifetime he worked to share his collection of American art with audiences worldwide. Today, we honour his legacy by fostering the exploration, understanding, and enjoyment of the visual arts of the United States through innovative exhibitions such this one, which inspires multi-national perspectives and meaningful cross-cultural dialogues. We also support research and educational programs across the globe, motivated by the belief that art has the potential both to distinguish cultures and to unite them.

The Terra Foundation for American Art is proud to be co-organizer and sponsor of *American Impressionism: A New Vision, 1880-1900*, which results from an inspiring, ongoing partnership with the musée des impressionnismes Giverny. I am deeply indebted to both Diego Candil, Director of the museum, and Jean Louis Destans, its Chairman, for their generosity of ideas and friendship throughout the years. This exhibition has also benefitted invaluably from the collaboration of two additional museums, the National Galleries of Scotland and the Museo Thyssen-Bornemisza, which have graciously shared the expertise of their curators and their collections. In particular, I'd like to thank Sir John Leighton, Director-General of the National Galleries of Scotland, Michael Clarke, Director of the Scottish National Gallery, and Guillermo Solana and Evelio Acevedo, Artistic Director and Managing Director, respectively, of the Museo Thyssen-Bornemisza. I am grateful to Richard R. Brettell, Margaret McDermott Distinguished Chair of Art and Aesthetics at the University of Texas, Dallas, and Frances Fowle, Senior Curator of French Art at the Scottish National Gallery, and Reader in History of Art at the University of Edinburgh, for their thoughtful catalogue texts and indispensable advice, and to the Boards of Directors of the musée des impressionnismes Giverny and the Terra Foundation for American Art. Lastly, I want to congratulate and acknowledge Katherine M. Bourguignon, Associate Curator at the Terra Foundation for American Art, for developing such an intelligent exhibition—her unyielding creativity and insightfulness have rendered a show that significantly augments the worldwide discourse about American Impressionism and honours the global mission of the Terra Foundation.

Elizabeth Glassman
President and CEO, Terra Foundation for American Art

After several years of collaboration, we are delighted to present this catalogue dedicated to the emergence of American Impressionism. It has been written to accompany a magnificent exhibition on a subject that remains relatively unfamiliar in Europe. The French, British and Spanish publics will now have the opportunity to discover the depth and richness of American Impressionism, which will be presented in three shows on the Old Continent with a large selection of works loaned from the United States.

The paintings are representative of the many fruitful connections and exchanges that took place between American and European artists during the conception and development of Impressionism in France. The paintings of the American artists are far from being pale copies of those produced by their French contemporaries. They present a different vision to eyes accustomed to the techniques and subjects of the French painters. Brightened by whites and violets, there is a different sense of colour in these works, whose modern, contemporary subjects express the mellowness and joy of life in the United States. In characteristic landscapes painted with patriotic pride we see a fresh view of the New World.

Our warm thanks are offered to the Terra Foundation for American Art for its loyal and generous support; to Katherine M. Bourguignon, who has led this project with verve and precision; to the directors of each of the three museums for the belief and dedication they have invested in this project, and of course to the museum staff, who have collaborated in exemplary fashion to organise this exhibition and publication in three languages.

We hope that this project will encourage greater interest in American Impressionism and offer due recognition in Europe to these great American artists.

Jean Louis Destans
Président du musée des impressionnismes Giverny

Sir John Leighton
Director-General of the National Galleries of Scotland

José Ignacio Wert
President of the Museo Thyssen-Bornemisza Board of Trustees

Impressionism was truly an international movement. Like a stone tossed into a still pond, the new colours, subjects, and compositions of Impressionism rippled outward from Paris and had repercussions throughout the world. The American example is in some ways similar to that of the United Kingdom and Spain: in the later decades of the nineteenth century, artists from these countries began to produce pictures with startling colours and everyday subjects. Artists like Joaquín Sorolla and Walter Sickert made friends among the artists of the impressionist group while living and working in Paris and took the new ideas back home, adapting and inventing highly diverse versions of Impressionism. American artists such as James McNeill Whistler, Mary Cassatt, and John Singer Sargent also worked among the avant-garde artistic circles in Paris, but, unlike so many of their younger compatriots, these three returned to the United States only for brief visits, spending most of their time in Europe. Through their paintings, they participated in the 'ripple effect' of Impressionism, not only among their fellow Americans, but also within the countries where they chose to live and work.

American Impressionism: A New Vision brings together iconic pictures by these three expatriate Americans and demonstrates their role in the development of Impressionism. It also includes important works by lesser known American impressionists—treasures shared with our audiences from major museums on both sides of the Atlantic. The musée des impressionnismes Giverny is proud to be co-organizer of this exhibition with the Terra Foundation for American Art and to have collaborated so successfully with the National Galleries of Scotland and the Museo Thyssen-Bornemisza. This ambitious project would not have been possible without the dedication of the curator of the exhibition, Katherine M. Bourguignon, Associate Curator at the Terra Foundation, and the help and contribution of Frances Fowle, Senior Curator of French Art at the Scottish National Gallery.

We are grateful to the Terra Foundation for their loans and their support, and we recognise the unfailing support of all the members of our Boards of Directors, Ministries and Ambassadors of each country, and local sponsors. We greatly appreciate the effort and expertise of friends and colleagues who have brought this project to a successful realization.

Diego Candil
Director of the musée des impressionnismes Giverny

Michael Clarke
Director of the Scottish National Gallery

Guillermo Solana
Artistic Director of the Museo Thyssen-Bornemisza

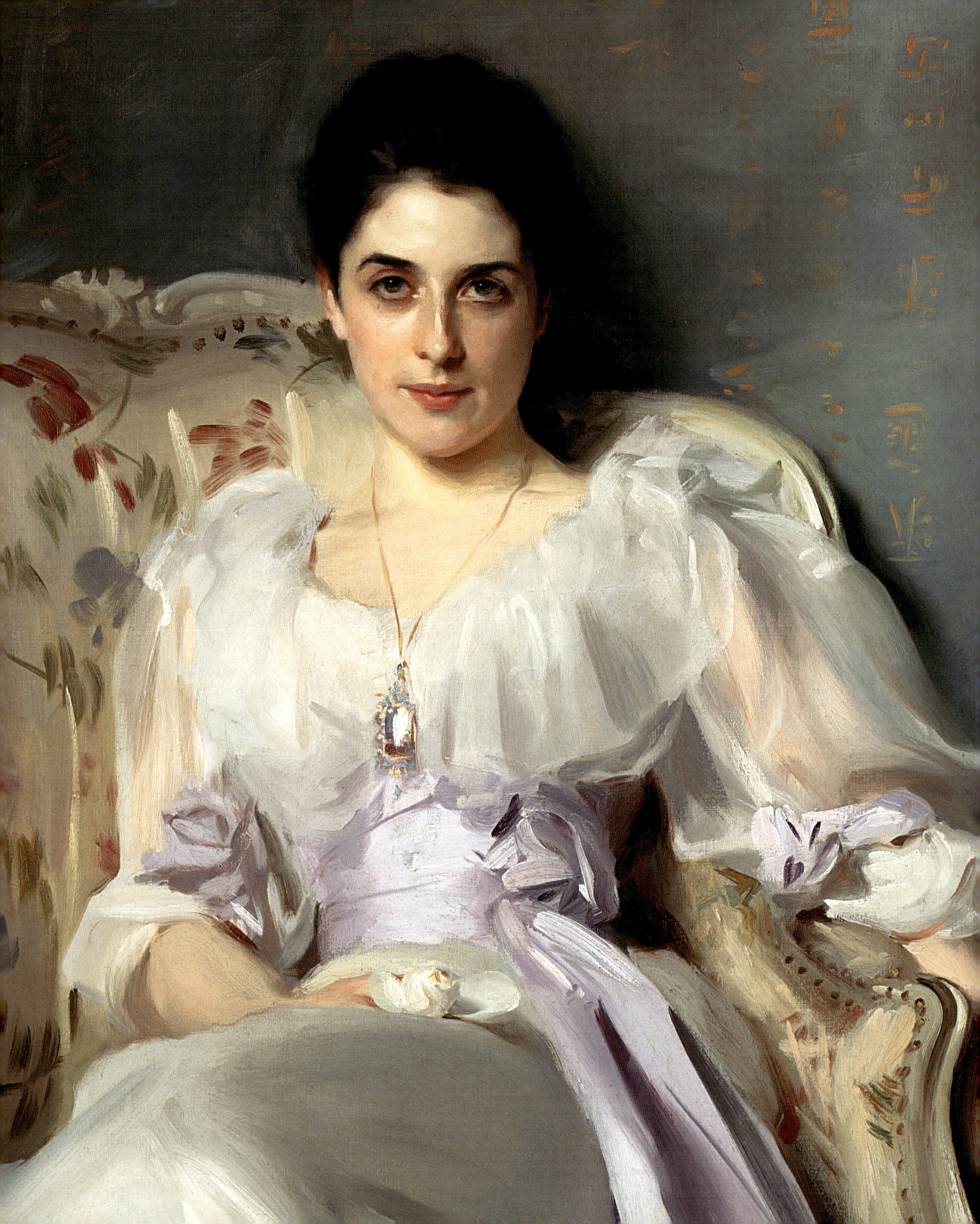

CONTENTS

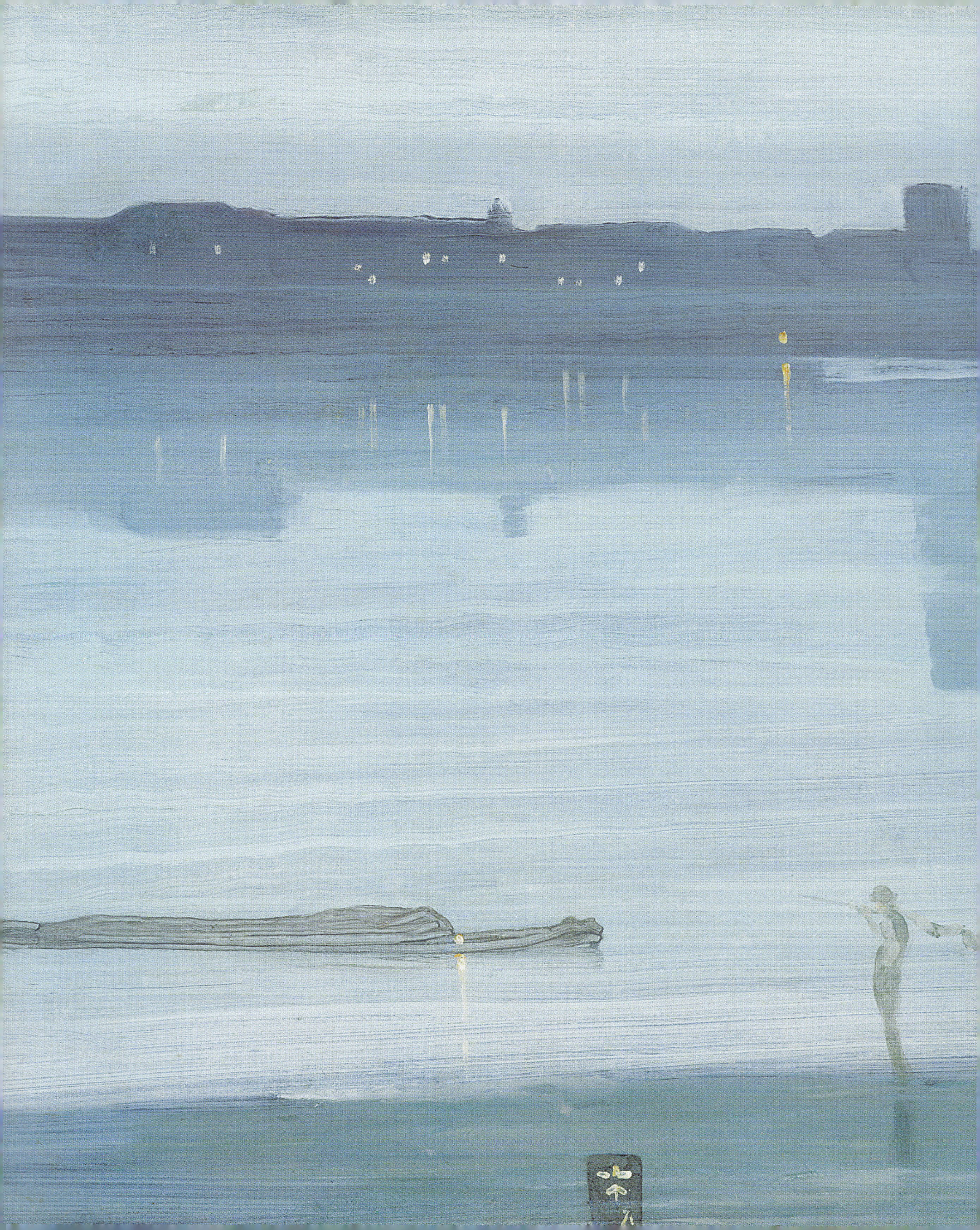

INTRODUCTION

Impressionism and Nationalism: The American Case

Richard Brettell

I confess that I experience a slight bout of intellectual indigestion every time I confront the words 'American Impressionism'. But, before raising the hackles of my countrymen, I have to say that I have the same problem with the words 'French Impressionism'. My discomfort has to do with the fact that, to me and many other students of artistic modernism, 'nationalism' is most often at war with 'the modern', and, if there is a premier form of artistic modernism, it is Impressionism. A term that is frequently applied to this trans-national or even anti-national modernism is 'cosmopolitan', which evokes both adaptability and rootlessness in equal measure and is an enemy of the kind of patriotism that words like 'American', 'French', 'German' or 'Polish' – indeed any national word – have at their core.

We have learned from many students of nationalism – from historians like Ernest Gellner to social scientists such as Benedict Anderson – that it is, paradoxically, the ultimate modern binding medium precisely because it is an antidote to the kind of placeless adaptability that is at the core of modern mobility.[1] Those of us who are less than successful at the art, or necessity, of adaptation want to find an enduring set of values somewhere, generally bound together by a shared language, religion or landscape. The endurance – one might better say the reocurrence – of this notion of shared values and ideals is absolutely fundamental to France, the birthplace of the movement called Impressionism shortly after its inauguration in an exhibition held in Paris in 1874, and it is the ways in which the impressionists strayed from those values that made their art unacceptable to the most nationalistic of art critics and commentators who saw the group's first exhibition.

Of the men and women who made up the inner circle of the movement, most were French and male, but certainly not all of them. Alfred Sisley and Camille Pissarro – essential to the group's ideals and survival – were British and Danish respectively, and Sisley almost died trying to become a French citizen, since he had been registered by his British parents as British at his birth in Paris – something Pissarro never bothered to do. Pissarro had been born Jacob Abraham Camille Pizarro on the Danish colonial island of St Thomas in the Caribbean and spoke Spanish, English and French fluently by the time he arrived in Paris to become a professional artist at the age of twenty-five. Claude Monet, Auguste Renoir, Gustave Caillebotte and Berthe

JAMES ABBOTT MCNEILL WHISTLER, *Nocturne: Blue and Silver – Chelsea*, 1871, detail (p.121)

Morisot were decidedly French, but were part of the Paris-based cosmopolitan society, which was increasingly global and sophisticated. Edgar Degas was more Parisian than French, although he was technically French, and most of his favourite relatives were Italian and lived in Naples and Florence, where he visited them and spoke fluent Italian. Degas also had a brother and other relatives in New Orleans, which he visited as a young artist, becoming the only 'French' impressionist actually to paint in America. Indeed, his painting *The Cotton Exchange at New Orleans* of 1873 (Musée des Beaux-Arts, Pau), one of the principal masterpieces of French Impressionism, represents the cotton-trading office of his relatives.

Degas, perhaps due to his own cosmopolitan origins, sponsored membership of the impressionist group for the Italian artists Federico Zandomeneghi and Giuseppe de Nittis, and for the American expatriate Mary Cassatt, whose name at birth was Cassat, to which the family added a 't' so that it would be more easily pronounced CasSAHT rather than CASSet.[2] When one considers the great 'post-impressionist' artists who first exhibited with the impressionists – Paul Cézanne, Paul Gauguin and Georges Seurat – we add another artist, this time Gauguin, who, though born in Paris, spent his childhood in Lima, his youth travelling around the world as a merchant marine, and the last dozen years of his life in Tahiti and the Marquesas. And the fourth great post-impressionist, Vincent van Gogh, whose career as a modern colourist took place in Paris in the lap of the impressionists, was Dutch.

All of this is to say that, if it is true that Impressionism was 'modern', it is not true that it was 'French'. What, then, do we do when we confront the words 'American Impressionism'? What we know now better than we did a generation ago is that Impressionism was the first major vanguard movement to appeal equally to 'foreign' and French collectors, critics and patrons. Indeed, it was perhaps Mary Cassatt and her friend the promoter Sarah Hallowell who brought an important group of American collectors to the cause – already in the 1870s, but more powerfully in the last two decades of the century. The English, Welsh, Scottish, Irish, German, Austrian and Russian collectors were equally important as the movement gained steam. Indeed, the Japanese began to buy towards the end of the nineteenth century, and the participation of foreigners in this Paris-based movement was essential to its success. Even the rather prudish American writer, Henry James, wrote a review of the second impressionist exhibition in 1876, by which date Americans in Paris were beginning already to discuss this group of artists and to put into words – and action, through purchase and, in some cases, art-making – their responses to the complex, decentred group.

First, we must deal with the knotty question of whether Impressionism was a 'group' or a 'movement'. In its most historically accurate form, it was more the former than the latter. Indeed, it was a 'group of groups', because no two of the eight impressionist exhibitions organised by the 'Corporation of Artist Painters' between 1874 and 1886 included the same artists, although there was a good deal of overlap. Of the 'famous' ones, only Pissarro showed work in all eight exhibitions, followed by Morisot in seven. Interestingly, Gauguin exhibited in as many as either Renoir or Monet. The study of the 'group' was started by John Rewald, who left out the minor artists altogether (including most of the foreigners), and it is a dramatic story, with defections, acrimony, deception, anger and defeat among the inner circle.[3] This is because, to some of the artists, Impressionism was a movement rather than a group, and a movement defined by style and attitude towards making as much as by avant-garde posturing against 'official' or 'academic' art. For Degas, who was keen on artists like Jean-Louis Forain, Jean-François Raffaëlli and other 'naturalists', Impressionism was not primarily about *plein-air* landscape painting, but about gritty modern subject-matter that dealt at its core with issues of social class and class tension. For Monet, Renoir, Morisot and Sisley – and increasingly Caillebotte, one of Degas's protégés – this was precisely not what Impressionism was. To these artists, although few of them ever put it into words, Impressionism was about spontaneous modern landscape and figure painting ostensibly freed from politics and ideology – impossible as that was to attain. If this tension was not enough, Pissarro allied himself with young painters of what was called 'scientific' Impressionism in 1884, forcing a showdown with the 'Romantic' impressionists, Monet, Renoir, Sisley and Caillebotte, which split the group even further and led to its collapse. So, we must conclude that Impressionism in France was a group searching for a viable, stylistically coherent movement – and failing.

How, then, should we define Impressionism? Is it the contrived and carefully prepared urban realism of Degas? The 'spontaneous' *plein-air* landscapes and figures of Monet, Renoir, Sisley and Morisot? The highly theorised and politically charged paintings of Pissarro, Seurat and Paul Signac? The brooding amateur investigation of personal life of Gauguin? The visual exploration of upper-middle-class friends and family by Cassatt and Caillebotte? The uncompromising urban naturalism of Raffaëlli, De Nittis or Zandomeneghi? The 'constructive stroke' aesthetic of Cézanne? The literary dreamscapes of Odilon Redon? All of these were included in one or more of the eight impressionist exhibitions, so we must consider them as we consider the term. When put in this way, it is easy to see that this 'avant-garde group in search of a movement' was fascinating to other artists – French and foreign – for reasons of an astounding variety.

It was this diverse and internally inconsistent Impressionism that was known to foreign artists affected by the group's work. Indeed, the almost caricature-clear idea of Impressionism familiar from twentieth-century books on the movement and university classes in the history of modern art is an invention of the twentieth century. The men and women who actually attended the exhibitions and read reviews of them in the 1870s and 1880s knew that Impressionism was neither a unified style nor a coherent movement. To them it was a group of artists rebelling for various reasons and in various ways against the domination of the Salon and state-sponsored culture in their lives and careers. For this reason, it is only natural that Americans in particular were drawn as much to its spirit of independence and its risk-taking as to its modes of making pictures.

The first American artist to claw his way into French vanguard painting of the nineteenth century was James Abbott McNeill Whistler. Although born in Lowell, Massachusetts, Whistler claimed St Petersburg in Russia, where he spent a good deal of his childhood, as his birthplace. His career began in the United States, but it was his arrival in Paris in 1855 that led him to adopt an avant-garde existence, and he was active in London, Paris and Venice throughout his long working life. Despite this, he was always considered – and always considered himself – to be 'American'. His vanguard career was initially centred in 1860s Paris, where he worked closely with Gustave Courbet, Edouard Manet, Degas and the young artists who were to become impressionists. There is circumstantial evidence that Degas invited Whistler to exhibit in one of the impressionist group exhibitions, but either the American declined or he never received the letter of approach. Indeed, Whistler's own self-organised solo exhibition was held in London in the same year as the first impressionist exhibition, 1874. Yet, whenever he came to Paris from London, he re-entered a circle of writers, critics and artists that overlapped extensively with the impressionists. His moody style of painting, which evokes precise conditions of light and atmosphere in particular places at particular times, was rarely linked to the group, and his art can be considered more persuasively in the context of the progressive artists of the earlier generation, especially Courbet and Manet. In spite of the self-enforced distance between Whistler and the younger impressionists, he was considered a modern and rebellious artist in America, whose aesthetic was independent of academic norms. Like them, his inspirations widened themselves to Asia and particularly to the art of Japan, but, in spite of this, even his 'Japonisme' was very different from that of Monet, Pissarro or Gauguin.

In the present exhibition, he plays a role that is, for all those reasons, central to the 'American' artistic tradition rather than to the Paris-based group.His fame pushed his brand of tonal painting to the attention of a small number of younger American vanguard artists who wanted something that was at once radical and emphatically not impressionist. This sub-group is recognised in the exhibition and, in a way, linked to the term Impressionism, that Whistler himself avoided in favour of words rooted in music and abstract ideas of composition derived from Edgar Allan Poe's famous essay of 1846, 'The Philosophy of Composition'.[4]

When we think of American artists in France in the 1870s who could have experienced the dawn of this anti-authoritarian movement, we gravitate towards Cassatt and John Singer Sargent, whose careers, like that of Whistler, were so entirely European that they have to be considered as a particular class of expatriate Americans. Cassatt came to the movement in the 1870s through her budding friendship with and admiration for the painting of Degas, who was to be her sponsor when she first exhibited with the impressionists in 1879. She had already painted with him, and there is an old tradition telling us that Degas actually worked on her picture *Little Girl in a Blue Armchair*, 1878 (National Gallery of Art, Washington D.C.), which was to have been her entry to the 1878 Exposition Universelle in Paris. In many ways, her experience of French art was very much through the lens of the avant-garde, and, unlike other American artists, she was not closely allied to an important Salon painter/mentor, although Manet's teacher, Thomas Couture, was also her teacher before she met Degas.

Cassatt was the only artist who was both an impressionist and an American, giving her a unique position among all the artists in this exhibition. Indeed, she would probably recoil at being called an 'American impressionist', although she would never have denied that both those words were true of her. The depth of her involvement with Impressionism, which was particularly strong with Degas and Pissarro, cannot be overstressed. If there is any such thing as 'American Impressionism', she was the only artist who qualifies unreservedly for it, and one should use her career, her aesthetic and her associates to define what we mean by that term. In this, one must also consider her collection and her circle of friends. She is known to have retained a close friendship with Monet and to have visited him in Giverny in 1894, perhaps at the very same time as the only visit to Monet's house of the reclusive Cézanne. She owned important paintings by all the artists, and her understanding of the mature figure painting of Pissarro embodied in her decision to purchase his *In the Garden at Pontoise: A Young Woman Washing Dishes* of 1882 (The Fitzwilliam Museum, University of Cambridge), among other works, makes it clear that she learned from them as they from her. Indeed, the colour etchings executed by Pissarro in the 1890s were made under the direct stimulus of Cassatt's series of twelve colour etchings shown at the Durand-Ruel Gallery in 1893, and their mutual respect as printmakers stemmed from their equal participation with Degas in a planned impressionist print journal called *Le Jour et la nuit* (Day and Night) in 1878–9. No American artist could even approximate Cassatt's knowledge and experience of Impressionism.

In her participation with the group, Cassatt is different from Sargent, for whom the experience of academic painting and specifically of the Salon was at the centre of his career strategy in the arts in Paris. His teacher, Carolus-Duran, was exclusively a Salon artist, and the arena in which Sargent strove for excellence was the annual Salon, which he conquered by applying some of the shock-value lessons learned from the career of Manet. Yet, both American artists, however different in their very sense of 'American-ness', were deeply affected by the impressionist exhibitions they either joined or visited. Sargent made works in the manner of Degas by 1877, the year that Cassatt met Degas, and was making work influenced by Monet and Renoir in the 1880s. Perhaps because of Sargent's success at the Salon and his deference to Carolus-Duran, he was never asked by Degas to join the impressionist group.But this did not prevent him from having a real effect on the movement and by being, himself, deeply affected by it.

Few Americans and fewer French art lovers know about the depth of the friendship between Sargent and Monet, or about Sargent's 'intervention' with the great, but shy French painter in introducing him to Auguste Rodin. It is probably true to say that the now famous Monet–Rodin exhibition held at the Georges Petit Gallery in 1889 would not have happened without Sargent, who in bringing the two men together initiated a bond that was strong enough to form the basis for this epochal exhibition of the greatest living French sculptor and a major French painter. Indeed, Sargent's social abilities and his sixth sense of the particularities of creative people gave him a role in French art of the 1880s that perhaps only an American – or a likeable and subtle foreigner – could play.

Yet, Sargent did more than introduce two great artistic lions to each other. He also began to make art that wrestled with the radical techniques and ideas of Monet and his colleagues. We must remember that, in the 1880s, Monet was in touch as much with 'academic' painters such as Paul-César Helleu and Sargent as he was with his impressionist colleagues, and his openness to these talented young artists surely came after Monet himself had some success in the Salon, with the exhibition of *The Seine at Lavacourt* in 1880 (Dallas Museum of Art) and its full-page reproduction in a review of the Salon in the *Gazette des Beaux-Arts*. This is precisely the same moment at which Degas essentially blackballed Monet and Renoir from the fifth impressionist exhibition because they were breaking ranks with the avant-garde and attempting to show works at both the Salon and the independent exhibitions.

We know that Sargent painted with Monet in Giverny on several occasions, and his now famous depiction of Monet in the act of *plein-air* painting by Sargent (see p.69) as is evidence that he knew more about Monet's working method than did many of the other impressionists because he witnessed it. This is, one must point out, a few years before the village of Giverny became a Mecca for American artists and it also explains why the present exhibition includes so many works by Sargent. But what the exhibition does not contain is any of the pictures by Monet that Sargent bought from the older artist. Indeed, Sargent had more works by Monet in his private collection than he did works by his teacher Carolus-Duran, and several of them are bracingly strong and aggressively painted, including Monet's single most powerful oil study of *The Cliff at Etretat (La Manneporte)* (private collection) and the oddly unsuccessful portrait of the Monet/Hoschedé children of 1888 (see fig.7). The most important reason for artists to collect the work of others – and it seems as if Sargent actually bought them from the market rather than 'trading' them (as Frances Fowle discusses elsewhere in this volume) – is to learn from their example, to study them intensively in private so as to adapt their formal and technical lessons to new purposes.

These two 'case studies' contrast in important ways, suggesting that the American path through the fields of Impressionism was neither straight nor singular. The older American painter, George Inness, was in Europe from 1870 to 1878, and in 1874–5 he spent much of the year in France and painted extensively at Etretat, a tourism and fishing town on the Normandy coast near Le Havre where Monet spent his childhood. Both Monet and his teacher Eugène Boudin had already worked in Etretat and were later to return. Yet, Inness's career was too advanced in the 1870s for him to align himself with such young and rebellious artists. He simply did not need them or their techniques of painting because his own career was launched and his ideas of painting set. That is what we are told time and time again, yet, in looking at his paintings made after his return from Europe to the United States and before his death in 1894, we see an artist whose attitude towards facture, colour and subject altered profoundly in ways that suggest he surely knew about these young rebels more than he or his biographers will admit.

And we must surely consider the increasingly dominant American collectors of Impressionism, men and women so carefully cultivated by the great dealer, Paul Durand-Ruel, who opened his highly successful New York branch in 1886, the year of the eighth and final impressionist exhibition in Paris. Durand-Ruel made sure his sons knew English so as to communicate with these new American collectors both on their French trips and in the United States. He also began a practice of hiring railroad cars on a seasonal basis, filling them with art, and taking them on American tours so that the art came directly to the nouveau riche of Pittsburgh, Cleveland, Toledo, Chicago, Minneapolis and St Louis, among other places. The works of art he displayed were not always impressionist – there was a fair share of pictures by Jean-François Millet, Eugène Delacroix, Camille Corot and other mid-century masters for more conservative clients – but he did include the impressionists, particularly as the 1890s continued and the spread of American collecting beyond New York, Philadelphia and Boston began to become commercially important.

Indeed, by 1890, it was impossible to be 'visually literate' in America and not know about Impressionism in some way. However, that knowledge was skewed and partial, frequently based on what one heard rather than what one saw. The discourse triumphed often over the actual experience of these paintings, drawings and prints. What we do know is that Impressionism was associated with two things in America – rebelliousness and modern independence from authority – both of which play a fairly strong role in the American character, whoever defines it.

What, then, did the young Childe Hassam see of Impressionism when he came to Paris for his three-year study stint sponsored by a patron in 1886? He was too late for the last impressionist exhibition, and the artist whose oeuvre affected him the most was that of Manet's teacher, Couture, whose daughter became a close personal friend. Couture himself was dead, but his role as a kind of grandfather of the avant-garde was surely known to the young Hassam, and we can see easily when looking at his own Salon pictures of 1887, 1888, 1889 and 1890 that he at first strove to make a contribution to urban naturalism like that practised by Degas, Raffaëlli, Jean Béraud, De Nittis and other impressionists. But, his aesthetic development took a change of direction beginning in 1888, when he turned to a freer touch and a sense of lightness both of palette and of social judgement. His art made a brief journey from the naturalist Impressionism of Degas to the spontaneous chromatic Impressionism of Renoir, Caillebotte and Monet. Both were modern, but one was socially inflected and the other more interested in facture, colour and a kind of subjective neutrality. So, without ever exhibiting with the impressionists or interacting with them personally, Hassam's career can be considered in large measure as a response to the kinds of painting they developed in their exhibitions.

It is, oddly, at the very end of this introduction, when one gets to its real subject – what we as art historians and art lovers have been taught to call 'American Impressionism'. That art was practised not in France, but in the United States and was generally centred in the countryside around the increasingly large and wealthy American cities of Boston, New York and Philadelphia. In modest small towns and fishing villages accessible by rail to the cities, American painters began to congregate to create a brand of summer-suburban art that descends directly from that of Monet, Sisley, Renoir and Pissarro. Whether painted in Cos Cob in Connecticut or Shinnecock on Long Island, these works are dependent on a kind of 'seasonal landscape painting' experienced by urbanites leaving the congested and hot city in the summer. It is not so much the style or look of these works that is important for us in this context, but the social links to a new form of modern seasonal life experienced by people wealthy enough to leave the city annually for extended periods in search of a simpler existence. This kind of life itself was a 'style' and the painters, whose livelihoods depended upon the very people who 'summered', followed their patrons and made works that can be linked at their most basic social level to the modern art of Impressionism. Oddly, they did not really need to know very much about the kind of painting they were aping, because it was just that – a kind of painting determined as much by social mobility as by style. One could paint a *plein-air* landscape in Cos Cob or Shinnecock without ever seeing a Monet or a Sisley, and it could evoke the same kind of world in the same direct way for the same kind of prospective client.

The 'American impressionists' painted the city as well, preferring to work in parks, as did Manet, Monet and Morisot, or looking down from the lofty urban vantage points. The latter was particularly important in New York, where the new American skyscrapers provided a view higher than anything one could experience in Paris, apart from the Eiffel Tower after 1889. In this vertigo-inducing form of new urban modernism, artists like Hassam could find their precedents in paintings by Monet or Caillebotte or, a little later, Pissarro, but particular works by these painters were not necessary for the development of this 'New Painting'. Rather, it was participation in a new urban mobility. Indeed, the Massachusetts native, Hassam, migrated from Boston to New York precisely because of the robust urban growth and livelier art markets of that larger city. He did exactly what the Normandy-based Monet did by deserting Le Havre for Paris or Pissarro by deserting St Thomas for the same great European city.

It was not 'art' that caused 'American Impressionism', but life. In each case, town- and agriculturally-based economic worlds gave way to the metropolis. The impressionist artists of France in the 1870s and 1880s did less to induce Americans to paint this modern world than the metropolis itself. What the movement provided the Americans with was a model of an aesthetic laboratory in which new ways of making art for new kinds of art markets enabled artists to bypass the state art apparatus of nationalist France. What they did was to invent a 'start-up' mode of art for a world that had changed fundamentally. Their practice was enough to spawn other start-ups worldwide. Oddly, their art was less important to the artists who borrowed their method than their social inventions.

1. See Gellner 1983 and Anderson 1991.
2. See Mathews 1994, pp.3–7.
3. Rewald 1946 (first of many editions).
4. Poe 1846, www.vahidnab.com/philocompo.pdf.

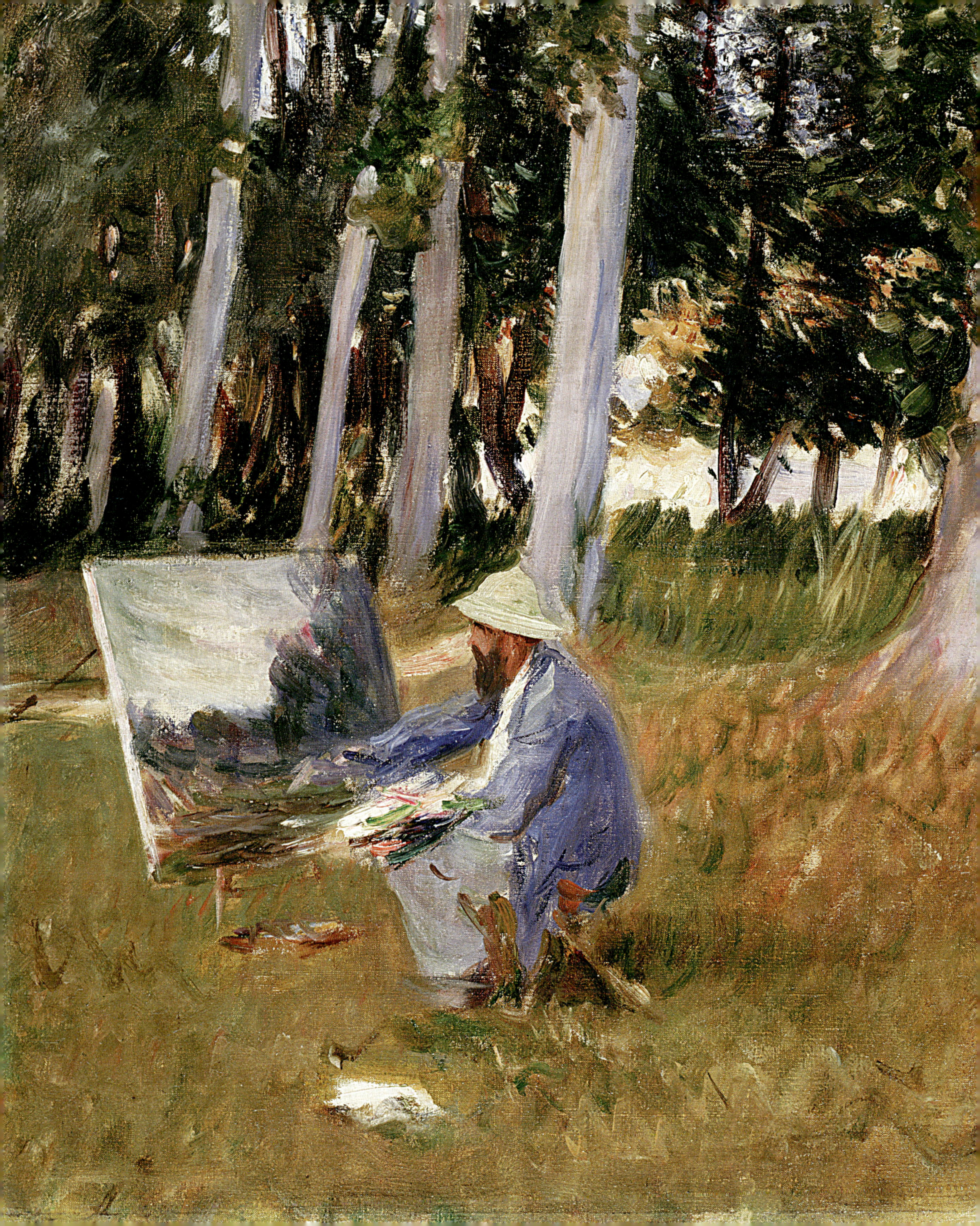

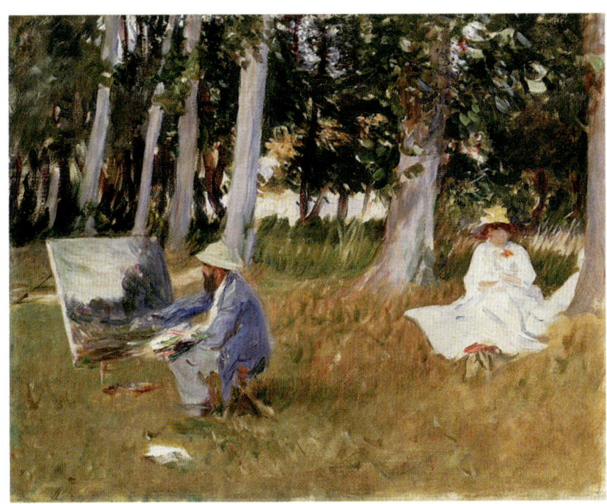

American Artists in Europe: Engaging with Impressionism

Frances Fowle

'My God, I would rather go to Europe than go to Heaven.'
William Merritt Chase[1]

To the American painter eager to engage with European modernism, a Paris 'sojourn' was a necessity. At the end of the Civil War, many aspiring artists made the arduous journey across the Atlantic, most to see the world-class collections at the Louvre and to visit the annual Salon; several to train at one of the numerous Paris ateliers. Among the first American visitors to the French capital during this period were James Abbott McNeill Whistler and Mary Cassatt. Both were welcomed into the impressionist fold in the 1870s and were invited by Edgar Degas to exhibit with the group. They were frequently labelled 'impressionists', even though they objected to the term, regarding themselves as 'independent' artists.[2] As we shall see, the majority of American artists of this period, although dubbed 'impressionist' by the critics, developed a style of painting that derived less from French Impressionism than from Salon naturalists such as Jules Bastien-Lepage and Jean-Charles Cazin. Their exposure to the impressionist inner circle was limited such that, as this essay will show, only a privileged few had direct access to the avant-garde.

It was Whistler who formed the advance guard of American artists who were to engage with French Impressionism. He spoke fluent French and was friendly with Edouard Manet and Claude Monet, but it was Degas for whom he had the greatest respect. In 1898 he is said to have boasted, 'As far as painting is concerned, there is only Degas and myself'.[3] Close in age, similar in temperament, and in their disdainful attitude towards the press and the artistic establishment, the two artists had a mutual respect for one another. Indeed, according to William Rothenstein, Degas was reputedly 'the only man of whom Whistler was a little afraid'.[4] 'When Degas is present,' agreed the critic George Moore, 'Mr Whistler's conversation is distinguished by "brilliant flashes of silence".'[5]

Whistler's affinity with Degas is evident early in his career, in works such as *At the Piano* (Taft Art Museum, Cincinnati) of 1858–9 and *Harmony in Green and Rose: The Music Room* of 1860–1 (Freer Gallery of Art, Washington D.C.), which share something in common with Degas's early portraits.[6] Conversely, Degas admired Whistler's seascapes of Trouville, and later remarked 'that fellow Whistler has really hit on something in those views of the sea and water'.[7] In 1869 Degas spent the summer at Beuzeval in Normandy and produced a series of more than forty minimalist studies in pastel, which have close stylistic parallels with Whistler's paintings.

JOHN SINGER SARGENT
Claude Monet Painting by the Edge of a Wood, 1885
Oil on canvas, 54 × 64.8 cm
Tate, London, Presented by Miss Emily Sargent and Mrs Ormond through the Art Fund, 1925, N04103

Whistler's seascapes developed in time into the Nocturnes of the early 1870s. When Monet took refuge in London during the Franco-Prussian war he very likely visited Whistler in his studio, where he would have seen *Nocturne: Blue and Silver – Chelsea* of 1871 (p.121), an atmospheric 'Japoniste' view of the city and the River Thames, transformed by the veil of evening.[8] Although Whistler's Nocturnes were painted from memory, they had a profound influence on Monet. The latter's *Impression – Sunrise* of 1872 (fig.1), included in the first impressionist exhibition in 1874, evokes the industrial harbour of Le Havre, viewed through an atmospheric haze (one critic even mistook it for a view of the Thames)[9]. According to Cassatt, Whistler was invited by Degas to participate in this initial exhibition, indicating how closely his work resonated with the impressionist group.[10]

By 1874 Paris was returning to normal after the horrors of the Franco-Prussian war and a second wave of Americans began to appear in the city. Opportunities for foreign artists improved with the establishment of the Académie Julian and the studio of Charles-Emile-Auguste Durand, known as Carolus-Duran.[11] A friend and admirer of Manet, Carolus-Duran was younger and more progressive than the majority of academic masters. He dressed with panache, often in his distinctive 'blue velvet coat and yellow silk shirt',[12] and was renowned not only for his dandyish appearance but also for his instinctive 'bravura' technique, applying the paint *au premier coup* (wet-on-wet). The young American artist R.C. Hinckley founded the studio in 1872, and around two-thirds of those who enrolled were American or British.[13] Nevertheless, the classes were taught in French and students were fined ten centimes if they lapsed into English.[14] They paid a monthly fee for rent, heating and the hire of models and Carolus-Duran instructed them two mornings a week.[15] None benefited from his training more than John Singer Sargent, who joined the studio on the Rue Notre Dame des Champs in 1874 at the age of eighteen. His fellow students included the American artist Will H. Low, the Irish painter Frank O'Meara, and Robert Mowbray Stevenson, first cousin of the writer Robert Louis Stevenson. Theodore Robinson joined the class in 1876.

Sargent also enrolled, in 1875, at the Académie Julian.[16] The studio, founded in 1868, had no entrance examinations and benefited from the teaching of eminent academic artists such as William Bouguereau, who had tremendous influence at the Salon.[17] It attracted a large number of American artists, among them several of the future 'impressionists': Robert Vonnoh (1881–3), Willard Leroy Metcalf (1883–4), John Henry Twachtman, Frank W. Benson (both 1883–5), Edmund C. Tarbell (1883–6) and Childe Hassam (1886–8). The academy also welcomed women, including Mary Fairchild MacMonnies (1887–8) and Cecilia Beaux (1888–9).

According to the Irish-born John Lavery, at the Académie Julian 'there was little stimulus owing to the fact that we foreigners kept together so much by going to the same cafés and rarely meeting any of our French atelier friends except at exhibitions'.[18] But for the language barrier, Lavery confessed, he would have 'learnt more and been more influenced by the influential and impressed by the Impressionists'.[19] Most American artists were influenced more by their British colleagues than by the French, and possibly vice versa. (Vonnoh, for example, overlapped with the future 'London impressionist' Philip Wilson Steer, as well as Lavery and George Clausen.) Outside the studio they could see the work of Camille Corot, Jean-François Millet and the Barbizon school at dealers in the Rue Laffitte, while at the Salon they had access to the naturalism of Bastien-Lepage and Cazin, as well as artists on the fringes of Impressionism, such as Giuseppe de Nittis, Jean-Louis Forain and Albert Besnard.

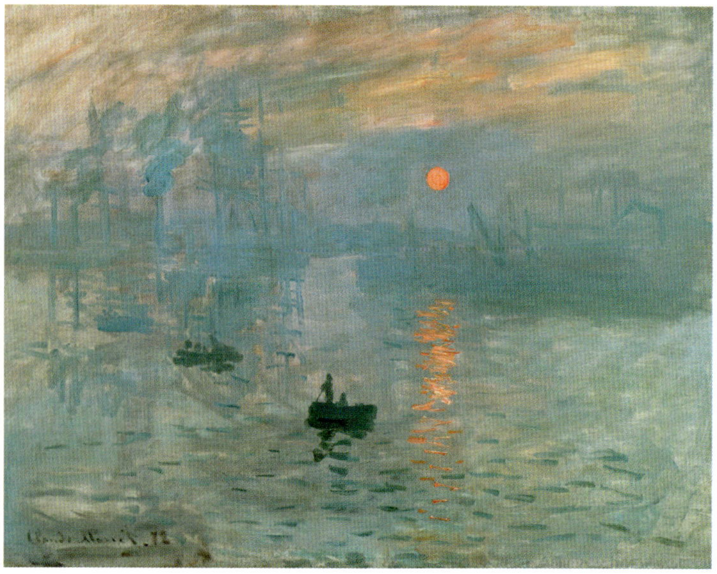

Fig.1 CLAUDE MONET
Impression – Sunrise, 1872
Oil on canvas, 48 x 63 cm
Musée Marmottan Monet, Paris, 4014

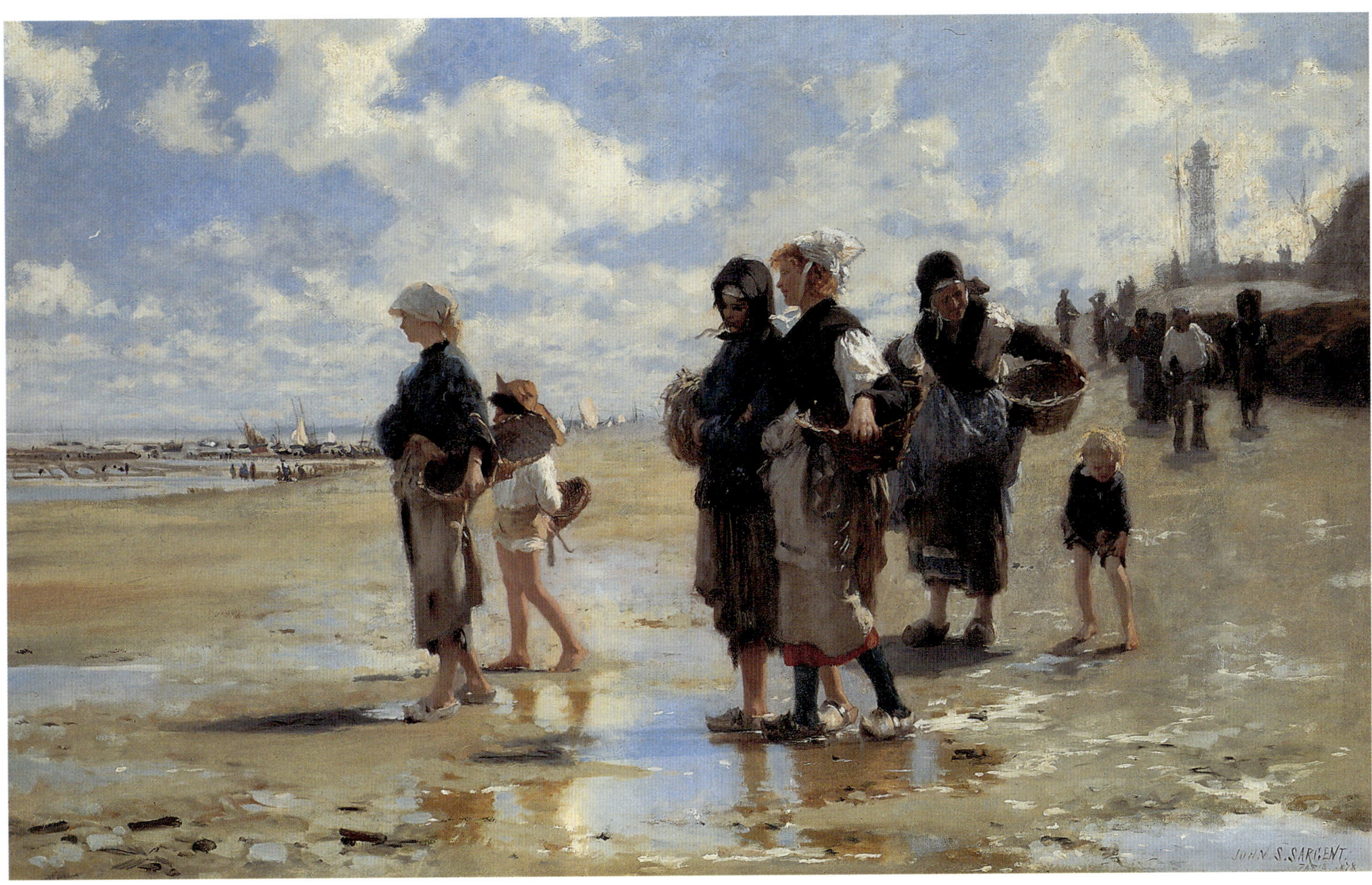

The latest craze among British and American artists was for sketching in oils out of doors (*en plein air*) and in the summer months they set off for the forest of Fontainebleau, or worked on the Brittany coast. Robinson was among the first to paint at the artist's colony of Grez-sur-Loing, where, in 1877, he encountered Low and other students from Carolus-Duran's atelier. According to Low, the English-speaking members of the colony alienated themselves from the rest through their rowdy behaviour: 'Our friends at Siron's [in Barbizon] of other nationalities ... looked on gravely when the little band of Anglais ... scaled garden walls in order to limber their muscles, or some of them, bearded men, gave themselves up to the childish game of leap-frog in the court.'[20] At Grez they stayed at the Hôtel Chevillon and 'brought to the quiet inn the clamour of our English tongue, and a freedom of manners and customs that escapes geographical definition ... ignoring completely the usages which, rude and simple as they are, centuries have imposed on the orderly country'.[21]

While Robinson was at Grez, Sargent was painting *en plein air* on the coast of Brittany. In the summer of 1875, J. Alden Weir reported that 'everybody' was 'going down there to paint Breton subjects'[22] but, while most Americans made for Pont-Aven or Concarneau, Sargent (accompanied by Eugène Lachaise) chose the small fishing port of Cancale, on the north-east coast. In 1877 he spent the summer making oil studies of the local oyster gatherers (pp.64, 65), with the aim of producing a large Salon painting. His sister Emily reported to the author Violet Paget (alias Vernon Lee) that Sargent 'had a good deal of rainy and cloudy weather' which had 'interfered a great deal with his work'.[23] Despite this, *En route pour la pêche* (*Setting Out to Fish*, also known as *Oyster Gatherers of Cancale*) (fig.2) is remarkable for its freshness, quality of light and high colour notes. It was exhibited at the 1878 Paris Salon and was admired by the French critic Roger-Ballu, who commented on the 'free, broad strokes, which seem confused when viewed up close, but which give a sense of relief and energy to the figures when seen

Fig.2 JOHN SINGER SARGENT
En route pour la pêche (*Setting Out to Fish*), 1878
Oil on canvas, 78.8 x 122.8 cm
Corcoran Gallery of Art, Washington D.C.,
Museum Purchase, Gallery Fund, 17.2

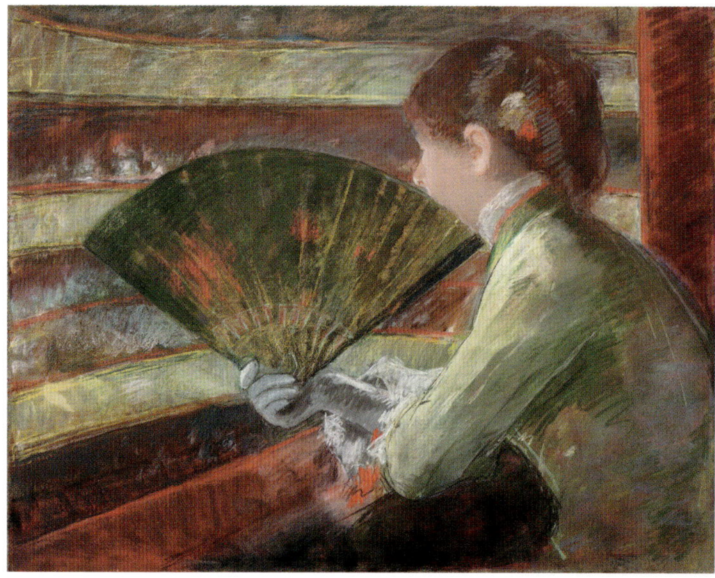

Fig.3 MARY CASSATT
In the Loge, *c.* 1879
Pastel and metallic paint on canvas prepared with a pastel ground, 65.1 × 81.3 cm
Philadelphia Museum of Art,
Gift of Mrs. Sargent McKean, 1950, 1950-52-1

at a distance'. In particular he commended Sargent for his ability to evoke 'the feeling of the sun shining on the wet sands of the beach, dappled here and there by the blue reflections of the sky in the shallow pools of water'.[24] The painting was Sargent's first success and had an important impact on British artists such as Stanhope Forbes who worked at Cancale in the summer of 1881.[25] In terms of subject, however, Sargent, like most American artists of this period, still preferred the rural naturalism of artists such as Jules Breton and Bastien-Lepage to the urban modernity of Impressionism.

Mary Cassatt and Edgar Degas

By contrast, Mary Cassatt, who returned to Europe after the Franco-Prussian war, engaged directly with French Impressionism. Degas admired her work and in 1877 invited her to join the newly formed 'impressionist' group. Like Degas she defined herself as an 'independent' artist, opposed to the Salon and its jury system, rather than an 'impressionist' *per se*, a term she considered more suited to Monet.[26] At that date the core group of 'independent' artists included Monet, Camille Pissarro, Auguste Renoir, Alfred Sisley, Paul Cézanne, Armand Guillaumin, Berthe Morisot and Gustave Caillebotte, but it was Degas's unusual compositions, acidic colours and use of pastel that most inspired Cassatt. In 1915 she recalled, 'The first sight of Degas's pictures was the turning point in my artistic life'.[27] Abandoning the dark palette and anecdotal subject-matter of her training under Charles Chaplin and Thomas Couture, she responded to Degas, who offered her advice and guided her towards more contemporary, urban motifs.

Several of the works that Cassatt contributed to the fourth impressionist exhibition of 1879 reveal the influence of the older artist. *In the Loge* (fig.3), for example, is strongly reminiscent, in subject and format, of Renoir's *The First Outing* of 1877 (The National Gallery, London), but Cassatt's interest in reflected light, the cropping of the woman's lower jaw, the almost jarring colours and the vigorous working of the pastel are closer to Degas. Even the decision to exhibit pastels shows Degas's influence and it was almost certainly Cassatt's willingness to experiment, combined with her graphic dexterity, which persuaded him of her talent.

Degas invited her, along with Pissarro, to participate in his next project to publish a collection of etchings under the title *Le Jour et la nuit* (*Day and Night*). Although the publication never materialised, the two artists continued to collaborate and support each other. Cassatt took part in the 1880 impressionist exhibition and showed solidarity with Degas in 1882 when he declined to exhibit with the rest of the group. She modelled for him on several occasions, not only for the two variations on *Mary Cassatt in the Painting Gallery at the Louvre* (p.144), but also for one of his best-known pastels, the dramatically cropped *At the Milliner's* of 1882 (Metropolitan Museum of Art, New York).[28] Degas clearly admired her work and acquired several prints and three pastels for his own collection, including *Study* of 1885–6 (National Gallery of Art, Washington D.C.), which hung in a prominent position in the salon of his Paris apartment at 37 Rue de Victor-Massé.[29] Cassatt, in return, was responsible for the wide dissemination of Degas's work to family and friends in the United States.

Cassatt valued Degas's advice, but he was a harsh critic and at times she was reluctant to show him her work.[30] 'Degas takes a pleasure in throwing me off track', she wrote to the American portrait painter Rose Lamb in November 1892.[31] She was influenced by Degas's compositional methods, but always insisted 'I don't copy him'.[32] Technically, she had a strong sense of design, but was also at home with the light palette and fragmented brushstroke of Impressionism. *On a Balcony* of 1878–9 (see fig.4), included in the 1880 impressionist exhibition, depicts a young woman, relaxing in the intimate space of a private garden, bathed in sunlight and coloured shadows. She is dressed informally in a loose, diaphanous morning dress, which reflects the light, enhancing the luminosity of the painting.

Like most women artists of her class, Cassatt was limited in the scope and variety of subjects she could depict.[33] The majority of her paintings focus on women in her immediate environment, their expressions often reflecting the stiffness and formality, as well as the boredom of their day-to-day lives. *Young Girl at a Window* of about 1883–4 (p.55), for example, shows a young girl in an elaborate but constricting dress and bonnet, stroking a small dog. As feminist art historians have observed, her position is 'liminal'; she is at once confined to her domestic location and 'debarred' or 'protected' from outdoor city life by the slender balcony to her right.[34] Cassatt's sister Lydia was the model for a number of these paintings, the most poignant example being *Autumn* of 1880 (p.53), painted in the autumn of her life, when she was suffering from the kidney disease from which she eventually died.

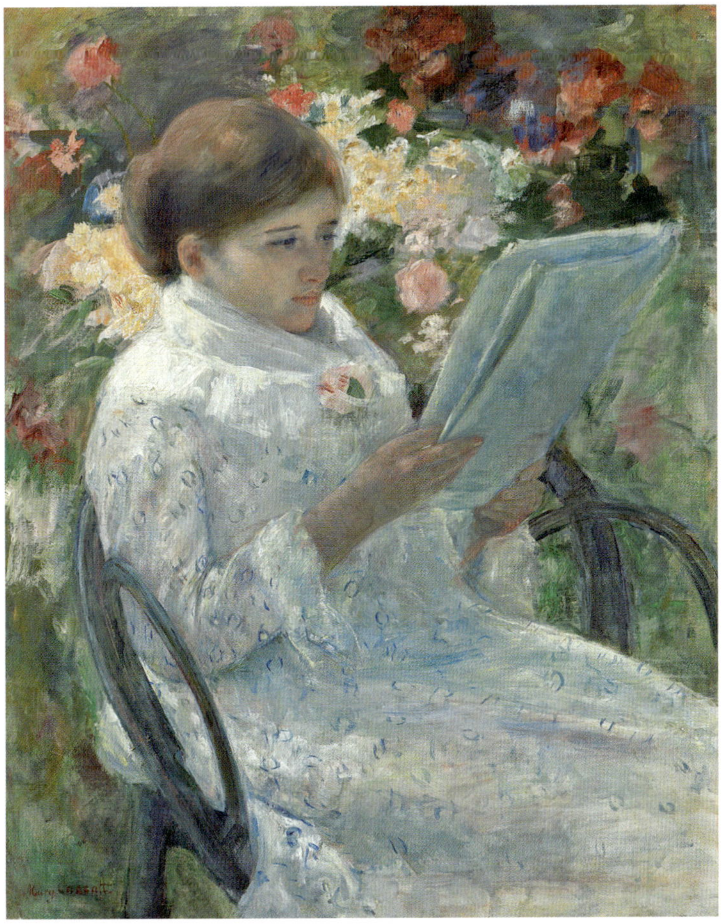

The pictures for which Cassatt was best known were her paintings of motherhood (pp.58, 59). As often as not, her sitters were not in fact mothers with their children, but family members, servants and even models posing as mothers with their offspring.[35] The critic Joris-Karl Huysmans approved of her approach to this subject because she avoided sentimentality; but there is an implied condescension in his 1881 comment that 'a woman is equipped to paint childhood. There is a special feeling men would be unable to render unless they are particularly sensitive and nervous.'[36]

Cassatt exhibited *Children Playing on the Beach* (p.57) at the eighth and final impressionist exhibition in 1886. The critic Gustave Geffroy commented on the painting's firm draughtsmanship, observing that it 'has the sharp outline that things and people have on the sand with the background of water and sky. The short arms and the dollish faces let you guess the flesh under a thick layer of suntan.'[37] Cassatt had an almost unsurpassed ability to infuse her compositions with an engaging naturalism, as illustrated by *Woman Sitting with a Child in her Arms*, painted around 1890 (p.58). The sleepy child and mother (or carer) are harmoniously interlocked, like a Renaissance tondo. The baby's warm, soft flesh acts as a foil to the cool white tones of the mother's dress, his contours echoing the sinuous lines of the jug, the woman's shoulder and the oval chair back. By contrast, *Summertime* (p.63) of 1894 is much more loosely handled, with broad strokes of green, violet, orange, blue and yellow. It depicts a woman and child boating on a pond near the Château de Beaufresne, which Cassatt had recently purchased. The broad brushstrokes and varied palette suggest a growing sympathy with Monet's Impressionism and especially a work such as *Young Girls in a Rowing Boat* of 1887 (National Museum of Western Art, Tokyo), painted in Giverny, which has the same cropped boat and high viewpoint.

Monet in Giverny: John Singer Sargent

In 1892 Cassatt appears to have paid a visit to Monet in Giverny.[38] By this date the village had been virtually taken over by the American colony, including a large number of women artists.[39] The Hôtel Baudy was forced to alter its cuisine to accommodate its foreign visitors, and regularly included 'American pie and Boston baked beans' on its menu.[40] Monet generally absented himself

Fig.4 MARY CASSATT
On a Balcony, 1878–9
Oil on canvas, 89.9 × 65.2 cm
The Art Institute of Chicago,
Gift of Mrs. Albert J. Beveridge in memory of her aunt, Delia Spencer Field, 1938.18

from the artists who congregated in Giverny, many of whom were taken under the wing of the painters Mary and Frederick William MacMonnies.[41] This had not always been the case, and some of the earliest visitors, such as Sargent and Robinson, were permitted to set up their easels alongside the master of Impressionism. Sargent commemorated his first trip to Giverny in 1885 with *Claude Monet Painting by the Edge of a Wood* (pp.22–3, 69). Monet is working on a canvas that has been identified as the painting now in the Museum of Fine Arts, Boston (p.68). To his right is a young woman, probably Suzanne Hoschedé, sitting in the shade of some poplars. Sargent's broken brushwork suggests a new direction but Monet recalled that Sargent was unable to paint without black pigment in the shadowed areas: 'I gave him my colours and he wanted black, and I told him "But I do not have any," "Then I cannot paint," he cried, and added, "How do you do it!"'[42] Significantly, the brightest colour notes in Sargent's painting are the bold strokes of complementary pinks and greens on Monet's palette.

Monet and Sargent first met at the Durand-Ruel Gallery in Paris in 1876.[43] Five years later they both exhibited at the Cercle des Arts Libéraux on the Rue Vivienne. In the intervening period, Sargent's style and subject-matter were extraordinarily eclectic. His two versions of *Luxembourg Gardens at Twilight* (p.66 and *In the Luxembourg Gardens*, 1879, Philadelphia Museum of Art) show the influence of Whistler and even Cazin, while *Woman in Furs* of around 1879–80 (Sterling and Francine Clark Art Institute, Williamstown) is in the style of Manet or Forain. Sargent's continued admiration for Carolus-Duran led him to darken his palette and it was not until 1883–5 that he began to work in a higher key and with more of an emphasis on landscape. He also produced several figure paintings that consciously reference Monet.

As Ormond and Kilmurray have demonstrated, the first painting that demonstrates this new departure is the remarkable oil sketch of Judith Gautier, entitled *A Gust of Wind* (private collection), thought to have been executed in the summer of 1883, when Sargent was working in Brittany.[44] The low vantage point and strong wind buffeting the sitter as she poses on a sand dune against a dramatic blue sky suggest that Sargent had seen Monet's *Woman with a Parasol – Madame Monet and her Son* (see fig.18), exhibited at the second impressionist exhibition of 1876. However, despite the sketchiness of handling, Sargent's colours are more opaque than Monet's and the handling is closer to Manet.[45] Sargent greatly admired Manet and after visiting the 'altogether delightful' retrospective at the Ecole Nationale des Beaux-Arts in Paris in January 1884 he took a keen interest in his work.[46]

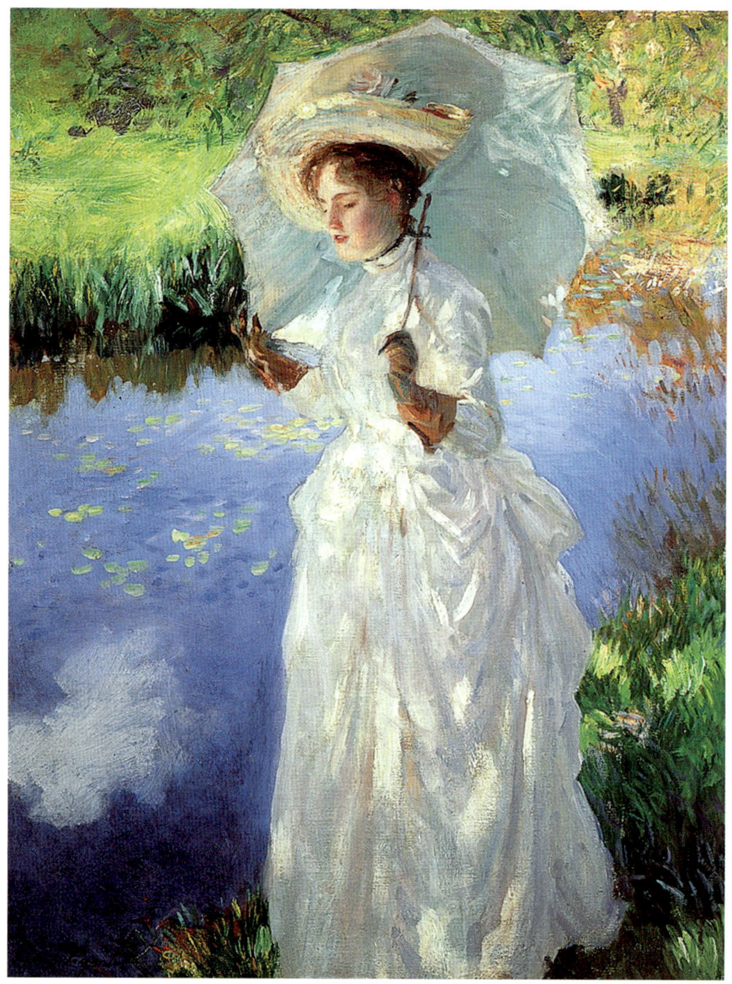

In October 1885, Sargent wrote to Monet with 'an unusual enquiry about the use of yellow and green'.[47] He was possibly working on *Reapers Resting in a Wheat Field* (p.71), although the date of this work is uncertain. It combines the rural subject-matter of Millet and Bastien-Lepage with a more experimental approach to colour. The figures are secondary to the flickering strokes of yellow and green that animate the hayfield, along with the bold, repeated curves of the reapers' sickles. The subject, choice of palette and format are reminiscent of Monet's 1885 views of the prairie in Giverny (p.72), even if Sargent's handling is less vigorous.

By this date, encouraged by the American artist Edwin Austin Abbey, Sargent had joined a group of British and American artists and writers – among them Henry James and

Fig.5 JOHN SINGER SARGENT
A Morning Walk, 1888
Oil on canvas, 67.3 x 50.2 cm
Private collection

Francis Davis Millet – at Broadway in the English Cotswolds. Here he began work on his masterpiece *Carnation, Lily, Lily, Rose* (Tate, London), painted out of doors over eighteen months, while he struggled to capture the precise effect of early evening light. In the spring of 1887 the critic Harry Quilter, reviewing the Royal Academy exhibition, hailed the picture as an exceptional example of 'the impressionist school'.[48] Even if the subject of two young girls with Chinese lanterns in a flower garden was more in keeping with English aestheticism, Sargent was continuing to develop his technique, modelling form with colour and lightening his palette.[49]

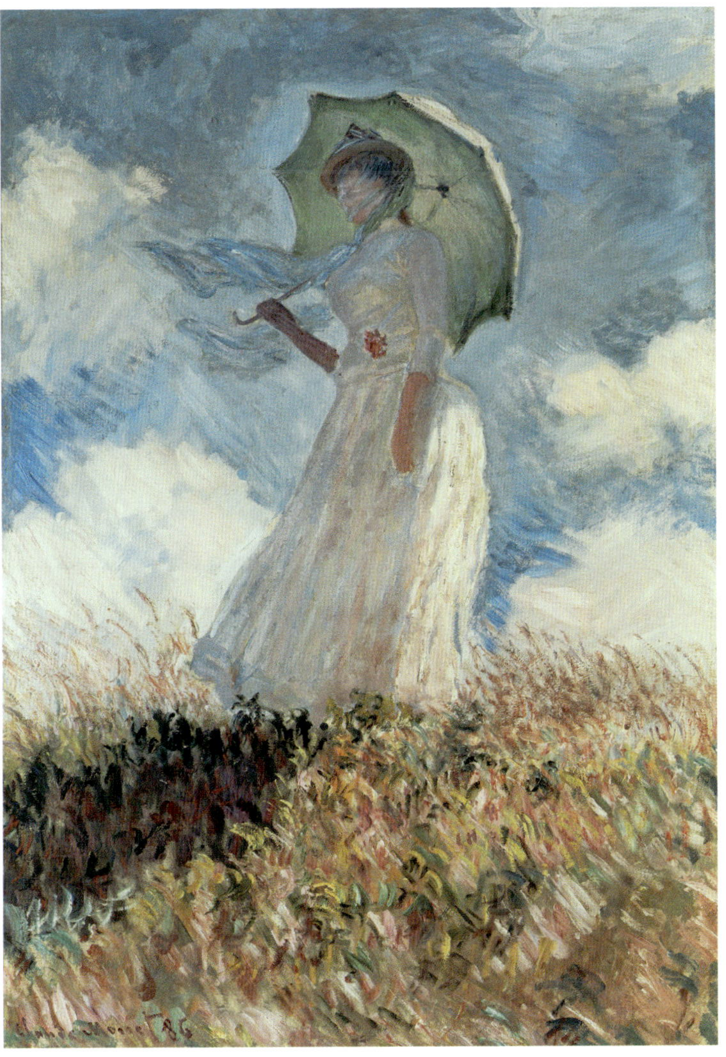

Sargent visited Giverny again in 1887, this time in the company of Auguste Rodin.[50] Like Cassatt, he was captivated by Monet's recent canvases of the Hoschedé girls boating on the river, which were quite Japoniste in conception. Returning to England he began work on a series of riverside studies at Henley and at Calcot Mill, his country house near Reading – where Monet visited him for two days in July 1888.[51] Emulating Monet, he sketched in oils from a studio boat and later wrote to his mentor, complaining about 'the practical difficulties of painting people on boats on the water, in between boats, etc'.[52] For *Two Women Asleep in a Punt under the Willows* (p.74) he chose a more convenient vantage point on the riverbank. This is one of Sargent's most strikingly modern canvases, freely painted with stabbing strokes of green to denote the reeds on the bank, and broader blues and whites to suggest reflections on the surface of the water.

Sargent's close association with Monet won him the approval of the New English Art Club and the inner circle of 'London impressionists', led by Walter Sickert. When Sargent exhibited *A Morning Walk* of 1888 (see fig.5) at the New English Art Club exhibition in the spring of 1889 Monet grumbled, 'I see that Sargent is engaged in this project [Impressionism] and proceeds by imitating me.'[53] The composition was directly inspired by Monet's *Study of a Figure Outdoors: Woman with a Parasol (Facing Left)* (fig.6), which Sargent would have seen in the studio in Giverny in 1887. Sickert defended Sargent, commenting 'to paint landscape in 1889 without knowing Monet by heart would be merely to betray a want of education, or worse, affectation'.[54]

Sargent may have had an ulterior motive for painting subjects so close to Monet, since the value of his pictures was steadily rising. Other art dealers besides Durand-Ruel were taking an interest in his work and in 1889 Monet was given exhibitions by Boussod, Valadon et Cie in Paris and London and by Georges Petit in Paris.[55] It was around this period that Sargent acquired four of his paintings.[56] These included *Five Figures in a Landscape* of 1888 (see fig.7), an evocative study of Monet's extended family posing against a hazy, sun-drenched landscape. Sargent may have been thinking of this mysterious work when he wrote to Monet: 'I am still haunted by the memory of your most recent paintings, full of unfathomable things.'[57] Later, Sargent tried to define Impressionism in a letter to D.S. MacColl:

Fig.6 CLAUDE MONET
Study of a Figure Outdoors: Woman with a Parasol (Facing Left), c. 1886
Oil on canvas, 131 x 88.7 cm
Musée d'Orsay, Paris, RF 2621

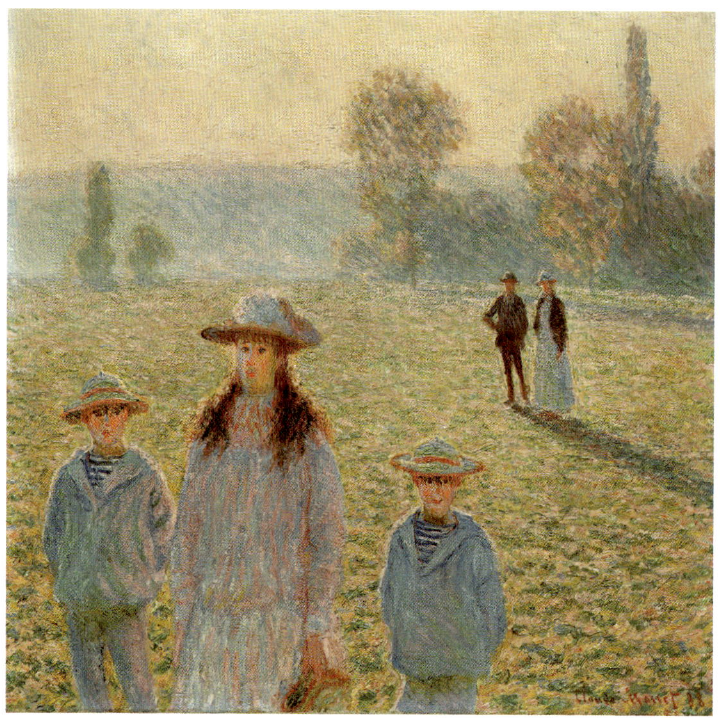

If you want to know what an impressionist tries for (by the way Degas said there is only one Impressionist 'Claude Monet') go out of doors and look at a landscape with the sun in your eyes and alter the angle of your hat brim and notice the difference of colour in dark objects according to the amount of light you let into your eyes – you can vary it from the local colour of the object (if there is less light) to something entirely different which is an appearance on your own retina where there is too much light.[58]

Monet himself did not recognise this definition of Impressionism, responding: 'Impressionism is simply the immediate sensation [of an object]. All the great painters were impressionists, more or less. Above all, it is a question of instinct. It is much simpler than Sargent believes.'[59]

Monet and Theodore Robinson

In 1926, shortly before his death, Monet remarked that Sargent 'was not an impressionist in the usual meaning of the word'.[60] Perhaps the same can be said for Theodore Robinson, who, like Sargent, probably visited Monet in Giverny for the first time in 1885. He was introduced by the landscape painter Ferdinand Deconchy and was immediately brought under the village's spell, 'writing longingly of it when he had to be away'.[61] Encouraged by his friend and fellow artist Kenyon Cox, Robinson had begun to take a closer interest in the impressionists. In 1886 he visited the fifth international exhibition at Georges Petit's gallery in the Rue de Sèze and reported back to Cox that he had seen 'some fine Monets, admirable in color and luminosity'.[62] Petit, and, more tentatively Theo van Gogh, had recently entered into competition with Durand-Ruel and were beginning to generate a sense of excitement around the impressionists. As Robinson noted, 'I know one or two picture dealers who prophesy great success in the near future for the impressionists and are making a kind of propaganda and are buying up their work'.[63] Perhaps Robinson, like Sargent, saw the commercial advantage of associating himself with the impressionist group.

Robinson returned to Giverny at the end of June 1887, when he rented a house along with Henry Fitch Taylor, Theodore Wendel, Metcalf and the Canadian artist William Blair Bruce.[64] In September he moved to the newly established Hôtel Baudy and remained in the village until early January 1888.[65] Thereafter he visited Giverny annually until 1892, arriving in the spring and leaving at the onset of winter.

Robinson was one of a select few welcomed into Monet's circle in Giverny. Apart from him, only Lilla Cabot Perry and Theodore Earl Butler were welcomed at his house, *Le Pressoir*, on a regular basis. A brief exception was John Leslie Breck, who visited the village between 1887 and 1891, but who was banished by Monet when he became romantically involved with Blanche Hoschedé.[66] Monet also disapproved of Butler's liaison with Blanche's sister Suzanne, but Robinson pleaded on his behalf and Monet relented.[67] Four days after Monet's own marriage to Alice Hoschedé, Suzanne and Butler were married on 20 July 1892, first in a civil ceremony at the *mairie*, and then at the church of Ste Radegonde in Giverny. It was one of those typical Giverny days, with periods of warm sunshine interspersed with sudden downpours, and Robinson described the 'frequent showers, champagne and gaiety'.[68] He recalled the scene in a letter to Thomas Sergeant Perry: 'Nearly all the wedding party were in full dress ... Most of the villagers and *all* the *pensionnaires* were there – guns were fired, two beggars held open the carriage doors and received alms.'[69] In *The Wedding March*, painted the same year (p.81), he captured the excitement and solemnity of the day by focusing on the wedding party parading through the village towards the church. Suzanne betrays her nervous anticipation as she clutches her veil and hangs on the arm of her new husband. In the same year Monet

Fig.7 CLAUDE MONET
Five Figures in a Landscape, 1888
Oil on canvas, 80 x 80 cm
Private collection, on loan at The Art Institute of Chicago, FLN 35.1989

painted Blanche working *en plein air*, and included Butler at his easel in the background, with Suzanne looking over his shoulder, a clear sign that he had been accepted into the fold.[70]

The extent to which Monet influenced the artists who worked in Giverny is questionable. Certainly, Monet's choice of motif appears to have been an important source of inspiration to artists such as Breck and Robinson, but to a certain extent Giverny and its surrounding landscape offered only a limited choice of subjects. The artists in the American colony were arguably influenced less by Monet than by Salon naturalists such as Cazin and Bastien-Lepage and by other artists on the edge of Impressionism.[71] Philip Leslie Hale's *French Farmhouse* of around 1893 (Museum of Fine Arts, Boston), for example, is reminiscent of Henri Le Sidaner, while Louis Paul Dessar's *Peasant Woman and Haystacks, Giverny* (fig.8) is directly inspired by Bastien-Lepage's etching *The Return from the Field* (fig.9), which was reproduced in Philippe Burty's *L'Eau Forte en 1878*.[72]

Similarly, the quiet atmosphere and muted tones of Robinson's *Giverny* of 1887 (private collection) suggests an awareness of Cazin's landscapes of the Pas-de-Calais. However, Robinson, who worked in the village over an extended period, soon lightened his palette and, from around 1889, developed a more vigorous brushstroke. He also began to adopt a high vantage point, especially in his views of the village. In *From the Hill, Giverny* of 1889–92 (p.78) the buildings are reduced to geometric shapes, absorbed into the surrounding landscape, while the paint is applied in bold strokes in the foreground, receding to cooler tones on the

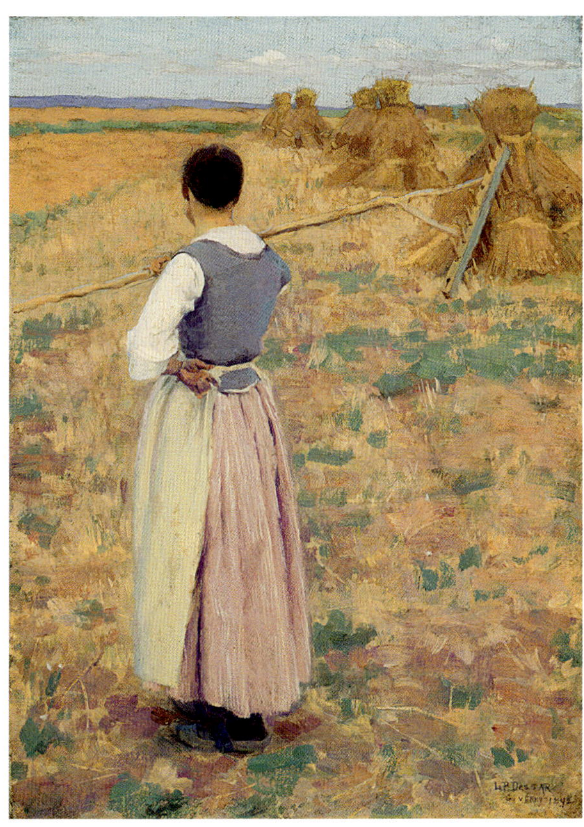

Fig.8 LOUIS PAUL DESSAR
Peasant Woman and Haystacks, Giverny, 1892
Oil on canvas, 46.4 x 33 cm
Terra Foundation for American Art, Chicago, Daniel J. Terra Collection, 1993.9

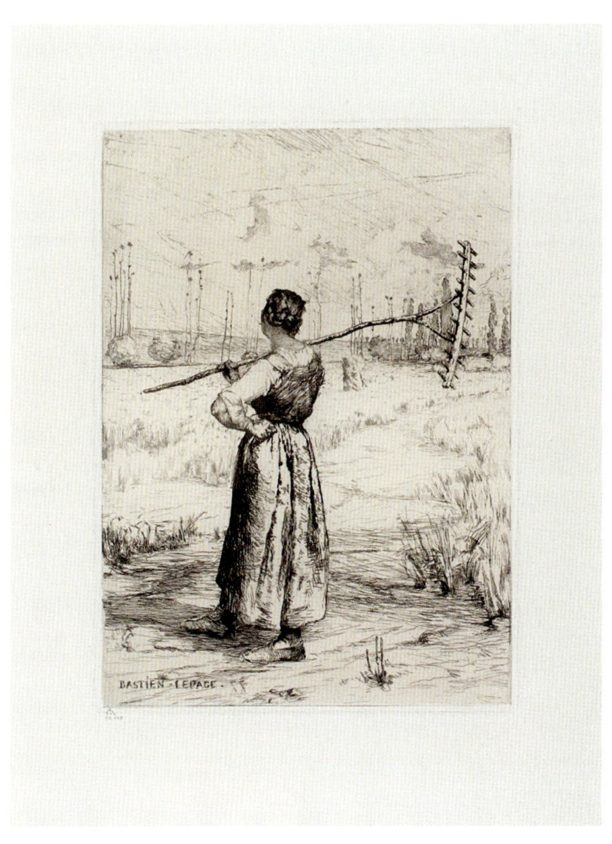

Fig.9 JULES BASTIEN-LEPAGE
The Return from the Field, 1878
Etching on ivory China paper laid down on heavy white wove paper (China paper collé), 28 x 20 cm
The Art Institute of Chicago, The Stickney Collection, 1887.448

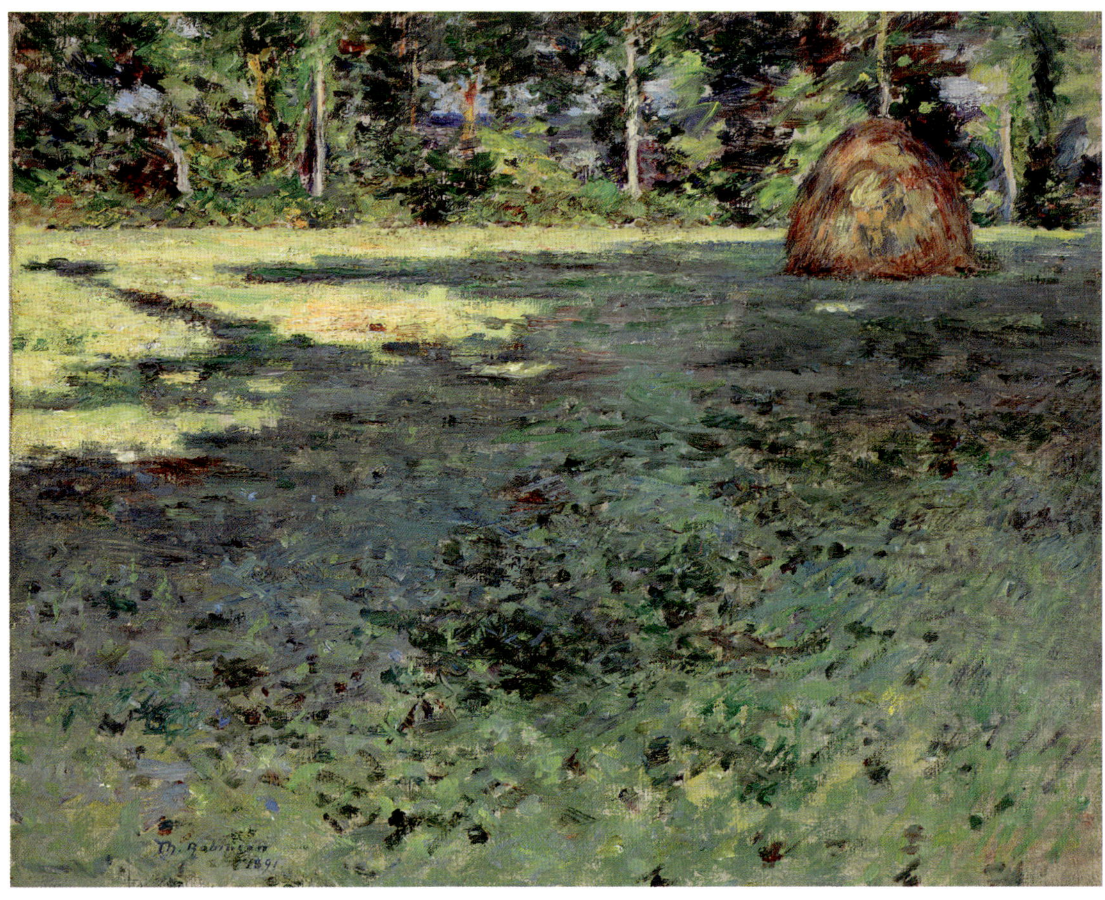

horizon. In *Winter Landscape* of 1889 (p.77), a rare snow scene, Robinson has chosen a similar angle and has applied the paint quickly, allowing the prepared ground to show through in places, while the sparse vegetation in the foreground is barely indicated.

One of the most effective uses of this elevated viewpoint is in a pair of canvases probably made in the spring of 1891, entitled *Blossoms at Giverny* (p.80) and *In the Orchard* (Princeton University Art Museum). Robinson almost certainly painted both scenes from a window although, as Sona Johnston has demonstrated, he worked frequently from photographs.[73] The view through blossoming trees may have been inspired by Caillebotte's *The Boulevard Seen from Above* of 1880 (private collection), which is an urban version of the same scene. Like Caillebotte, Robinson was fascinated by the transformative effect of the high vantage point and the way in which the white blossoms and tree branches obscure our view of the figures below, creating a vivid pattern. His handling is much sketchier than Caillebotte's, however, and for Robinson the real challenge of the painting was the evocation of coloured shadows and dappled light.

Another aspect of Robinson's oeuvre that suggests an engagement with Impressionism was his practice of painting pairs or groups of paintings of the same motif, viewed in different atmospheric conditions. With the success of Monet's Haystacks (or, more precisely, Grainstacks) series, which was exhibited at the Durand-Ruel Gallery in 1891, both he and Breck began to look again at the possibilities for this familiar motif.[74] In 1891 Robinson produced two canvases entitled *Afternoon Shadows* (fig.10 and private collection). Both approach the same subject from the same viewpoint, the artist's main concern being the variation in light and shadow on different days. However these canvases lack the mood of intensity and decorative impact of Monet's series paintings of 1890–1 (p.82) and are much closer in handling and conception to a work such as *Haystacks, Giverny* (private collection, W993) of 1885 where the grainstacks are set against a screen of trees.

Breck comes closer to Monet in his atmospheric *Morning Fog and Sun* of 1892 (p.83), even if this work has almost symbolist overtones. Moreover, in direct response to Monet, he produced a series of twelve oil studies of haystacks entitled *Studies of an Autumn Day* of 1891 (pp.84–5). This may have been

Fig.10 THEODORE ROBINSON
Afternoon Shadows, 1891
Oil on canvas, 47 x 55.9 cm
Museum of Art, Rhode Island School of Design, Providence, Gift of Mrs. Gustav Radeke, 20.206

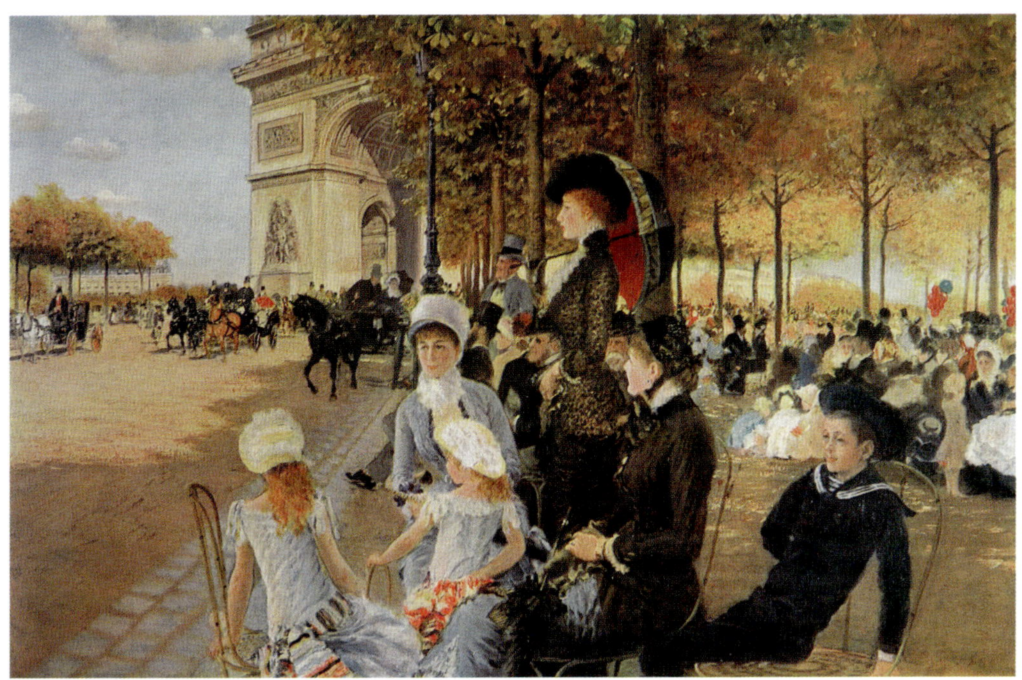

the final straw for Monet who, as we know, objected to being copied, and may have confirmed his decision to banish Breck from the village. He had no such concerns with Robinson, who visited Giverny for the last time in 1892, just as the number of American artists reached its peak.

Childe Hassam in Paris

In contrast to most of the artists discussed above, Childe Hassam, who settled in Paris from 1886 until 1889, failed to engage with the core group of impressionists. This was not due to lack of opportunity, since his first apartment at no.11 Boulevard de Clichy, on the edge of Montmartre, was a popular area with the avant-garde. Other residents at this address included Degas's Italian friend Giovanni Boldini and the American artist Frank Boggs. The apartment was not far from the Atelier Cormon at no.104, where Vincent van Gogh and Henri de Toulouse-Lautrec were enrolled as students; and both Georges Seurat and Paul Signac had studios in the same street.[75] However, although fluent in French, Hassam eschewed the bohemian life of Montmartre in favour of a more sedate existence, suited to his age and marital status. He also remained aloof from the American colony, apart from Boggs, and did not travel to either Grez or Giverny.

Hassam later concluded that his 'Paris instruction was superfluous'.[76] Nevertheless, his three years in the city had a considerable impact on his technique. His contribution to the Salon of 1887, *Une Averse – Rue Bonaparte* (p.88), with its dramatic perspective, hansom cabs and rain-soaked street, betrays a fascination with reflected light. Theodore Child, writing for the New York journal *The Art Amateur*, commented perceptively on the artist's 'sensitiveness to the values of objects in ambient atmosphere', comparing Hassam's cityscape with 'the gray opalescence' of Giuseppe de Nittis's Paris scenes.[77]

Hassam, like several genre artists of the period, was more influenced by artists such as Besnard, Forain and, above all, De Nittis than by any of the impressionists.[78] De Nittis specialised in images of the modern city and often experimented with unusual viewpoints and asymmetry. His paintings of the racecourse and of the fashionable streets and boulevards were extremely popular with the Parisian bourgeoisie and he enjoyed even more prominence after his death in August 1884. A friend of Degas, he participated in the first impressionist exhibition and according to Child he was 'often classed among the "impressionistes" [*sic*] ... [but] he was too conscientious and too complete an artist to disdain perfection of drawing, truth of coloring, and order of composition as the ordinary super-disdainful impressionist is inclined to do'.[79]

Hassam's next major work, *Le Jour du Grand Prix* of 1887 (p.89) shows how closely he must have studied works such as *The Avenue du Bois with the Arc de Triomphe* of 1880 (fig.11) by De Nittis. In both paintings the most fashionable members of society are promenading in their carriages near the Arc de Triomphe, and we know from the title of Hassam's painting that

Fig.11 GIUSEPPE DE NITTIS
The Avenue du Bois with the Arc de Triomphe, Paris, 1880
Oil on canvas, 60 x 90 cm
Private collection

they will proceed shortly to the Bois de Boulogne for the races at Longchamp. The composition of *Le Jour du Grand Prix* is comparable with several of De Nittis's paintings in its treatment of space, as well as subject. It also shows him experimenting with impressionist broken brushwork in the trees and sky, and colour in the shadows, whereas the horses and carriages are carefully painted, following his academic training. Degas, too, occasionally included race-goers in his compositions, as in *At the Races in the Countryside* of 1869 (Museum of Fine Arts, Boston) and some of Hassam's works on this subject – such as the pastel *Au Grand Prix de Paris* of 1887 (Corcoran Gallery of Art, Washington D.C.), with its asymmetrical composition, and *Carriage Parade* of 1888 (The Haggin Museum, Stockton, CA), with its cropped carriages viewed from behind – suggest an awareness of Degas, as well as De Nittis.

In 1889 the French critic, Maurice Hamel, commenting on the American works on display that year at the Exposition Universelle, observed that Hassam 'has Renoir in mind'.[80] Around November 1887 Hassam moved to a new apartment at 35 Boulevard Rochechouart, which Renoir had recently vacated, and where he discovered 'all sorts of little experiments'.[81] Hassam later recalled, 'I did not know anything about Renoir or care anything about Renoir [but] I looked at these experiments in pure colour and saw what I was trying to do myself'.[82] The influence of Renoir on Hassam's work is questionable, but he was becoming more aware of Impressionism, since several of the canvases of the Blumenthals' garden at Villiers-le-Bel show him experimenting with a vivid palette and unusual compositions. In works such as *Geraniums* of 1888–9 (The Hyde Collection, Glens Falls, New York), he uses pale pinks and lilacs in the shadows reflected on the whitewashed wall and vivid reds for the geraniums; while *Gathering Flowers in a French Garden* of 1888 (Worcester Art Museum, Massachusetts), with its rising central path, recalls Monet's *The Artists' Garden at Vétheuil* of 1880 (National Gallery of Art, Washington D.C.).[83]

It can be no coincidence that the impressionists who had the greatest following among their American counterparts were Monet and Degas, who enjoyed greater commercial success than their colleagues. It was almost inevitable that they would attract an admiring group of acolytes, eager to share in their achievement. Robinson and Sargent may well have seen the commercial potential of aligning themselves with Monet, while Cassatt benefited enormously from her association with Degas. However it was only those who spoke fluent French – Whistler, Cassatt, Sargent and Robinson – who developed close and meaningful friendships with the impressionists, even if they rejected Monet's particular brand of Impressionism. The majority of Americans were relatively isolated from the avant-garde and as a result their version of Impressionism was concerned less with the application of pure, unmixed colour than with painting *en plein air*. Nevertheless, to a greater or lesser extent, these artists embraced modernity and challenged the very tenets of the academy, adopting the heightened colour values and broken brushwork associated with the modern movement. For this reason they were quickly labelled 'impressionists' when they returned to the United States.

1. William Merritt Chase, 'The Picture that First Helped me to Success', *New York Times*, 28 January 1915, section 5, p.5, quoted in London, Boston and New York 2006, p.14.
2. On Whistler and Impressionism see Robins 2007, especially pp.5–6.
3. J. Engelhart, 'Meine Erlebnisse mit James McNeill Whistler aus dem Jahre 1898', *Der Architekt*, vol.21, 1916–18, p.53, quoted in Theodore Reff, 'The Butterfly and the Old Ox', in Reff 1976, p.15.
4. William Rothenstein, *Men and Memories*, 3 vols, New York, 1931–8, vol.1, p.101, cited in Reff 1976, p.18.
5. George Moore, 'Degas, the Painter of Modern Life', *Magazine of Art*, vol.13, 1890, p.425, cited in Reff 1976, p.18.
6. Reff has compared these two pictures to Degas's *The Bellelli Family* of 1858–67 (Musée d'Orsay, Paris), which Whistler could have seen in Degas's studio as early as 1858. See Reff 1976, pp.26–7.
7. Reff 1976, p.16.
8. Katharine Lochnan states that Monet 'probably visited Whistler's studio in 1870–71'. Toronto, Paris and London 2004, p.22.
9. Ibid.
10. This is mentioned in a letter dated 12 September (no year given) from Mary Cassatt to Joseph Pennell (Pennell Collection, Library of Congress): 'long ago M. Degas told me he had once written a very urgent letter to Whistler asking him to join a group of painters who were intending to exhibit together, the same group afterwards nicknamed impressionists, but Whistler never replied to the letter.' Lochnan 1998, p.223. Degas's letter has never been located.
11. On the Académie Julian see Morris 2005, p.38.
12. Low 1908, p.22.
13. Morris 2005, p.39.
14. Low 1908, p.13.
15. Low 1908, p.16.
16. Morris 2005, p.290.
17. Morris 2005, p.38.
18. Lavery 1940, p.52
19. Ibid.
20. Low 1908, p.132.
21. Low 1908, p.176.
22. Dorothy Weir Young, *The Life and Letters of J. Alden Weir*, New Haven 1960, p.77, cited in Morris 2005, p.167.
23. Letter dated 29 July 1877 from Emily Sargent to Violet Paget, Vernon Lee Papers, Special Collections, Millar Library, Colby College, Waterville, Maine, cited in Ormond and Kilmurray 2006, p.85.
24. Roger-Ballu, *Gazette des Beaux-Arts*, vol.18. no.1, July 1878, p.185, cited in Ormond and Kilmurray 2006, p.108.
25. Sarah Cash, 'Testing the Waters: Sargent and Cancale', in Washington, Houston and London 2009, pp.98–9.
26. On 15 March 1904 she wrote to Harrison Morris, Director of the Pennsylvania Academy of Art, 'Our first exhibition was held in 1879 and was a protest against official exhibitions and not a grouping of artists with the same art tendencies. We have been dubbed "Impressionists", a name which might apply to Monet but can have no meaning when attached to Degas's name.' Mathews 1984, pp.291–2.

27. Letter dated 28 February 1915 from Mary Cassatt to Colonel Paine, in Mathews 1984, pp.321–2.

28. In addition Cassatt posed around 1879 for a series of drawings of street women and for two other pastels, *Woman Tying the Ribbons of her Hat* 1882 (Musée d'Orsay, Paris) and another version of *At the Milliner's*, 1882 (The Museum of Modern Art, New York, acc. 141.57). See George T.M. Shackelford, 'Pas de deux: Mary Cassatt and Edgar Degas', in Chicago, Boston and Washington 1998–9, pp.125–7.

29. Chicago, Boston and Washington 1998–9, p.129.

30. In 1892 she confessed, to the Chicago art collector Mrs Potter Palmer, that Degas was 'the only man ... whose judgement would be [of] help'. See letter from Mary Cassatt to Bertha Palmer, 1 December 1892, in Mathews 1984, p.241.

31. Mary Cassatt to Rose Lamb, 30 November 1892, in Mathews 1984, pp.239–40.

32. Letter dated 12 March 1915 from Mary Cassatt to Louisine Havermeyer, in Mathews 1984, pp.322–3.

33. On this see Griselda Pollock, 'Modernity and the Spaces of Femininity', in Pollock 1988, pp.59–90.

34. Hollis Clayson, 'Threshold Space: Parisian Modernism Betwixt and Between (1869–1891)', in Dublin 2008, pp.19–20. See also Chicago, Boston and Washington 1998–9, p.66.

35. See Judith A. Barter, 'Mary Cassatt: Themes, Sources and the Modern Woman', in Chicago, Boston and Washington 1998–9, p.73.

36. J.K. Huysmans, 'L'Exposition des indépendants en 1881', *L'Art moderne*, Paris, 1883, in Berson 1996, vol.1, pp.348–55.

37. Gustave Geffroy, 'Salon de 1886: Hors du Salon: Les Impressionnistes', *La Justice*, 26 May 1886, pp.1–2, in Berson 1996, vol.1, pp.449–52.

38. To be precise, Robinson mentions Cassatt in his diary on 3 October 1892, but does not actually state that she is staying in Giverny. See Chicago, Boston and Washington 1998–9, p.342, and Giverny and San Diego 2007, p.204. Rewald and Gerdts have also suggested that she returned to Giverny with Cézanne in 1894, but there is no documentary evidence for this.

39. On Giverny and its colony of American artists, see Katherine M. Bourguinon, 'Giverny, a Village for Artists' and Kathleen Pyne, 'Americans in Giverny: The Meaning of a Place', in Giverny and San Diego 2007, pp.17–27; 45–53.

40. Low 1908, p.450.

41. See Kathleen Pyne, 'Americans in Giverny: The Meaning of a Place', in Giverny and San Diego 2007, pp.49–51.

42. Gimpel 1966, p.75.

43. Charteris 1927, p.130.

44. See New York 2010, [p.8], and Ormond and Kilmurray 2010, p.41.

45. Sargent acquired Manet's *Portrait of Mlle Claus* of 1868 (Ashmolean Museum, Oxford) and a watercolour of irises (private collection) at the atelier sale at the Hôtel Drouot on 4 and 5 February 1884.

46. See letter dated 18 January 1884 from Sargent to Charlotte Ida Popert, Boston Athenaeum, Sargent Papers, box 1, folder 18, cited in New York 2010, p.19, n.28.

47. Wildenstein letter 592. Wildenstein 1974–91, vol.II, p.262; Ormond and Kilmurray 2010, p.52.

48. See, for example, Quilter 1887.

49. For an extended analysis of this painting and its critical reception in the context of current British debates around Impressionism, see Helmreich 2003. See also Prettejohn 1998, pp.48–51.

50. It was probably on this occasion that he painted a profile study of Monet (National Academy of Design, New York).

51. Monet referred to this visit in a letter to Paul-César Helleu, written around 20 July 1888. Département des arts graphiques, Musée du Louvre, Paris. Cited in Ormond and Kilmurray 2010, p.56.

52. 'Les difficultés matérielles faire des gens en bateau sur l'eau, entre bateaux etc.' Cited in Charteris 1927, p.97; see also Ormond and Kilmurray 2010, p.55.

53. 'Je vois surtout que Sargent est très pris à partie et qu'il passe pour m'imiter.' Claude Monet to Alice Hoschedé, 12 April 1889, in Wildenstein 1974–91, vol.III, no.959, p.245.

54. 'The New English Art Club' (First Notice), New York Herald, 16 April 1889, cited in Ormond and Kilmurray 2010, p.42. See also Robins 2008, pp.35–6.

55. Frances Fowle, 'Making Money out of Monet: Marketing Monet in Britain 1870–1905', in Fowle 2006, p.146.

56. These were an 1887 landscape with trees of Bennecourt in the Ile de France; a sketch of the dramatic *Manneporte* at Etretat on the Normandy coast of about 1883; *Paysage avec figures, 'Figures au soleil' (Five Figures in a Landscape)* of 1888 (fig.7); and *Maison de Jardinier (The Gardener's House, Bordighera)* of 1884 (private collection).

57. Sargent to Monet, 'Sunday', summer 1889. Reproduced in Ormond and Kilmurray 2010, p.60.

58. This letter is reproduced in full in Charteris 1927, p.124.

59. 'L'Impressionisme [*sic*] ce n'est que la sensation immédiate. Tous les grands peintres étaient plus ou moins impressionistes [*sic*]. C'est surtout une question d'instinct. Tout cela est plus simple que ne le croit Sargent.' Cited in Charteris 1927, p.129.

60. 'Il n'etait pas un Impressioniste, au sens où nous employons ce mot, il était trop sous l'influence de Carolus Duran.' Charteris 1927, p.130.

61. Pierre Toulgouat, 'Skylights in Normandy', *Holiday*, no.4, August 1948, p.67, cited in Baltimore, Phoenix and Hartford 2004, p.51.

62. Theodore Robinson to Kenyon Cox, 3 July 1886, Kenyon Cox Papers, cited in Baltimore, Phoenix and Hartford 2004, p.50.

63. Ibid.

64. Baltimore, Phoenix and Hartford 2004, p.54.

65. He may have rented a house through the Baudys. I am grateful to Katherine M. Bourguignon for this information.

66. Margaret Werth, '"Long Entwined Effort" – Colonizing Giverny', in Giverny and San Diego 2007, p.63. Blanche eventually married Monet's son Jean in 1897.

67. Theodore Butler married Monet's stepdaughter Suzanne Hoschedé on 20 July 1892. After Suzanne's death he married her sister Marthe in 1900.

68. Theodore Robinson diary, 20 July 1892, cited in Baltimore, Phoenix and Hartford 2004, p.140.

69. Letter from Theodore Robinson to Thomas S. Perry, 23 July 1892, Thomas Sergeant Perry papers, Special Collections, Miller Library, Colby College, Waterville, Maine, cited in Baltimore, Phoenix and Hartford 2004, p.140.

70. Claude Monet, *Blanche Monet Painting*, 1892, oil on canvas, 73 x 92 cm (private collection).

71. Cazin was particularly influential, since from 1888 he began to specialise in pure landscape and in 1889 he received a gold medal at the Exposition Universelle, where a large number of American artists also exhibited their work. In 1893 he held an exhibition in New York, at which date his work was worth considerably more than Monet's. Mrs Potter Palmer's collection included eight works by Cazin and nine by Monet. See R. Thomson 'La "dune mélancolique": Jean-Charles Cazin, la création et la transmission d'une esthétique régionale vers 1880–1905', in Cousinió 2013, p.145.

72. Burty 1878. I am grateful to Richard Thomson for pointing out the original source of Dessar's painting.

73. Baltimore, Phoenix and Hartford 2004, see especially pp.116–35; 154–5.

74. These 'haystacks' were unique to Normandy and were used for storing wheat, including stalks, after threshing. Later the wheat grain would be divided from the chaff. This was first noted by Robert Herbert; Herbert 1979, p.106.

75. Signac was at no.130 from 1886 to 1888 and Seurat was at no.128bis from 1887 to 1891. See New York 2004a, p.54.

76. Frederick W. Morton, 'Childe Hassam, Impressionist', *Brush and Pencil*, vol.8, June 1901, p.146, quoted in New York 2004a, p.58.

77. Child 1887.

78. On the influence of De Nittis's cityscapes, see Igra 1999.

79. Child 1884. On De Nittis's friendship with Degas, see Edinburgh 2003.

80. 'pense à Renoir.' Hamel 1889, p.382.

81. DeWitt McClellan Lockman, *Five Interviews with Childe Hassam*, 31 January 1927, pp.19–20, DeWitt McClellan Lockman Papers, New York Historical Society, Archives of American Art microfilm, reel 503, cited in New York 2004a, p.60.

82. Lockman interview with Hassam, 31 January 1927, pp.19–20, quoted in New York 2004a, p.60.

83. Gerdts points out that he could have seen this painting at Durand-Ruel's 1886 impressionist exhibition in New York, even before moving to Paris. Gerdts 1984, p.94; Edinburgh and Madrid 2010–11, p.153.

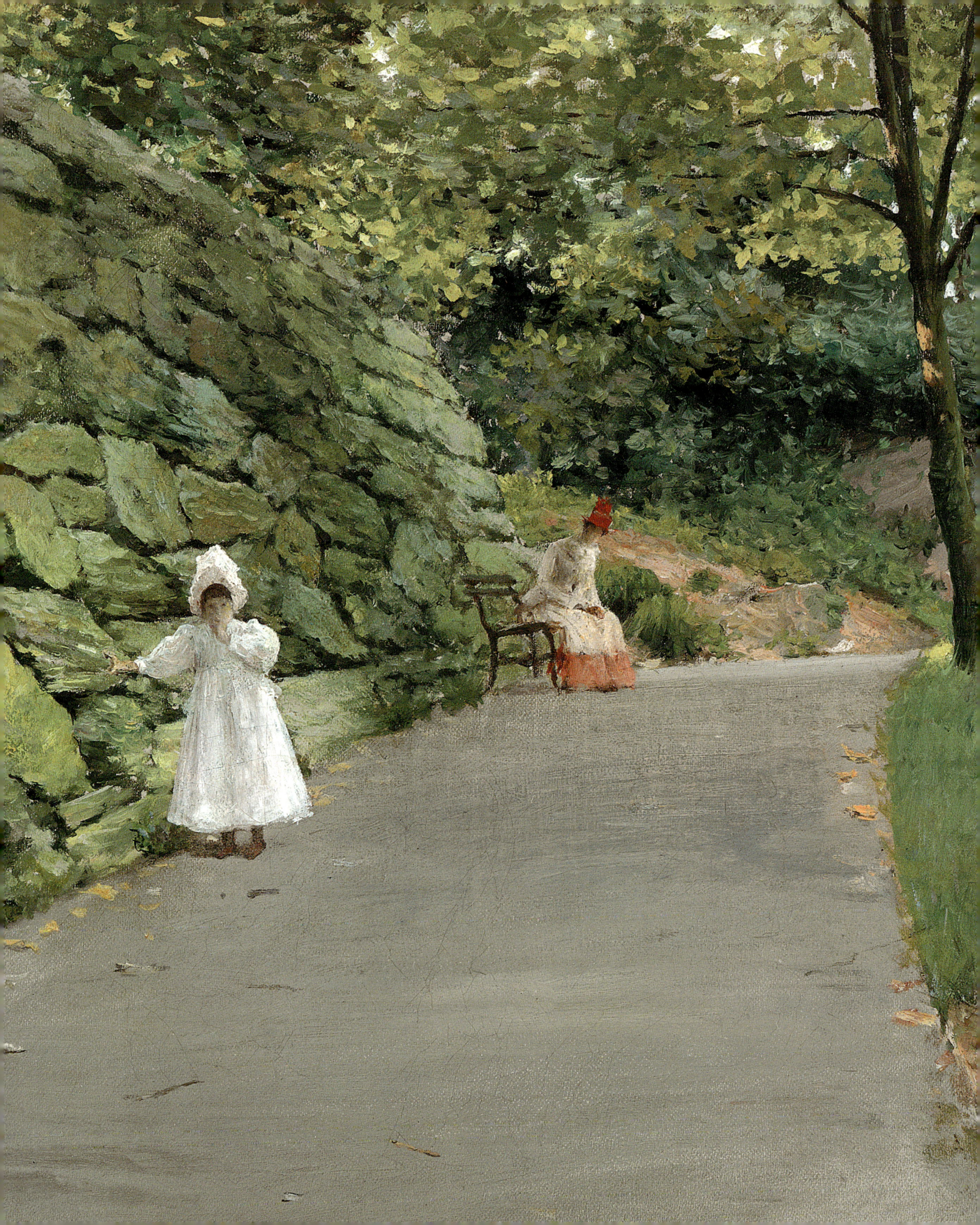

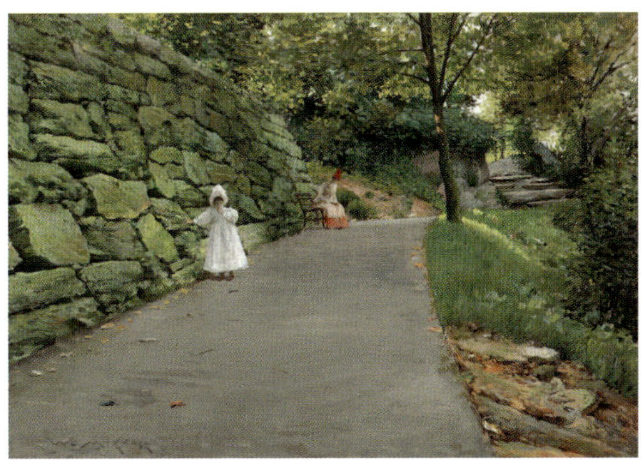

Painting **Impressionism** in America

Katherine M. Bourguignon

American painters came late to Impressionism. When the independent artists now known as the impressionists held their first exhibition in Paris in 1874, the event was barely noticed on the other side of the Atlantic. When the group exhibited again in the coming years, Americans expressed surprise, even outrage. In letters home, the painter J. Alden Weir wrote in 1877, 'I never in my life saw more horrible things'. Artist Ellen Day Hale in 1882 explained, 'It all makes you feel rather sick the first minute', though she conceded that, 'on looking at the pictures separately you find that you like a great many of them'.[1] It was not until the mid-1880s that American artists truly paid attention to the new colours, everyday subjects and loose brushwork characteristic of Impressionism. There were exceptions, of course. As Frances Fowle has discussed elsewhere in this volume, expatriates Mary Cassatt and John Singer Sargent helped shape the style, and James Abbott McNeill Whistler in many ways preceded it.[2] But for American artists working on native soil, Impressionism did not enter their visual vocabulary until at least ten years after its emergence in the Parisian art world.

American critics also puzzled over the meaning of Impressionism during its first ten years. In 1879, they associated it with bright colours, non-traditional pictures, 'pictorial riddles' and fidelity to nature. 'In viewing the various works offered for inspection,' wrote one reviewer of the annual exhibition at the National Academy of Design in New York that year, 'it is striking how quickly the new tendencies and the old tendencies ... the Hudson River school and the impression school, separate themselves out and assert their families'.[3] A few months later, another critic admitted, 'It is difficult to get at precisely what is meant by "impressionism," as the word is popularly used'.[4] He continued to wonder if it referred to puzzles and riddles left for the viewer to solve. A third, however, struck by the strangeness of purple shadows in such works, defended the impressionists for their faithfulness to nature and light, arguing that if an artist saw colours this way, he or she should paint them.[5]

During the 1880s, as opportunities to view impressionist pictures in America increased, critics and writers continued to respond to the new aesthetic. American collectors who travelled to Europe returned home with examples of paintings by Claude Monet, Camille Pissarro and Auguste Renoir. Encouraged by this potential new market, the French art dealer, Paul Durand-Ruel, organised two exhibitions of French impressionist works in America, the first in 1883 in Boston and the second larger display in New York in 1886. This latter exhibition brought Impressionism to America in full force, with 290 paintings by artists including Monet, Edgar Degas, Renoir, Gustave Caillebotte, Pissarro and Cassatt, as well as Eugène Boudin, Edouard Manet and Georges Seurat. Reviewers commented on the surprising

WILLIAM MERRITT CHASE
In the Park – A By-Path, c. 1889
Oil on canvas, 35.5 x 49 cm
Carmen Thyssen-Bornemisza Collection,
on loan at the Museo Thyssen-Bornemisza, Madrid, CTB. 1979.15

colours – 'It is the repetition of strange and violent coloring, and of discords, that the visitor first remarks...'[6] – and the purple shadows, a feature that would become almost a trademark of the new style of painting.[7] They likened the exhibition to a friendly 'invasion' as if an entire country had been 'brought to our doors'.[8]

Shock gave way to more serious, scholarly discussions and enthusiastic responses, and by 1887, the growing popularity of Impressionism in America led one journalist to write, 'There are Monets all along Sixth Avenue. The waterfronts present a succession of Boudins. The truncated compositions of Degas, especially applied to figures, strike one unexpectedly at the turn of a street...'[9] Her words reveal a knowledge of particular French impressionists as well as a desire to see New York through their eyes. The possibility that an American city could become the inspiration for such modern pictures challenged American artists returning from Europe. How could they adapt their foreign training for a native audience, not so much by painting 'Monets all along Sixth Avenue', but by depicting Sixth Avenue and other American subjects using new pictorial techniques? How could they employ Impressionism in America?

In this essay, I will study a series of concurrent moments when individual Americans began responding to and experimenting with Impressionism around 1890. These various and overlapping beginnings occurred along the East Coast between 1888 and 1892, as artists including Dennis Miller Bunker, Theodore Robinson, William Merritt Chase, Edmund C. Tarbell and John Henry Twachtman incorporated and adapted the colours, techniques and subjects of the impressionists. Studying individual paintings from this period, I do not seek to identify differences between 'American' and 'French' Impressionism, as if to suggest that Americans fell short of a model. In fact, American artists in 1890 faced a different audience than their French predecessors in the 1870s, and they had a very different agenda.[10] In turn, there was not a unique 'model' to emulate. By 1890, the impressionist revolution in France had already reached new challenges and departures, from artists such as Vincent van Gogh, Paul Gauguin, Seurat and Paul Signac. Delay can be a good thing. It allowed more freedom to the American artists who looked to Impressionism in the late 1880s. They found inspiration not only in the bright hues and *plein-air* immediacy of Monet, for example, but also in the abstracted use of colours of Seurat and Gauguin and the soft monochromes of Whistler.[11] Finally, as we will see, American artists working to adapt the style to native subjects also participated in a larger cultural phenomenon, that of constructing a national identity through art, and they did so over a short period of time. In 1889, Impressionism had barely taken root in the United States; by 1900 it had become the predominant style, associated with celebrated artists and transmitted to younger generations.

Painting 'local'

> 'Rather be a *bona fide* American than a sham Frenchman.'
> Frederic D. Crowninshield[12]

In the late 1880s, as hundreds of American art students returned to the United States after years of study in Europe, most struggled to appeal to home audiences and collectors. Indeed, in a climate of growing nationalism, critics called repeatedly for American subjects and denounced foreign scenes as 'counterfeit', 'imitation', 'reminiscences' and 'conventional'.[13] Some complained that their artists were under the influence of Europe and urged them to focus on the United States. 'Sheltering themselves under the convenient saying that art has no country, our painters either remain abroad and paint Europe, or return to their own land and paint Europe still', wrote Charles De Kay in 1891, warning 'Do not attempt to paint America through French spectacles'.[14] Sadakichi Hartmann echoed this idea in 1894, 'So many of our artists are foreigners, living abroad, and those who return to this country bring a foreign technique with them, either Munich or Paris, and it takes them half their lives to free themselves from its influence'.[15] Hartmann objected to the over-confidence of artists recently returned from Europe who, he felt, produced 'pale imitations' of their European teachers. American collectors also shunned the American impressionists, preferring to invest in art by French artists rather than pictures of France by Americans.

The writer and critic Hamlin Garland was the most influential of the voices calling for a national art. In 1894, he too encouraged artists to study abroad and learn new techniques, but he told them to return home and work in their native land. 'Each painter should paint his own surroundings ... art, to be vital, must be local in its subject.'[16] Not only would this 'local colour' add interesting, American details to a picture, but such attention to the 'local' would also make a painting authentic. An artist could demonstrate a sense of belonging by painting American landscapes to show he was not a tourist or visitor. Nature alone would be the 'teacher' for the new generation of artists, and, according to Garland, local, familiar Nature would be best. 'The light floods the Kankakee marshes as well as the meadows and willows of Giverny', he wrote, 'The Muscatatuck has its subtleties of color as well as the L'Oise, and a little young haymaker on the banks of the Fox River is certainly as admirable ... as a clumsy Brittany peasant in wooden shoes'.[17] For Garland, America offered just as many picturesque possibilities as France. Hartmann pushed the idea of nationalism still further, writing, 'We have to search in our own day and in our immediate surroundings to solve the enigma of future American art'. He called on artists to depict native subjects and on collectors to buy their works: 'Above all else be patriotic!'[18]

Garland also advocated the use of new techniques, specifically Impressionism. For him, the idea of painting 'local' was not restricted to geographical boundaries but also encompassed time. An artist needed to paint his own moment. 'Presentness' is at the origin of modernism, and new ways of seeing grew from new notions of time. Indeed, such attention to individual, fleeting moments is at the heart of Impressionism as artists sought to depict contemporary life, with no story, past or memory. Americans, by focusing on their own country, could embrace modernity and modern techniques. They could adapt the new style to capture the rich, sophisticated modernity of the Gilded Age, a period of great economic development in the United States following the end of the Civil War, from the late 1860s until 1900. Impressionism – with its new colours, methods, compositions and subjects – would be appropriate for representing American modern life.

Finally, painting local could allow artists to express spiritual depth and feeling because, as Garland suggested, they responded emotionally to familiar, local sites. Critics denounced Monet's art, for example, because they felt it lacked such depth and was too scientific and superficial.[19] American sites could help provide this emotional content and artists chose New England cities and rural landscapes imbued with social and national significance as well as nostalgia.[20] Painting local could allow American artists a three-fold advancement: to express a growing nationalism, experiment with modernist techniques and generate an emotional response to familiar subjects. But it often also required struggle and a new beginning. After years abroad, it was not always easy to paint one's own country or to find transcendence in its landscapes.

'Knowing every bull-frog'

> 'I know every bush and bird and bull-frog in this place and they are all very friendly.'
> Dennis Miller Bunker[21]

Dennis Miller Bunker and Theodore Robinson began experimenting with Impressionism at almost the same time but in different situations. Robinson worked in Giverny between 1887 and 1892, learning from Monet the importance of close observation of nature. Bunker met Sargent in Boston in 1887, and learned of Impressionism through his example. Both Robinson and Bunker had received a traditional training in America and France before adopting impressionist techniques and maintained academic structure in their art. Both also made a conscious decision to paint American landscapes, often struggling to train their eyes to find beauty in their own country.[22]

In 1888, the successful, flamboyant Sargent invited Bunker to Calcot Mill in England for a summer of painting. During those few months, Sargent produced colourful, daring pictures, which reflect his most advanced explorations of Impressionism and his recent exchanges with Monet. Bunker watched and learned, experimenting on his own, but not yet ready (or able) to integrate these ideas. He wrote to a friend about his lack of progress, 'I've done nothing – ab-so-lu-ment rien'.[23] The following year, back in Boston, Bunker made a decision to reproduce the experience. He travelled fifteen kilometres from the city to Medfield, working alone outdoors in a rural environment reminiscent of the English countryside. Meandering brooks and blue skies invited him to concentrate on applying impressionist methods. The summer resulted in masterful pictures such as *Roadside Cottage* of 1889 (p.102), which depicts an eighteenth-century New England home typical of this area. The cottage is unassuming, even uninteresting, but specifically American. Bunker also painted a series of close observations of an ordinary stream including *The Pool, Medfield* of 1889 (p.103) and *The Brook at*

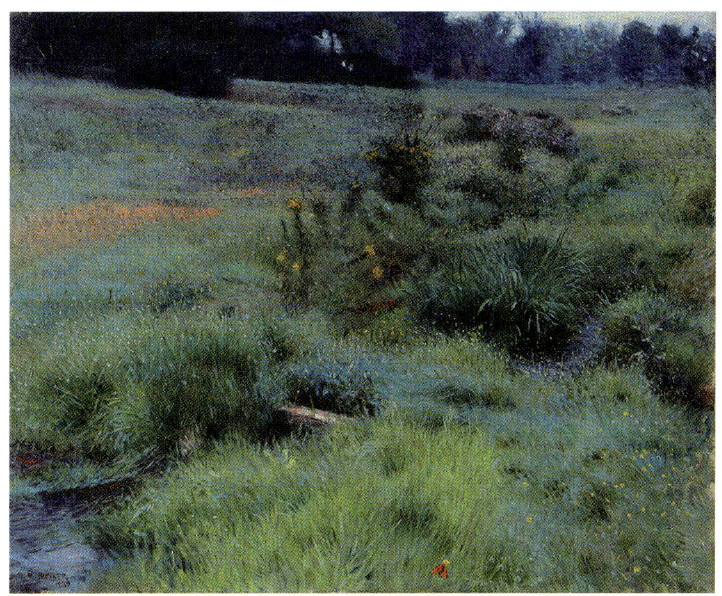

Fig.12 DENNIS MILLER BUNKER
The Brook at Medfield, 1889
Oil on canvas, 62 × 76 cm
Isabella Stewart Gardner Museum, Boston, P3s19

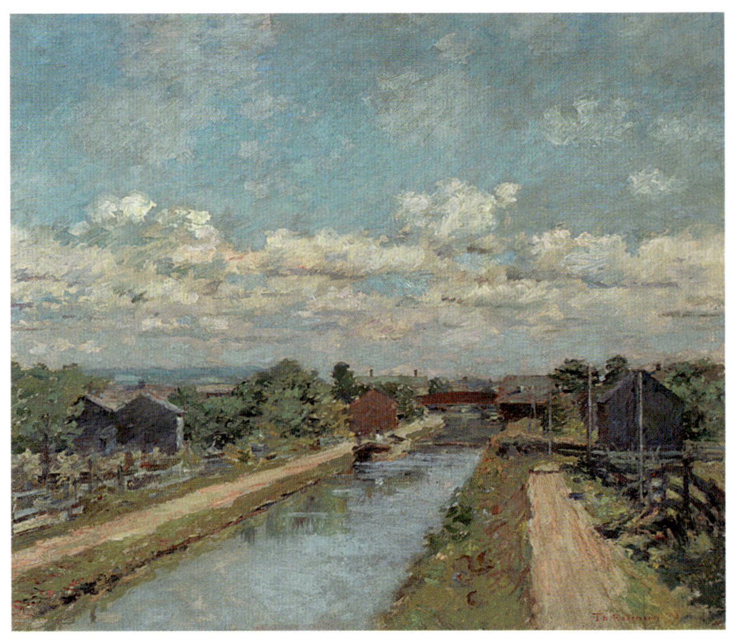

Medfield (see fig.12). The high horizon line helps flatten the composition, while the free brushwork and application of colour in individual, unblended strokes demonstrates a full understanding of Impressionism. Bunker anticipated the call for a 'local' art, combining European painting techniques with American subjects.

When he exhibited these pictures in Boston in 1890 alongside works by Sargent, critics made favourable comparisons, calling them 'very pretty, startling, undoubtedly, and somewhat unique'.[24] Bunker's impressionist summer did not, however, lead the artist to abandon his more traditional, academic portraits, and he would continue to fluctuate between bright, colourful landscapes and darker, moodier, figurative works such as *The Mirror* of 1890 (fig.13). His art demonstrates the notion that for many Americans, Impressionism was not a final destination but a process.

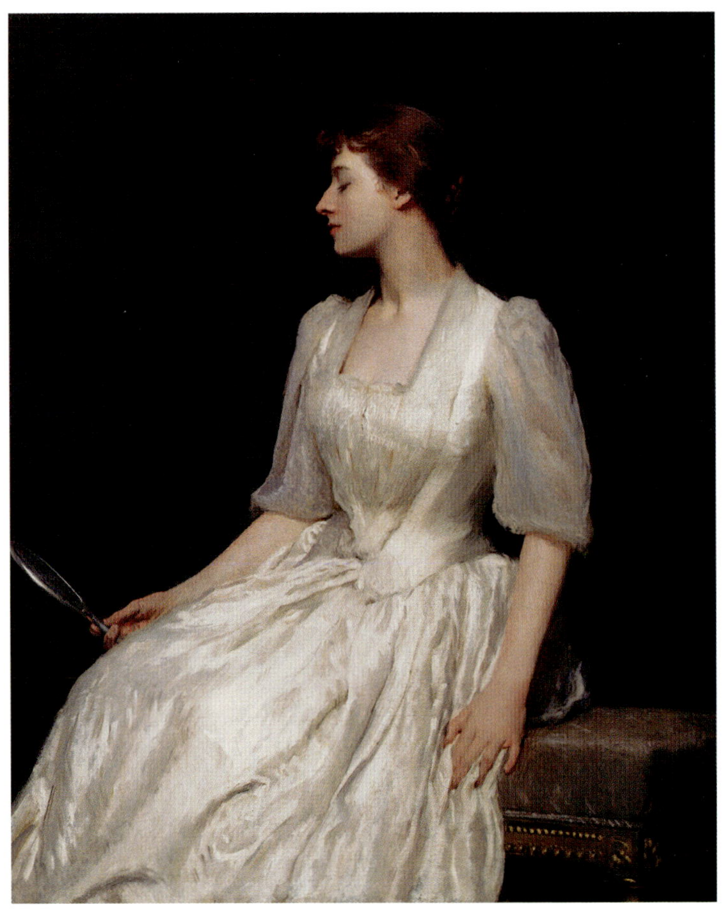

Of all the artists who returned from Europe and focused their attention on their native landscape, Robinson did so in the most self-conscious way and – perhaps because of that – he struggled. When Garland called on artists to paint 'local', he failed to consider how someone like Robinson, after years living and working in Giverny, might in fact be more familiar with the gentle hills and everyday life of the French village than with his native country (pp.77-81). Encouraged by Monet, Robinson returned to America in 1892 with the specific desire to paint the American landscape. Early works owe much to his Giverny experiments, but some examples reveal a new vision. Two views of canals painted in 1893 in upstate New York depict a mode of moving goods that was already nearly obsolete (*Port Ben, Delaware and Hudson Canal*, above and p.100; *Canal Scene*, p.101). The absence of human activity makes these works nostalgic, poetic renderings of nature, rather than commentaries on labour or man-made progress. They look back rather than forwards, but demonstrate the impressionist desire to find interest in the ordinary or commonplace. Robinson commented on this choice of subject: 'We have been too much afraid of certain

Fig.13 DENNIS MILLER BUNKER
The Mirror, 1890
Oil on canvas, 128 × 102.6 cm
Terra Foundation for American Art, Chicago, Daniel J. Terra Collection, 1999.22

THEODORE ROBINSON
Port Ben, Delaware and Hudson Canal, 1893
Oil on canvas, 71.8 × 81.9 cm
Pennsylvania Academy of the Fine Arts, Philadelphia, Gift of the Society of American Artists as a memorial to Theodore Robinson, 1900.5

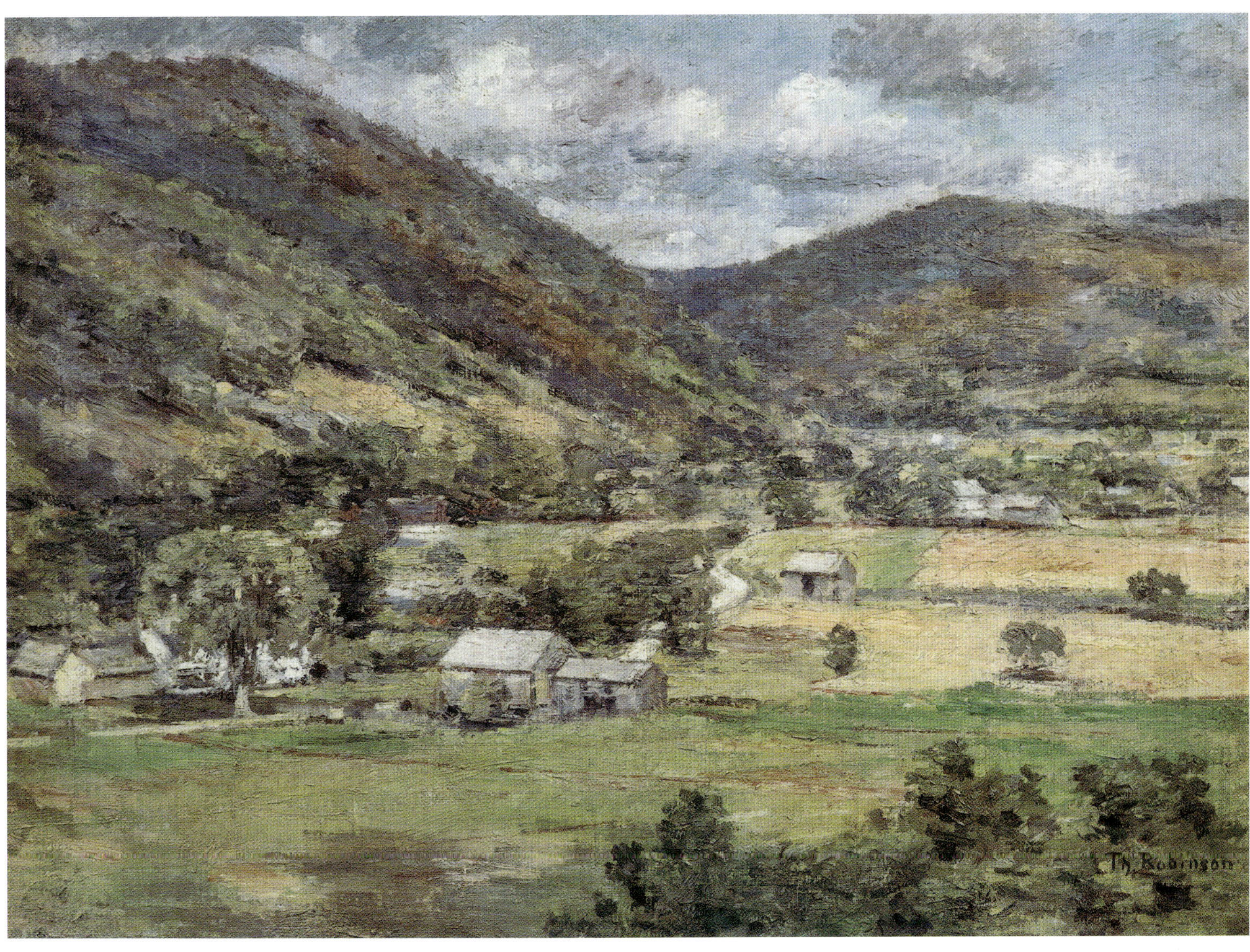

things, and have been choosing things we have painted abroad or similar ones – instead of painting as the Dutchmen did ... their own kind of house, ugly as it may appear to some. And new beauties, new oddities, new points of interest are waiting discovery.'[25] His desire to paint American scenes and instil them with an emotional response never reached fulfilment. Just before his sudden death at the age of forty-three, Robinson had begun a series of landscape scenes of rural Vermont, 'among the hills I knew when a boy'.[26] He had purposefully and consciously chosen a part of the country where he felt emotionally attached to the landscape. These paintings, however, do not signal a new or final phase in his art; instead works such as *West River Valley, Vermont* of 1895 (fig.14) are reminiscent of his pictures from Giverny a decade earlier.

'Right out under the sky'

At the same moment that Bunker experimented with Impressionism near Boston, and Robinson in Giverny, William Merritt Chase produced radically new pictures near New York. In 1889, he sent several city and park scenes to Paris for inclusion in the Exposition Universelle. These small, unassuming paintings, including *A City Park* of around 1887 (fig.15), depict ordinary corners of public spaces. They differed from the other American paintings on view, most of which featured French subjects. Several critics remarked on the fresh, new nature of these everyday scenes.[27]

Fig.14 THEODORE ROBINSON,
West River Valley, Vermont, 1895
Oil on canvas, 80 × 118.1 cm
Owen Yost Collection, New York

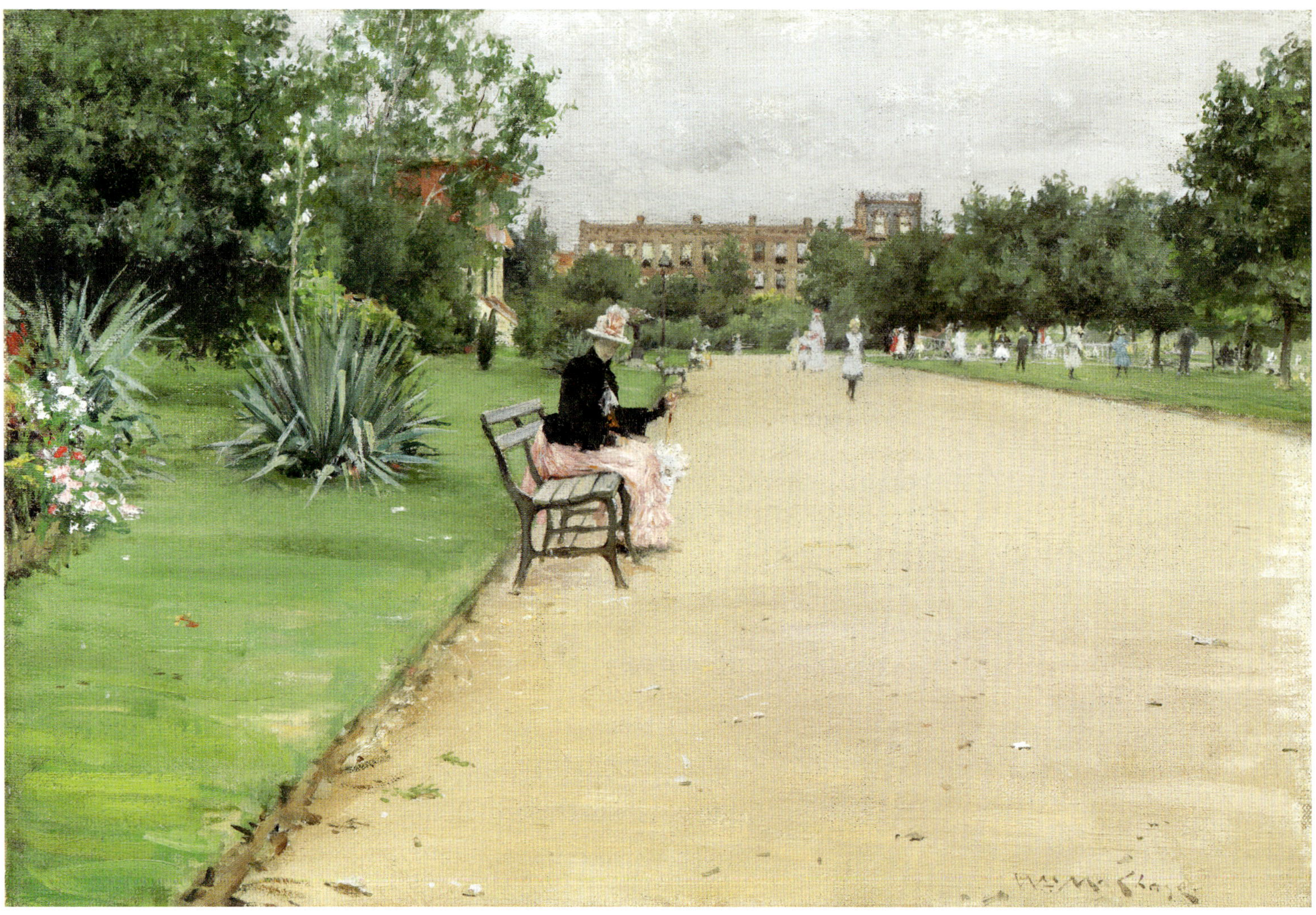

When exhibited in the United States, the series received praise as American in both subject and technique. 'Nothing in the artist's work is better than these flashing jewels, which give the lie to the familiar moan of many American artists, who persist in painting much bepainted Holland because there is nothing worth painting in America', wrote one Chicago critic in 1889.[28] A New York critic noted in 1891 that, 'In the parks of Brooklyn and New York he has found subjects which, although so close at hand, none of our other painters had appreciated'.[29] Yet another praised the parks as being more beautiful than those of Paris.[30]

These park scenes (pp.94-6) came at an important moment in Chase's career. Back from Europe and firmly established in New York a decade earlier, he had earned a strong reputation for bravura brushwork and a dark manner inspired by his artistic training in Munich. By the late 1880s, critics and collectors had tired of his art, and perhaps in response to poor reviews, the artist began to reinvent his artistic style, introducing new techniques and brighter colours. His park subjects may have been, as Barbara Gallati has noted, 'a means to renovate his artistic reputation by essentially "Americanizing" it'.[31] And it is clear that these scenes, coming so quickly after the large exhibition of French Impressionism organised in New York by Durand-Ruel, marked a major shift for Chase who devoted himself to *plein-air* painting.

During the 1890s, Chase spent his summers on the Eastern seashore, teaching art students in Shinnecock on Long Island and capturing the sandy, open landscapes surrounding his house. 'You must be right out under the sky', he remarked in 1891, 'You must try to match your colors as nearly as you can to those you see before you, and you must study the effects of light and shade on nature's own hues and tints'.[32] Chase espoused many

Fig.15 WILLIAM MERRITT CHASE
A City Park, *c.* 1887
Oil on canvas, 34.6 x 49.9 cm
The Art Institute of Chicago,
Bequest of Dr. John J. Ireland, 1968.88

ideas of the impressionists, such as close attention to nature and changing light effects. He did not, however, adopt scientific colour theories or represent industrialised landscapes. Instead, works such as *At the Seaside* of around 1892 (fig.16) show bright, summer days and children at play (pp.105, 108, 109). This preference for uncomplicated weather and carefree, upper-class leisure marked Impressionism as a selective vision of America. Chase had no interest in rural scenes of hard-working farmers or urban visions of immigrant labourers. Instead, the 'local' for him, was a world in which upper-middle-class Americans enjoyed genteel pursuits in a sun-filled outdoor paradise.

Fig.16 WILLIAM MERRITT CHASE
At the Seaside, c. 1892
Oil on canvas, 50.8 × 86.4 cm
The Metropolitan Museum of Art, New York, Bequest of Miss Adelaide Milton de Groot (1876-1967), 67.187.123

'Learning of the Impressionists to paint sunshine'

The sun is also always shining in the figurative paintings of Edmund C. Tarbell and Frank W. Benson from the 1890s. Friends and colleagues throughout their careers, Tarbell and Benson travelled to Paris around the same time and later taught in Boston at the School of the Museum of Fine Arts. Both artists adopted the bright colours and rough brushwork of Impressionism but avoided dissolution of the figure or atmospheric effect. Their women are solid and pleasing – never mottled by purple shadows or blotches of sunlight. Theirs was a conservative Impressionism, which blended academic technique with modern painting ideas. Tarbell made a sudden shift to the impressionist style in 1890, producing several large canvases of outdoor scenes over the next few years. Bold colour combinations such as a bright red hat against a green and yellow background in *Three Sisters – A Study in June Sunlight* of 1890 (p.90, 110) demonstrate his

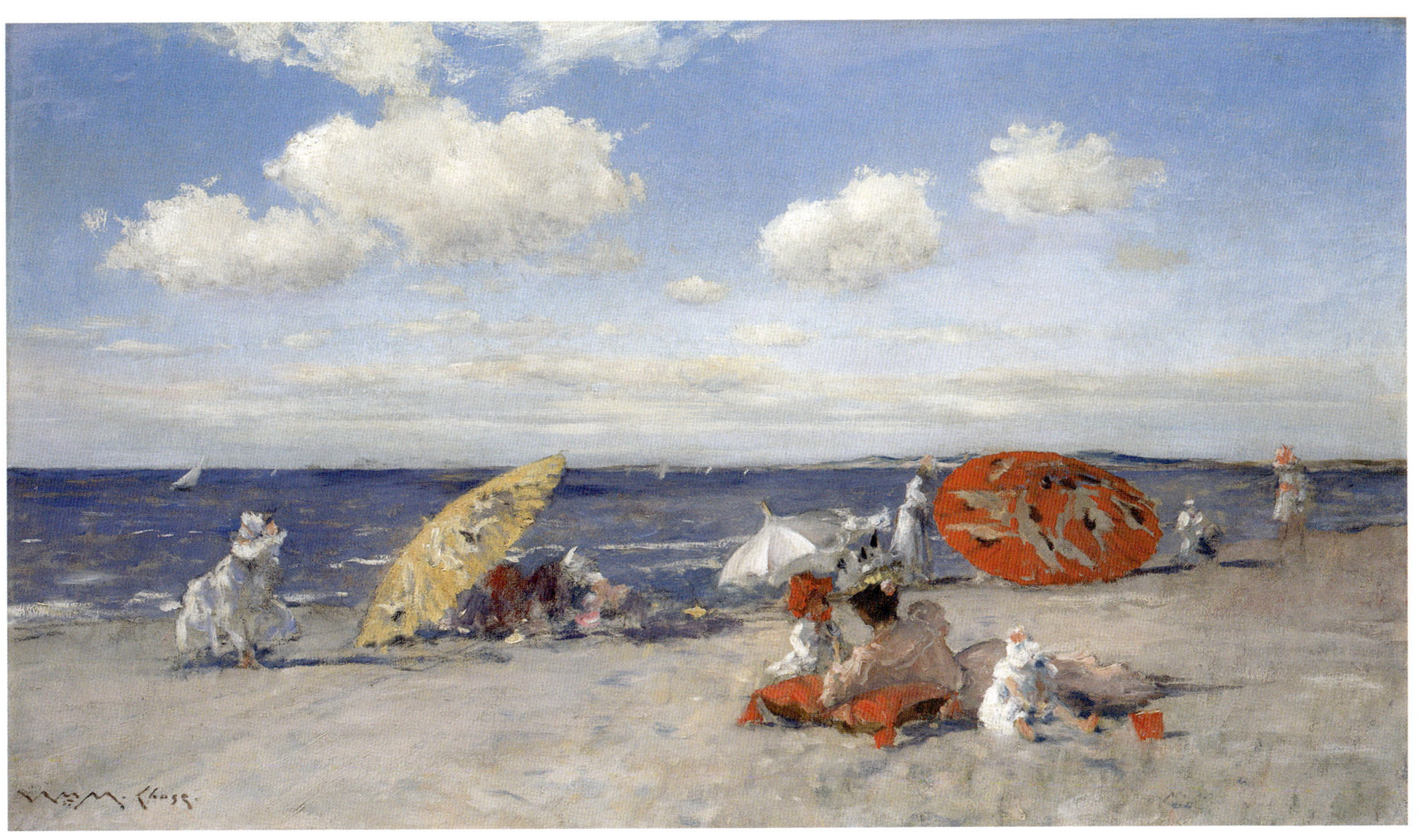

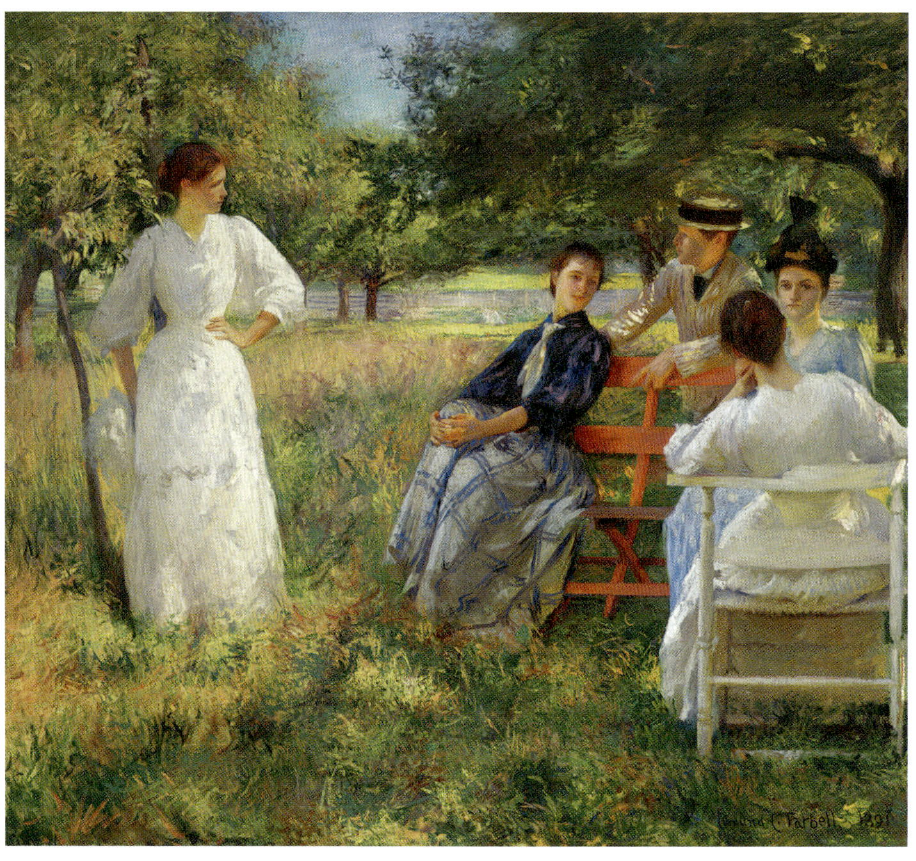

knowledge of modern colour theories,[33] while the balanced composition points to the artist's priorities, creating beautiful scenes of a refined Gilded Age. When Tarbell exhibited *In the Orchard* of 1891 (above and p.111) at the Chicago World's Columbian Exposition in 1893, William Howe Downes called it 'one of the happiest examples of [Tarbell's] style, audacious yet reserved, beautifully sound and sweet in color, splendid in its light and warmth, in a word one of the most remarkable paintings American art can boast of'.[34] The painting established Tarbell as a leader of Impressionism, and critics upheld his art as specifically American.[35] Such nationalistic praise may seem surprising for a work that owes a clear debt to French Impressionism in its brushwork, palette and subject. Painted in France and America, the canvas lacks site-specificity, so its 'American-ness' may refer more to its artist than its subject.[36] Nonetheless, for contemporary viewers, the picture somehow represented America – in clothing, manner and attitude, Tarbell's female figures pointed to a new American ideal, and depictions of women (often clothed in white) became popular among American impressionists during this period.[37] Though Tarbell turned away from the bright, sun-filled pictures of 1890 and 1891, he continued to focus on female figures with attention to a more subtle, moodier atmosphere, depicting them quietly lost in thought in numerous interior scenes from the turn of the century.

Benson turned to outdoor subjects in the 1890s and especially after 1901, when he began to spend summers on North Haven Island off the coast of Maine. The artist's academic training is visible in the skilful drawing and respect for the figure, while his penchant for Impressionism can be found in his colours, paint application and *plein-air* motifs. Like Tarbell, he received praise for his emphasis on sunshine and bright colours. A critic wrote in 1892 that Tarbell 'has been learning of the Impressionists to paint sunshine', while another wrote in 1909 that Benson must own a 'little jar marked "Sunshine," into which he dips his brush when he paints his pictures of summer'.[38] Paintings like *Summer* of 1909 (fig.17) and *Sunlight* from 1909 (p.119) pay homage to works by Monet, such as *Woman with a Parasol – Madame Monet and her Son* of 1875 (fig.18) or *Study of a Figure Outdoors: Woman with a Parasol (Facing Left)* from about 1886 (see fig.6) and to Sargent, *A Morning Walk* of 1888 (already a reference to Monet; see fig.5). Benson has removed the protective parasol and turned his female figure to face the sun. Still dressed in white, she is hatless and

EDMUND C. TARBELL
In the Orchard, 1891
Oil on canvas, 154.3 × 166.4 cm
Terra Foundation for American Art, Chicago,
Daniel J. Terra Collection, 1999.141

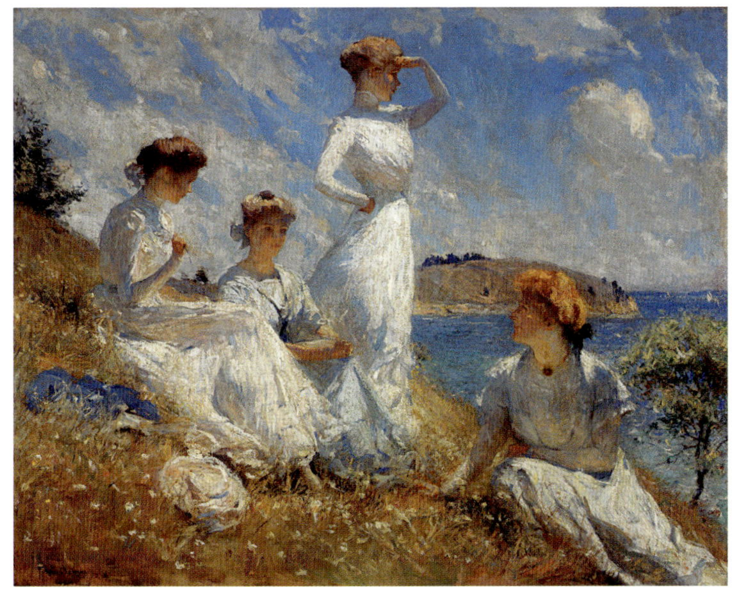

Fig.17 FRANK W. BENSON
Summer, 1909
Oil on canvas, 91.8 × 113 cm
Museum of Art, Rhode Island School of Design, Providence, Bequest of Isaac C. Bates, 13.912

stands erect, her bright, optimistic confidence evoking a new, American woman for the twentieth century, genteel and sophisticated but also liberated and modern.

'A page from Thoreau's note books'

John Henry Twachtman veered away from high-keyed colours, purple shadows and women in white. A 'master of nuance',[39] he found a way to intertwine quiet, familiar landscapes with mystical, otherworldly spirituality. His art shows a debt to the soft, muted nocturnes of Whistler, whom he met in Europe in 1880. Yet even Twachtman's hazy, monochromatic snow scenes painted in the early 1890s could be hailed as local and familiar to American eyes (pp.124, 126, 127). Critics described not only the visible scene but also the atmosphere of winter, 'One feels the temperature, and recalls the scream of the blue jay, the black-green leaves of the sapling pines turning gray in the wind. It is like a page from Thoreau's note books. This likeness to Thoreau is, of course, due to the fact that they were both original observers, observers at first hand.'[40] Comparisons of Twachtman to the American author, poet and naturalist Henry David Thoreau allowed critics to insist on the artist's 'American-ness'.[41] They compared the artist's unpopulated landscapes with the poet's seclusion in nature in the 1840s, suggesting that both men had found artistic inspiration through isolation in nature. Twachtman sought peaceful transcendence in the familiar landscape around his rural Connecticut home and developed new painterly techniques to express a different unity with the natural environment. At times he applied paint in a thick, rich impasto, while for other works he thinned his paint to allow for subtle layering. He also experimented by exposing his canvases to sunlight, in an attempt to bleach and brighten the delicate dematerialised effects of his landscapes.[42] In *Winter Landscape* of 1890–1900 (p.127), the pale blue stream, meandering from foreground to background, encourages the eye to linger on bits of straggly, bare trees and to be dazzled by the brightness of the white snow. In *Round Hill Road* painted between 1890 and 1900 (fig.19), the nebulous atmosphere and broad, blinding expanse of snow in the foreground confuse the viewer who finds refuge in the solid rooftops in the background. For Twachtman,

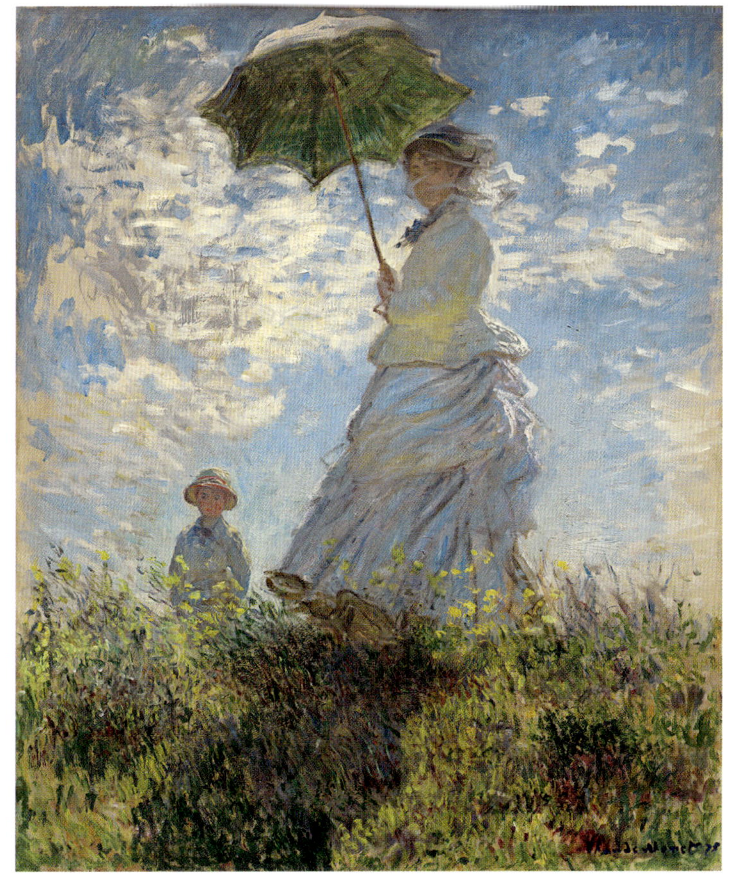

Fig.18 CLAUDE MONET
Woman with a Parasol – Madame Monet and her Son, 1875
Oil on canvas, 100 × 81 cm
National Gallery of Art, Washington D.C., Collection of Mr. and Mrs. Paul Mellon, 1983.1.29

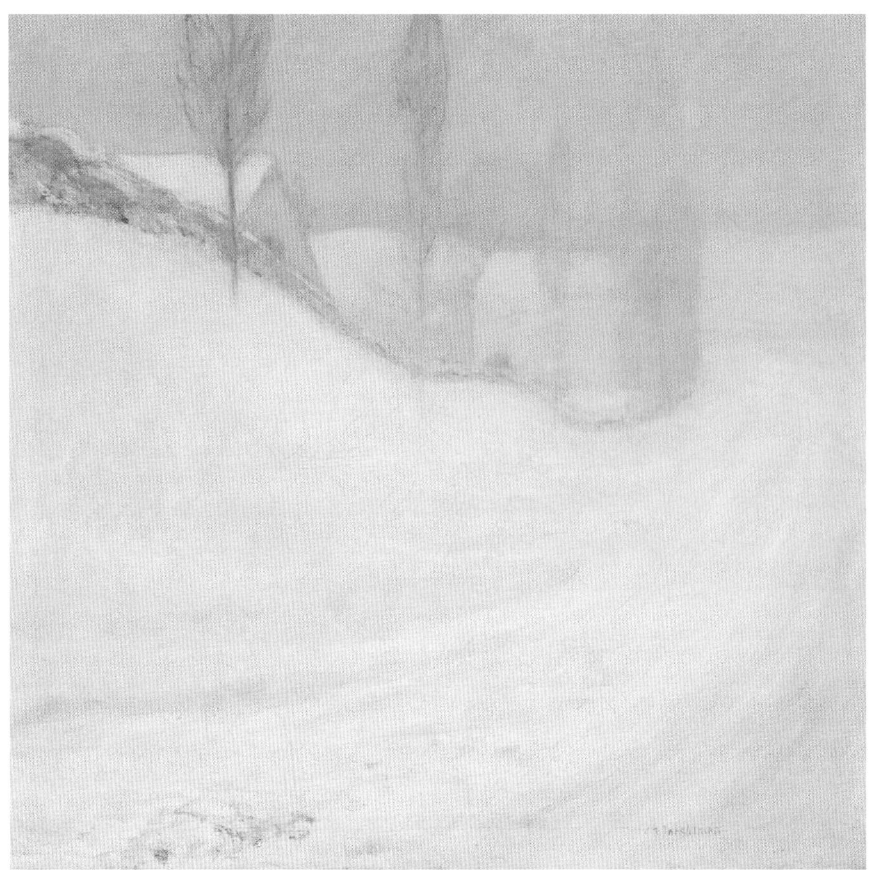

Impressionism merged with a poetic, quiet approach to nature and snow offered the ideal subject for studying light and atmosphere.

Ten American Painters

In calling for art to be both local and of the present moment, Garland and Hartmann encouraged painters to look around them for inspiration. It is unlikely, however, that either critic would have welcomed scenes of poverty, immigrants, crowded cities or industrial landscapes. 'The impressionist is a buoyant and cheerful painter', wrote Garland.[43] These artists painted through a lens of nostalgia and enthusiasm and edited out signs of the present that might be uncomfortable or unwanted to produce idealised pictures, tinged forever with bright sunshine and unthreatening, domestic nature. The men and women depicted are well-dressed and sophisticated, and shown at leisure. The landscapes are peaceful, sunny and positive.

Disruption did occur in late 1897 when a group of impressionists chose to break away from the Society of American Artists and organise separate exhibitions. Known as the 'Ten American Painters' or 'The Ten', they rejected the crowded exhibitions and lack of quality leadership at the American academy.[44] The media stir they created quickly subsided, however, and their almost annual exhibitions soon became part of the artistic mainstream. The group's rebellion from the academy bore little resemblance to the more radical rejection of the French Salon system by the French impressionists in the 1870s. Instead, the Ten represented a continuation of the optimism of the Gilded Age well into the twentieth century. A younger generation was needed to truly embrace the harsher realities of everyday life. Just after the turn of the century, artists such as Robert Henri, John Sloan and George Bellows began to tackle the rough, dark side of modern American life. Their scenes of urban crowds and low-rent tenements pointed to the fast pace and social inequalities of twentieth-century America. In comparison, the works of the American impressionists appeared utterly reassuring. Their human-scale landscapes welcome and shelter: children play on the beach; women walk along sunlit avenues. Rather than 'presentness', then, these impressionist paintings came to represent 'timelessness' – an enduring, undisturbed moment of peaceful leisure.

Fig.19 JOHN HENRY TWACHTMAN
Round Hill Road, c. 1890–1900
Oil on canvas, 76.8 × 76.2 cm
Smithsonian American Art Museum, Washington D.C., Gift of William T. Evans, 1909.7.64

1. Weir continued by saying: 'It was worse than the Chamber of Horrors. I was there about a quarter of an hour and left with a head ache... ' Weir to his parents, 15 April 1877, Archives of American Art. Hale to her family, 16 March 1882, Sophia Smith Collection, Smith College. Both letters can be found in Burns and Davis 2009, p.969.

2. See especially Lochnan 2003 and Toronto, Paris and London 2004.

3. Strahan 1879. It is worth noting that Strahan referred to American works of art inspired by *plein-air* paintings of the Barbizon school rather than to pictures now associated with Impressionism.

4. Brownell 1879.

5. Lejeune 1879.

6. Hitchcock 1886.

7. Hamilton 1886. References to purple shadows can be found throughout the criticism of the period.

8. 'A part of Paris, of intellectual France, has been brought to our doors; Mahomet has come to the mountain; and we cannot but gladly and gratefully acknowledge the compliment, as well as the unique character of the invasion, and feel the rites of hospitality would be violated if a courteous reception were not accorded the strangers.' 'The Impressionists. II' 1886.

9. Charlotte Adams, 'Color in New York Streets', *Art Review*, September–November 1887, p.19, cited in Brooklyn, Chicago and Houston 2000, p.168.

10. Kathleen Pyne has made a convincing argument about American Impressionism as a conscious response to a very different social and artistic context than French Impressionism. See Pyne 1996, pp.220–39. See also New York, Fort Worth, Denver and Los Angeles 1994–5.

11. See Atlanta and Detroit 2003–4.

12. 'Our feeling for subjects indigenous to France is but cultivated, the feeling of a feeling. Let our transatlantic students stock their minds with the experience of the past and the present ... and then let them return home to adapt themselves to their native environments...' Crowninshield 1883, p.223.

13. Crowninshield 1883. See also Van Rensselaer 1883, 'it is just as conventional for an American to keep on painting his reminiscences of French scenes, as it is for a Frenchman to cling to the classic subjects of his fathers.'

14. De Kay 1891, p.327. Van Rensselaer had voiced similar concerns, 'even when a landscape was American in name it was too often French or Dutch in aspect – that while the artist's corporeal eye had been resting upon some local scene, his mental eye had been remembering foreign scenes and the manner of their interpretation by foreign brushes.' Van Rensselaer 1886.

15. Hartmann 1894, p.44.

16. Garland 1960, p.104.

17. Garland, Introduction to the Palette and Cosmopolitan Art Clubs exhibition, Chicago 1895; quoted in Seattle and Los Angeles 1980, p.104. Garland also voiced national pride when he wrote: 'I have just come in from a bee-hunt over Wisconsin hills, amid splendors which would make Monet seem low-keyed.' Garland 1960, p.103. It is important to note this inferiority complex among artists who complained that America lacked picturesque landscapes. See the discussion 'The Return from Europe', in Burns and Davis 2009, pp.752–5. Midwestern scenes inspired Impressionism by the late 1890s. See Charles C. Eldredge, 'American Impressionism Goes West', in Eiland 1996, pp.100–17.

18. Hartmann 1894, p.48.

19. 'Many of his pictures are downright ugly,' complained one reviewer of Monet, 'his manner of work is often coarse and crude. The first thing and the last thing one sees in his pictures is not nature, but paint.' In 'The Fine Arts: Exhibition of Mr. Breck's Paintings at the St. Botolph Club', *Boston Evening Transcript*, cited in Meixner 1982, p.158 n. 35. See Kathleen Pyne's excellent discussion of the American reception of Monet in Pyne 1996, pp.235–8.

20. See H. Barbara Weinberg *et al.*, 'The Country: Modern Painters in Landscape', in New York, Fort Worth, Denver and Los Angeles 1994–5, pp.51–87.

21. Bunker to Isabella Stewart Gardner, n.d. [summer 1890], ISG Papers, cited in David Park Curry, 'Reconstructing Bunker', in Boston, Chicago and Denver 1994–5, p.98.

22. Robinson wrote to Hamlin Garland in 1895, 'I've got to go back to what is my country. I am now beginning to see its beauties and possibilities and to feel that affection for a country, so indispensable to paint it well.' Robinson letter to Hamlin Garland, as cited in New York, Fort Worth, Denver and Los Angeles 1994–5, p.58.

23. Bunker to Joe Evans, 11 September 1888, in Boston, Chicago and Denver 1994–5, p.91.

24. 'Fine Arts', *Boston Herald*, 2 February 1890, p.12. For a detailed discussion of Bunker's time in Medfield, see Boston, Chicago and Denver 1994–5, pp.65–9.

25. Cited in New York, Fort Worth, Denver and Los Angeles 1994–5, p.69 n.98.

26. Robinson quoted in Garland 1899. See also Pyne 1996, pp.243–54.

27. It is surprising that Chase's paintings received any attention, given the fact that there were 336 pictures by 189 artists in the American fine arts section as well as numerous drawings, sculptures and prints. Because Chase won a silver medal and exhibited more paintings than his fellow Americans, reviewers may have been attracted to his selections. For more information about American art at the Exposition Universelle see Philadelphia, Norfolk and Memphis 1989.

28. 'Mr. Chase's Pictures', *Chicago Tribune*, 15 September 1889, p.24, as cited in Brooklyn, Chicago and Houston 2000, p.170.

29. 'Some Questions of Art. Pictures by Mr. William M. Chase', *Sun*, 1 March 1891, p.14, cited in Brooklyn, Chicago and Houston 2000, p.172.

30. 'Indeed, why should not these exquisite scenes of Central park find their way from the artist's easel to the walls of citizens as easily as pictures of Niagara, or views taken in Lutetia Parisiorum. Few cities can boast so beautiful a park as New York.' De Kay 1891, p.328.

31. Brooklyn, Chicago and Houston 2000, p.163.

32. Chase quoted in 'Suburban Sketching Grounds', *Art Amateur*, vol.25, September 1891, p.80.

33. The colour theories of Michel-Eugène Chevreul and Ogden Rood found a following among the French impressionists and less frequently, among certain American painters. Laurene Buckley suggested that Tarbell was one of the artists familiar with these ideas. See Buckley 2001, pp.44–5.

34. Downes 1893, pp.360–3.

35. Sadakichi Hartmann wrote, for example, that Tarbell's depictions of girls 'are American girls, make no mistake about that – and also his technique might have American qualities, if he remained true to himself, without paying attention to Zorn and other fashionable technicians'. See Hartmann 1894, p.47.

36. Tarbell painted the landscape background in France but added the figures after his return to the United States. See Buckley 2001, p.44.

37. For an excellent discussion of painting of women from this period, see Sarah Burns, 'Fashioning the Transatlantic Woman', in Giverny and Bordeaux 2008, pp.116–24.

38. For Tarbell, see 'The Society of American Artists' Exhibition' 1892. For Benson, see M.W.F., 'Vacation Days', *St. Nicholas*, vol.36, no.10, August 1909, p.883, cited in New York 1989, p.57.

39. Clark 1924, p.556.

40. New York 1903, p.2.

41. Childe Hassam, for example, emphasised the artist's 'American sensibility' and 'manliness' in 'John H. Twachtman: An Estimation', *North American Review*, vol.176, April 1903, as cited in Burns and Davis 2009, pp.994–5.

42. Kathleen Pyne wrote, 'The quiescence of Twachtmans' imagery was also accomplished by a suitably rarefied painterly process. Transferring his pastel technique to oil painting around 1890, his pigment was thinned out with a medium called mastic and his canvases exposed to the sun for periods of time in order to enhance the delicate dematerialized effects of his images.' Pyne 1996, p.279.

43. Garland 1960.

44. See New York 1991, in which Hiesinger makes clear that the Ten were associated with Impressionism in the minds of critics and the general public. Indeed, their first exhibition held in March 1898 at the Durand-Ruel Gallery in New York strengthened their ties to the impressionist movement. The Ten included Benson, Joseph Rodefer De Camp, Dewing, Hassam, Metcalf, Robert Reid, Edward E. Simmons, Tarbell, Twachtman and Weir. Chase joined the group upon Twachtman's death in 1902.

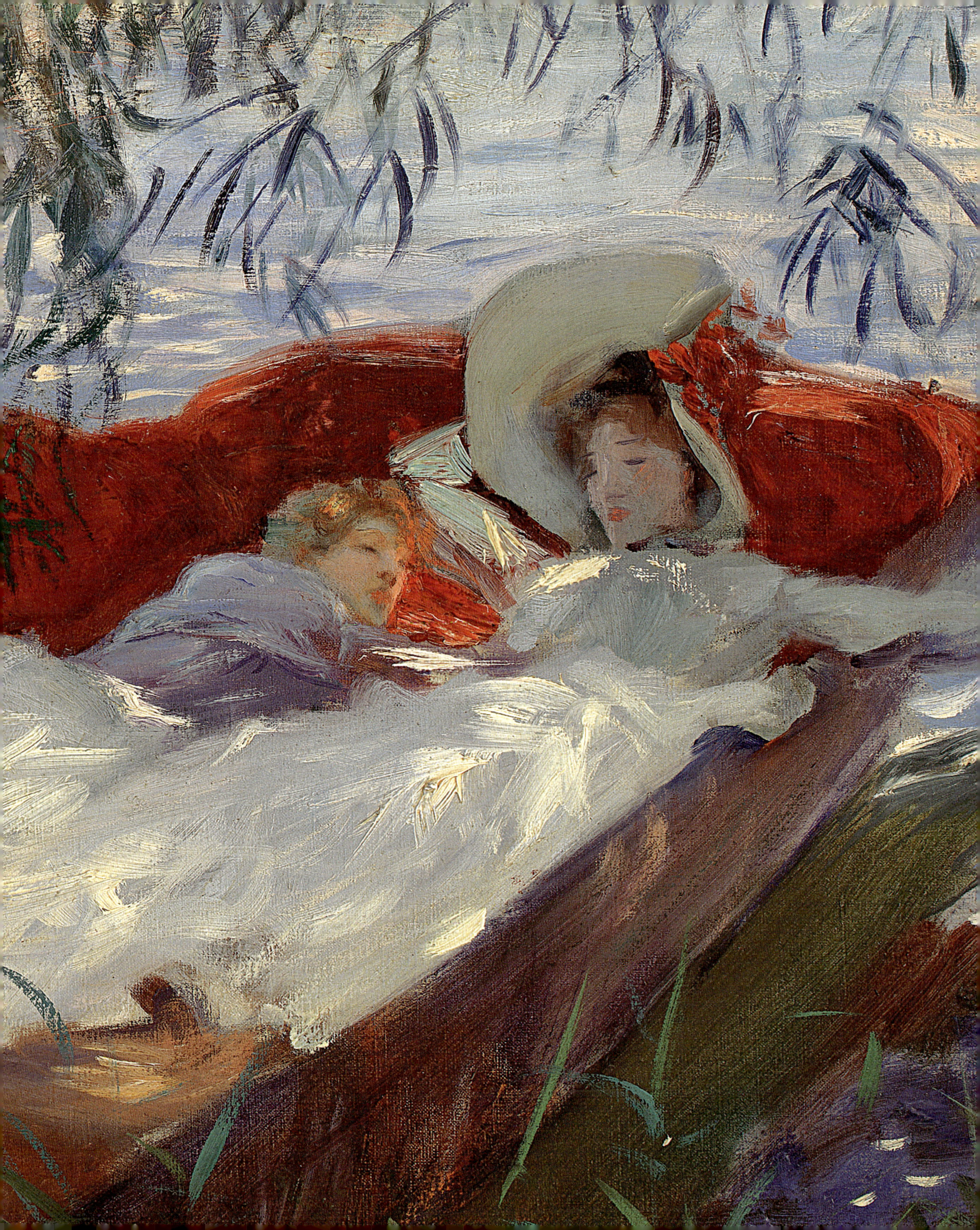

CATALOGUE OF EXHIBITED WORKS

The Beginnings of American Impressionism **in Europe, 1880–90**

American artists began to experiment with Impressionism in Europe just before 1880. While living in Paris, Mary Cassatt and John Singer Sargent developed close friendships with French artists and played a leading role in the advancement of avant-garde ideas. By the mid- to late 1880s, several younger Americans working in France also began to incorporate the new techniques while still adhering to academic training.

Through her friendships with Edgar Degas and Berthe Morisot, Cassatt was invited to exhibit with the impressionists between 1879 and 1886 and received praise for her depictions of upper-middle-class women and children at leisure. *Young Girl at a Window* of around 1883–4 (p.55) and *Children Playing on the Beach* of 1884 (p.57) appeared in the eighth and final impressionist exhibition in Paris in 1886. These two works demonstrate Cassatt's mastery of the new aesthetic, with flattened picture planes, cropped compositions and a heightened interest in painting the ordinary moments of modern life. Cassatt devoted herself to this cause, avoiding the official Salon and promoting French impressionist works among American collectors. More than any other American artist working in France at this time, Cassatt helped shape Impressionism.

In 1883 Sargent, working in the French countryside, began experimenting with loose brushwork and less structured compositions, perhaps in response to the landscapes of Camille Pissarro. A few years later, during a period of close friendship with Claude Monet, Sargent produced impressionistic outdoor scenes in rural England. These freely painted works demonstrate his usual flamboyance

JOHN SINGER SARGENT, *Two Women Asleep in a Punt under the Willows*, c. 1887, detail (see p.74)

as well as a new, wilful sketchiness and brighter palette. Throughout the 1880s, Sargent experimented with broken brushwork, relaxed poses and modern subjects in works such as *A Boating Party* of about 1889 (p.75). The artist did not devote himself exclusively to Impressionism, however. Instead, he maintained a smoother, more finished treatment of the figure in commissioned society portraits, incorporating only occasional impressionistic flourishes, such as the loosely painted white dress and background in *Lady Agnew of Lochnaw* of 1892 (p.112).

Younger Americans working in France also began to explore the brighter palette and spontaneous effects of the impressionists by the late 1880s. During *plein-air* sessions in Giverny, Theodore Robinson and John Leslie Breck started to use lighter colours and to focus on the changing effects of light and shadow at different times of day. Robinson employed a seemingly random, broken brushstroke in landscapes but maintained an academic rigour and careful finish when painting people. In his journal, he lamented his reliance on the model and on photography, and voiced a desire to focus more wholeheartedly on the ephemeral moment, just as Monet was doing nearby in the village. A similar combination of impressionist brushstrokes with more traditional compositions can also be found in the work of Childe Hassam who spent three years in France. In two large Salon pictures, Hassam consciously moved from a dark, rainy scene in 1887 (p.88) to a sun-filled, more loosely painted one (p.89). These Salon paintings, with their careful compositions designed in the studio, are not entirely impressionist. Hassam would only devote himself completely to the new style on his return to America in 1889.

THEODORE ROBINSON, *Blossoms at Giverny*, 1891–2, detail (see p.80)

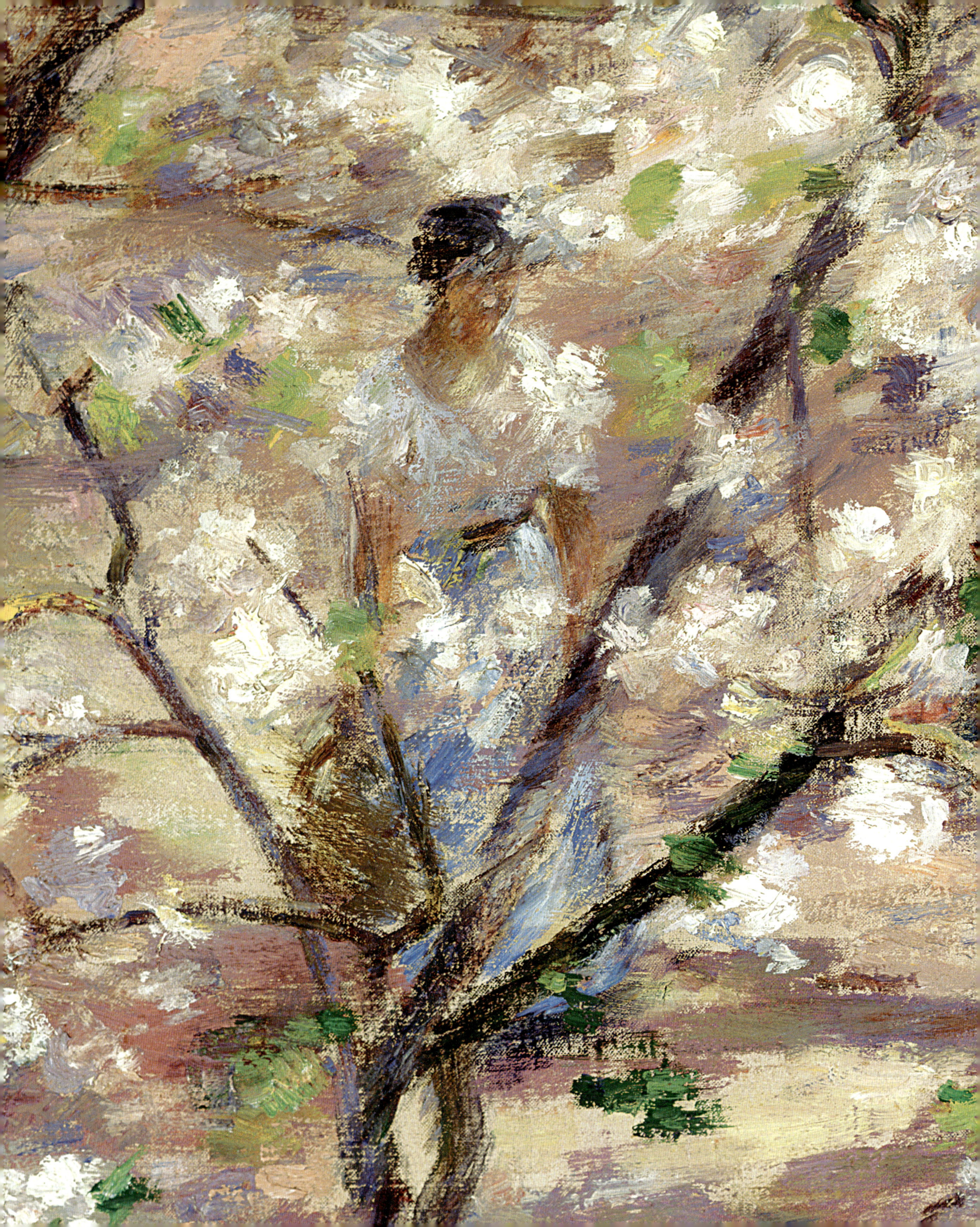

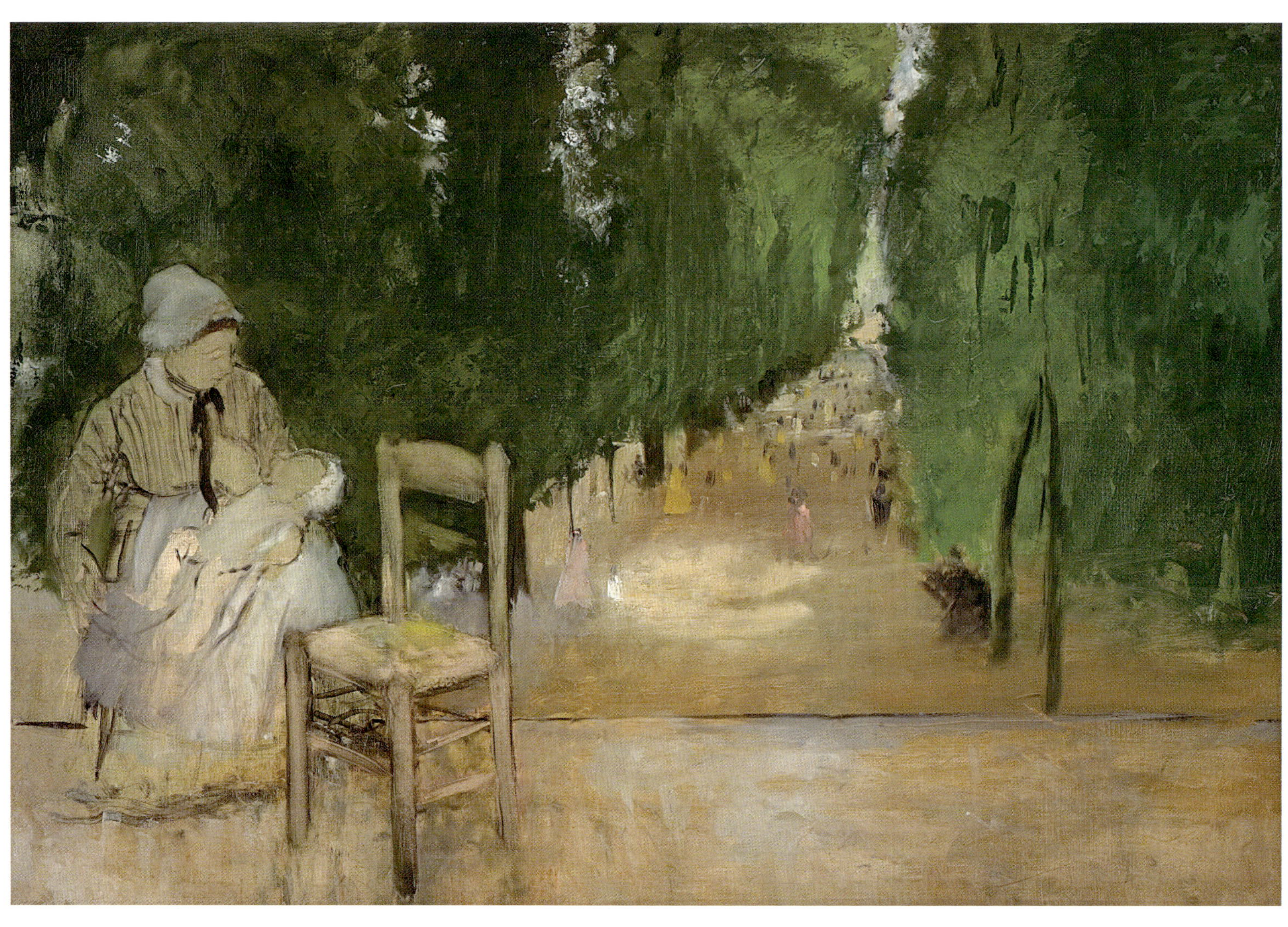

EDGAR DEGAS, *A Nanny in the Luxembourg Gardens, Paris*, *c.* 1872
Oil on canvas, 65 × 92 cm
Musée Fabre, Montpellier Agglomération, 58.3.1

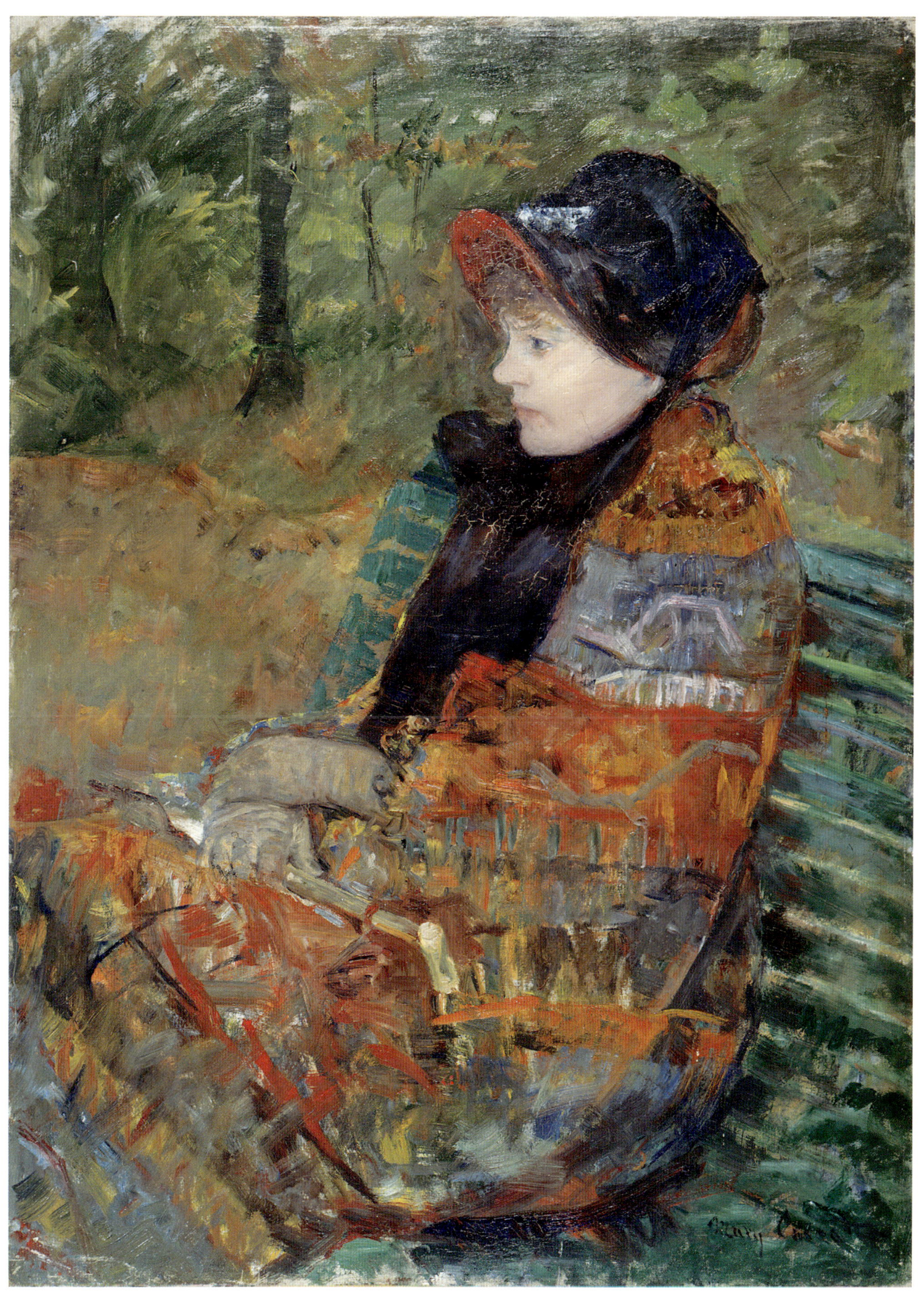

MARY CASSATT, *Autumn*, 1880
Oil on canvas, 92.5 × 65.5 cm
Musée des Beaux-Arts de la Ville de Paris, Petit Palais, PPP00706

MARY CASSATT, *Young Girl at a Window*, *c.* 1883–4
Oil on canvas, 100.5 × 64.8 cm
Corcoran Gallery of Art, Washington D.C.,
Museum Purchase, Gallery Fund, 09.8

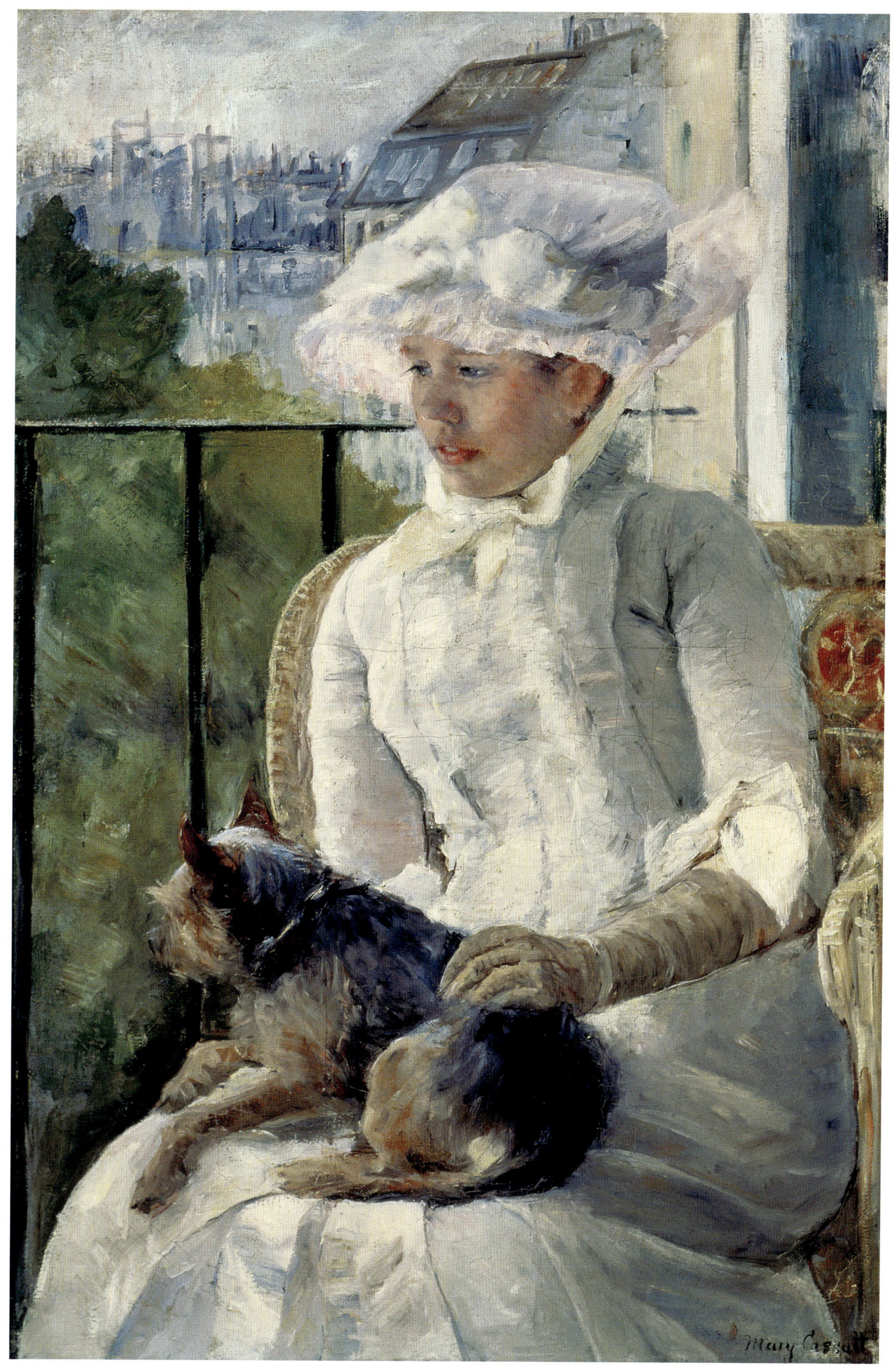
Mary Cassatt

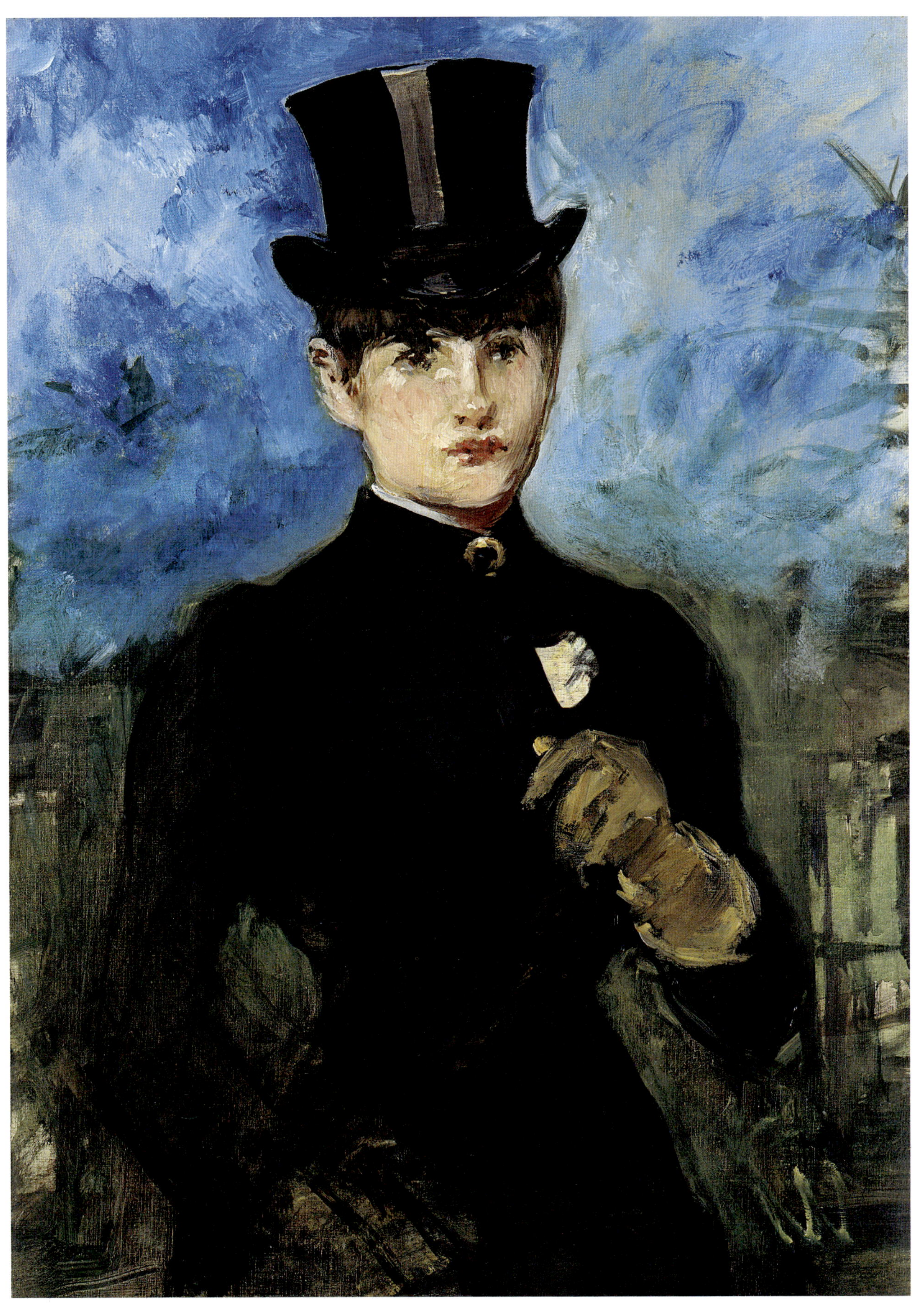

EDOUARD MANET, *Horsewoman, Full-Face* (*L'Amazone*), *c.* 1882
Oil on canvas, 73 × 52 cm
Museo Thyssen-Bornemisza, Madrid, 659 (1980.5)
[Shown in Madrid only]

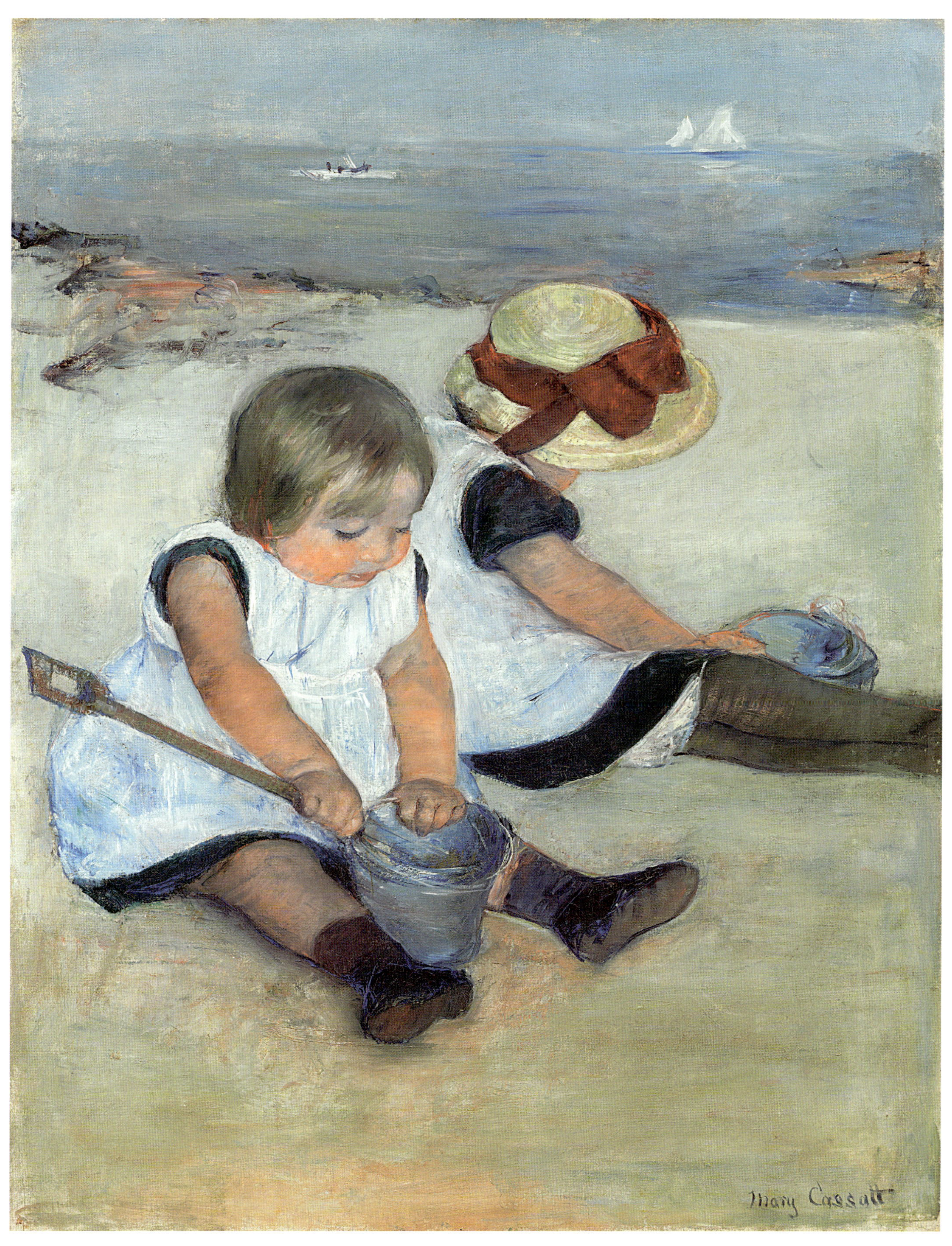

MARY CASSATT, *Children Playing on the Beach*, 1884
Oil on canvas, 97.4 × 74.2 cm
National Gallery of Art, Washington D.C.,
Ailsa Mellon Bruce Collection, 1970.17.19

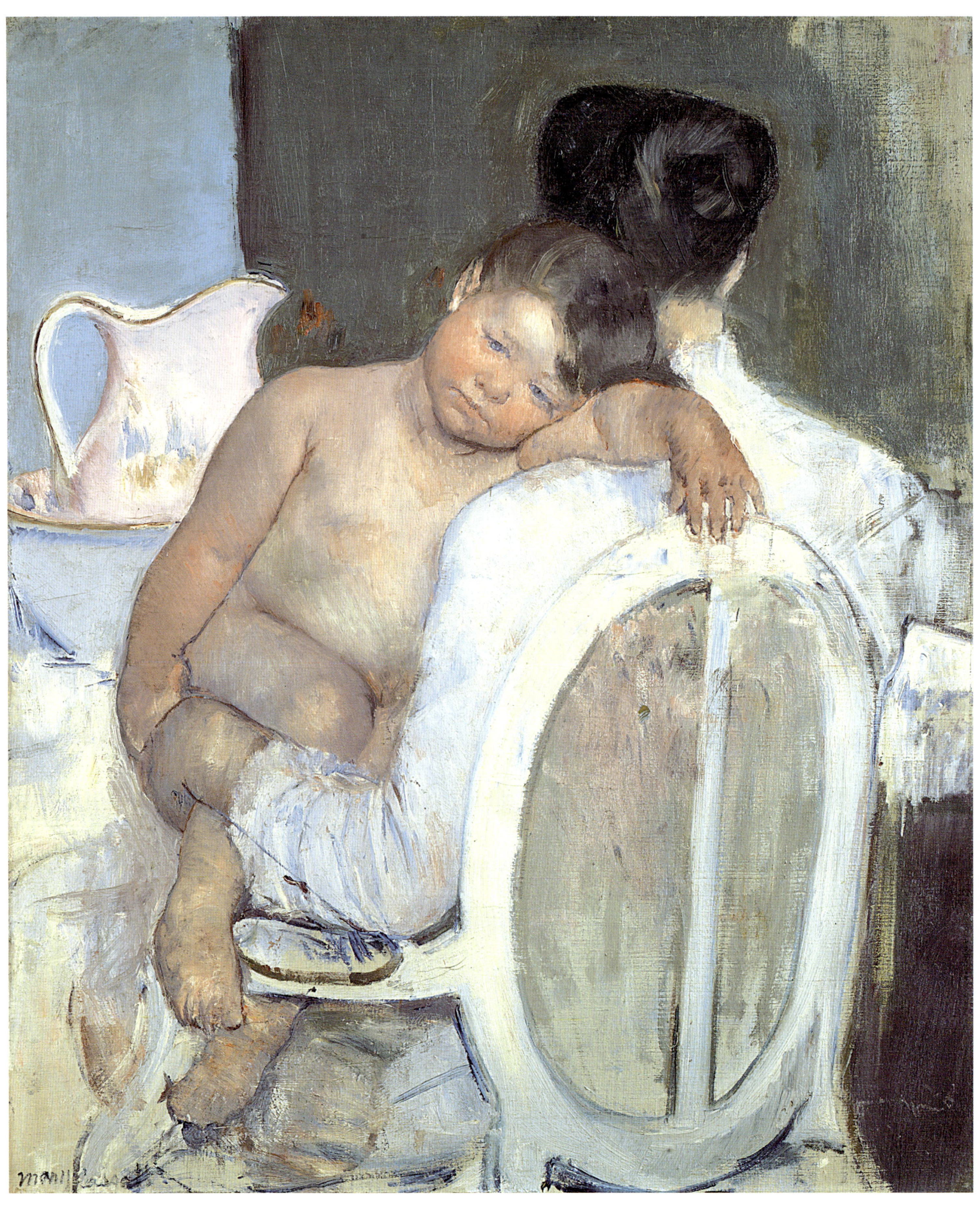

MARY CASSATT, *Woman Sitting with a Child in her Arms*, *c.* 1890
Oil on canvas, 81 × 65.5 cm
Museo de Bellas Artes de Bilbao, 82/25

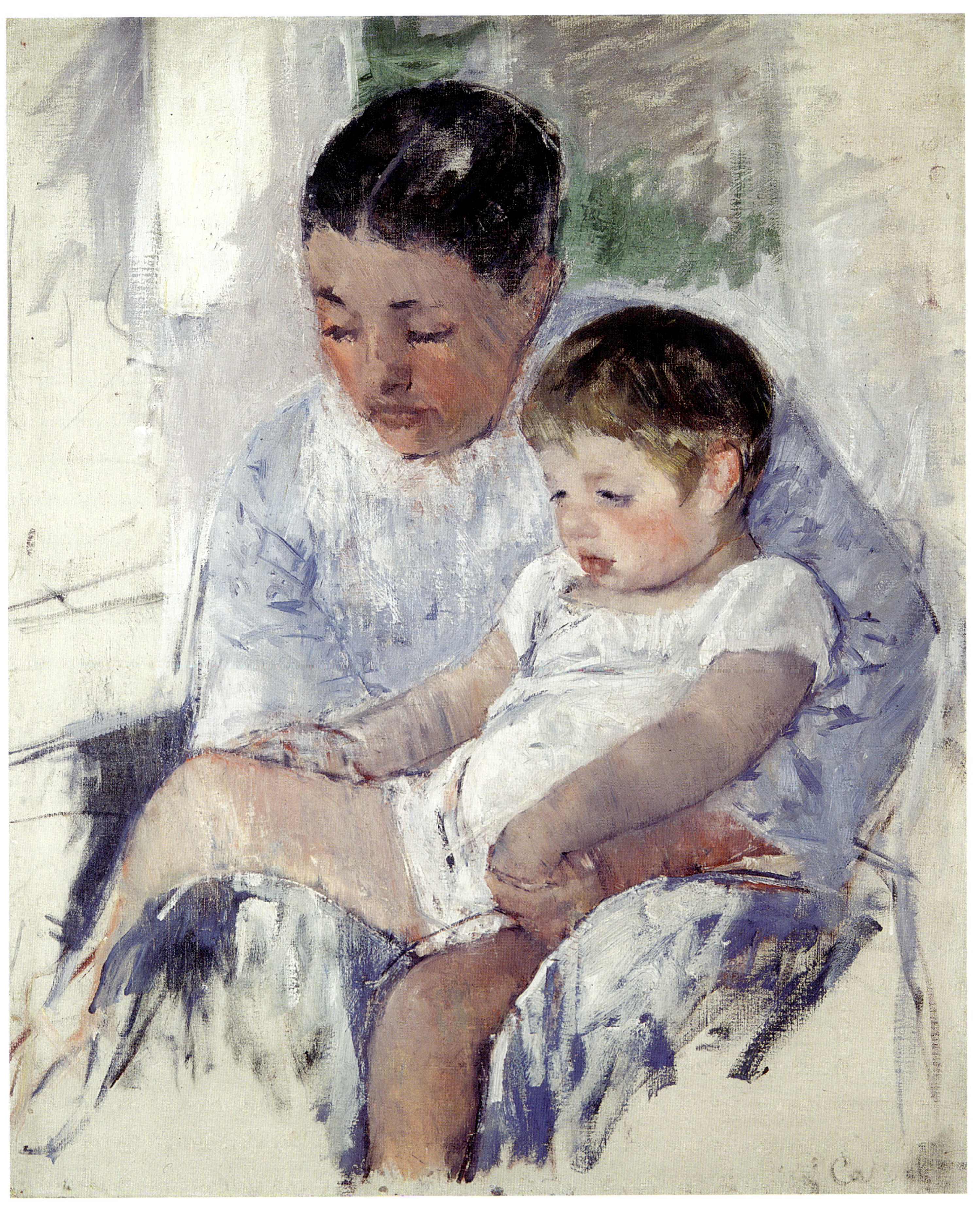

MARY CASSATT, *Jenny and her Sleepy Child*, between 1891 and 1892
Oil on canvas, 73.5 × 60.3 cm
Terra Foundation for American Art, Chicago,
Daniel J. Terra Collection, 1988.24

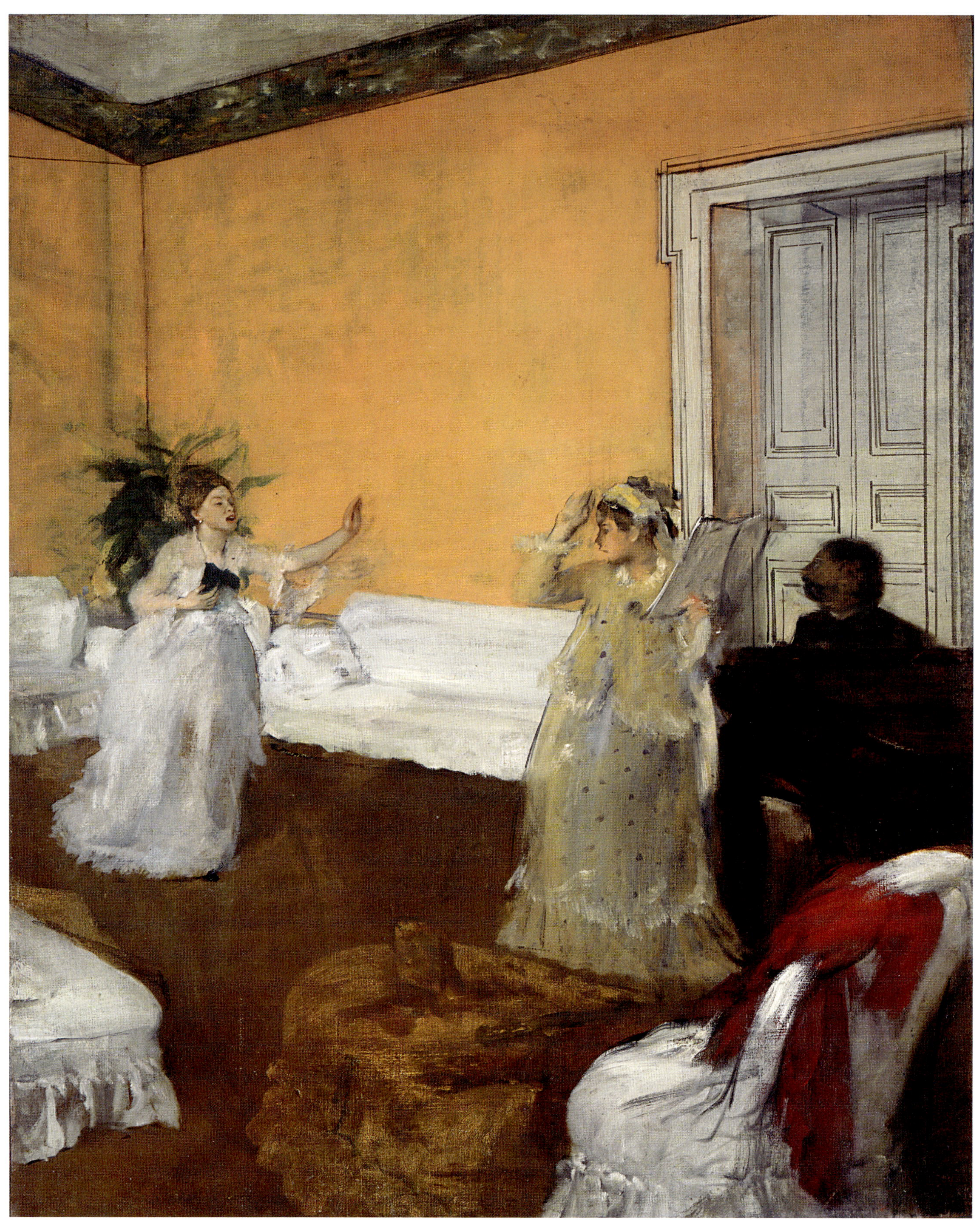

EDGAR DEGAS, *The Song Rehearsal*, *c.* 1872–3
Oil on canvas, 81 × 64.9 cm
House Collection, Dumbarton Oaks, Washington D.C., HC.P.1918.02.(O)
[Shown in Giverny only]

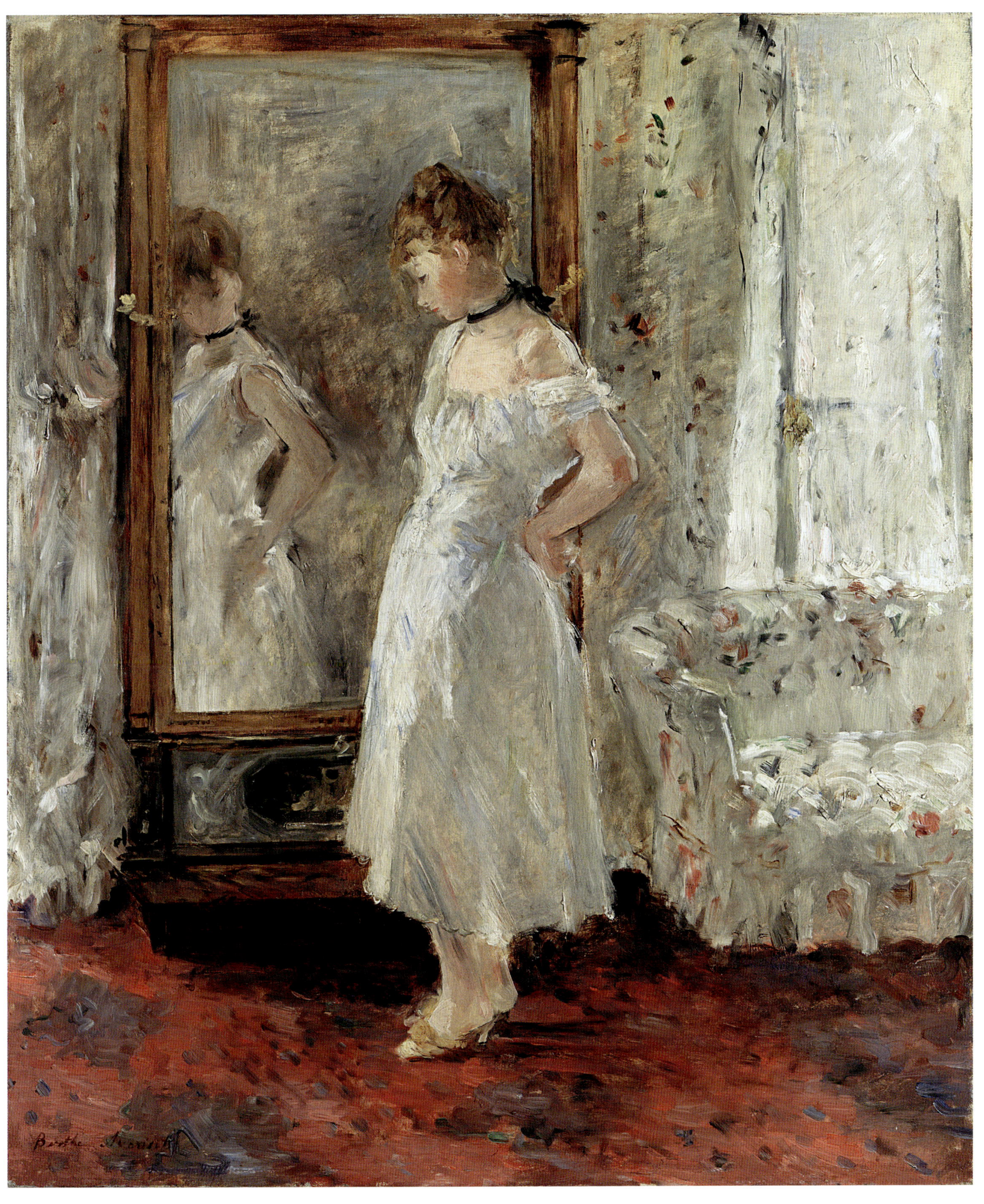

BERTHE MORISOT, *The Cheval-Glass*, 1876
Oil on canvas, 65 × 54 cm
Museo Thyssen-Bornemisza, Madrid, 686 (1977.87)
[Shown in Edinburgh and Madrid only]

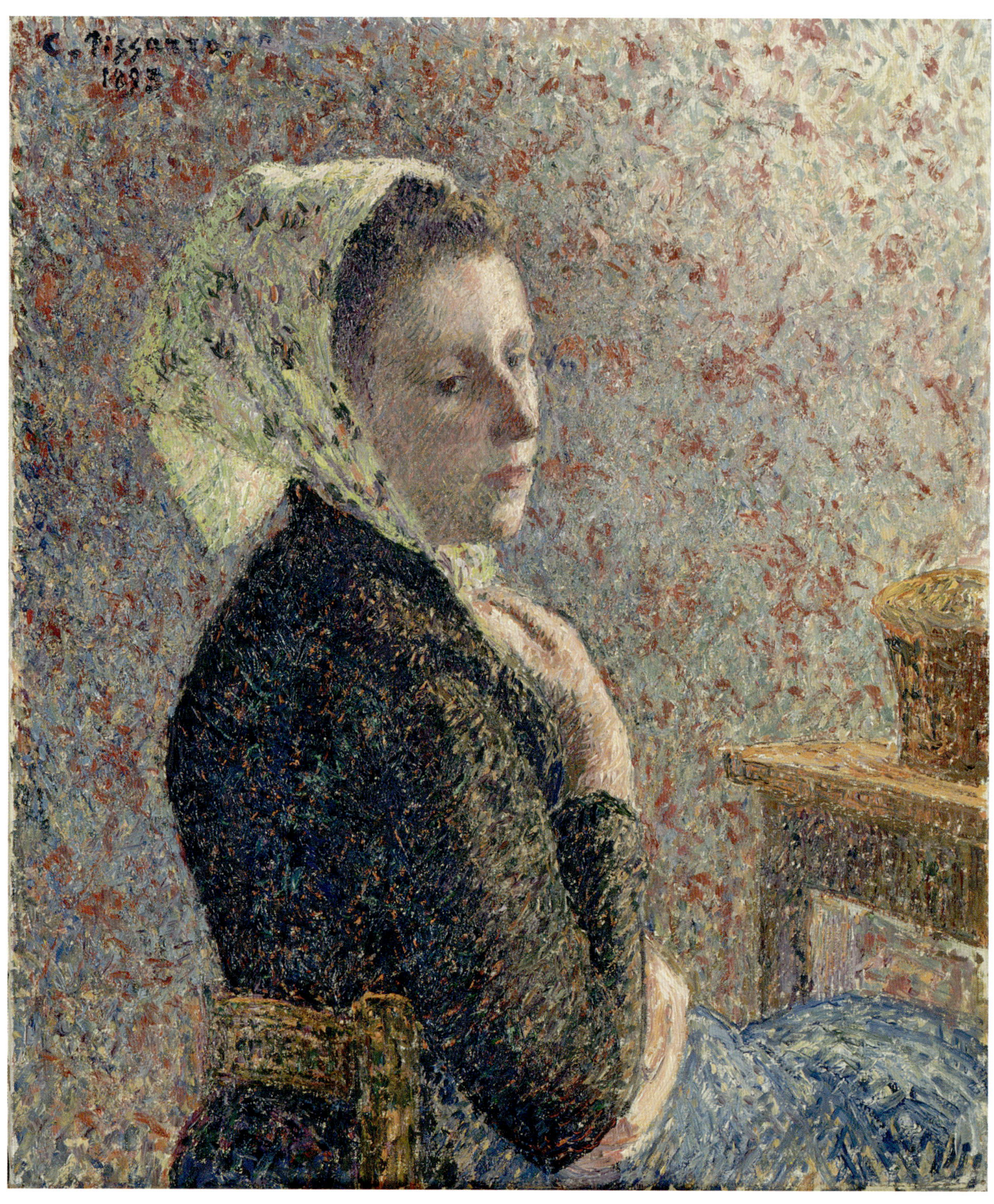

CAMILLE PISSARRO, *Woman with a Green Headscarf*, 1893
Oil on canvas, 65.5 × 54.5 cm
Musée d'Orsay, Paris, bequeathed by Enriqueta Alsop, in memory of Dr Eduardo Mollard, 1972 RF 1972-30
[Shown in Giverny only]

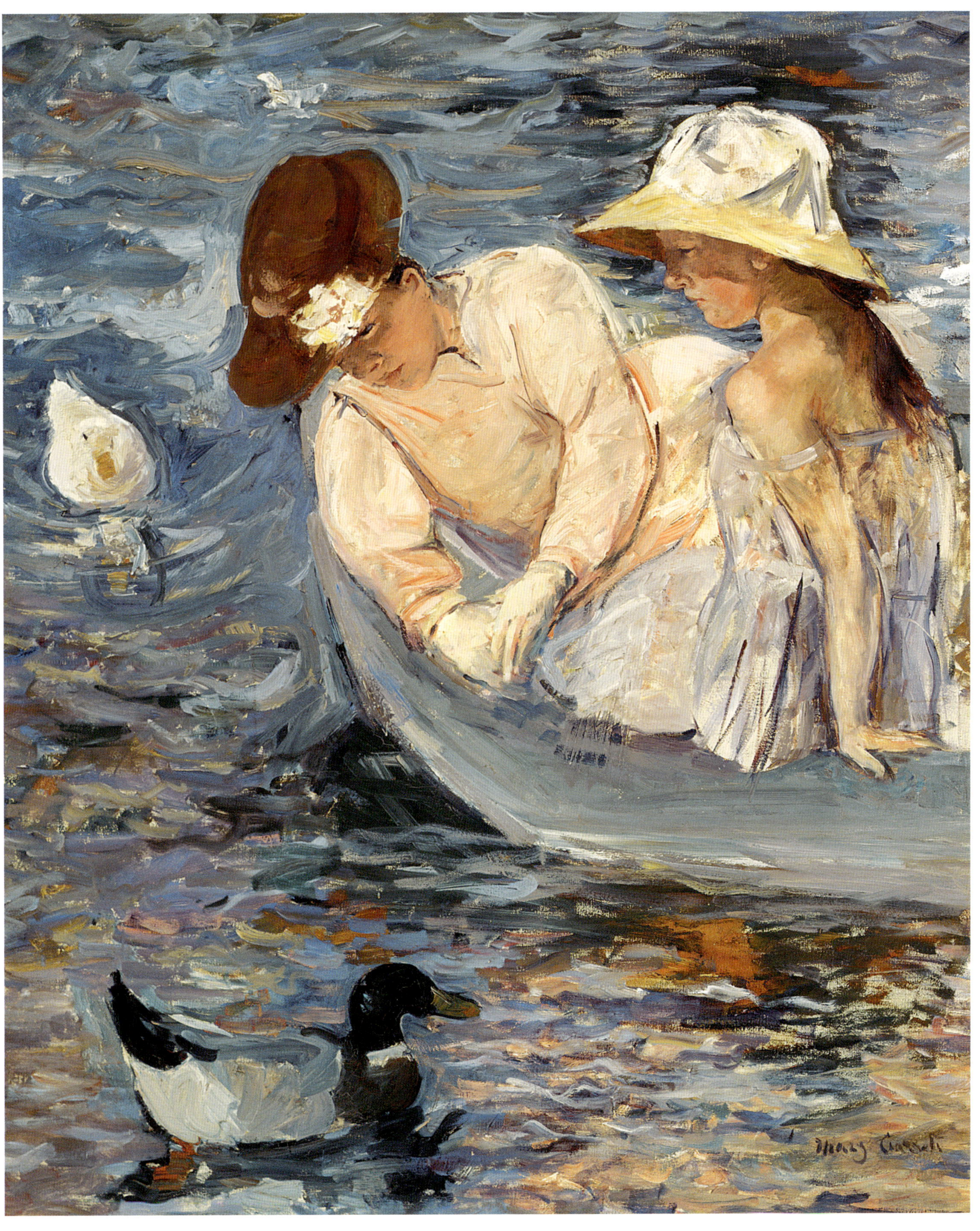

MARY CASSATT, *Summertime*, 1894
Oil on canvas, 100.6 × 81.3 cm
Terra Foundation for American Art, Chicago,
Daniel J. Terra Collection, 1988.25

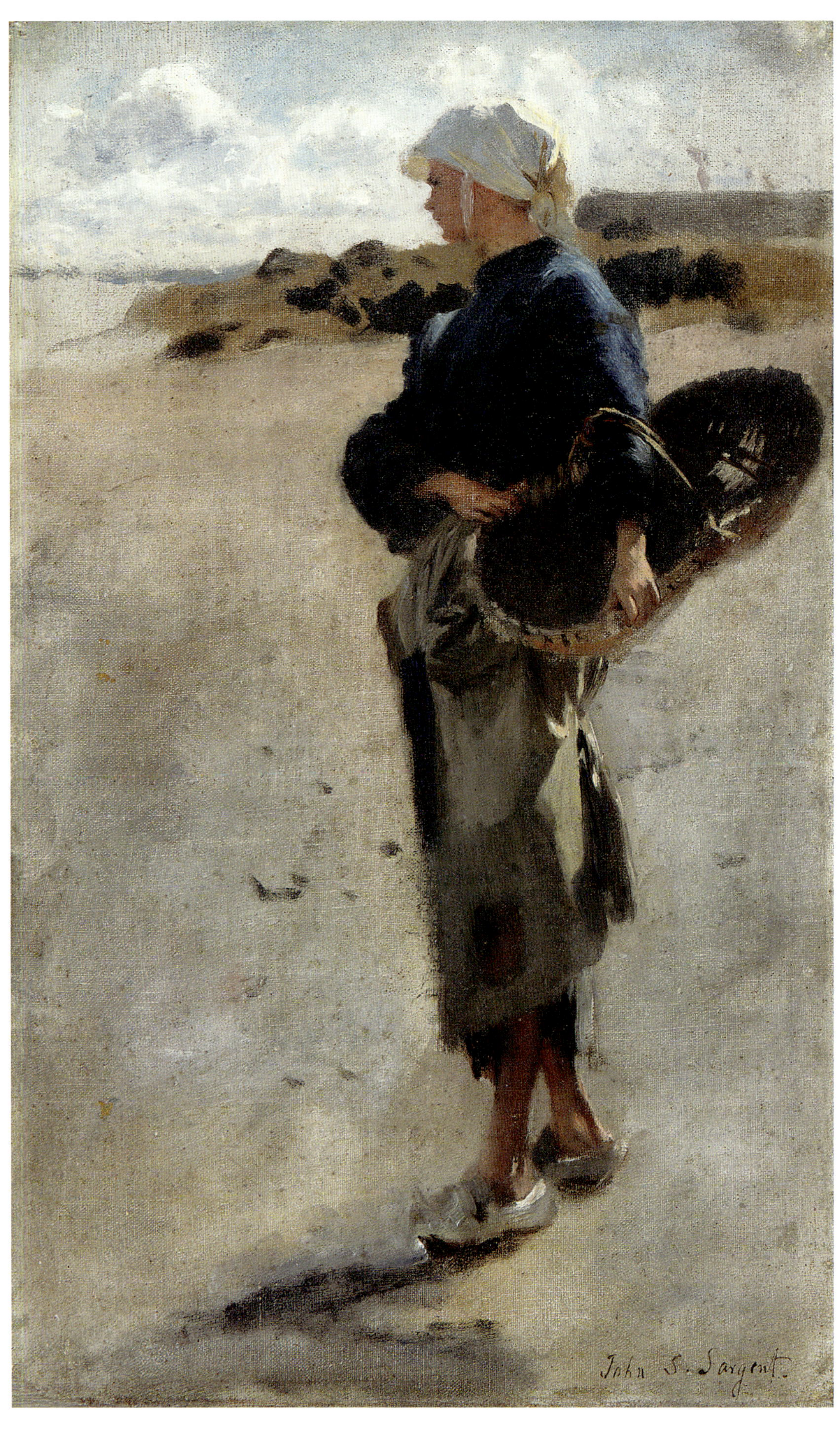

JOHN SINGER SARGENT, *Breton Girl with a Basket, Sketch for 'Oyster Gatherers of Cancale'*, 1877
Oil on canvas, 48.3 × 29.2 cm
Terra Foundation for American Art, Chicago,
Daniel J. Terra Collection, 1999.129

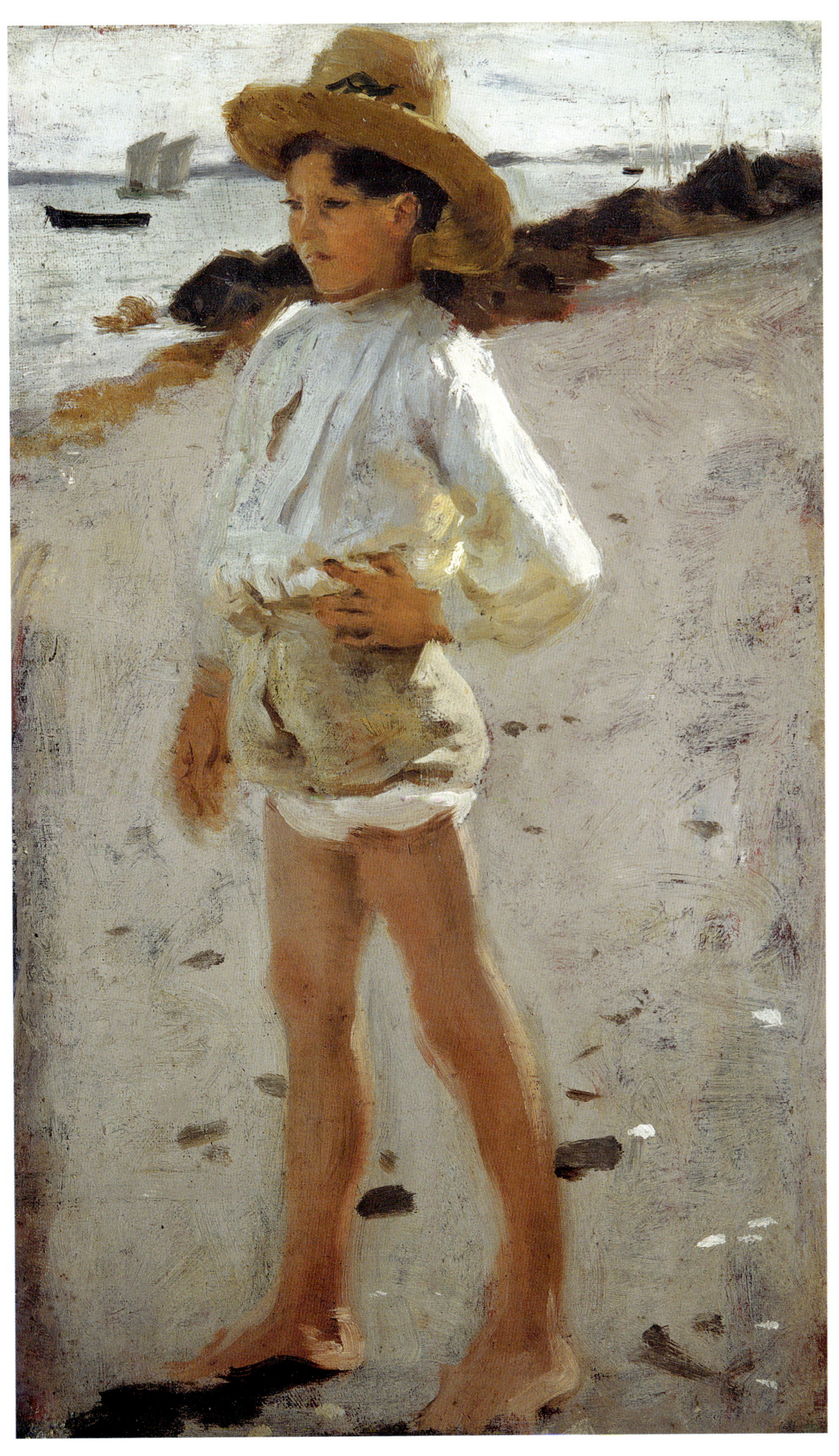

JOHN SINGER SARGENT, *Young Boy on a Beach, Sketch for 'Oyster Gatherers of Cancale'*, 1877
Oil on canvas, 43.8 × 26 cm
Terra Foundation for American Art, Chicago,
Daniel J. Terra Collection, 1999.132

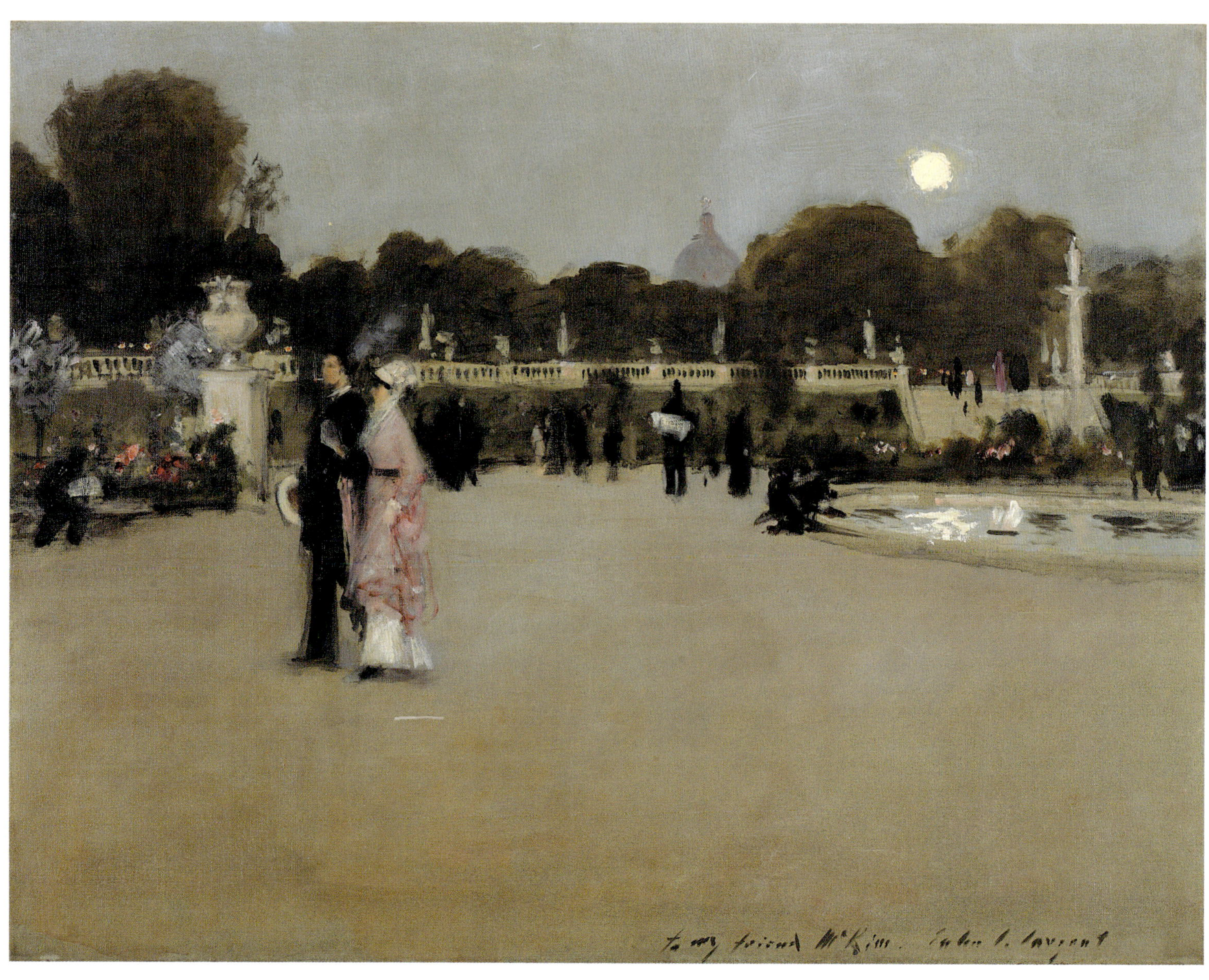

JOHN SINGER SARGENT, *Luxembourg Gardens at Twilight*, 1879
Oil on canvas, 66 × 92.7 cm
Minneapolis Institute of Arts, Minnesota,
Gift of Mrs. C.C. Bovey and Mrs. C.D. Velie, 16.20
[Shown in Giverny and Edinburgh only]

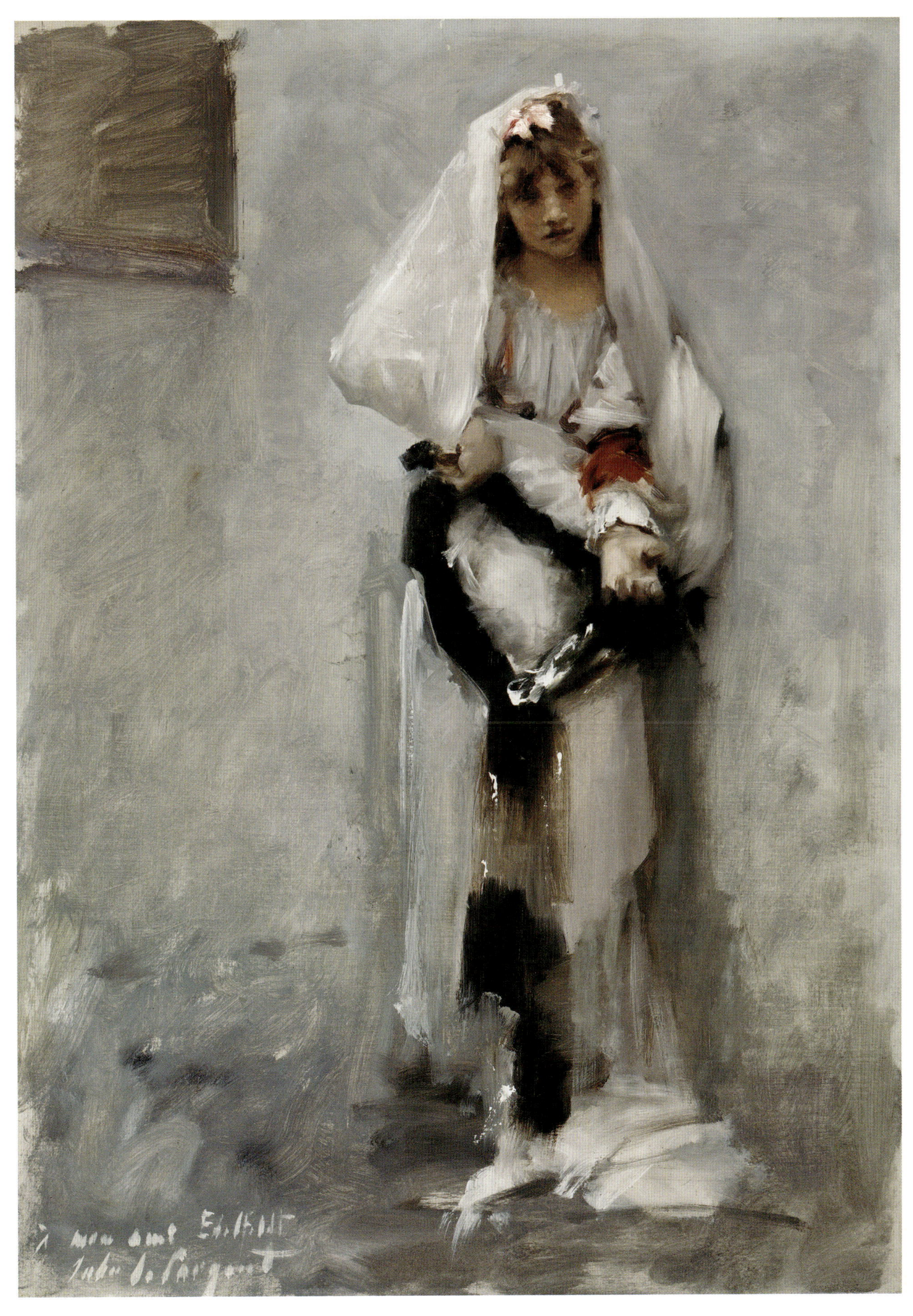

JOHN SINGER SARGENT, *A Parisian Beggar Girl*, *c.* 1880
Oil on canvas, 64.5 × 43.7 cm
Terra Foundation for American Art, Chicago,
Daniel J. Terra Collection, 1994.14

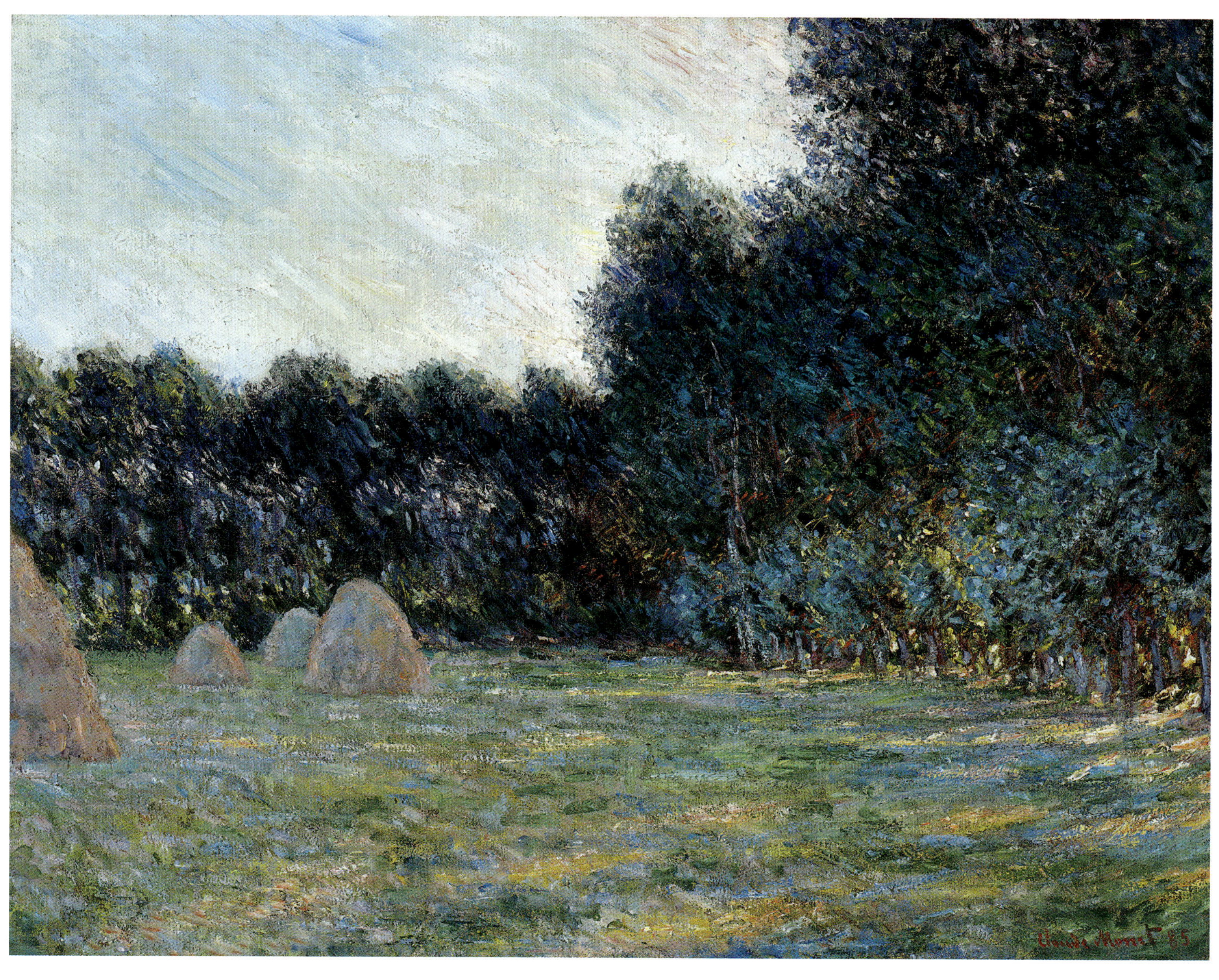

CLAUDE MONET, *Meadow with Haystacks near Giverny*, 1885
Oil on canvas, 74 × 93.5 cm
Museum of Fine Arts, Boston,
Bequest of Dr. Arthur Tracy Cabot, 42.541

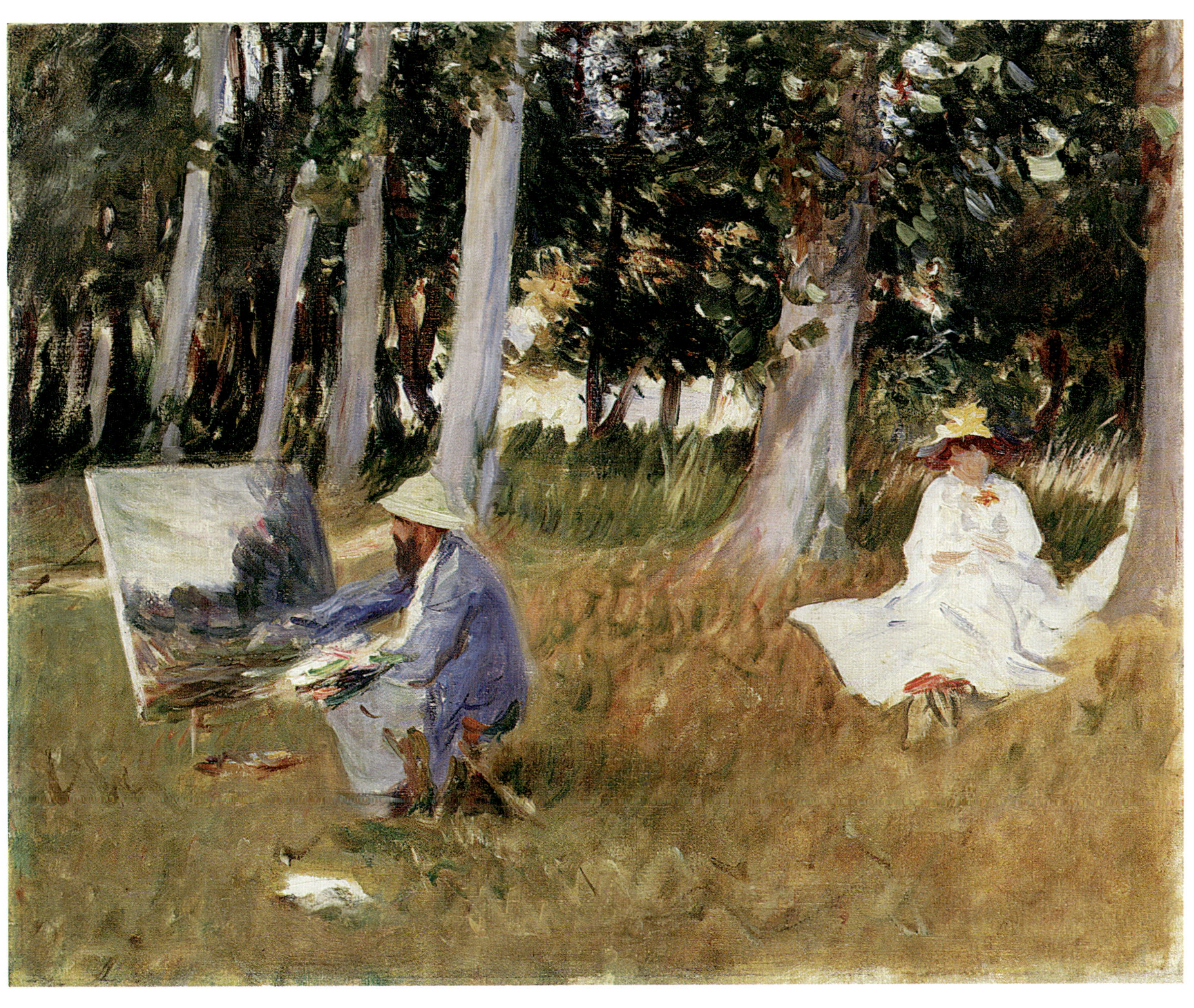

JOHN SINGER SARGENT, *Claude Monet Painting by the Edge of a Wood*, 1885
Oil on canvas, 54 × 64.8 cm
Tate, London, presented by Miss Emily Sargent and Mrs Ormond
through the Art Fund, 1925, N04103

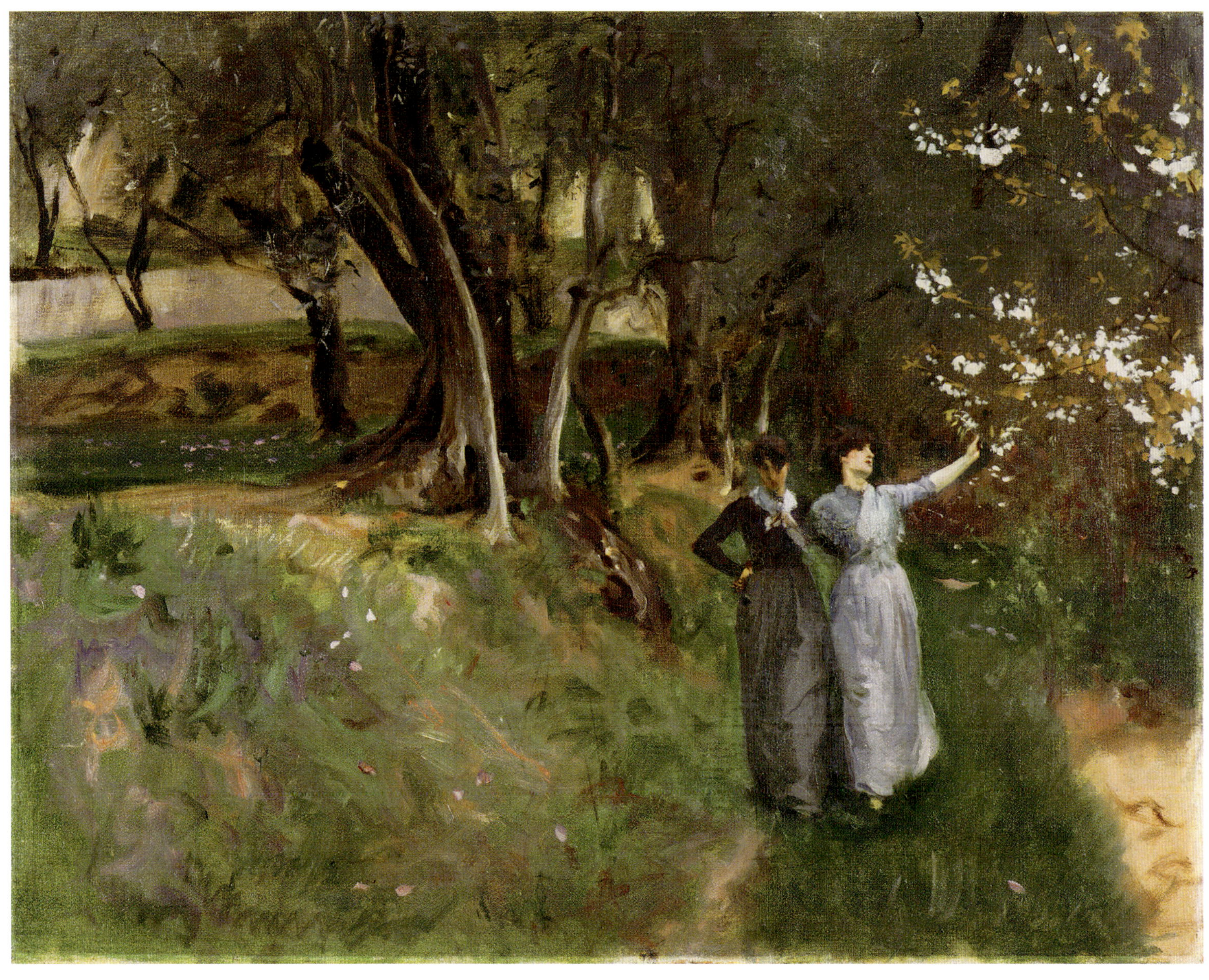

JOHN SINGER SARGENT, *Landscape with Women in Foreground*, *c.* 1883
Oil on canvas, 63.5 × 77.5 cm
Philadelphia Museum of Art, 125th Anniversary Acquisition,
Gift of Joseph F. McCrindle, 2002, 2002-49-1

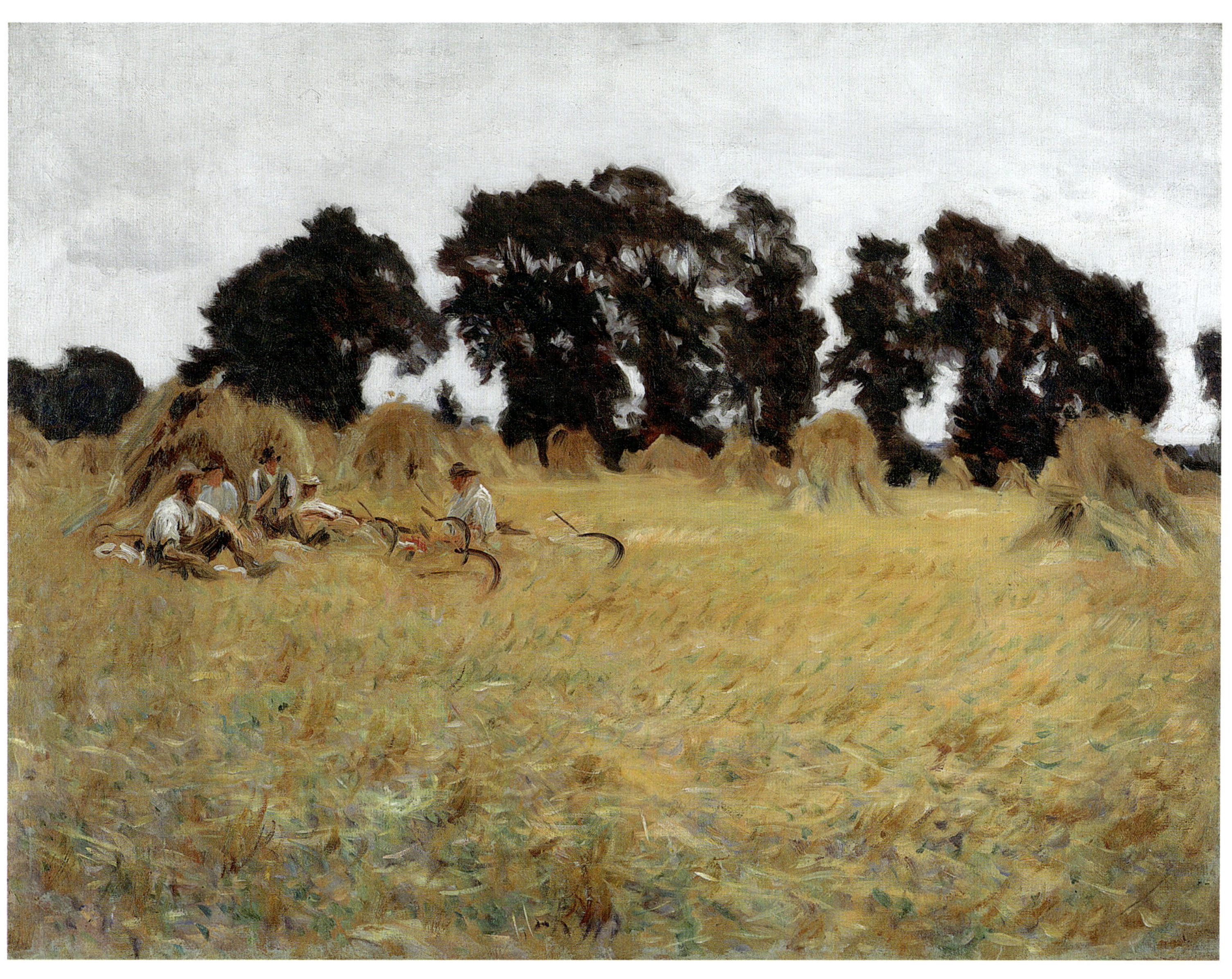

JOHN SINGER SARGENT, *Reapers Resting in a Wheat Field*, 1885
Oil on canvas, 71.1 × 91.4 cm
The Metropolitan Museum of Art, New York,
Gift of Mrs. Francis Ormond, 1950, 50.130.14

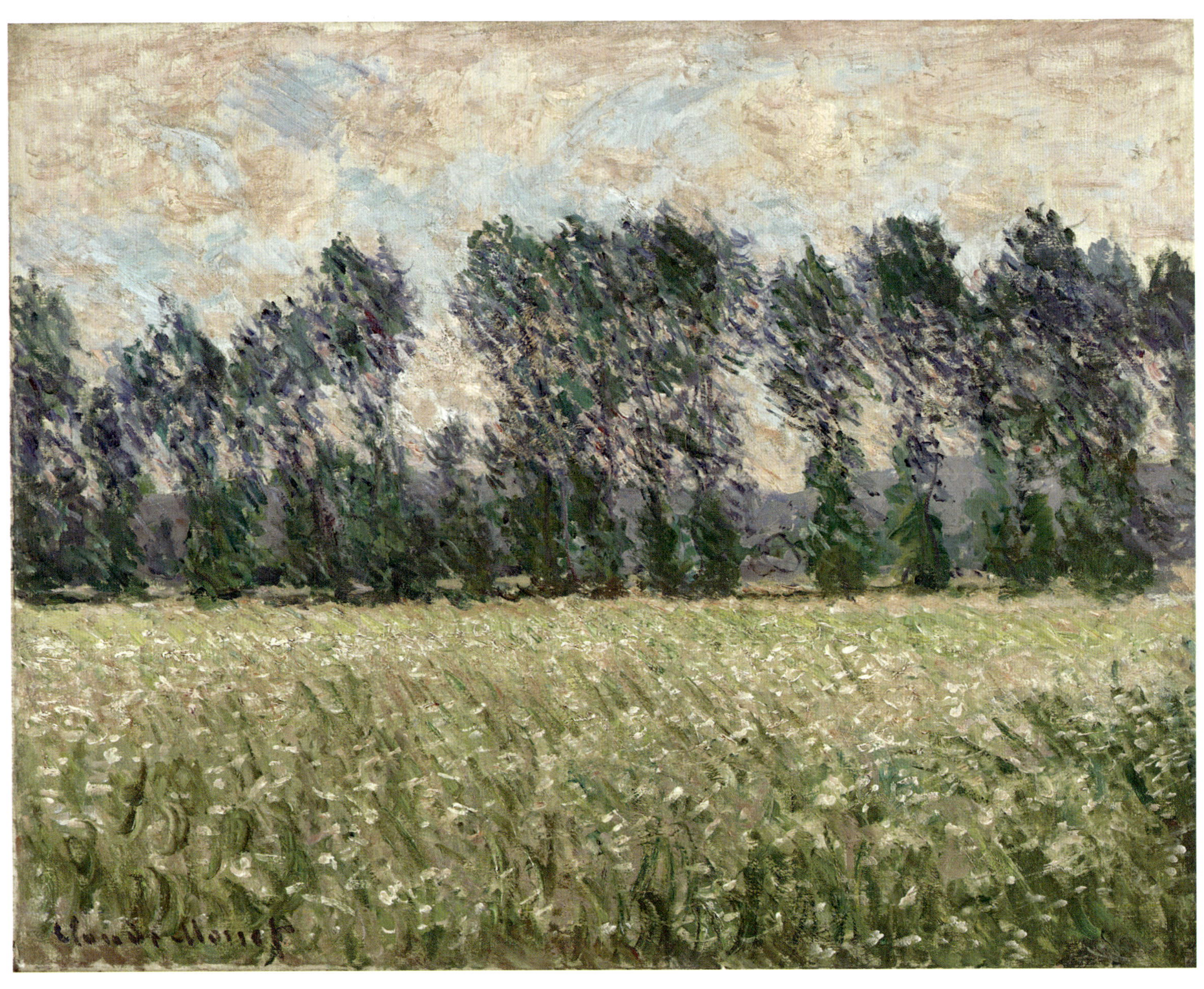

CLAUDE MONET, *Prairie at Giverny*, 1885
Oil on canvas, 65 × 81 cm
Private collection,
on loan to the Scottish National Gallery, Edinburgh

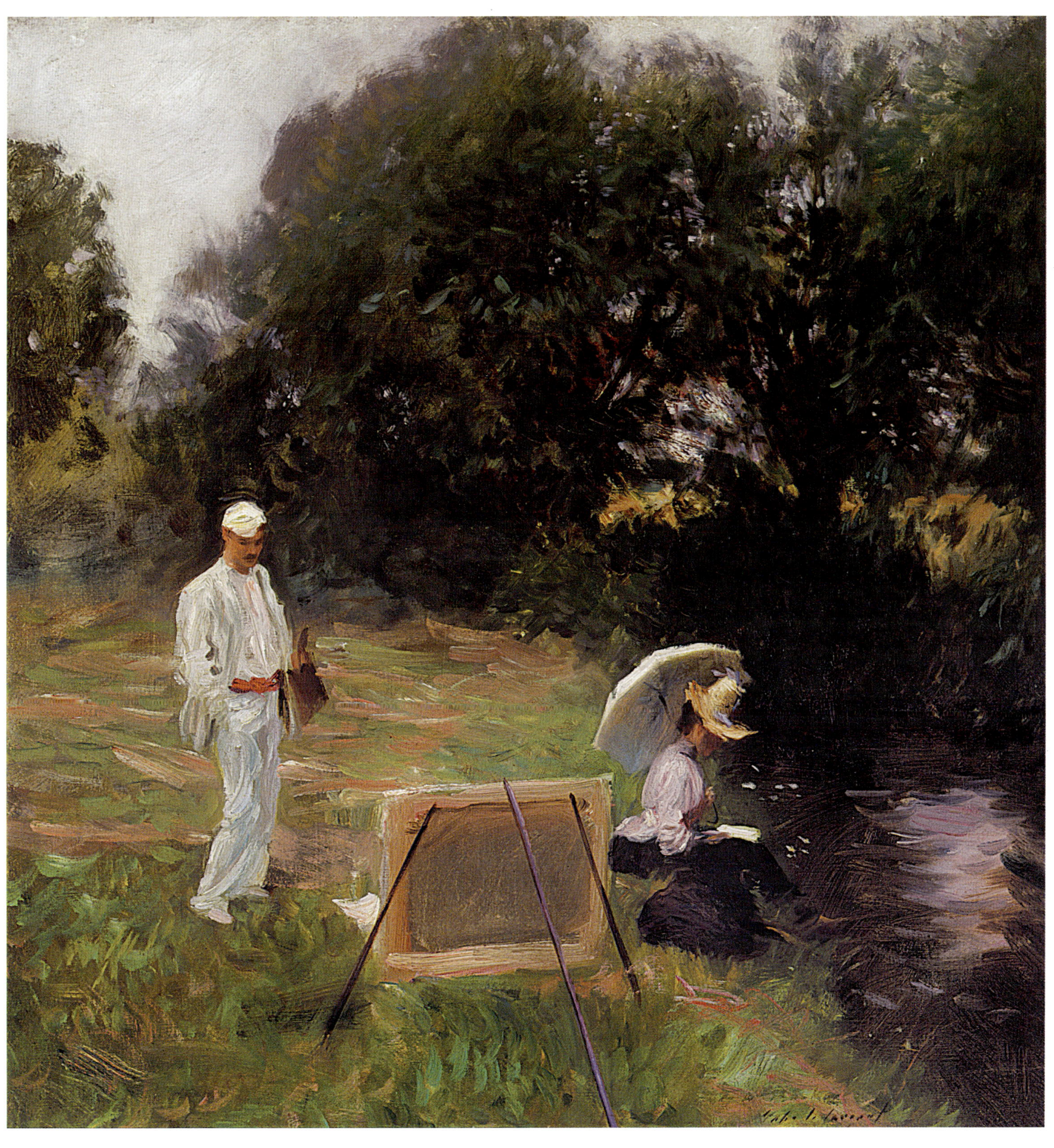

JOHN SINGER SARGENT, *Dennis Miller Bunker Painting at Calcot*, 1888
Oil on canvas, 68.6 × 64.1 cm
Terra Foundation for American Art, Chicago,
Daniel J. Terra Collection, 1999.130

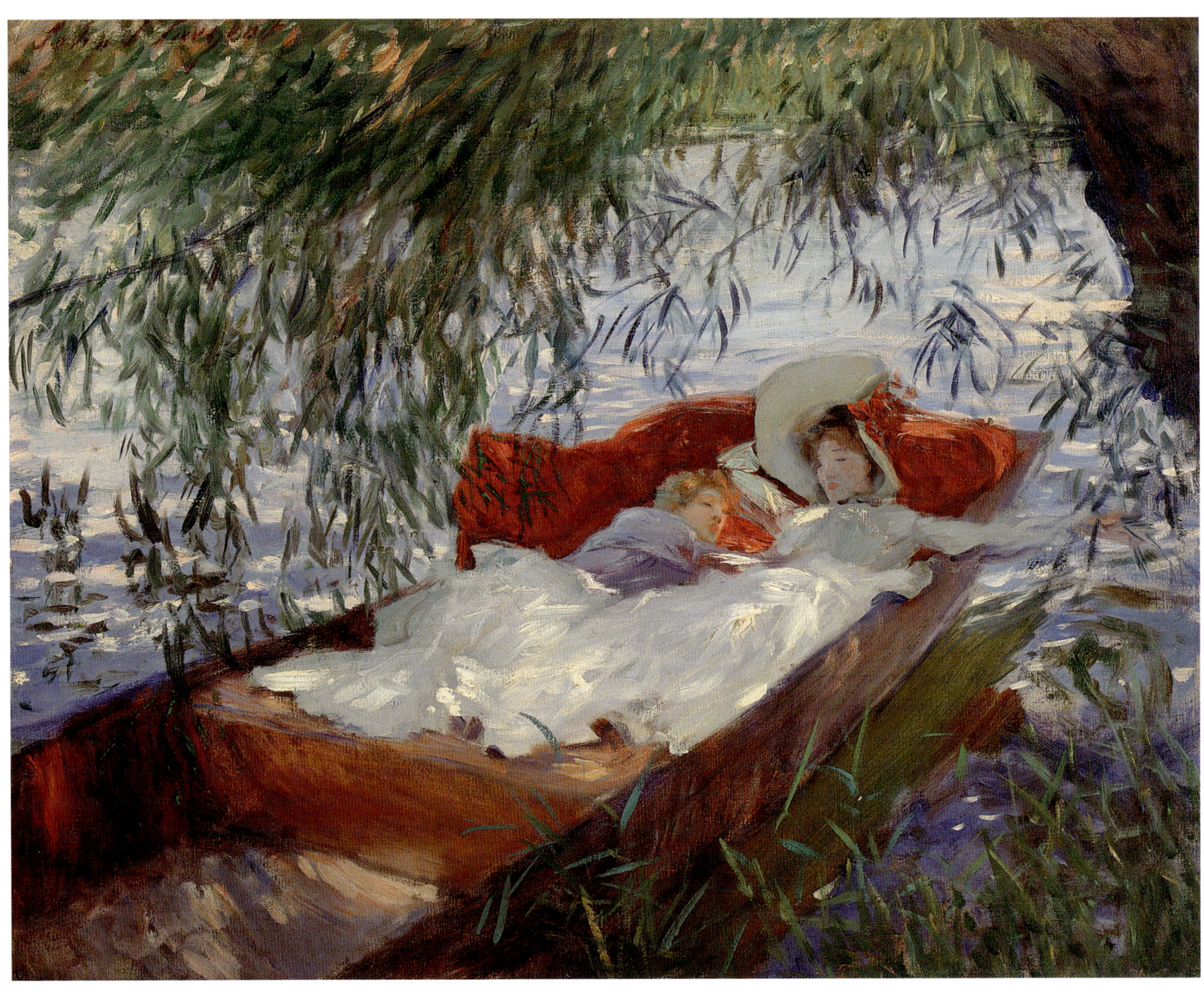

JOHN SINGER SARGENT, *Two Women Asleep in a Punt under the Willows*, *c*. 1887
Oil on canvas, 56 × 68.6 cm
Museu Calouste Gulbenkian, Lisbon, 73
[Shown in Madrid only]

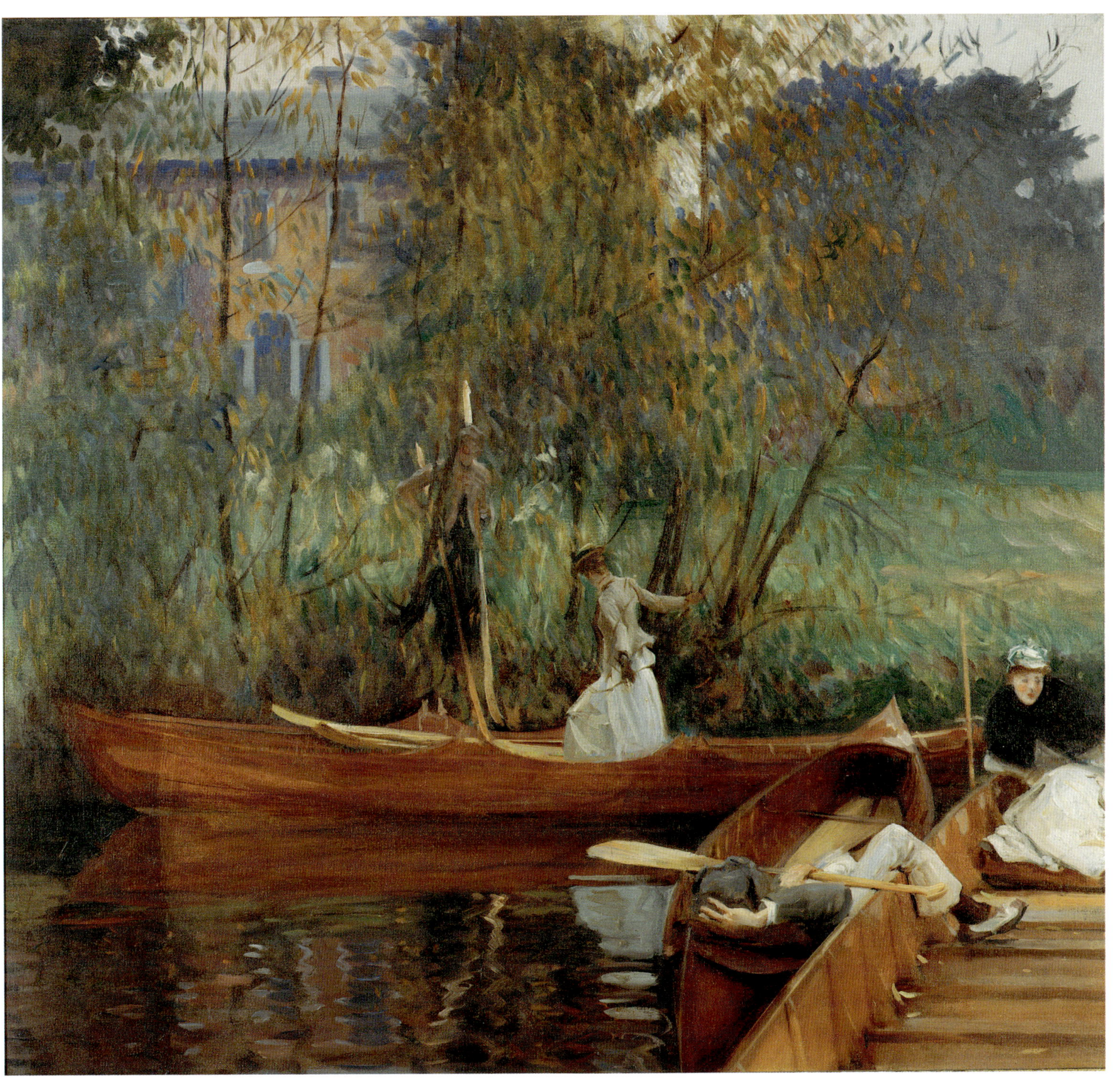

JOHN SINGER SARGENT, *A Boating Party, c.* 1889
Oil on canvas, 88.3 × 91.4 cm
Museum of Art, Rhode Island School of Design, Providence,
Gift of Mrs. Houghton P. Metcalf in memory of her husband, Houghton P. Metcalf, 78.086

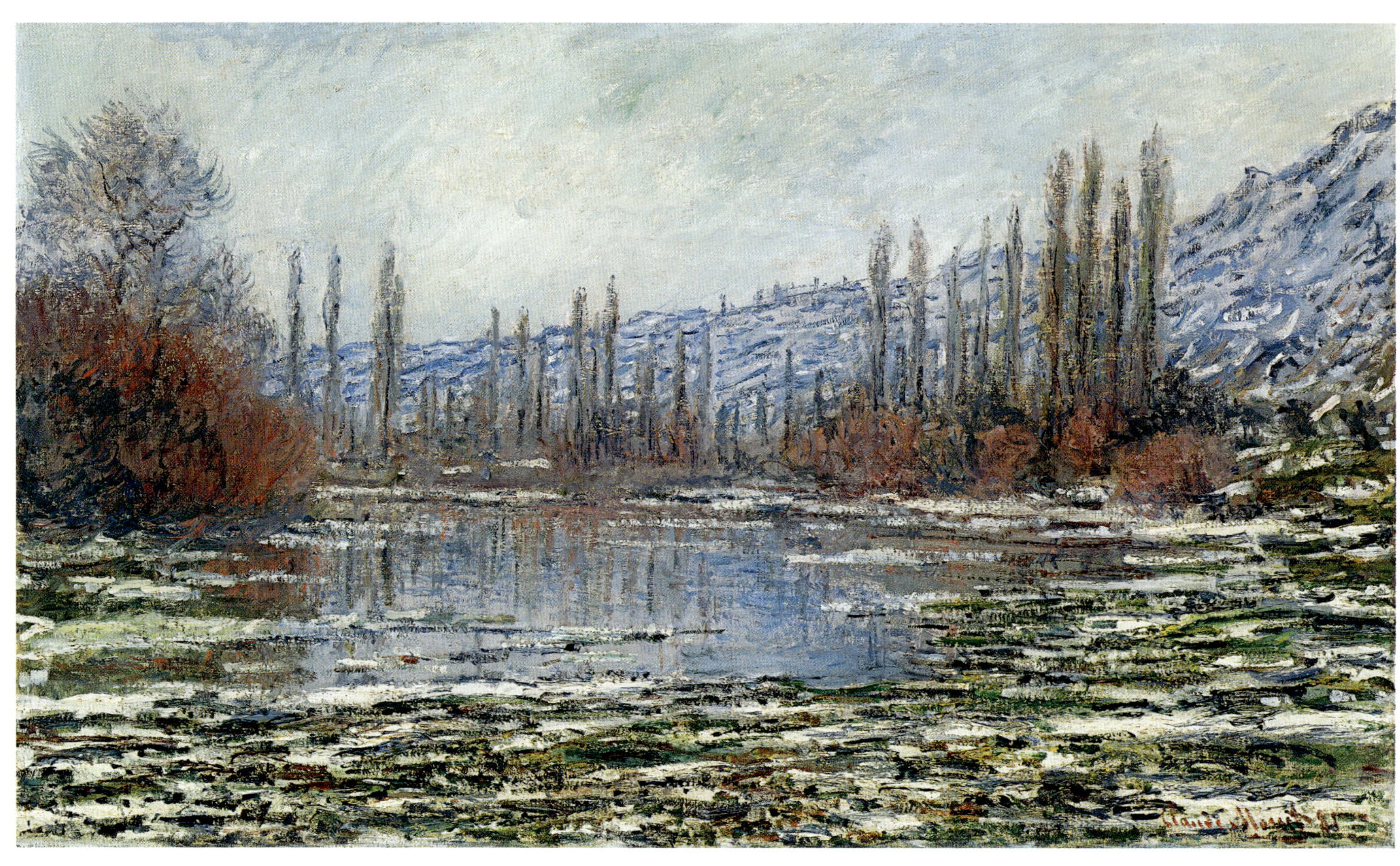

CLAUDE MONET, *The Thaw at Vétheuil*, 1880
Oil on canvas, 60 × 100 cm
Museo Thyssen-Bornemisza, Madrid, 680 (1977.86)
[Shown in Giverny only]

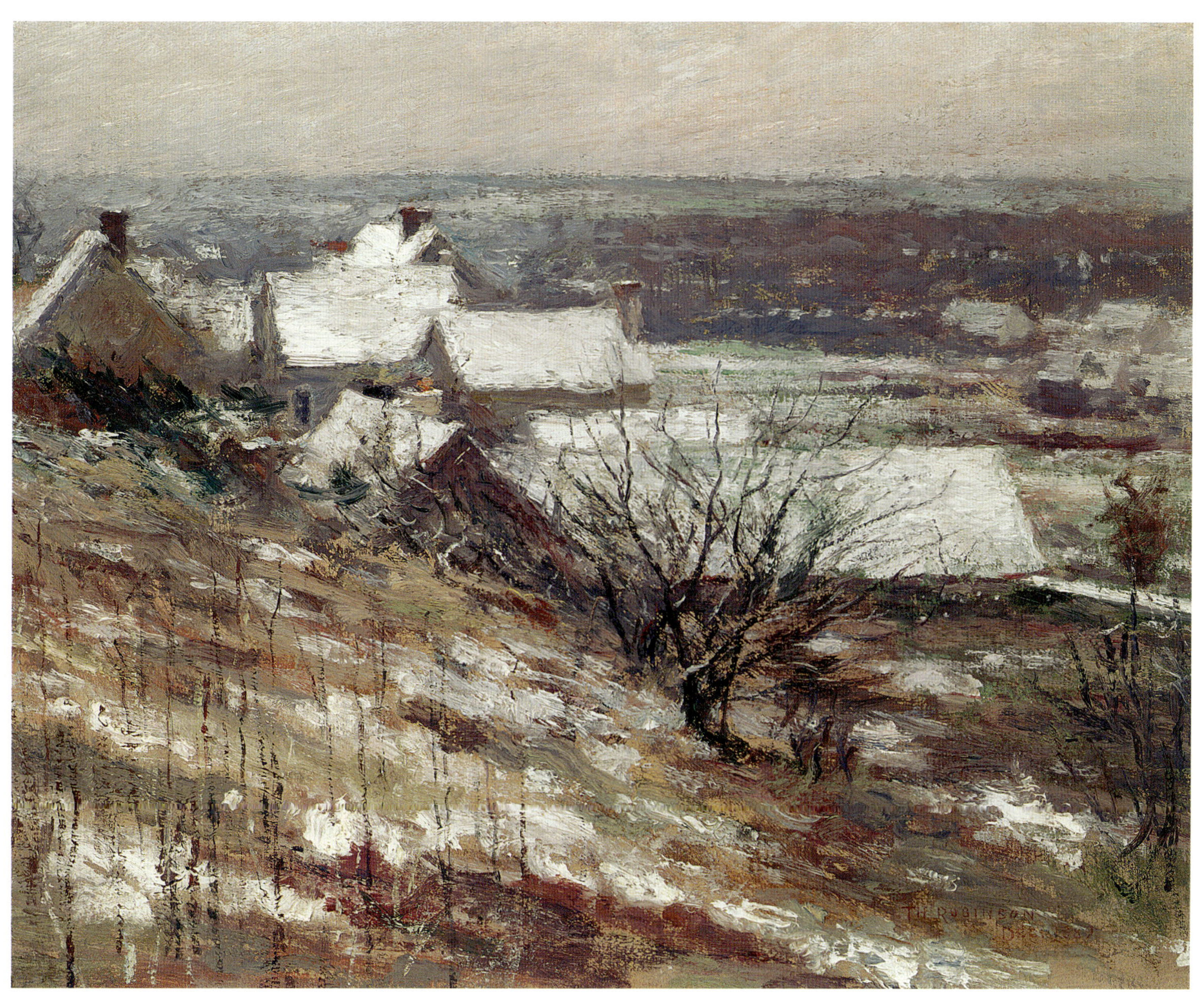

THEODORE ROBINSON, *Winter Landscape*, 1889
Oil on canvas, 46.4 × 55.9 cm
Terra Foundation for American Art, Chicago,
Daniel J. Terra Collection, 1999.128

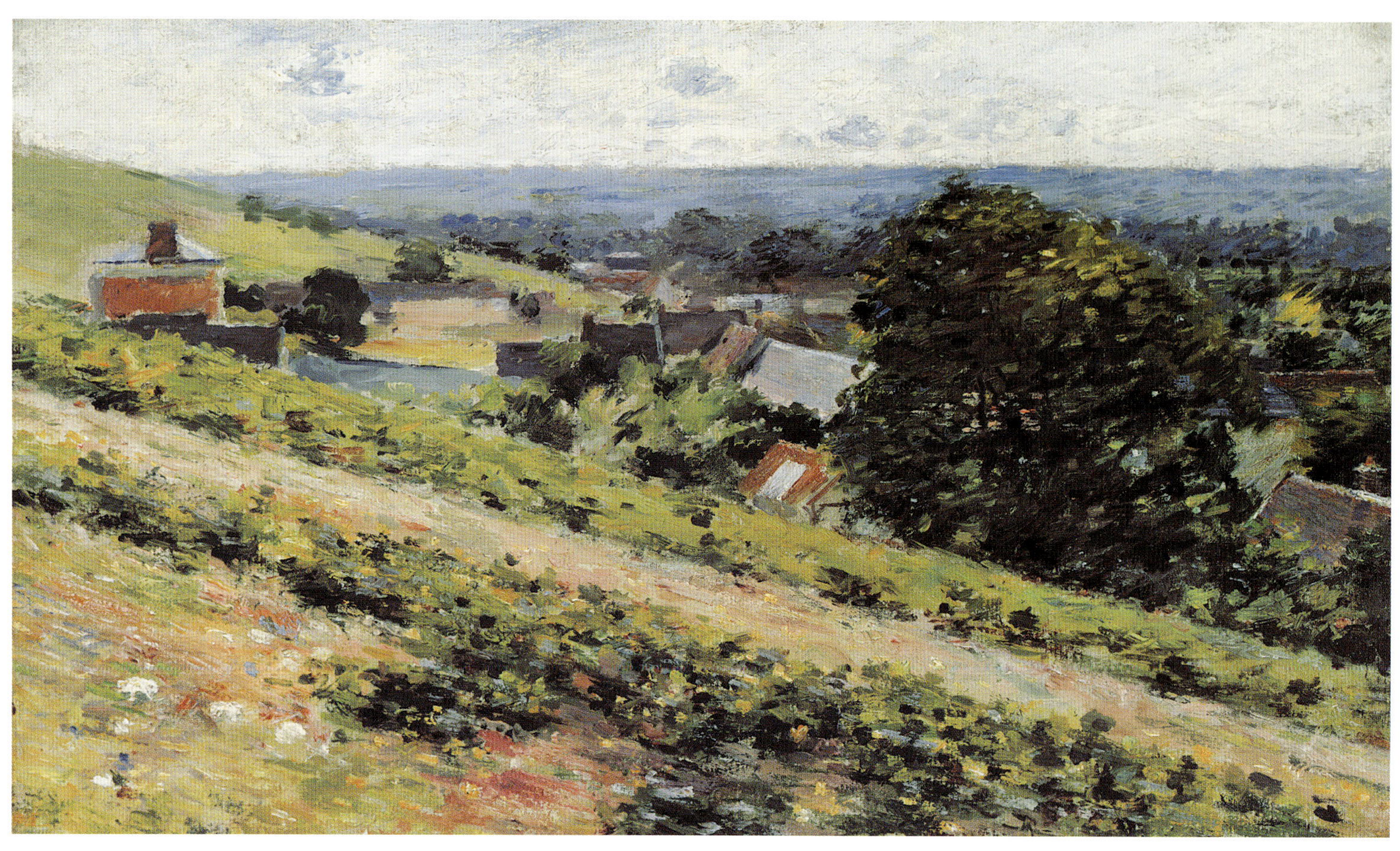

THEODORE ROBINSON, *From the Hill, Giverny*, between 1889 and 1892
Oil on canvas, 40.3 × 65.7 cm
Terra Foundation for American Art, Chicago,
Daniel J. Terra Collection, 1987.6

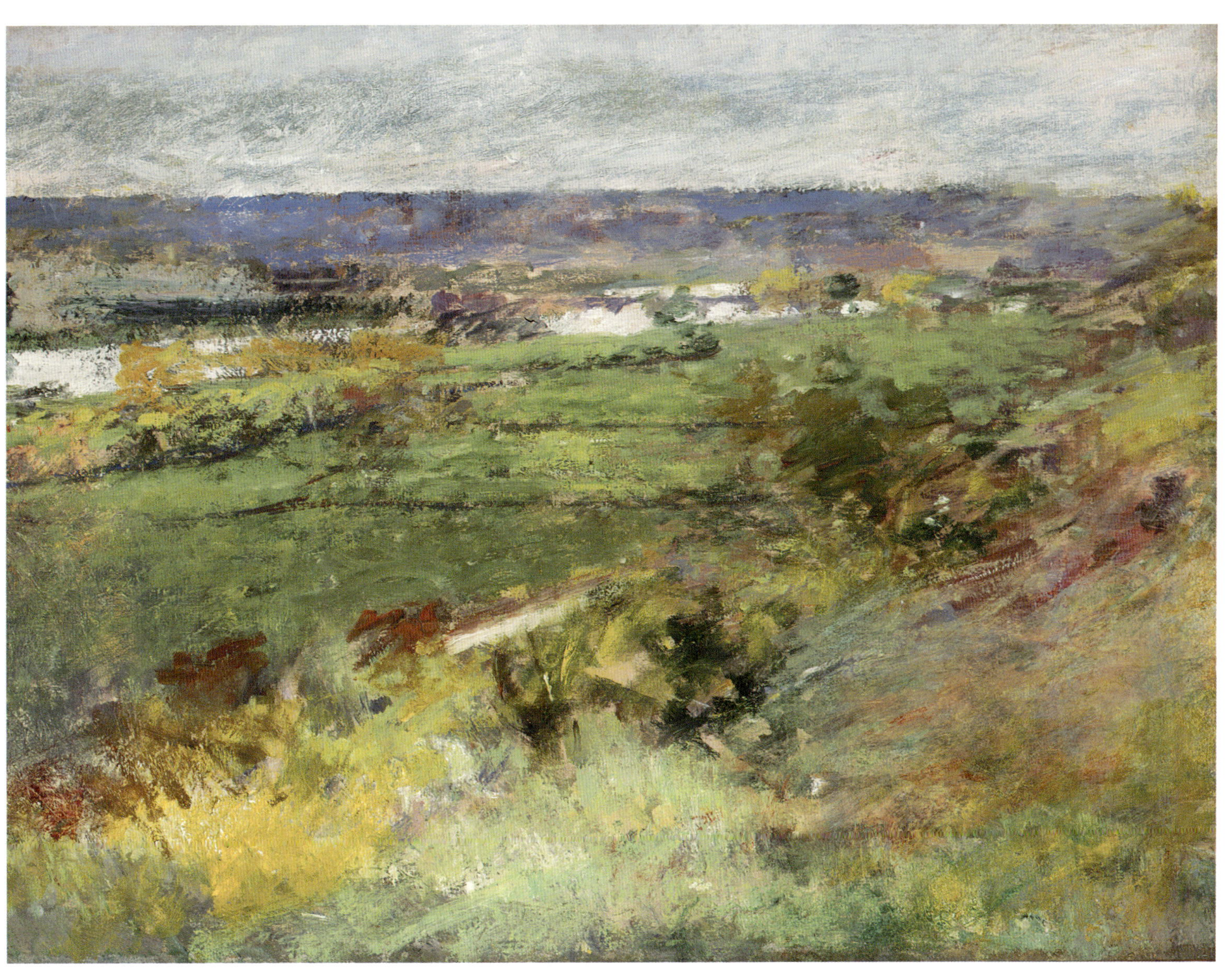

THEODORE ROBINSON, Study for *'Vallée de la Seine vue des hauteurs de Giverny'*, 1892
Oil on canvas, 58.1 × 73.3 cm
Terra Foundation for American Art, Chicago,
Daniel J. Terra Collection, 1992.9

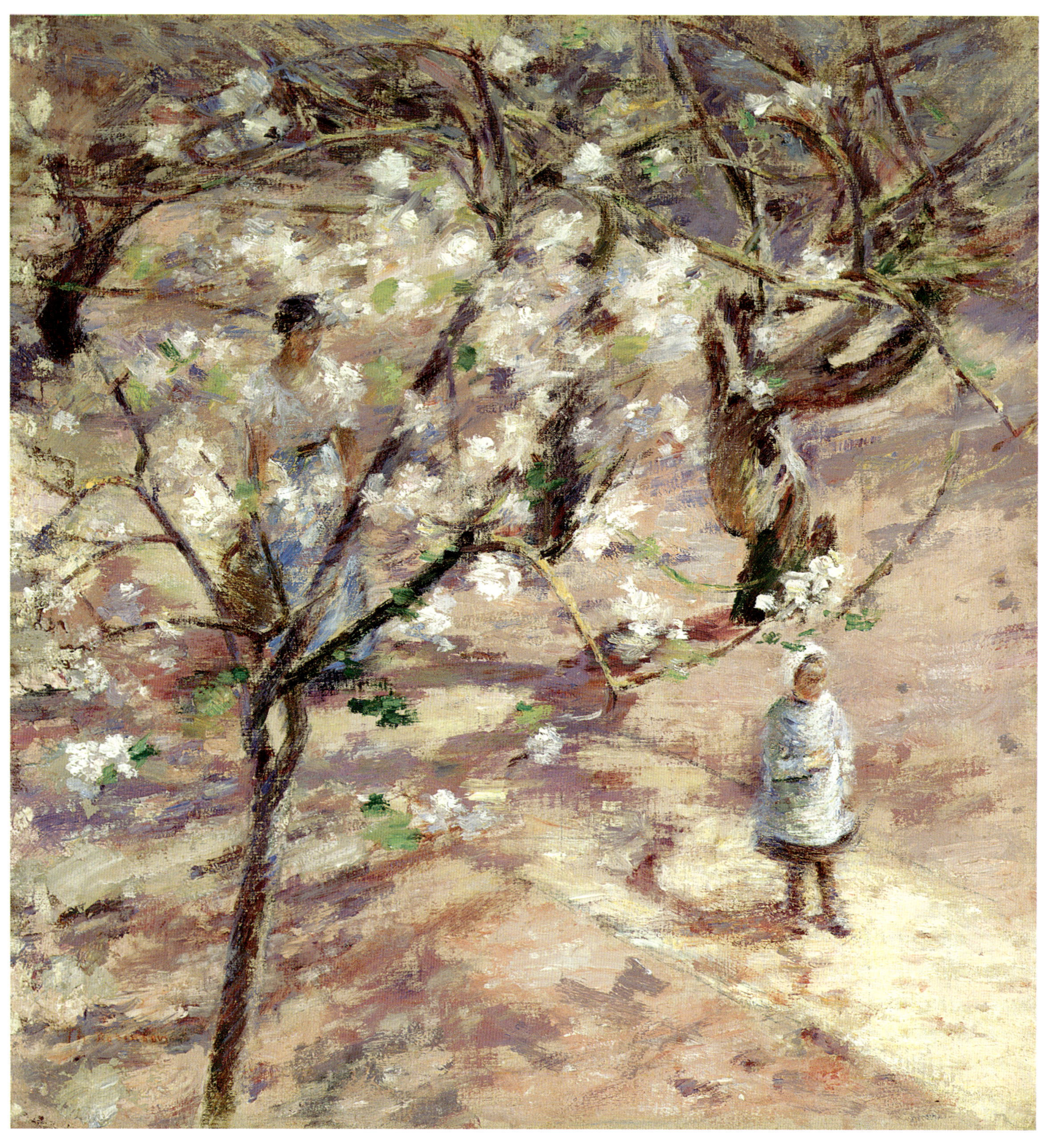

THEODORE ROBINSON, *Blossoms at Giverny*, 1891–2
Oil on canvas, 54.9 × 51.1 cm
Terra Foundation for American Art, Chicago,
Daniel J. Terra Collection, 1992.130

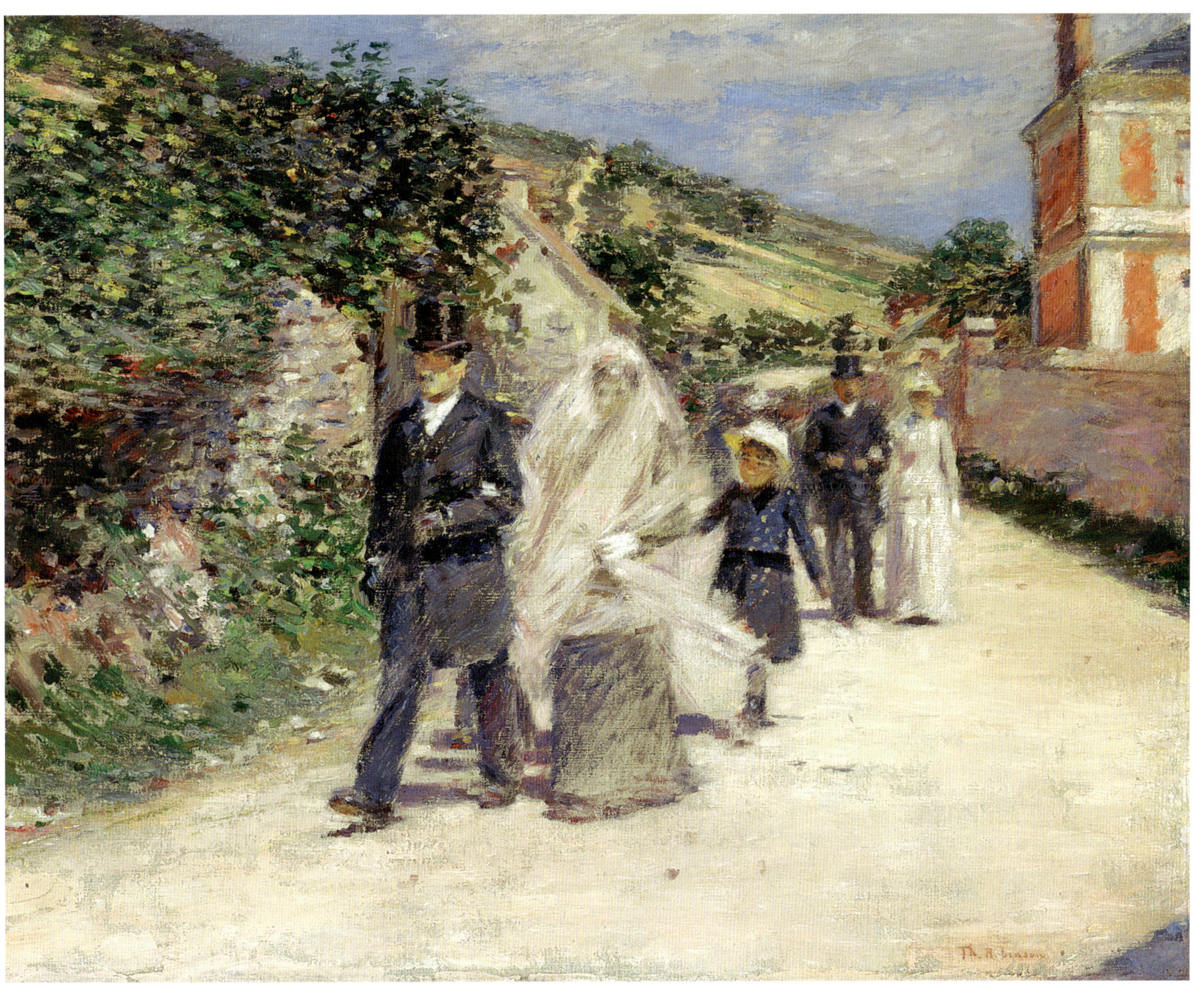

THEODORE ROBINSON, *The Wedding March*, 1892
Oil on canvas, 56.7 × 67.3 cm
Terra Foundation for American Art, Chicago,
Daniel J. Terra Collection, 1999.127

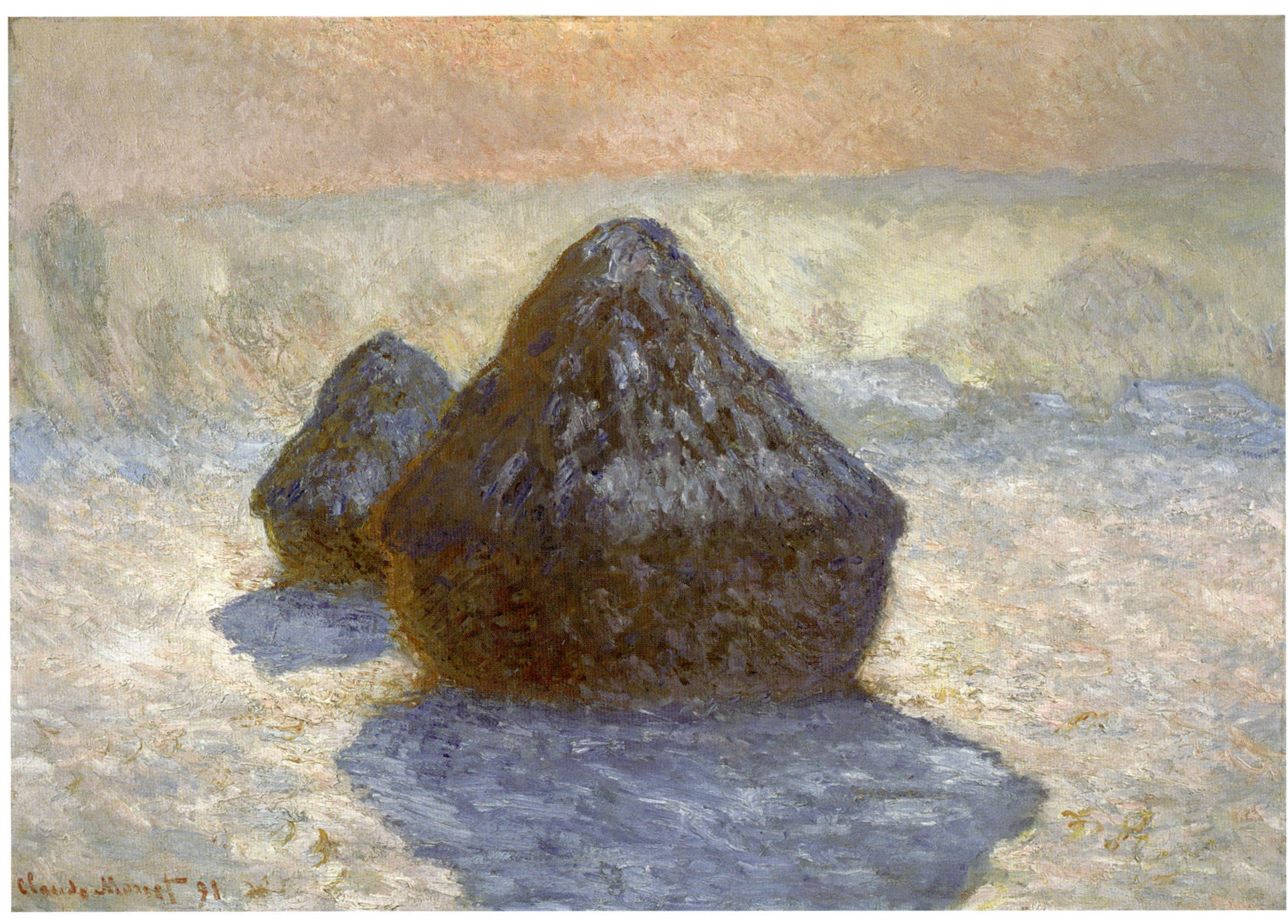

CLAUDE MONET, *Haystacks: Snow Effect*, 1891
Oil on canvas, 65 × 92 cm
Scottish National Gallery, Edinburgh,
Bequest of Sir Alexander Maitland, 1965, NG 2283

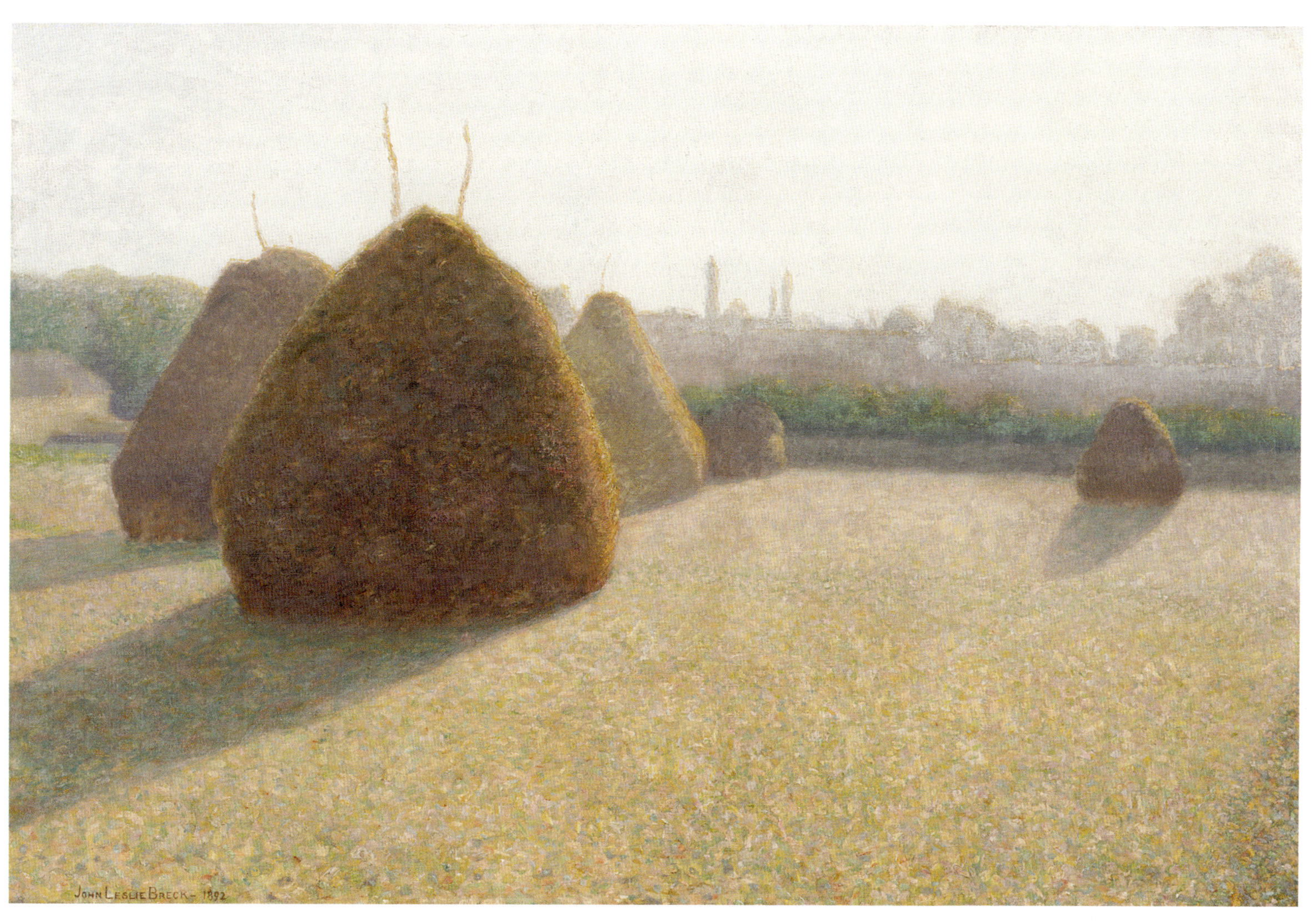

JOHN LESLIE BRECK, *Morning Fog and Sun*, 1892
Oil on canvas, 81.3 × 117.3 cm
Terra Foundation for American Art, Chicago,
Daniel J. Terra Collection, 1999.19

PAGES 84–5
JOHN LESLIE BRECK, *Studies of an Autumn Day*, 1891
Series of 12 paintings
Oil on canvas, each 32.7 × 40.8 cm
Terra Foundation for American Art, Chicago,
Daniel J. Terra Collection,1989.4.1-12

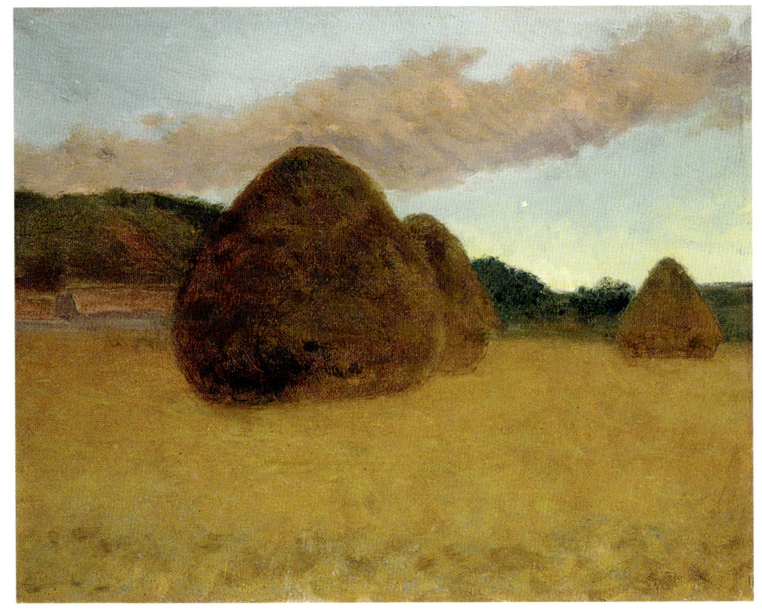

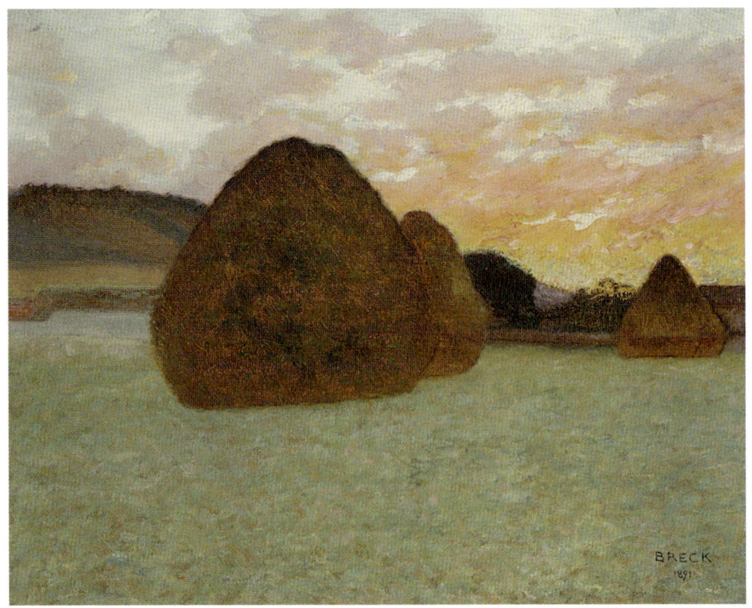
BRECK
1891

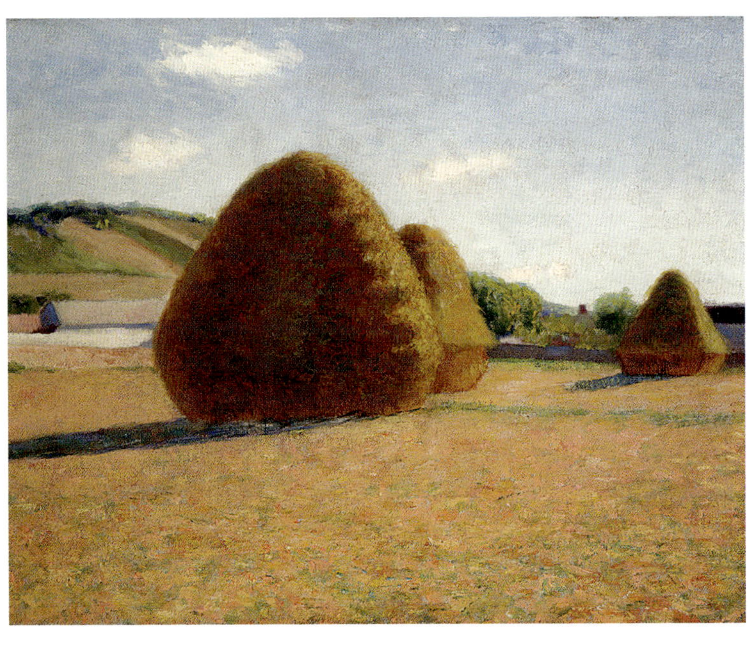

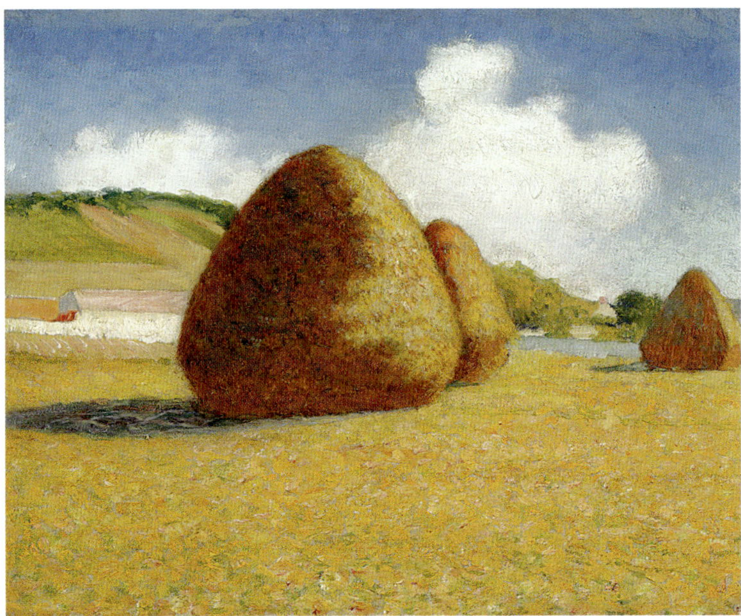

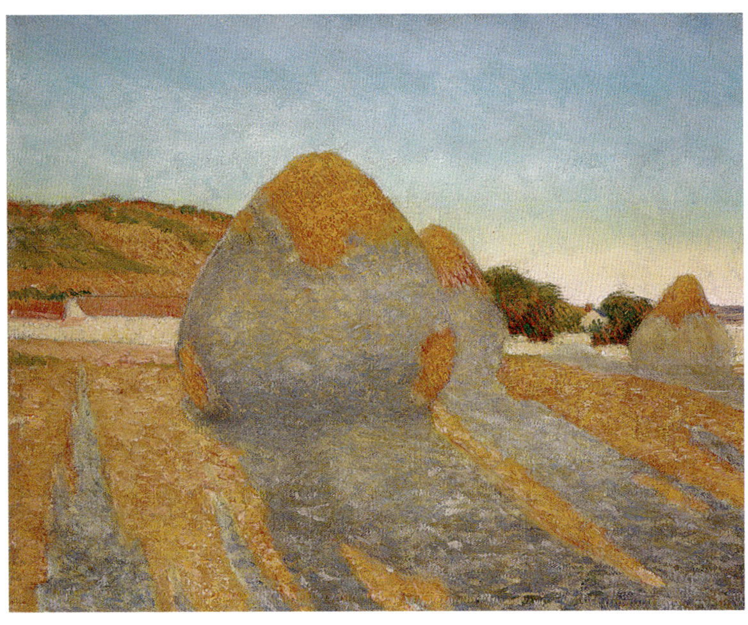

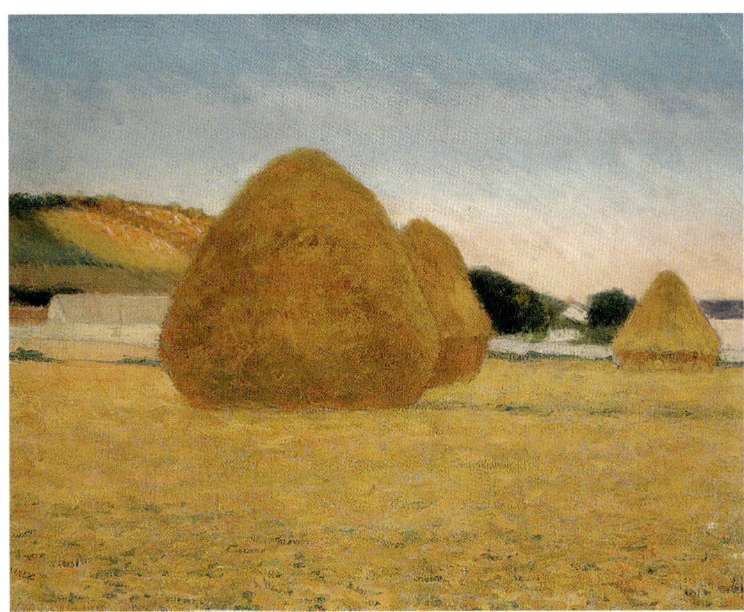

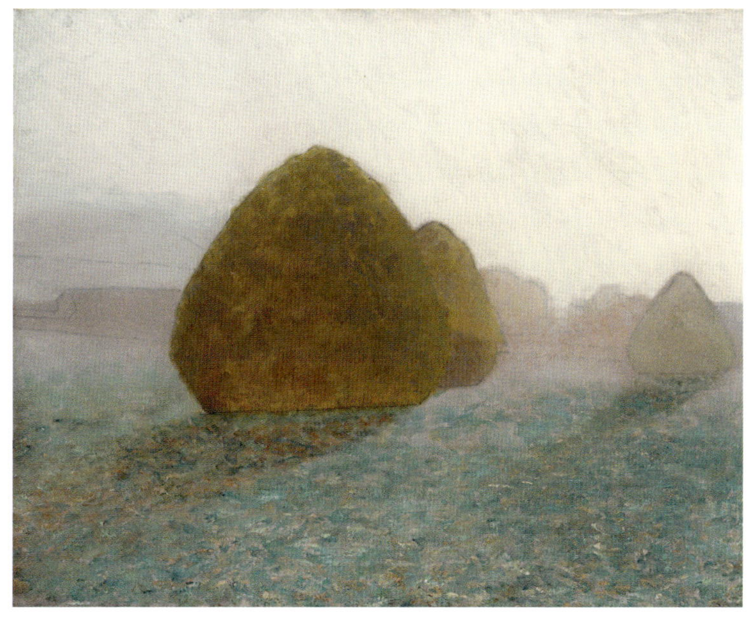
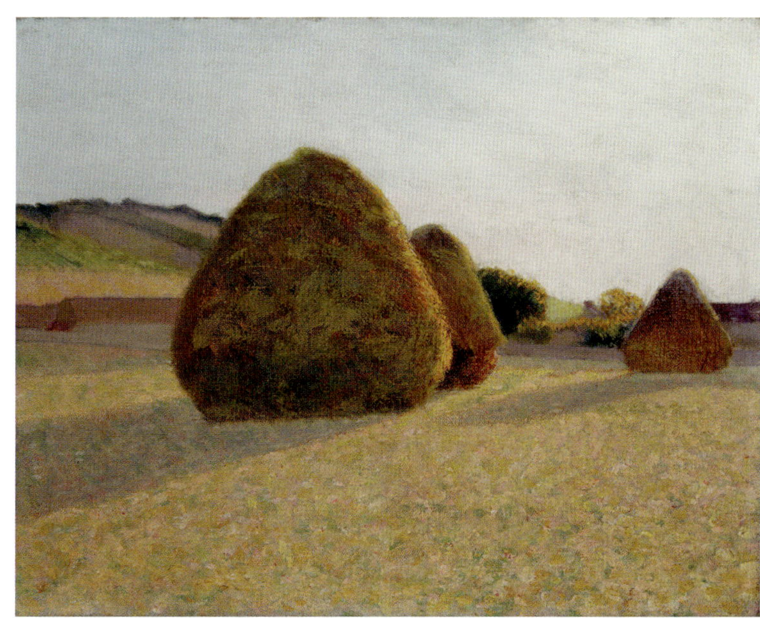
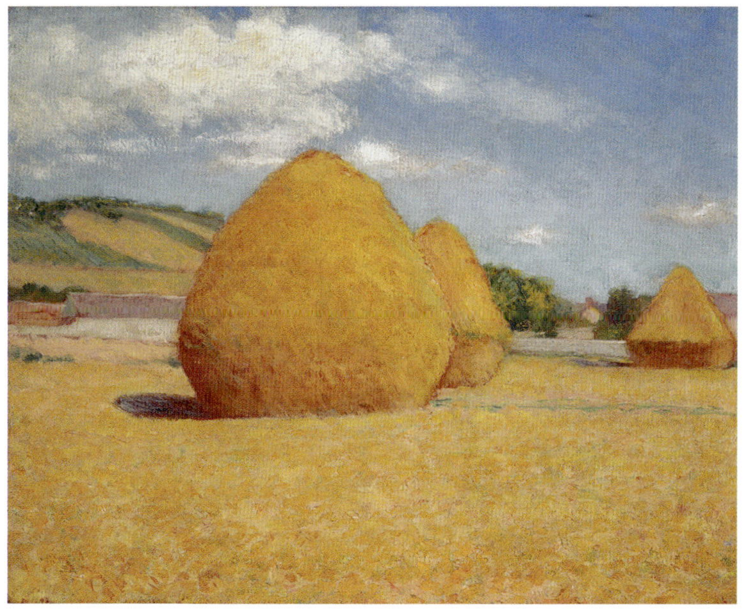
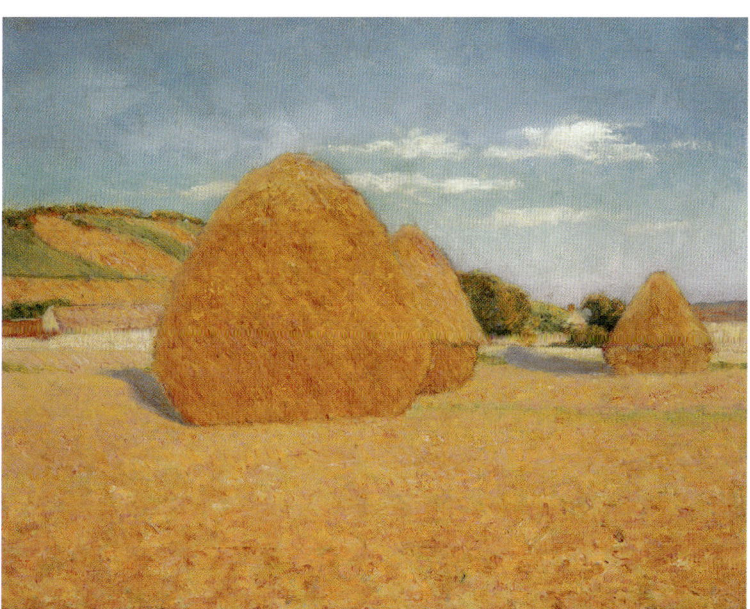
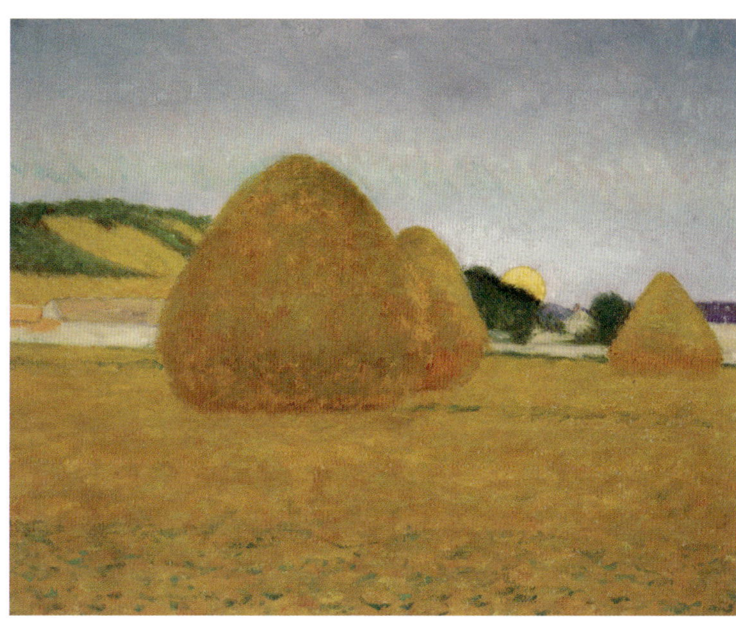
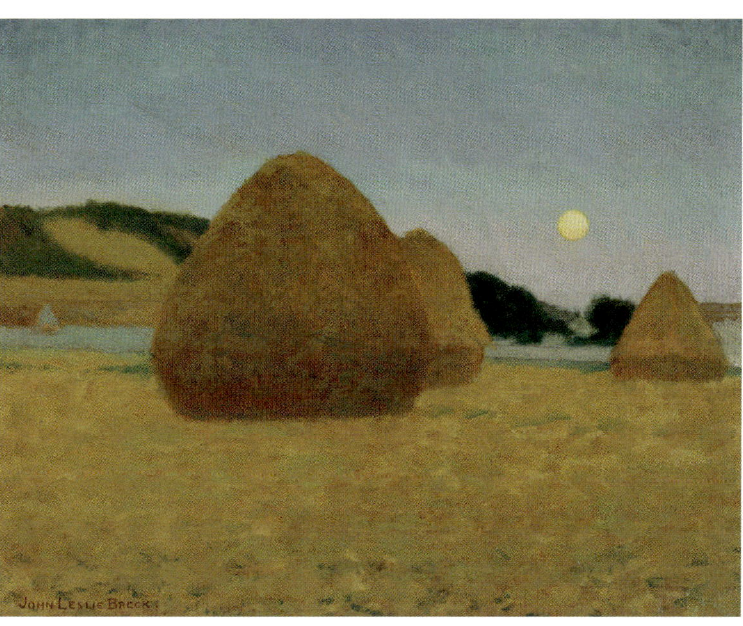
JOHN LESLIE BROOKS

CHILDE HASSAM, *Peach Blossoms – Villiers-le-Bel*, 1887–9
Oil on canvas, 54.6 × 46 cm
The Metropolitan Museum of Art, New York,
Gift of Mrs. J. Augustus Barnard, 1979.490.9

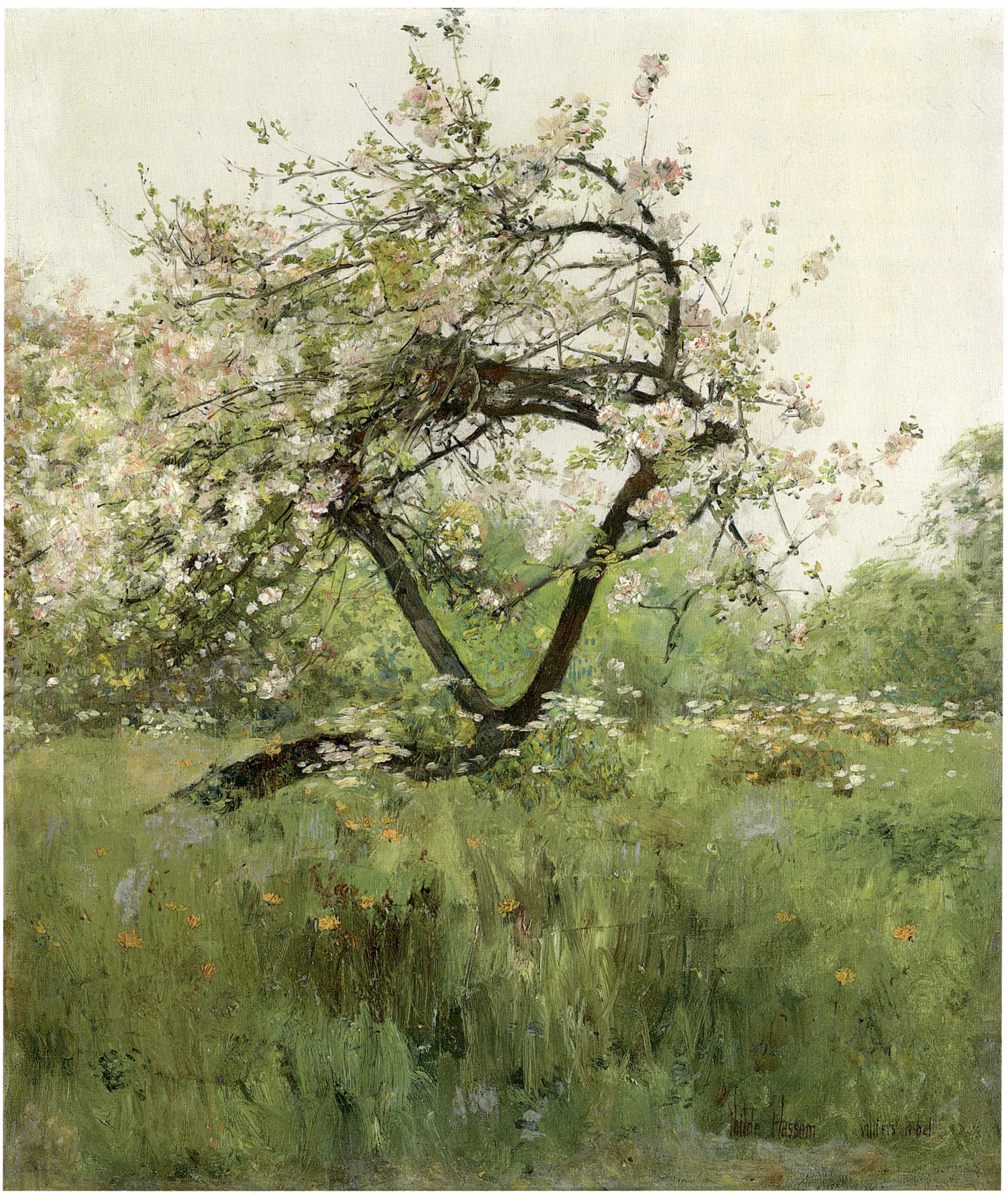

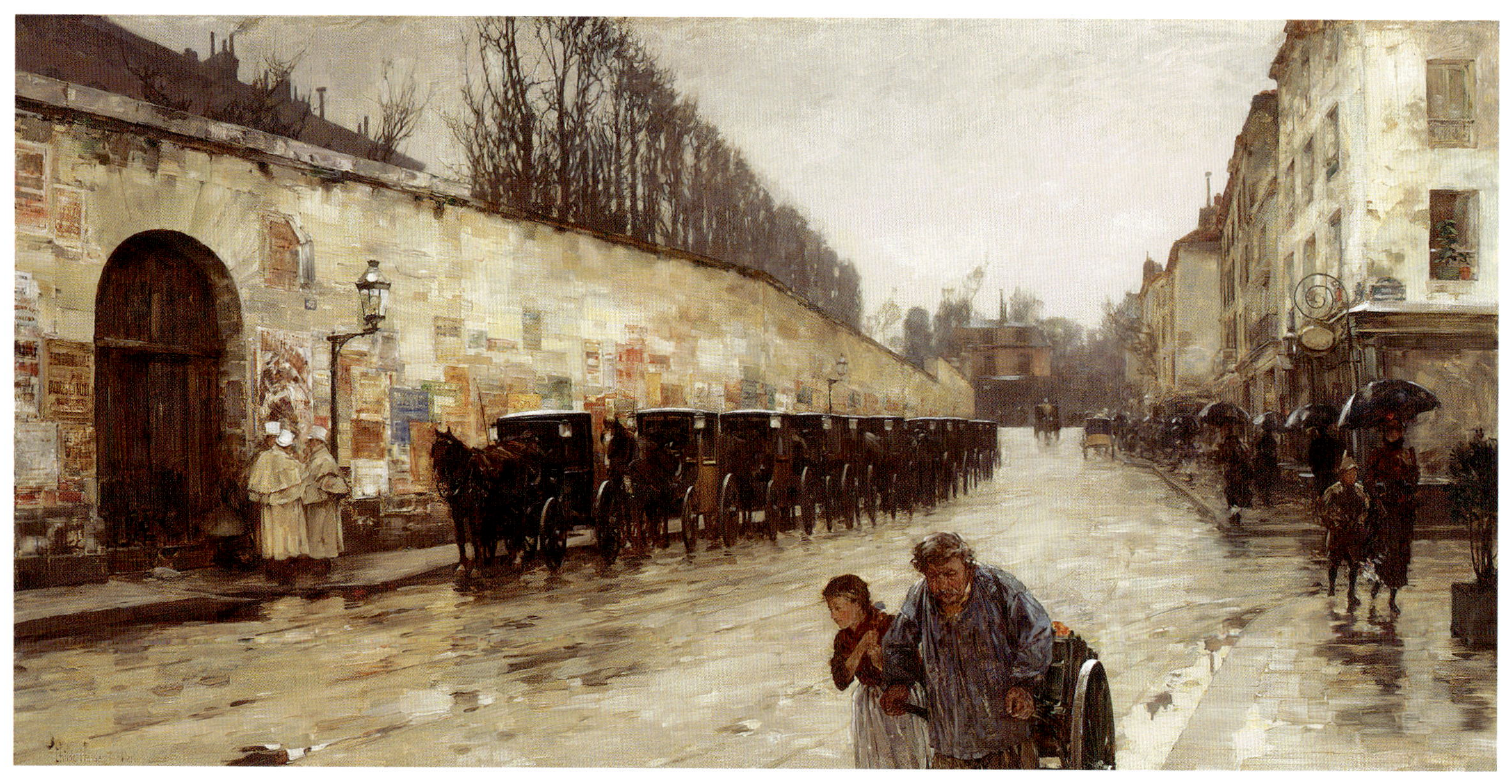

CHILDE HASSAM, *Une Averse – Rue Bonaparte*, 1887
Oil on canvas, 102.6 × 196.7 cm
Terra Foundation for American Art, Chicago,
Daniel J. Terra Collection, 1993.20

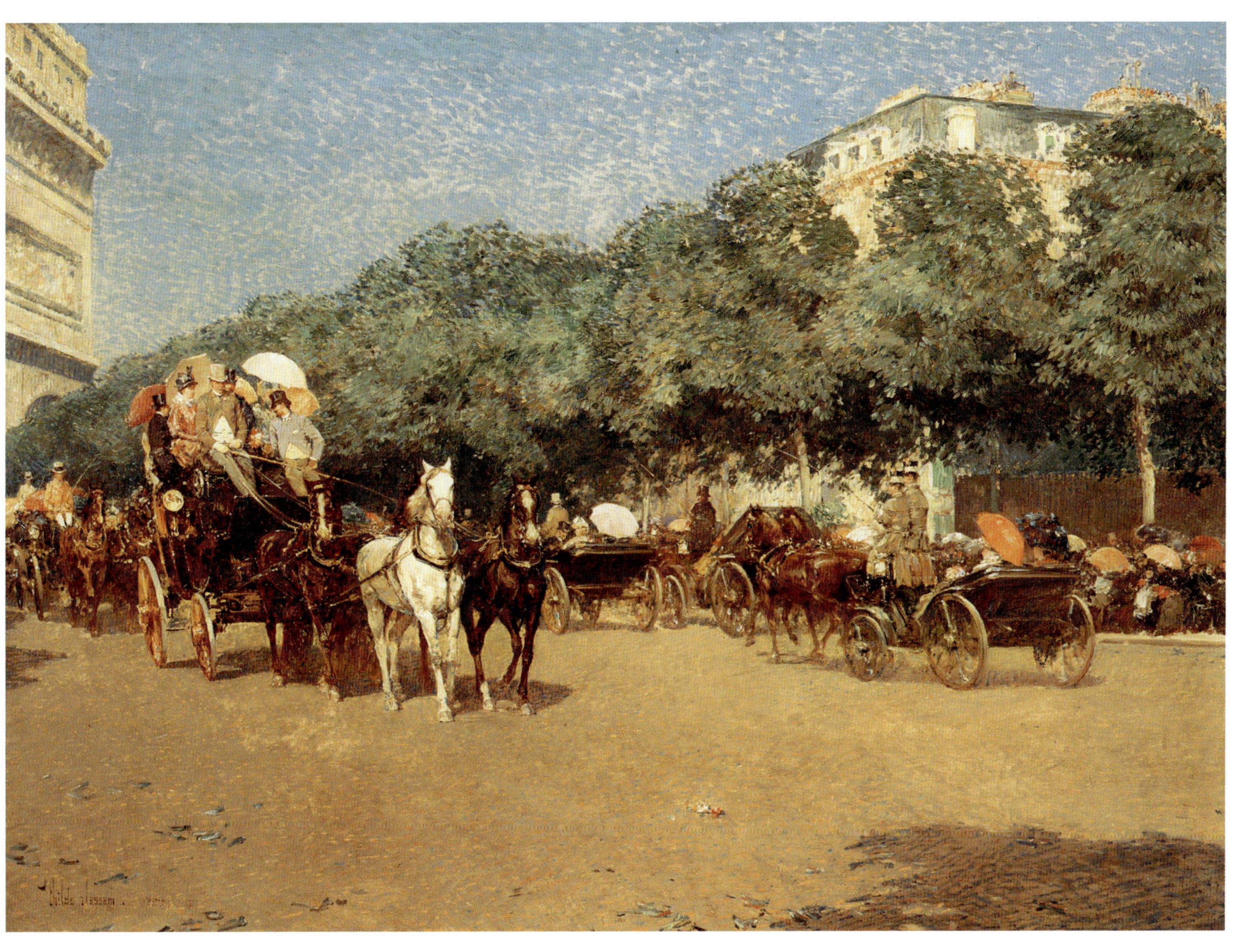

CHILDE HASSAM, *Le Jour du Grand Prix*, 1887
Oil on canvas, 91.4 × 121.9 cm
New Britain Museum of American Art, New Britain, Connecticut,
Grace Judd Landers Fund, 1943.14

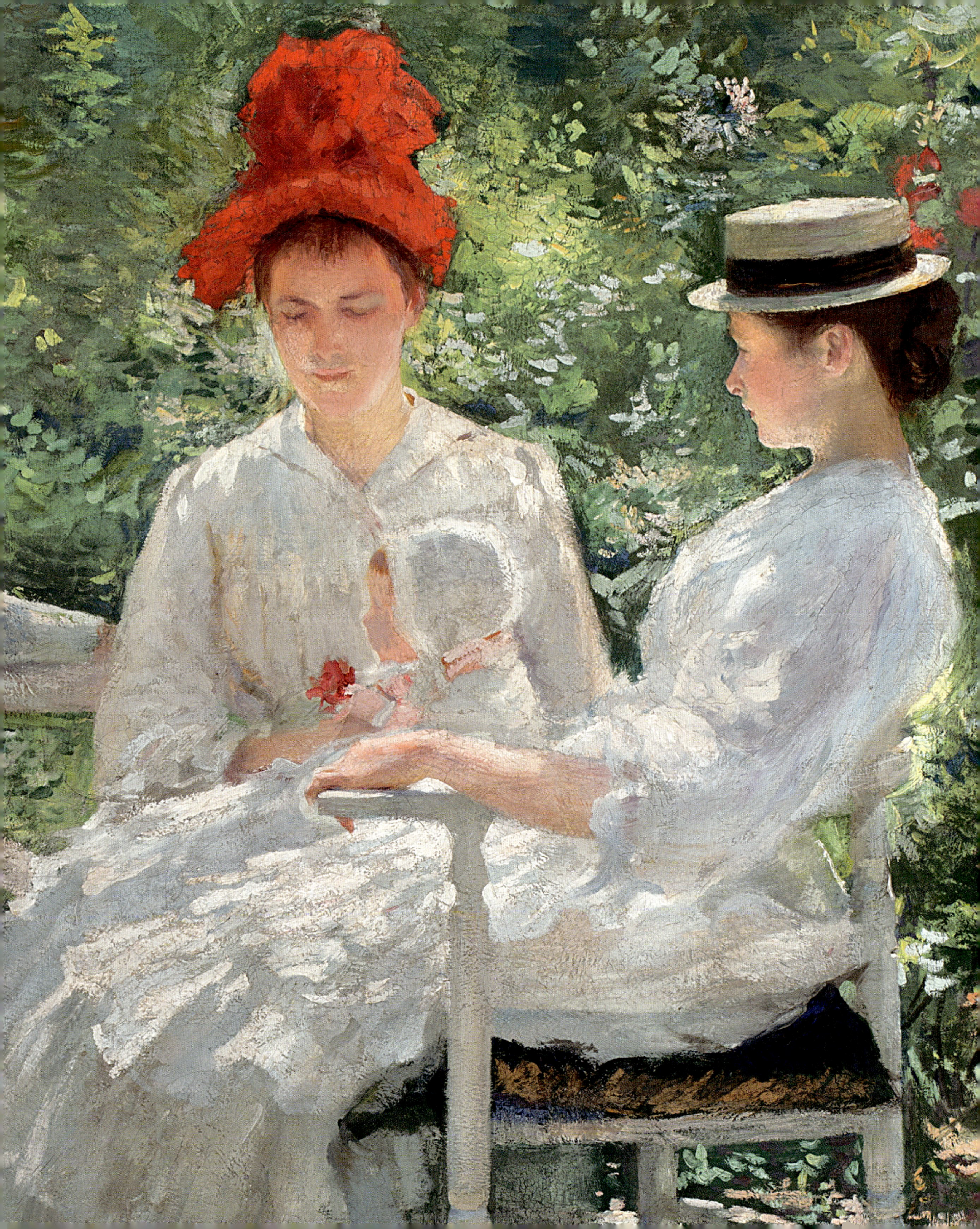

The Beginnings of American Impressionism **at Home, 1890–1900**

Around 1890, several American artists back from Europe began to respond to the new subjects, compositions and colours of Impressionism in scenes depicting their native country. Their pictures of New York and Boston represent individual points of departure rather than a unified pictorial style. Throughout the 1890s, increasing numbers of Americans responded to the growing popularity of Impressionism, and, by 1900, prismatic colour, broken brushwork and purple shadows had become the predominant style at American exhibitions.

William Merritt Chase and Childe Hassam focused on upper-class leisure in their depictions of urban parks in Boston, Brooklyn and New York in the late 1880s and early 1890s. Women and children occupy public spaces in these intimate, *plein-air* pictures filled with sunshine. Chase and Hassam employed the asymmetrical compositions and surprising aerial views of artists such as Edgar Degas and Gustave Caillebotte, and experimented with coloured shadows and sketch-like handling (pp.94-9). In the 1890s, both artists began to spend summers on the Eastern seashore – Chase on Long Island and Hassam on the Isles of Shoals off the coast of New Hampshire and Maine – and their cheerful, luminous paintings found favour with collectors.

It was also in the early 1890s that Dennis Miller Bunker and Theodore Robinson turned their attention to the rural American landscape as a subject for impressionist paintings. After his return from France in 1892, Robinson heeded critical advice to paint distinctly 'American' sites and travelled to Vermont and upstate New York. Works such as *Canal Scene* of 1893 (p.101) could be claimed as American because of their subjects as well as their vibrant colours and fresh, vigorous application of paint.

EDMUND C. TARBELL, *Three Sisters – A Study in June Sunlight*, 1890, detail (see p.110)

Edmund C. Tarbell and Frank W. Benson produced bright paintings of women and children in gardens or on the seashore throughout the 1890s. Although they used friends and family as models, such works functioned more broadly than portraits. Instead, these well-dressed, healthy women came to represent a new American ideal. While several of their canvases echo impressionist works created by Claude Monet and Auguste Renoir twenty years earlier, Tarbell's and Benson's have a decidedly American touch. In late 1897 they abandoned the Society of American Artists and joined the breakaway group known as the 'Ten American Painters', espousing modern principles and individual artistic expression.

Paintings by artists such as John Henry Twachtman and Thomas Wilmer Dewing from the 1890s hover on the fringes of Impressionism, combining attenuated brushwork with more subdued colours to encourage mystical interpretations. These artists found inspiration in the work of James Abbott McNeill Whistler. The legendary American expatriate embraced aestheticism in the 1870s in London when he painted a series of views of the River Thames as if seen through a blue mist. His simplified brushwork and lack of concern with 'finish' link these Nocturnes to the impressionists, even though the artist never exhibited with the group (pp.120, 121). More than any other American artist, Whistler preceded and informed a new generation who celebrated his emphasis on individual artistic sensibility and interest in atmospheric phenomena. For Americans like Twachtman and Dewing, Impressionism was not limited to sunny scenes of bourgeois leisure, but could incorporate ethereal landscapes inspired by Whistler.

THOMAS WILMER DEWING, *Summer*, *c.* 1890, detail (see p.129)

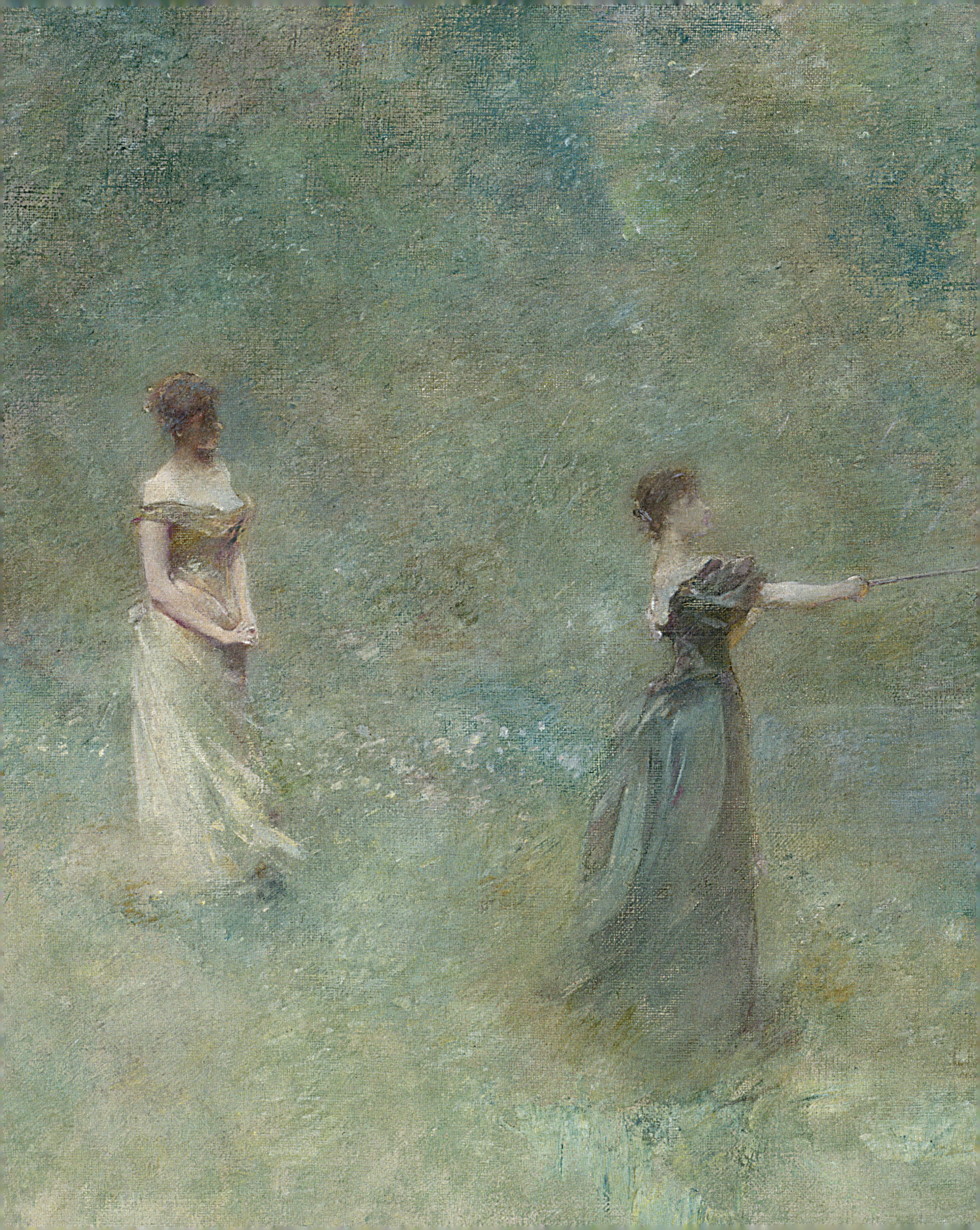

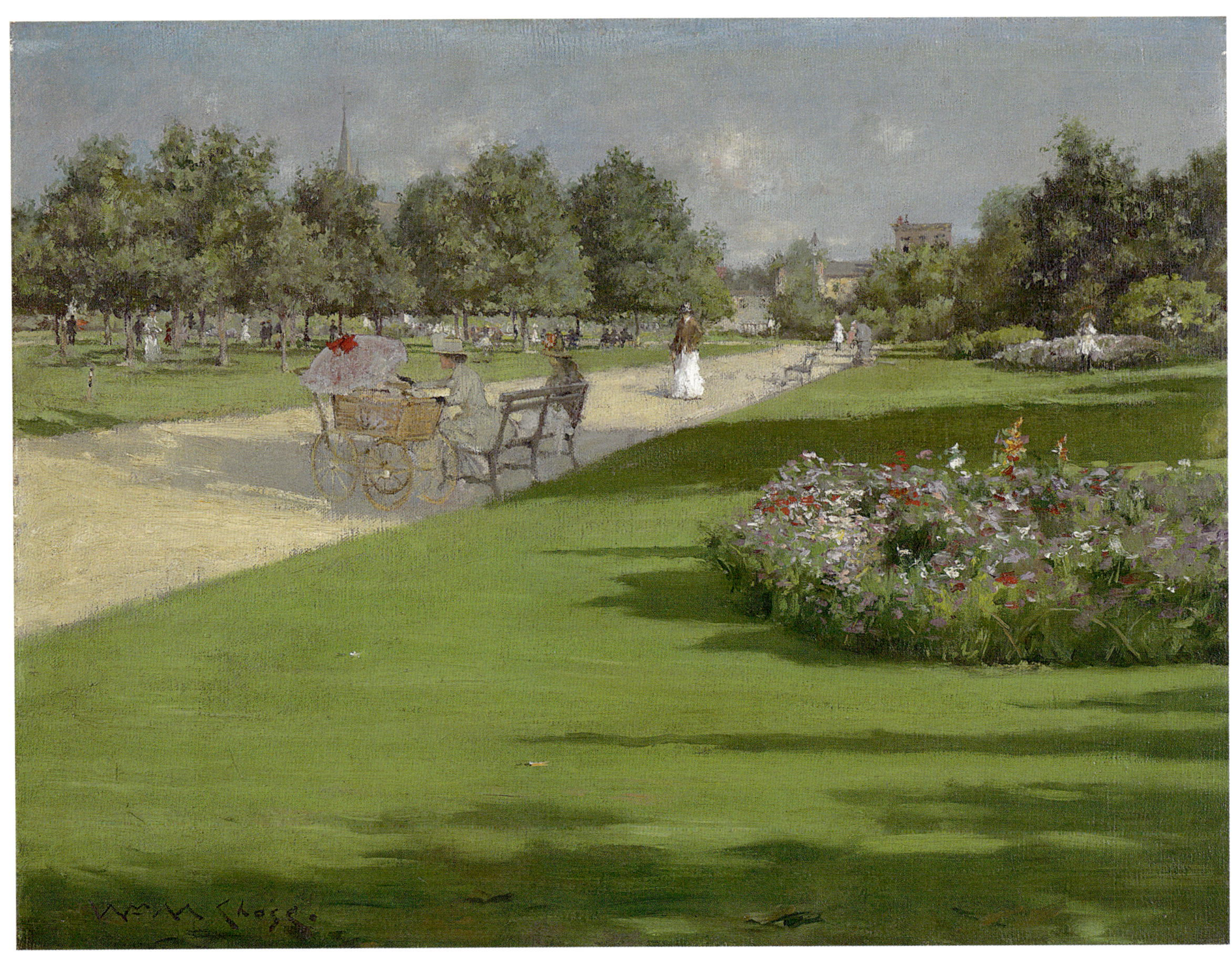

WILLIAM MERRITT CHASE, *Tompkins Park, Brooklyn*, 1887
Oil on canvas, 44.1 x 56.8 cm
Colby College Museum of Art, Waterville, Maine,
Gift of Miss Adeline F. and Miss Caroline R. Wing, 1963.040

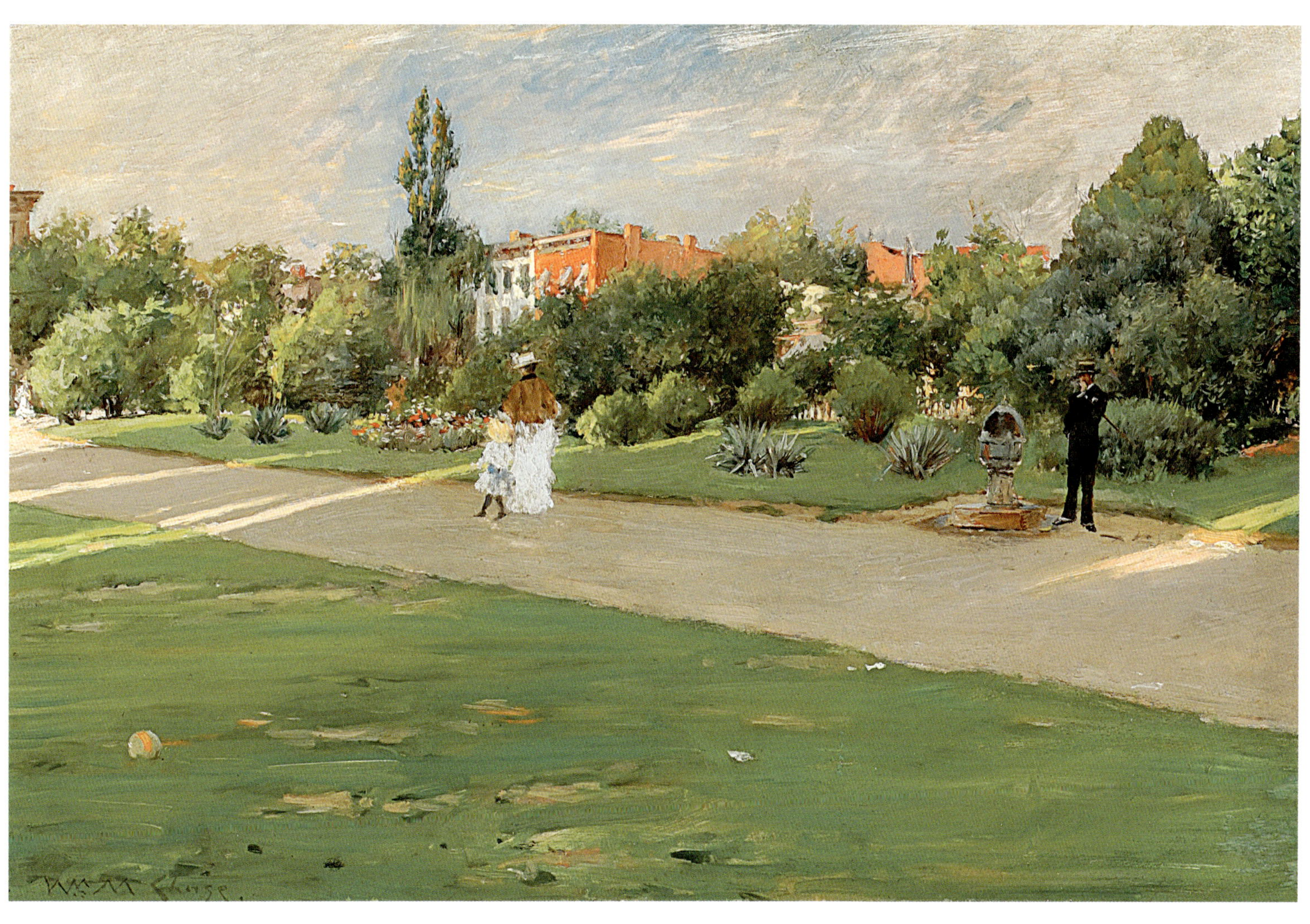

WILLIAM MERRITT CHASE, *Park in Brooklyn (Prospect Park, Brooklyn)*, *c.* 1887
Oil on panel, 41 x 61.3 cm
Parrish Art Museum, Water Mill, New York,
Littlejohn Collection, 1961.5.11

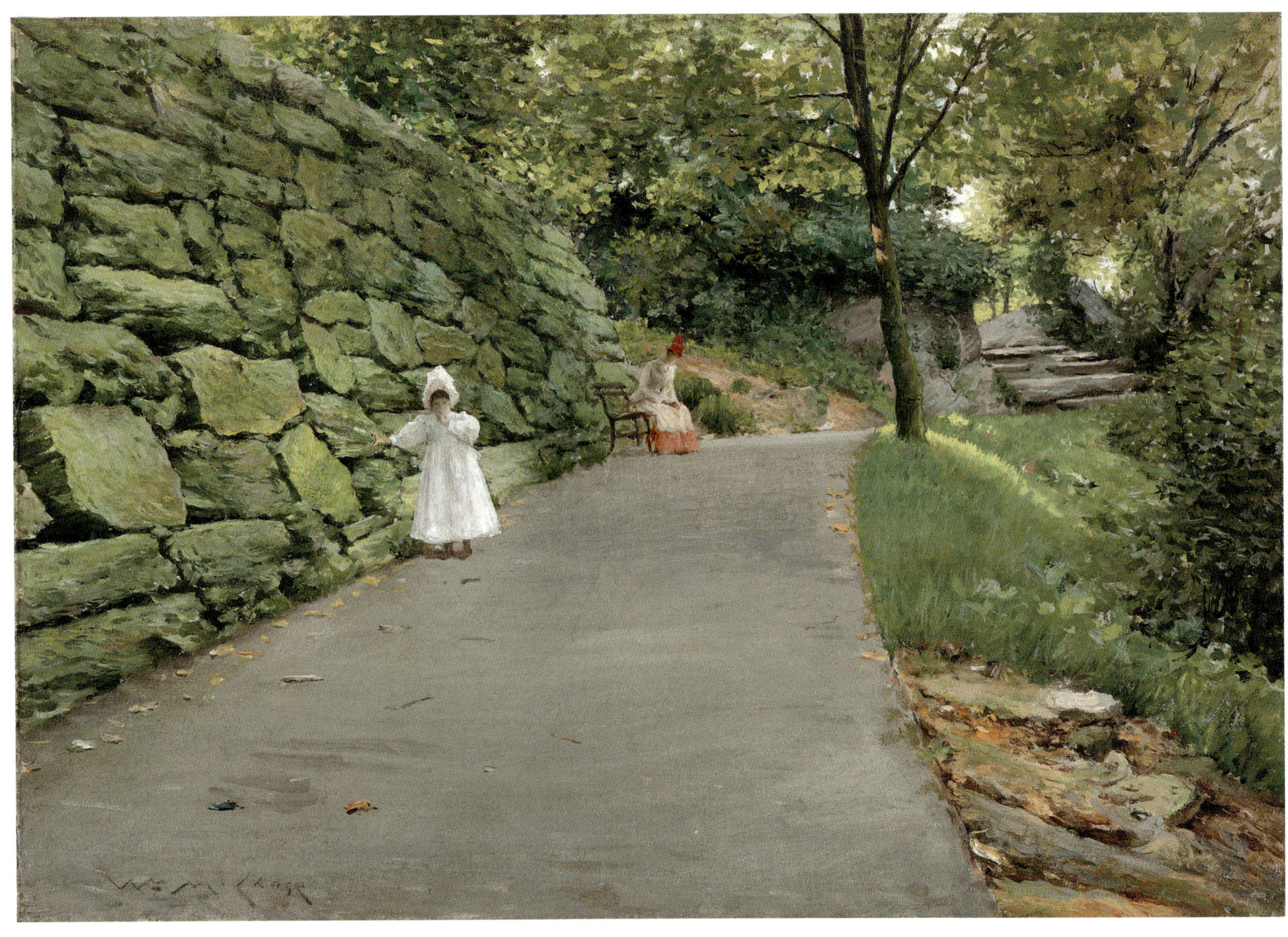

WILLIAM MERRITT CHASE, *In the Park – A By-Path*, c. 1889
Oil on canvas, 35.5 x 49 cm
Carmen Thyssen-Bornemisza Collection,
on loan at the Museo Thyssen-Bornemisza, Madrid, CTB. 1979.15

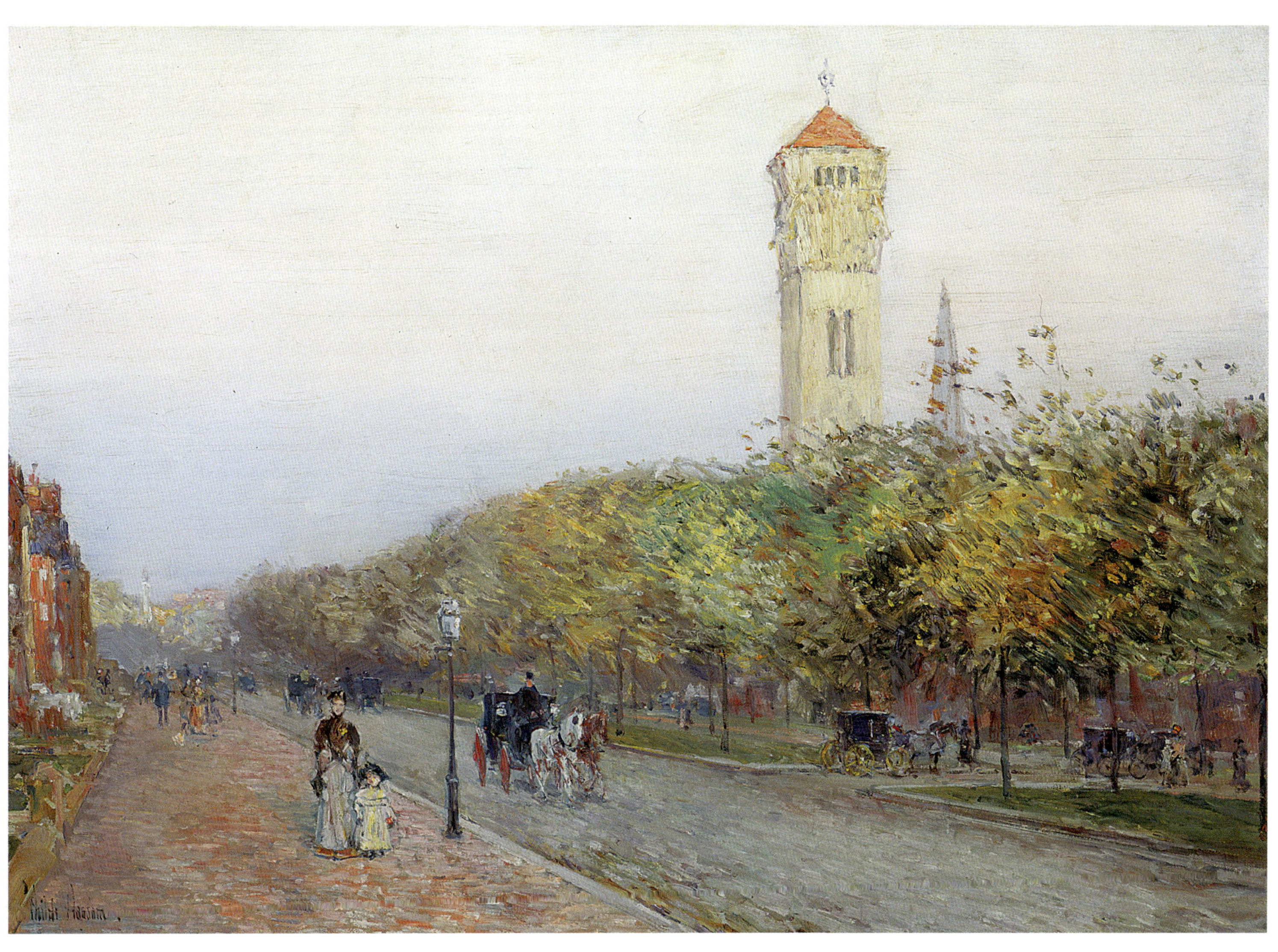

CHILDE HASSAM, *Commonwealth Avenue, Boston*, c. 1892
Oil on canvas, 56.5 x 76.8 cm
Terra Foundation for American Art, Chicago,
Daniel J. Terra Collection, 1992.39

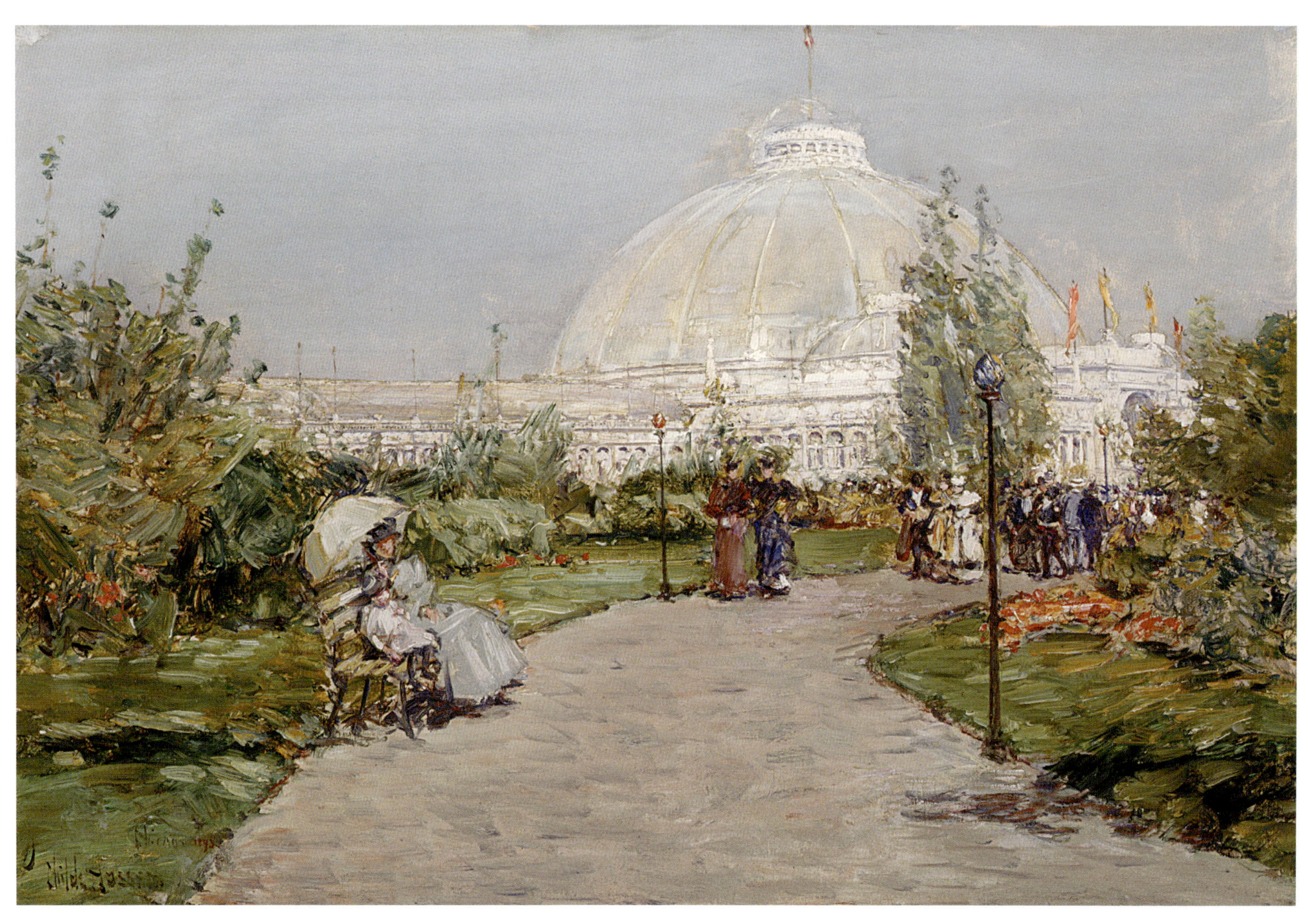

CHILDE HASSAM, *Horticulture Building, World's Columbian Exposition, Chicago*, 1893
Oil on canvas, 47 x 66.7 cm
Terra Foundation for American Art, Chicago,
Daniel J. Terra Collection, 1999.67

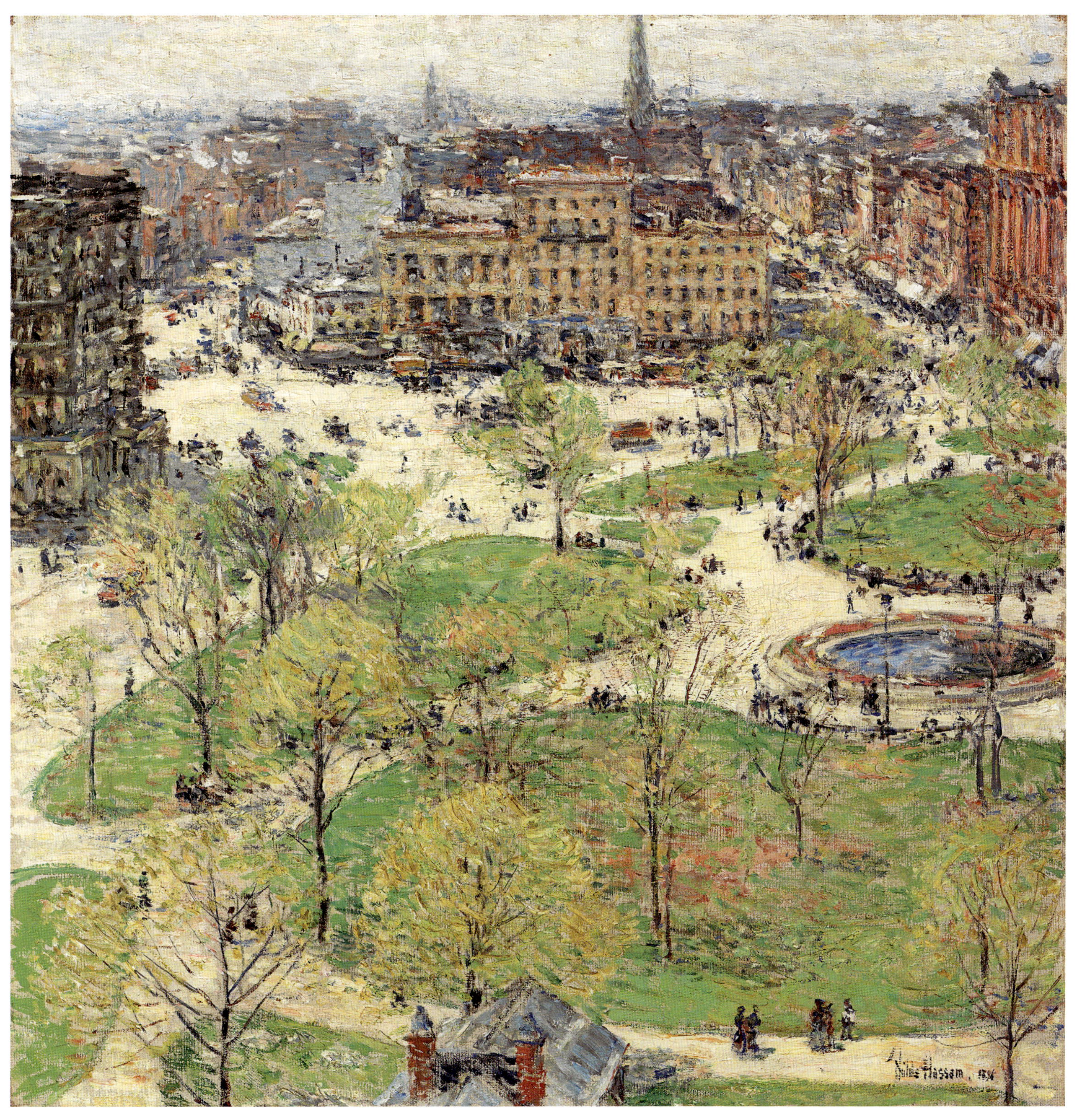

CHILDE HASSAM, *Union Square in Spring*, 1896
Oil on canvas, 54.6 x 53.3 cm
Smith College Museum of Art, Northampton, Massachusetts,
Purchased with the Winthrop Hillyer Fund, 1905:3.1

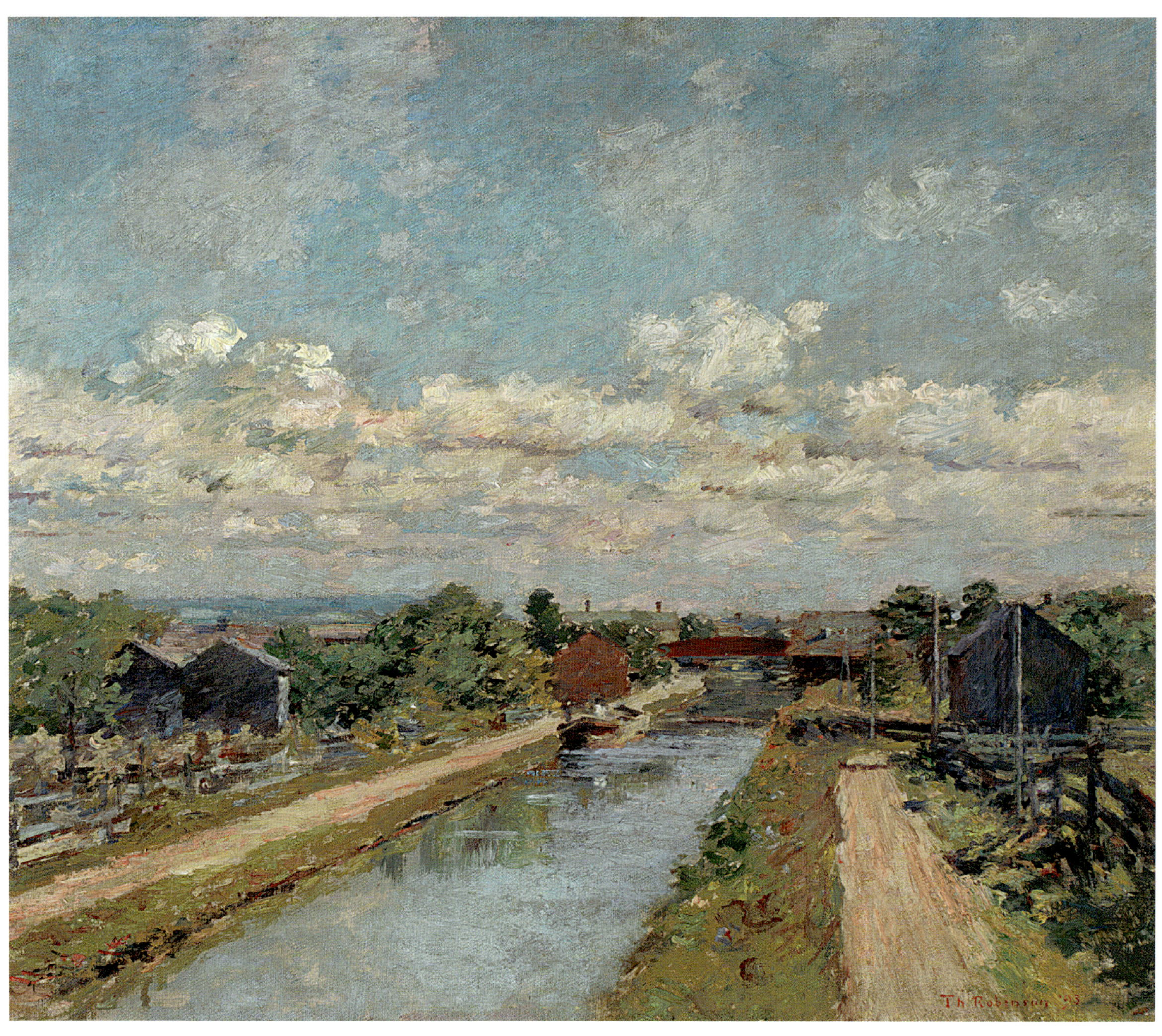

THEODORE ROBINSON, *Port Ben, Delaware and Hudson Canal*, 1893
Oil on canvas, 71.8 x 81.9 cm
Pennsylvania Academy of the Fine Arts, Philadelphia,
Gift of the Society of American Artists
as a memorial to Theodore Robinson, 1900.5

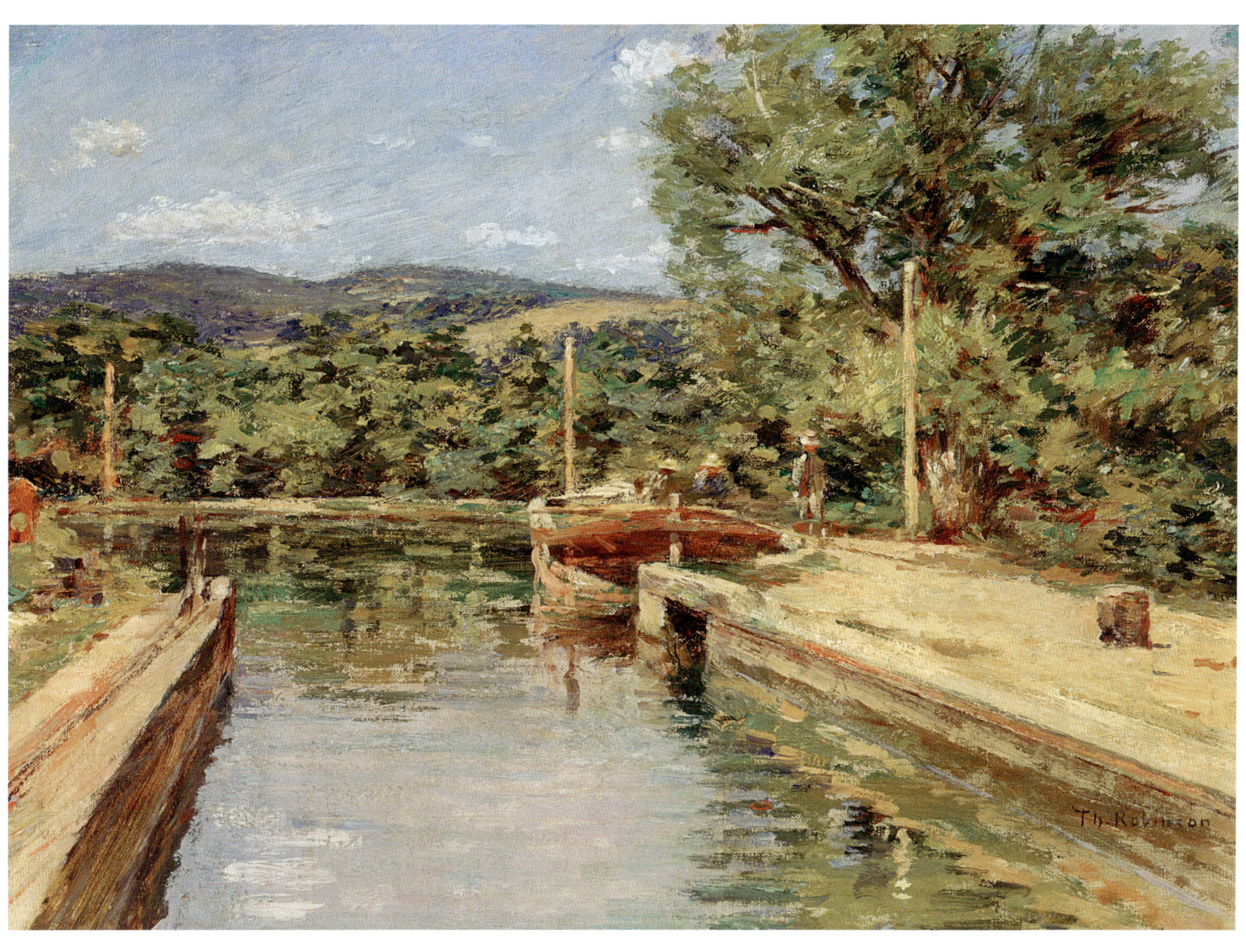

THEODORE ROBINSON, *Canal Scene*, 1893
Oil on canvas, 42.9 x 56.8 cm
Terra Foundation for American Art, Chicago,
Daniel J. Terra Collection, 1992.131

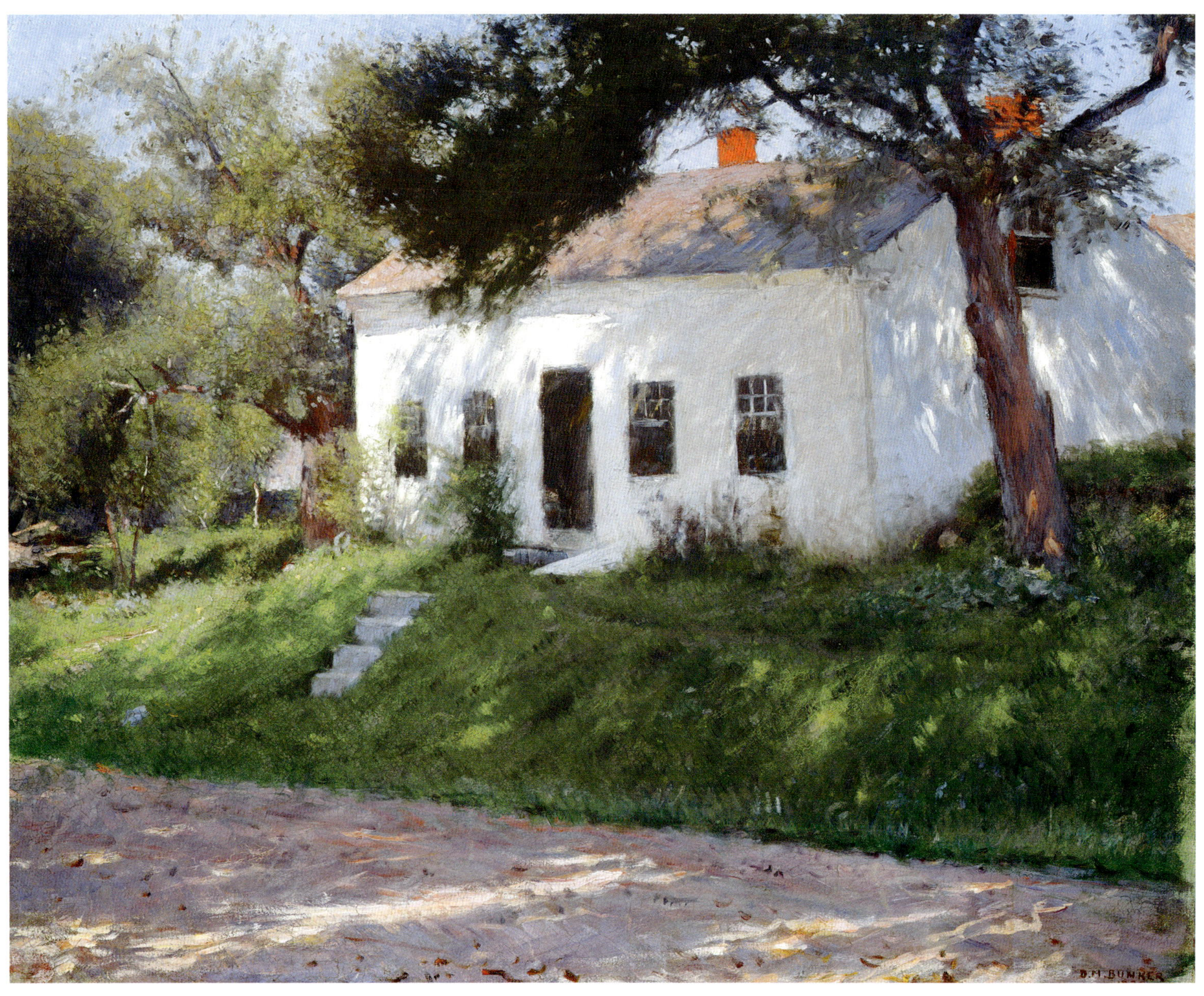

DENNIS MILLER BUNKER, *Roadside Cottage*, 1889
Oil on canvas, 63.7 x 76.2 cm
National Gallery of Art, Washington D.C.,
Gift of Raymond J. and Margaret Horowitz, 2007.94.1

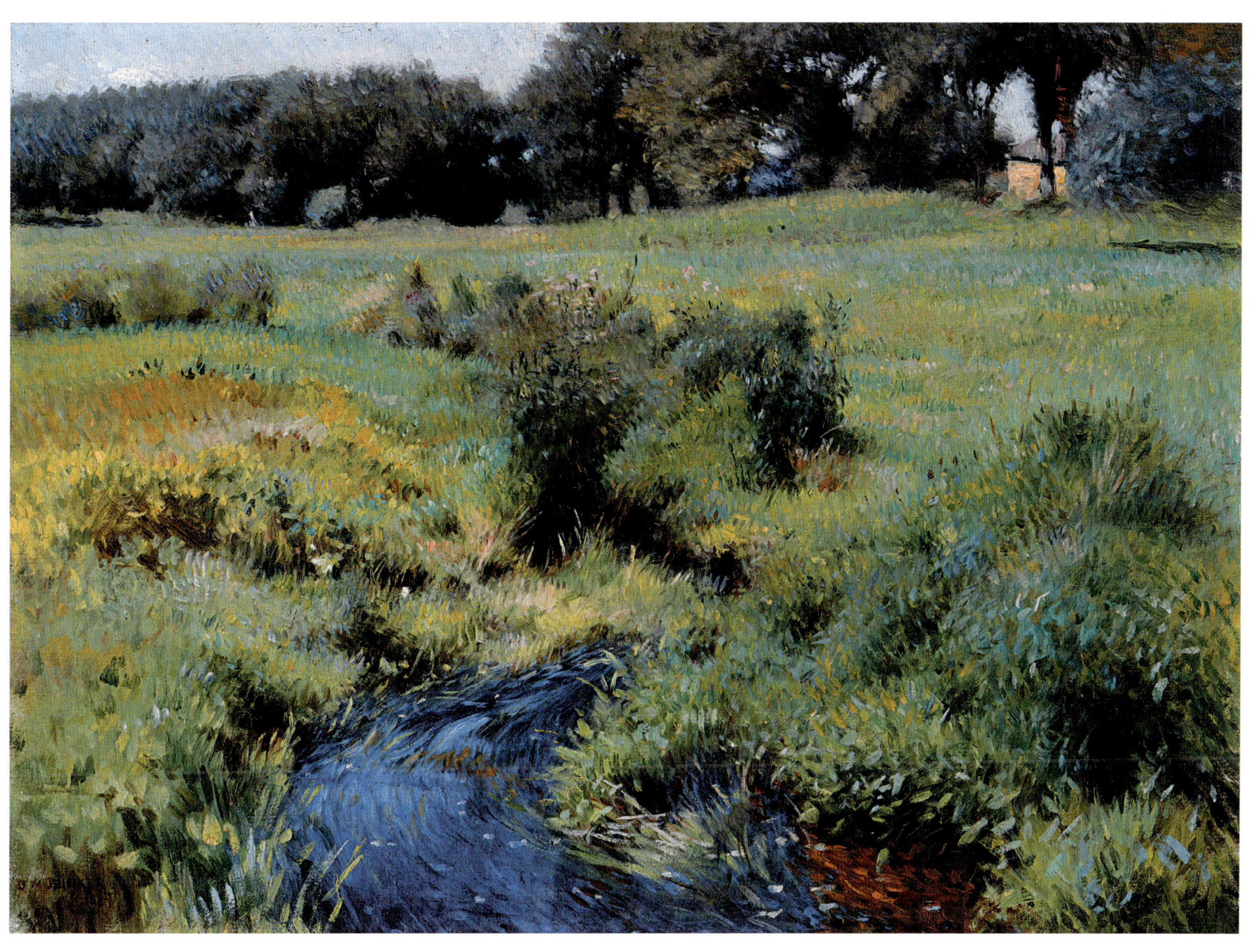

DENNIS MILLER BUNKER, *The Pool, Medfield*, 1889
Oil on canvas, 47 x 61.6 cm
Museum of Fine Arts, Boston,
Emily L. Ainsley Fund, 45.475

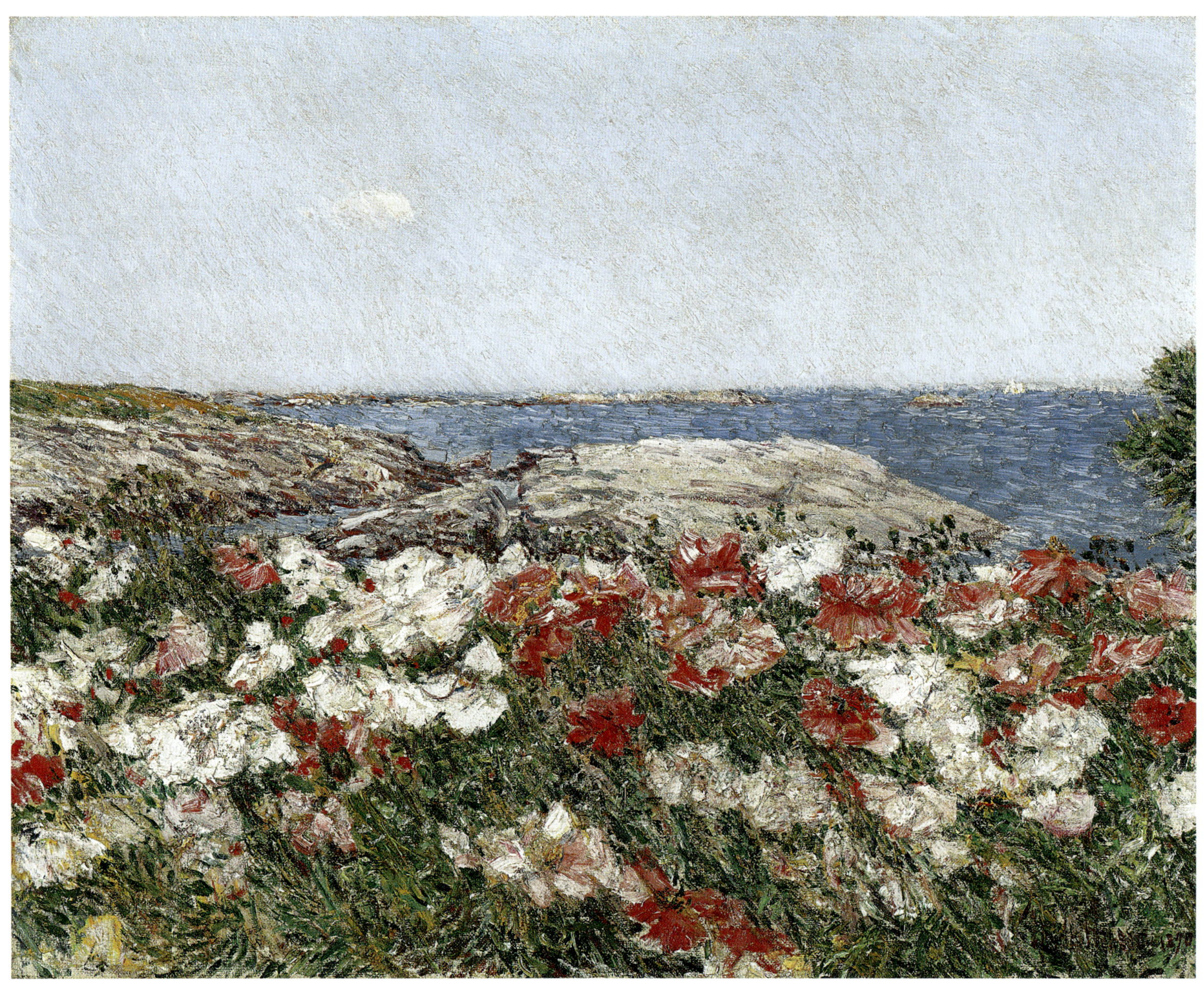

CHILDE HASSAM, *Poppies on the Isles of Shoals*, 1890
Oil on canvas, 45.7 x 55.7 cm
Brooklyn, Brooklyn Museum, Gift of Mary Pratt Barringer and Richardson Pratt, Jr.
In memory of Richardson and Laura Pratt, 85.286

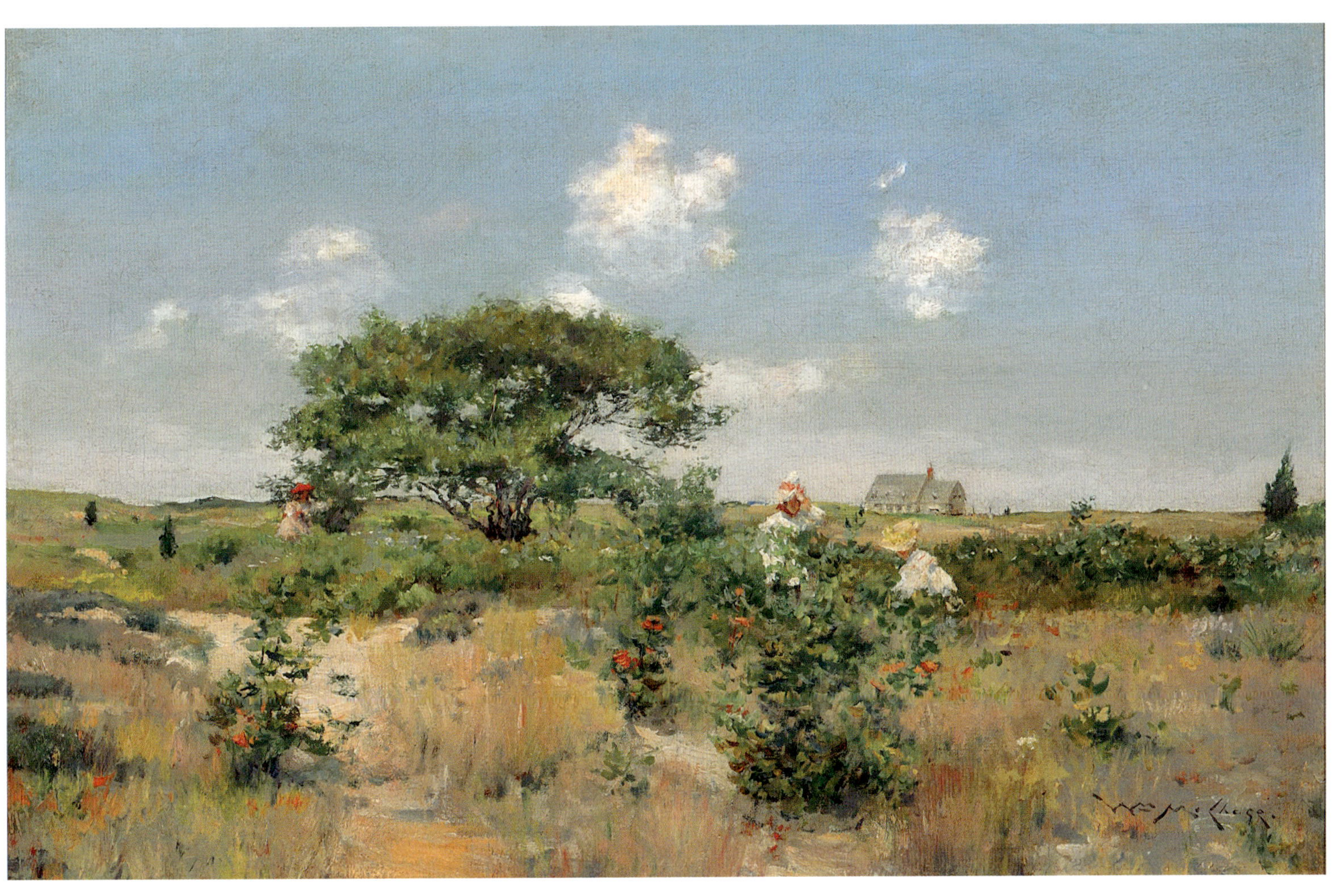

WILLIAM MERRITT CHASE, *Untitled (Shinnecock Landscape)*, c. 1894
Oil on canvas, 40.6 x 61 cm
Parrish Art Museum, Water Mill, New York,
Museum Purchase, 1978.5

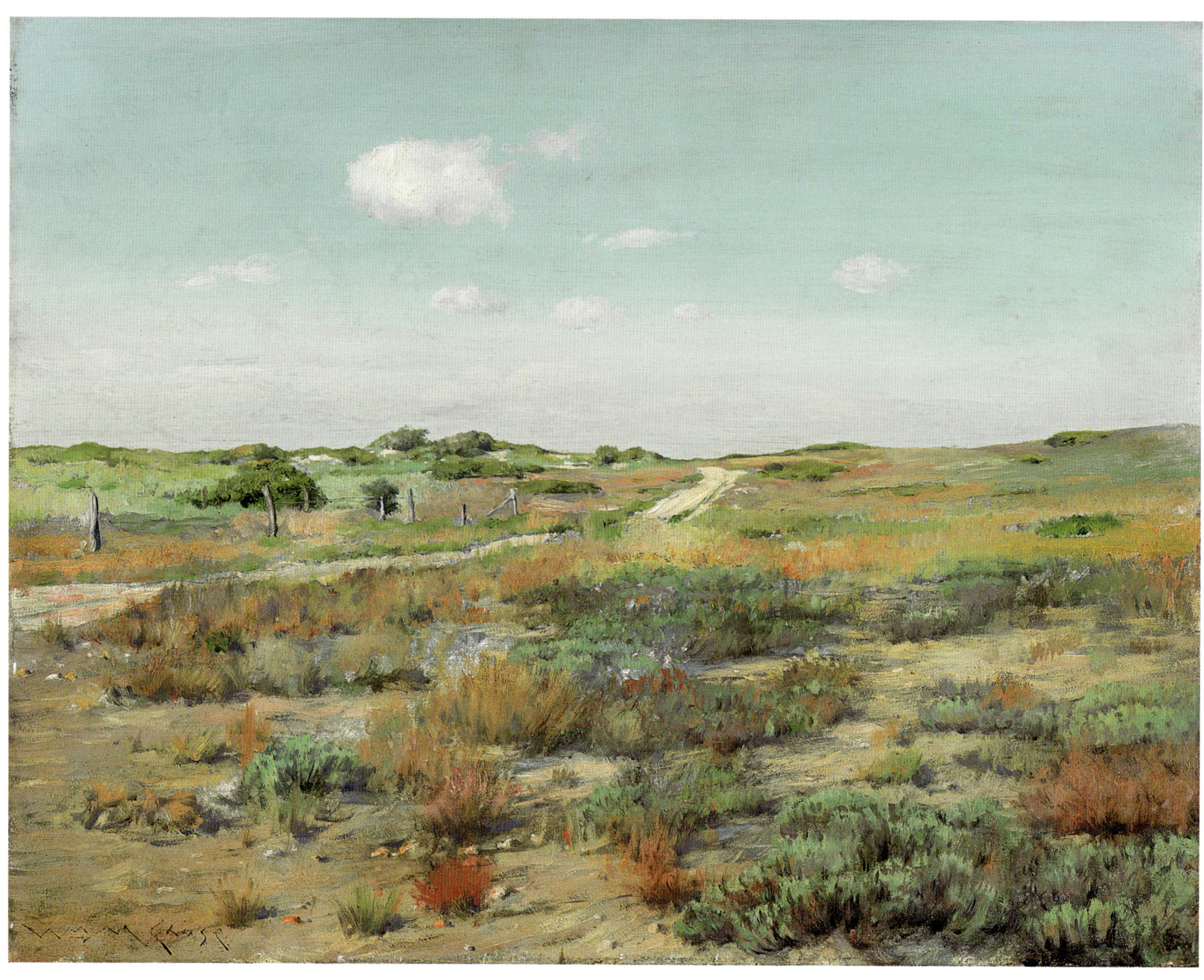

WILLIAM MERRITT CHASE, *Shinnecock Hills*, 1893–7
Oil on panel, 44.4 x 54.6 cm
Museo Thyssen-Bornemisza, Madrid, 502 (1979.30)
[Shown in Giverny and Madrid only]

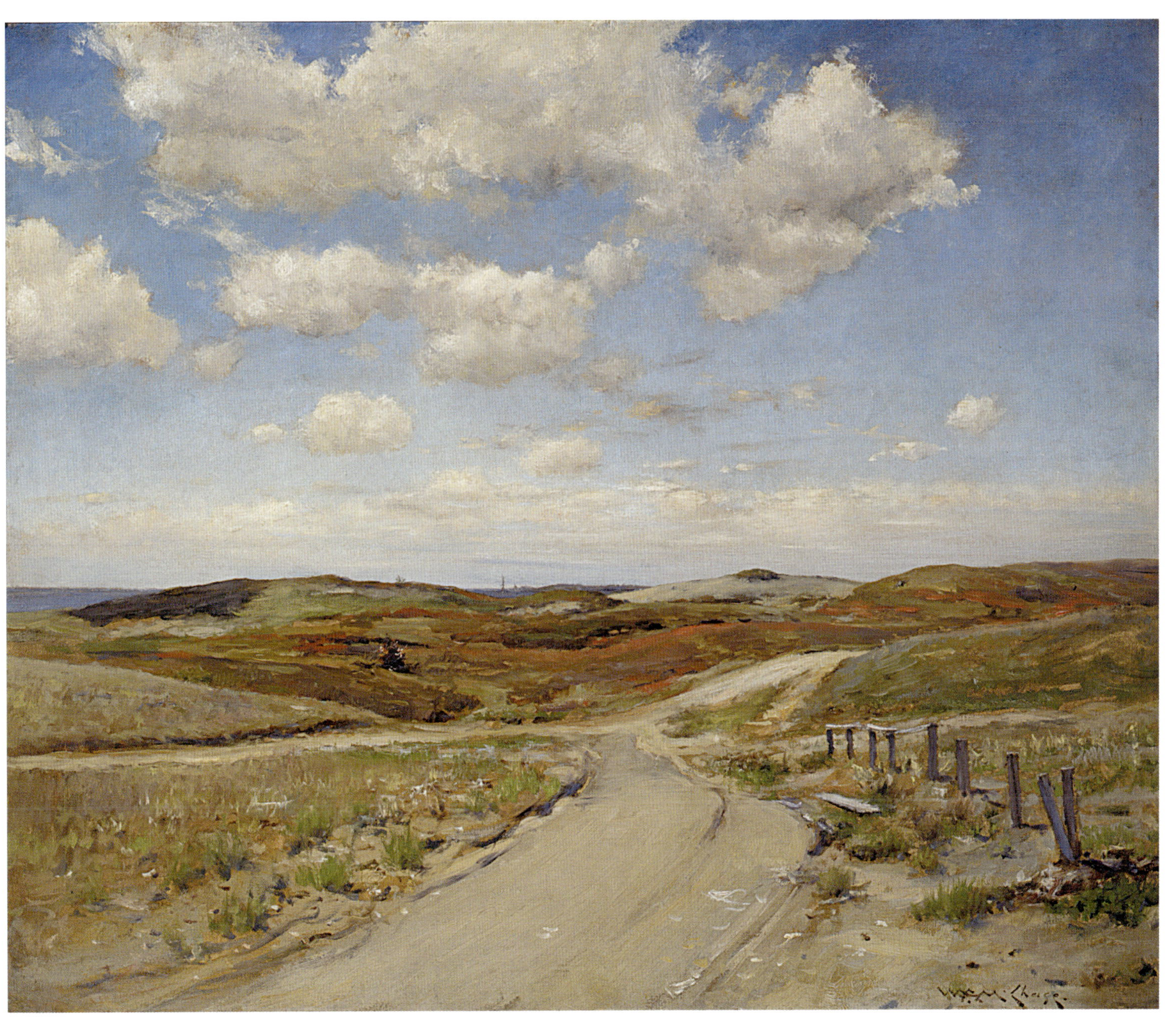

WILLIAM MERRITT CHASE, *Shinnecock Hills*, c. 1895
Oil on canvas, 88.6 x 100.4 cm
Smithsonian American Art Museum, Washington D.C.,
Gift of William T. Evans, 1909.7.11

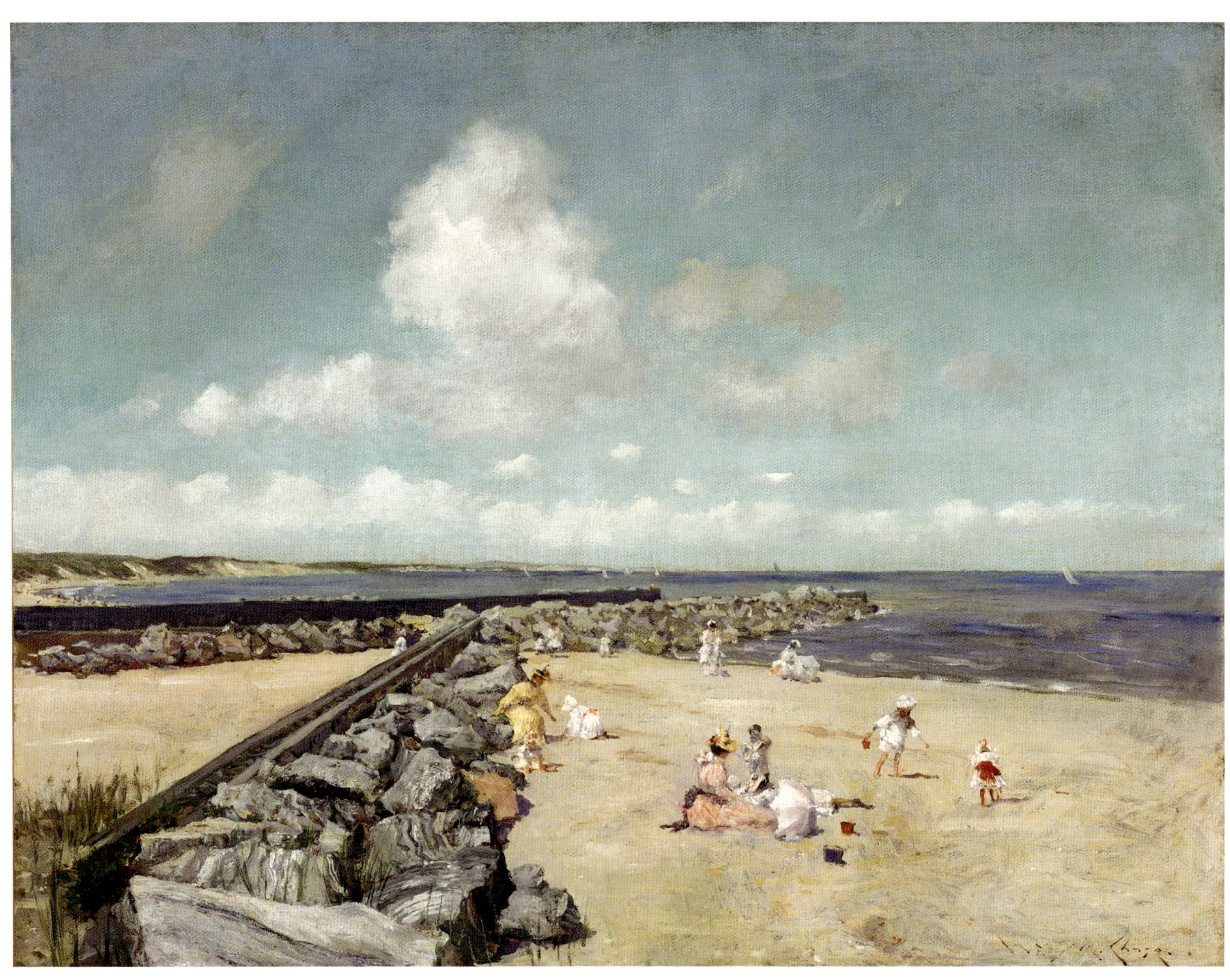

WILLIAM MERRITT CHASE, *Morning at Breakwater, Shinnecock*, *c.* 1897
Oil on canvas, 101.6 x 127 cm
Terra Foundation for American Art, Chicago,
Daniel J. Terra Collection, 1999.30

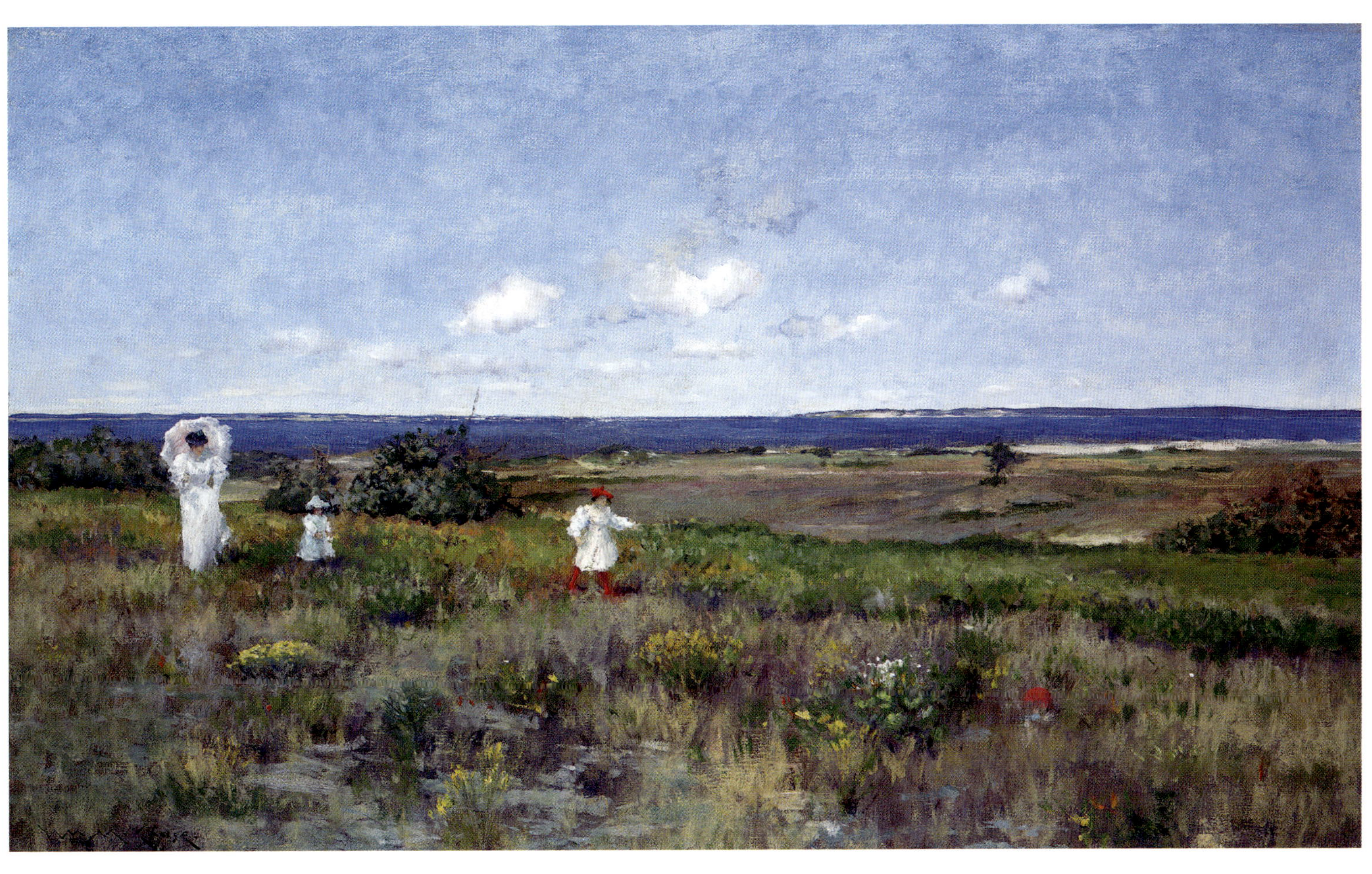

WILLIAM MERRITT CHASE, *Near the Beach, Shinnecock*, 1895
Oil on canvas, 76.2 x 122.2 cm
Toledo Museum of Art, Toledo, Ohio,
Gift of Arthur J. Secor, 1924.58

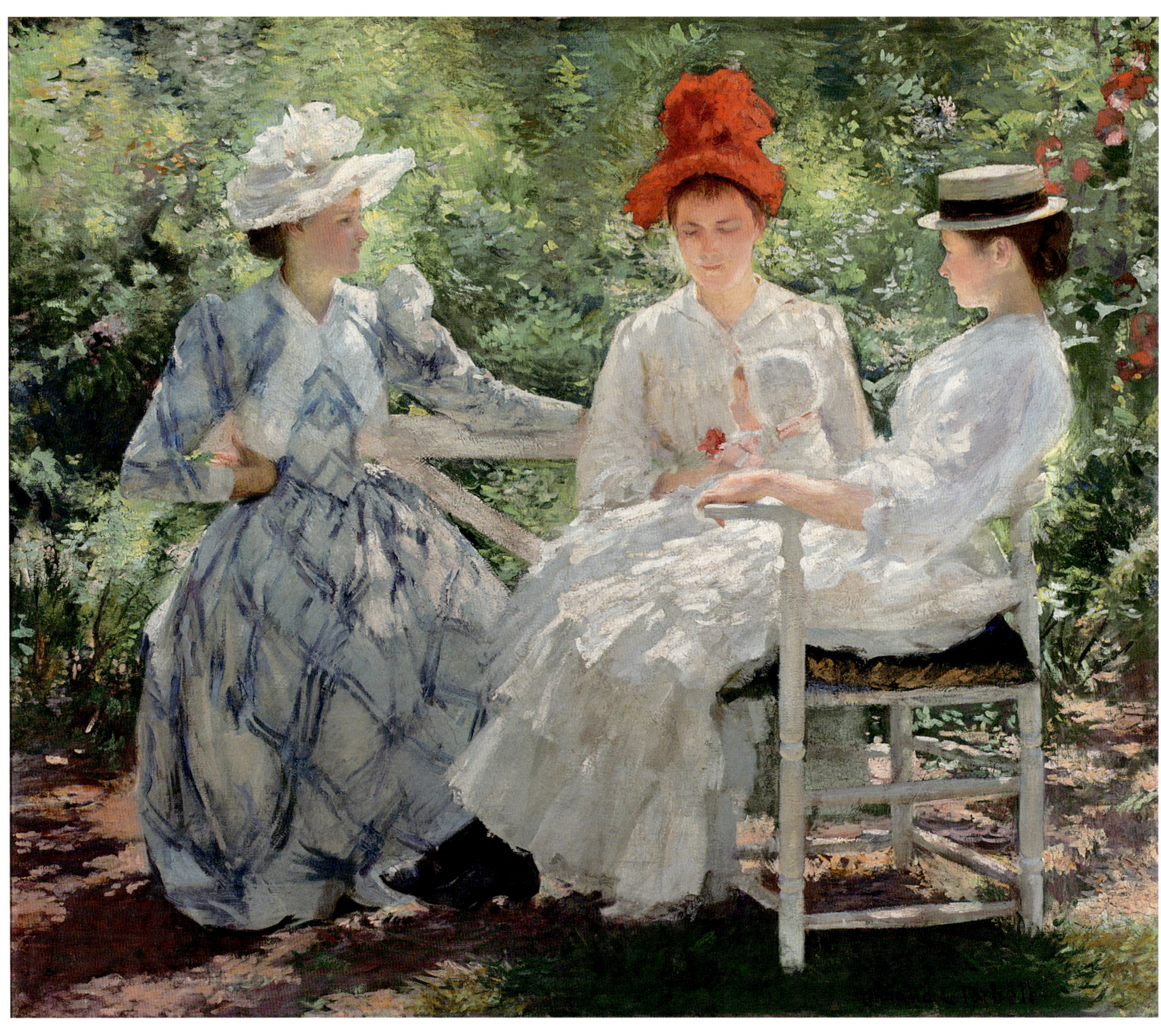

EDMUND C. TARBELL, *Three Sisters – A Study in June Sunlight*, 1890
Oil on canvas, 89.2 x 101.9 cm
Milwaukee Art Museum, Milwaukee, Wisconsin,
Gift of Mrs. Montgomery Sears, M1925.1

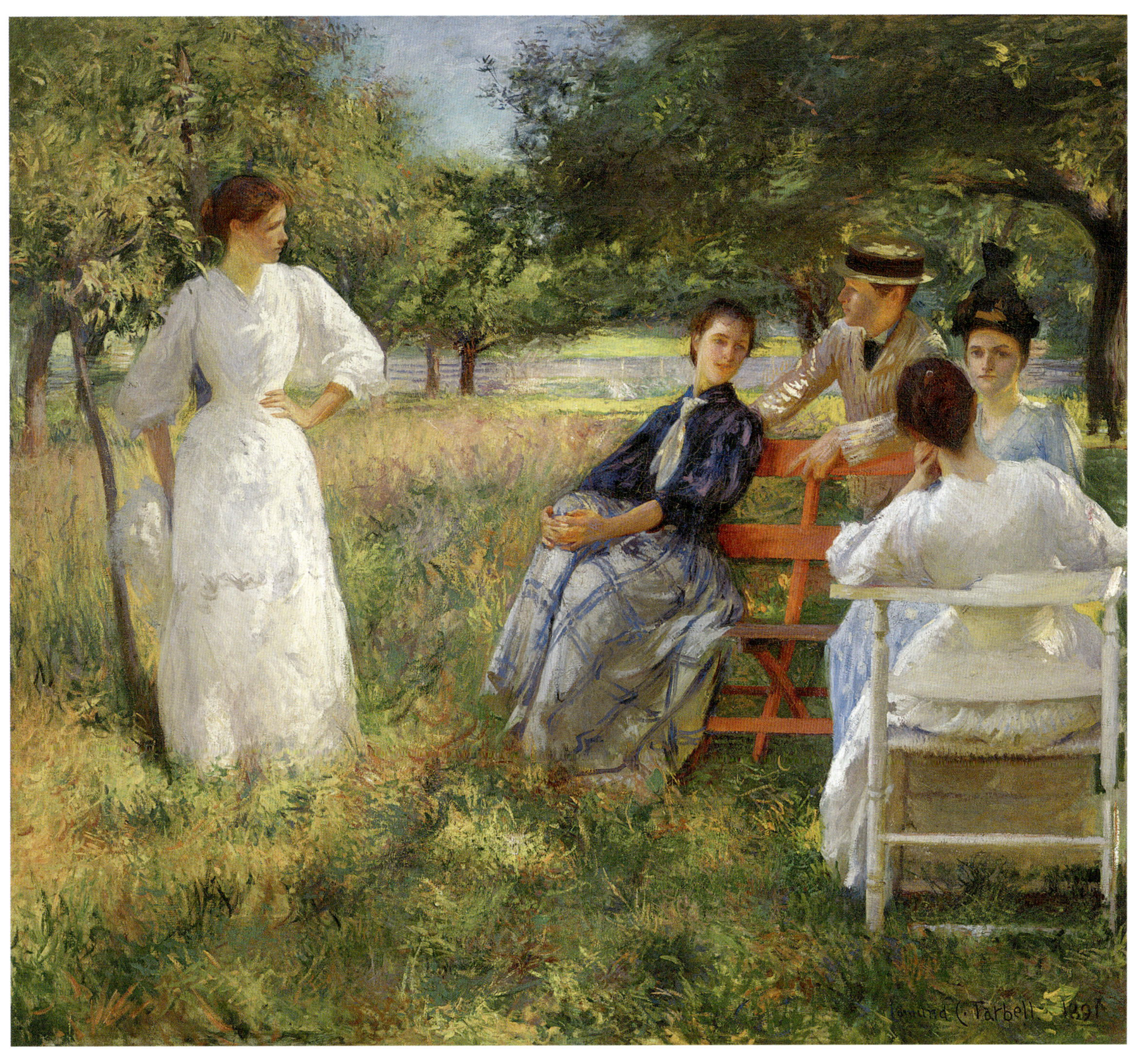

EDMUND C. TARBELL, *In the Orchard*, 1891
Oil on canvas, 154.3 x 166.4 cm
Terra Foundation for American Art, Chicago,
Daniel J. Terra Collection, 1999.141

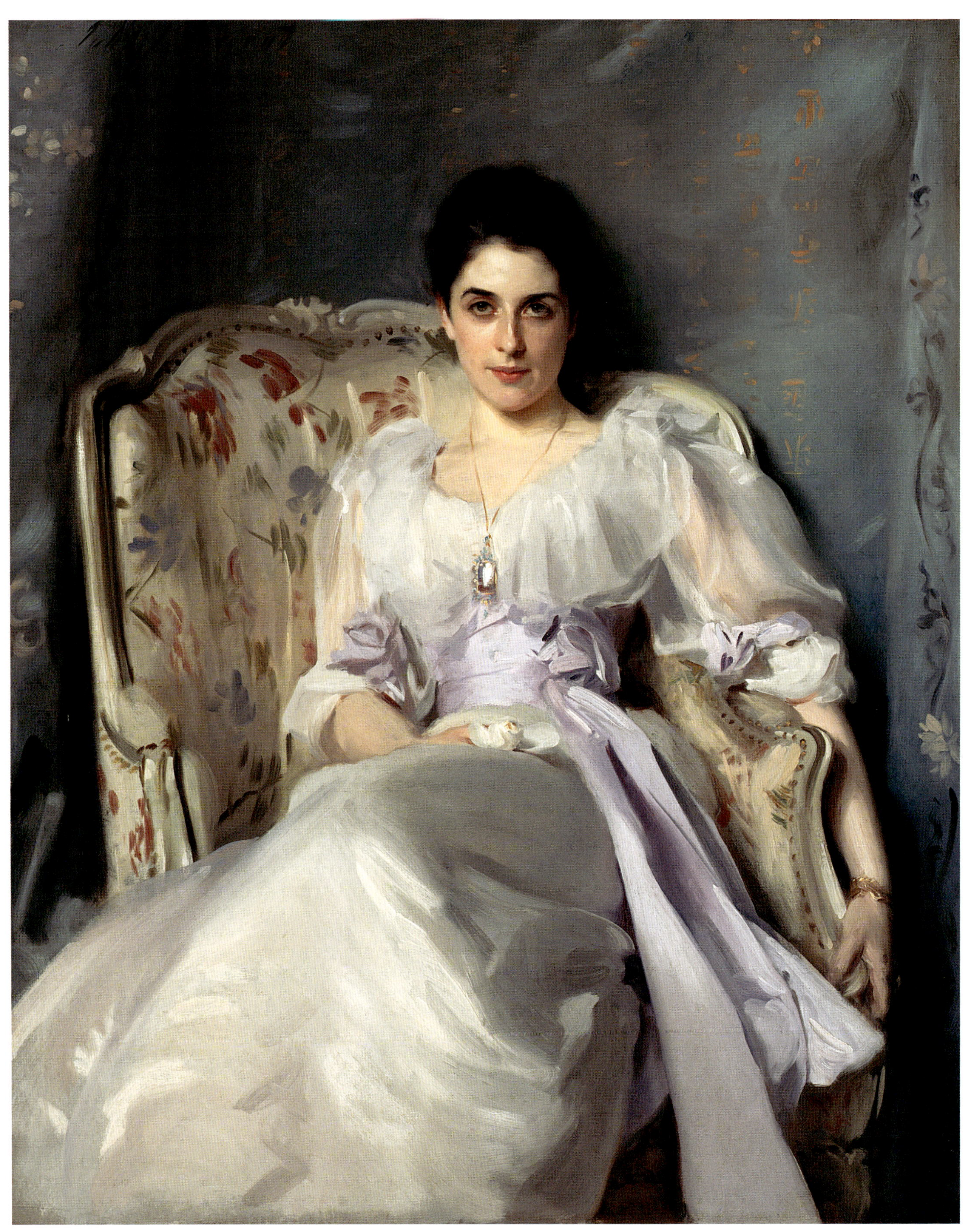

JOHN SINGER SARGENT, *Lady Agnew of Lochnaw (1865–1932)*, 1892
Oil on canvas, 127 x 101 cm
Scottish National Gallery, Edinburgh,
Purchased with the aid of the Cowan Smith Bequest Fund, 1925, NG 1656
[Shown in Giverny and Edinburgh only]

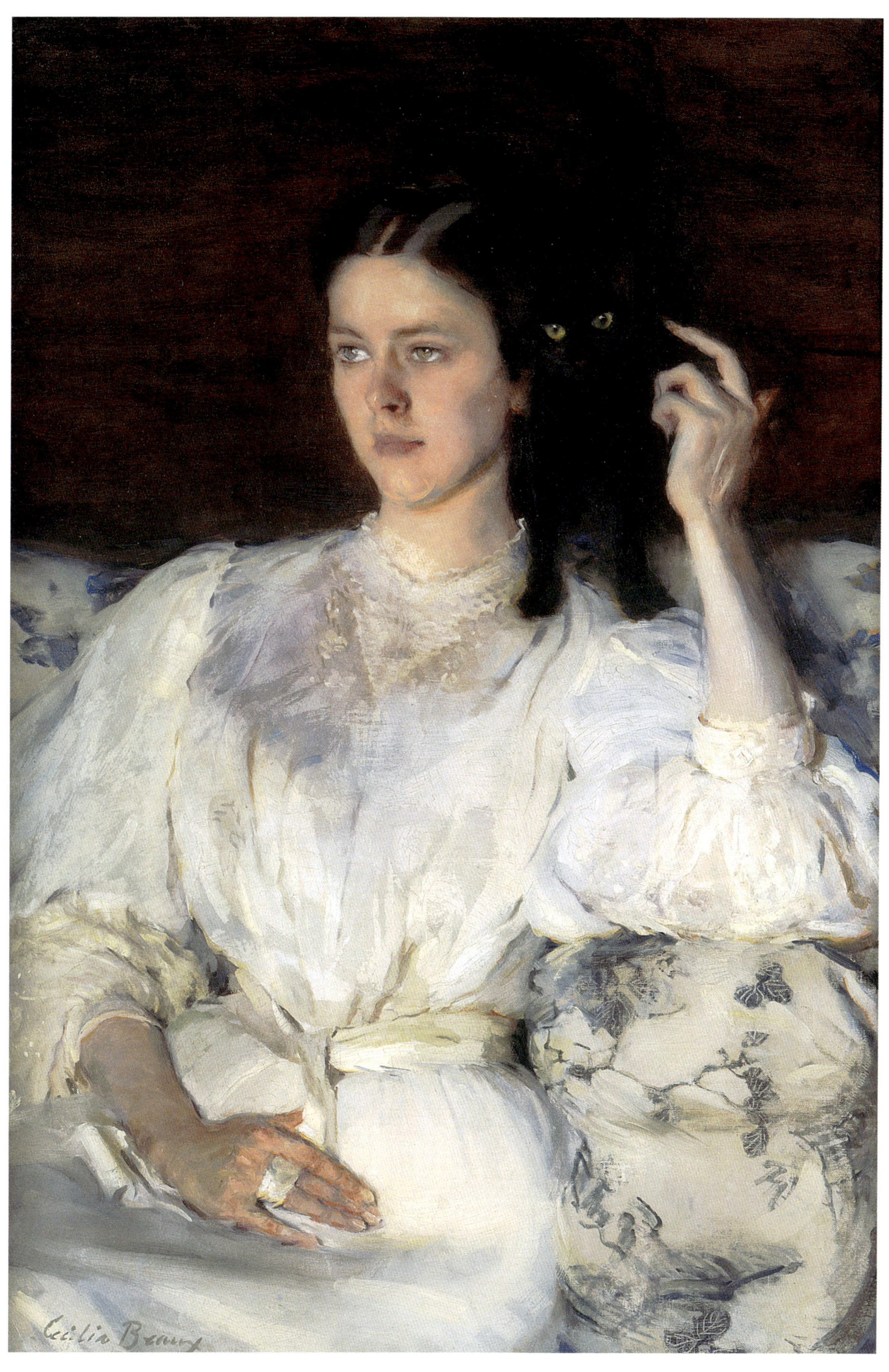

CECILIA BEAUX, *Sita and Sarita*, 1893–4
Oil on canvas, 94.5 x 63.5 cm
Musée d'Orsay, Paris,
Gift of the artist, 1921, RF 1980-60

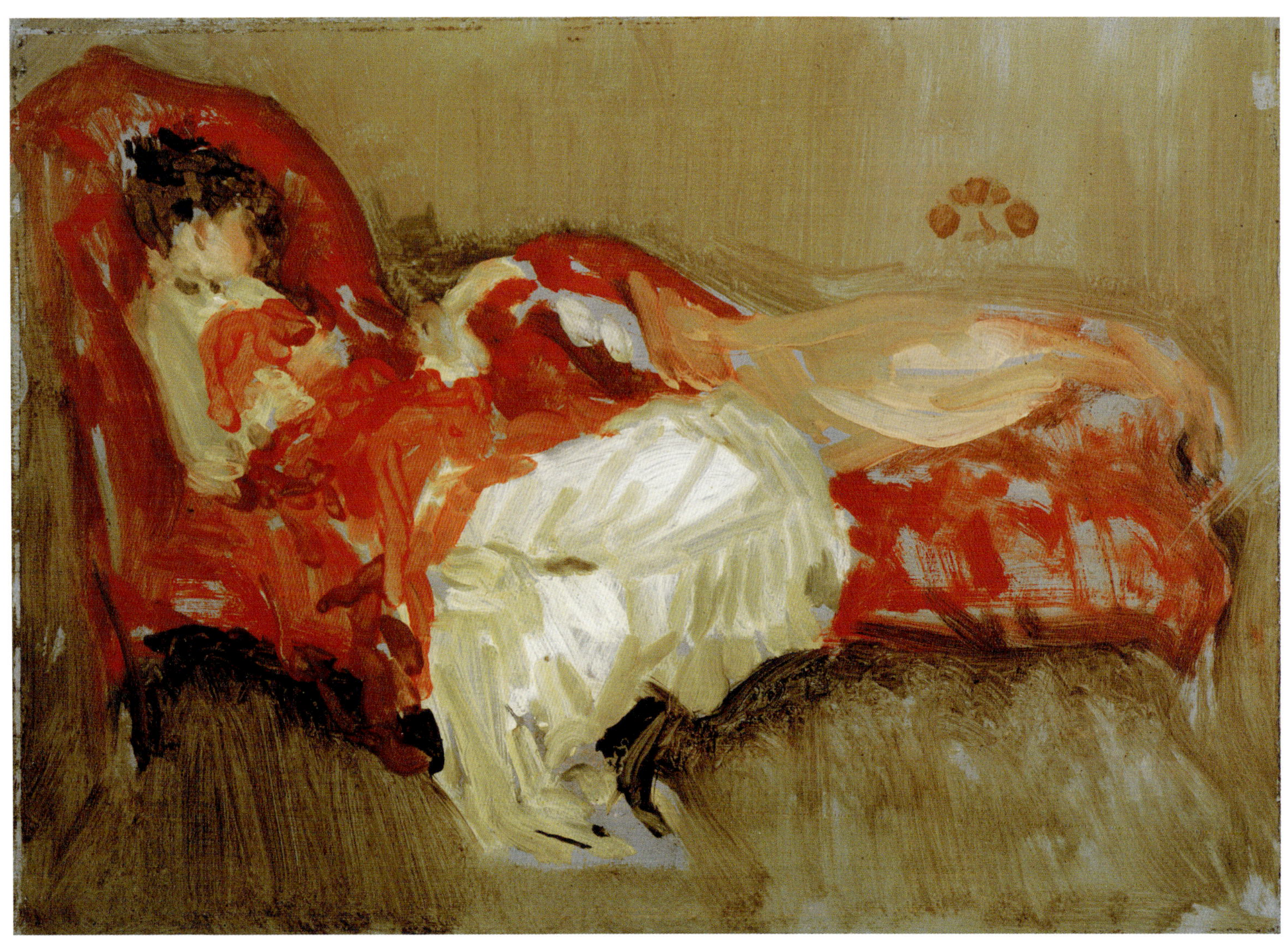

JAMES ABBOTT MCNEILL WHISTLER, *Note in Red: The Siesta*, by 1884
Oil on panel, 21.1 × 30.5 cm
Terra Foundation for American Art, Chicago,
Daniel J. Terra Collection, 1999.149

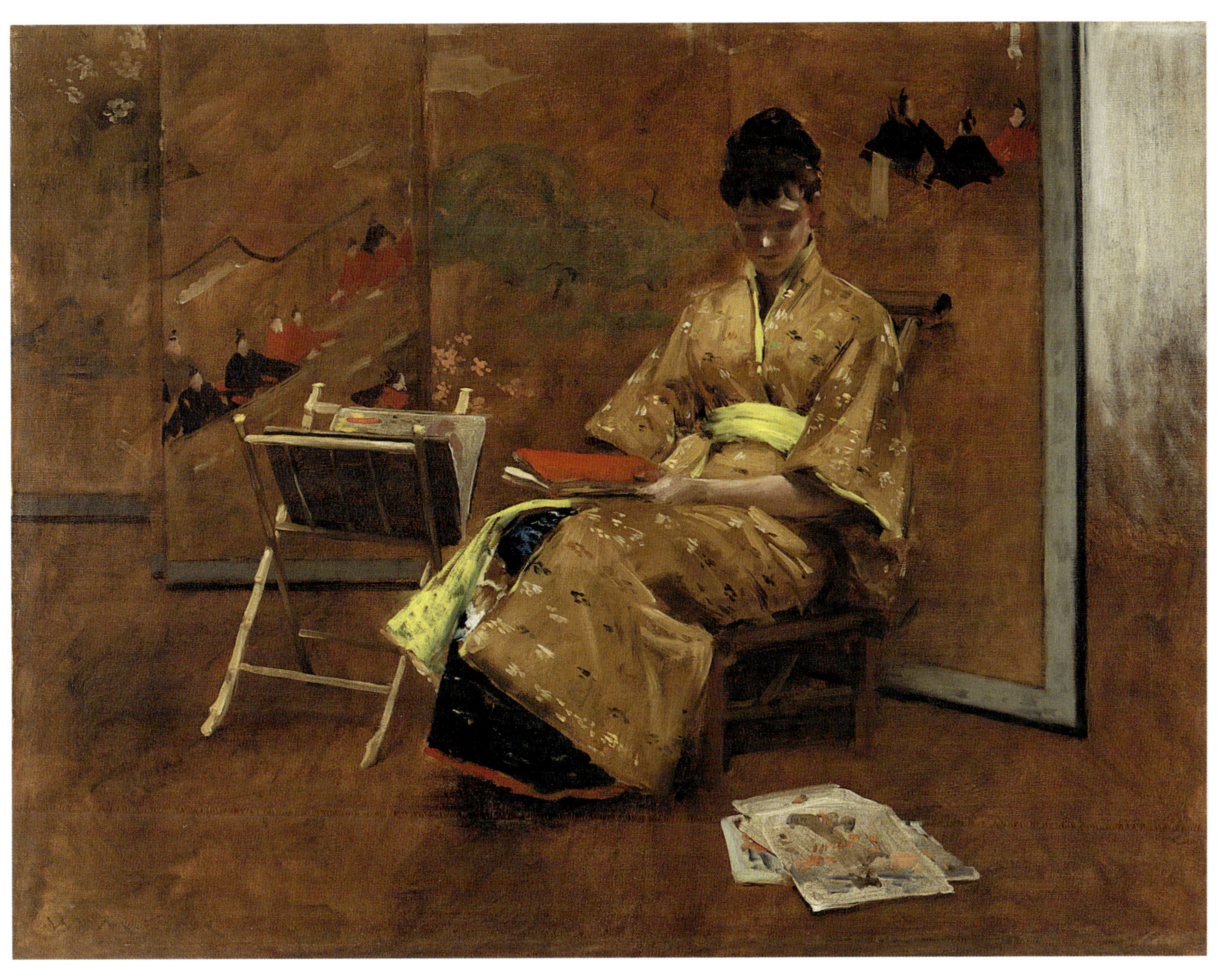

WILLIAM MERRITT CHASE, *The Kimono*, c. 1895
Oil on canvas, 89.5 x 115 cm
Museo Thyssen-Bornemisza, Madrid, 501 (1979.24)
[Shown in Edinburgh and Madrid only]

FRANK W. BENSON, *Eleanor*, 1901
Oil on canvas, 76.2 x 64.1 cm
Museum of Art, Rhode Island School of Design, Providence,
Gift of the Estate of Mrs. Gustav Radeke, 31.079

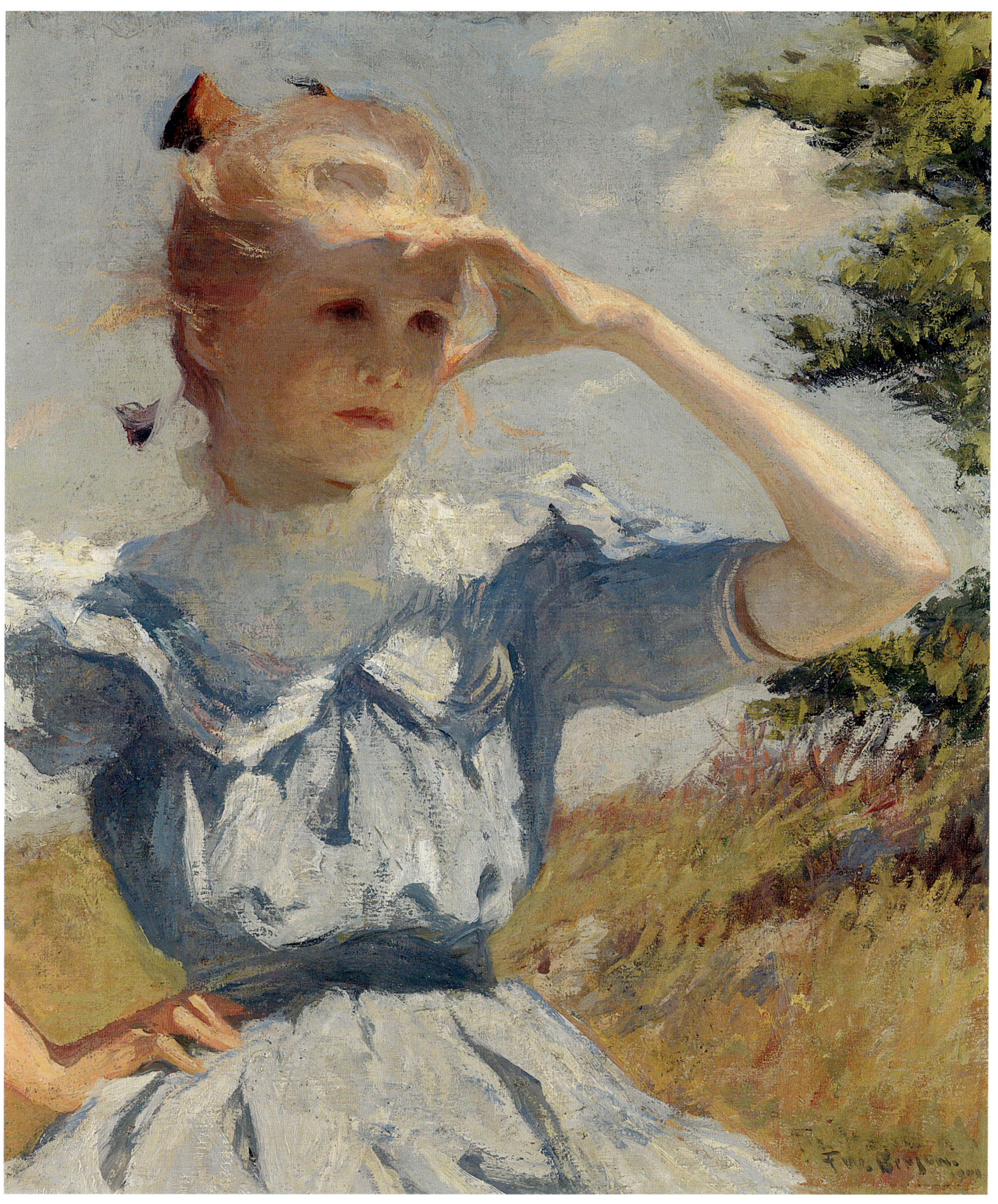

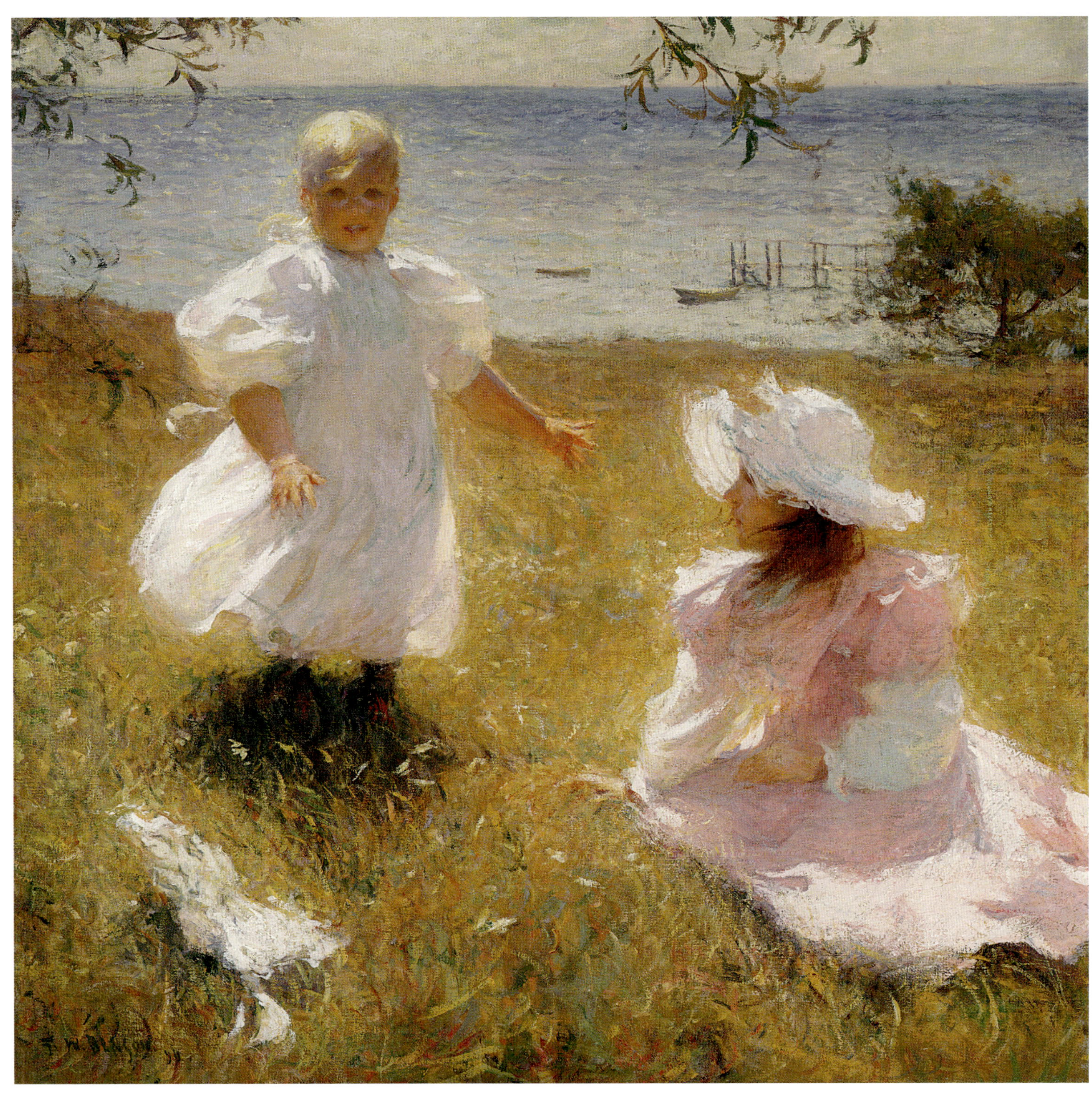

FRANK W. BENSON, *The Sisters*, 1899
Oil on canvas, 101.6 x 101.6 cm
Terra Foundation for American Art, Chicago,
Daniel J. Terra Collection, 1999.11

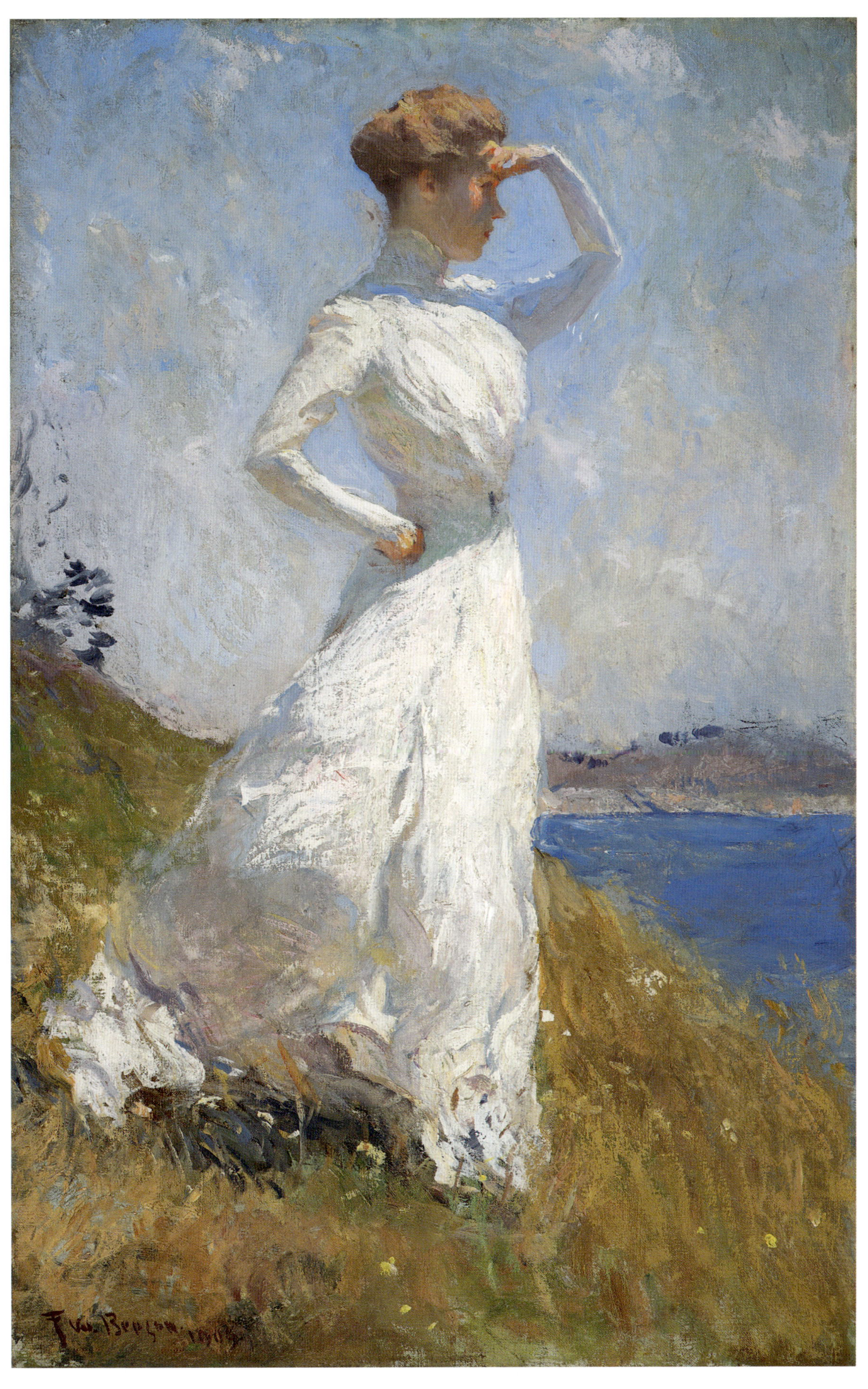

FRANK W. BENSON, *Sunlight*, 1909
Oil on canvas, 81.3 x 50.8 cm
Indianapolis Museum of Art, Indianapolis, Indiana,
John Herron Fund, 11.1

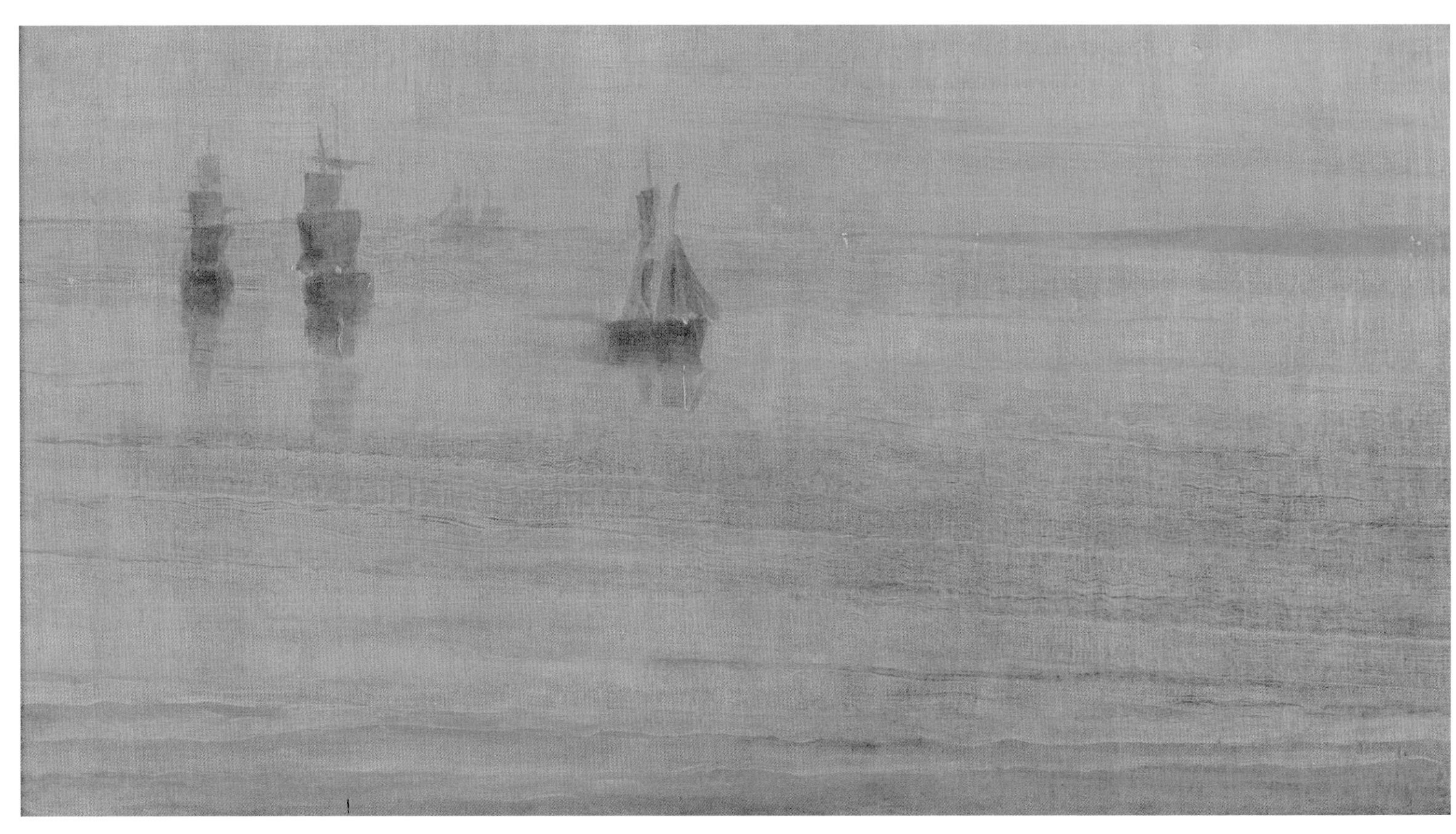

JAMES ABBOTT MCNEILL WHISTLER, *Nocturne: The Solent*, 1866
Oil on canvas, 48.9 x 90.2 cm
Gilcrease Museum, Tulsa, Oklahoma, GM 0176.1185
[Shown in Giverny only]

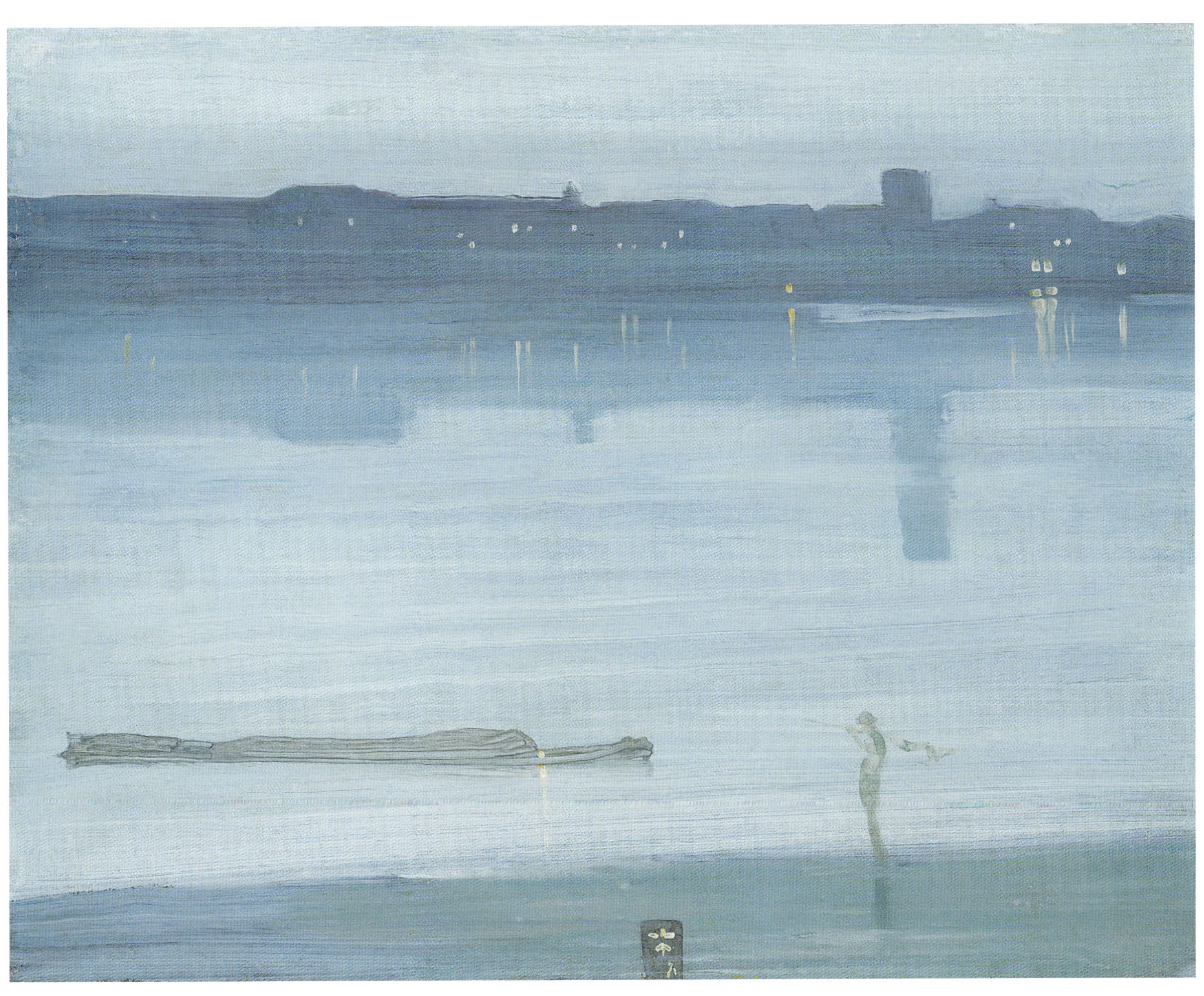

JAMES ABBOTT MCNEILL WHISTLER, *Nocturne: Blue and Silver – Chelsea*, 1871
Oil on wood, 50.2 x 60.8 cm
Tate, London,
Bequeathed by Miss Rachel and Miss Jean Alexander, 1972, T01571

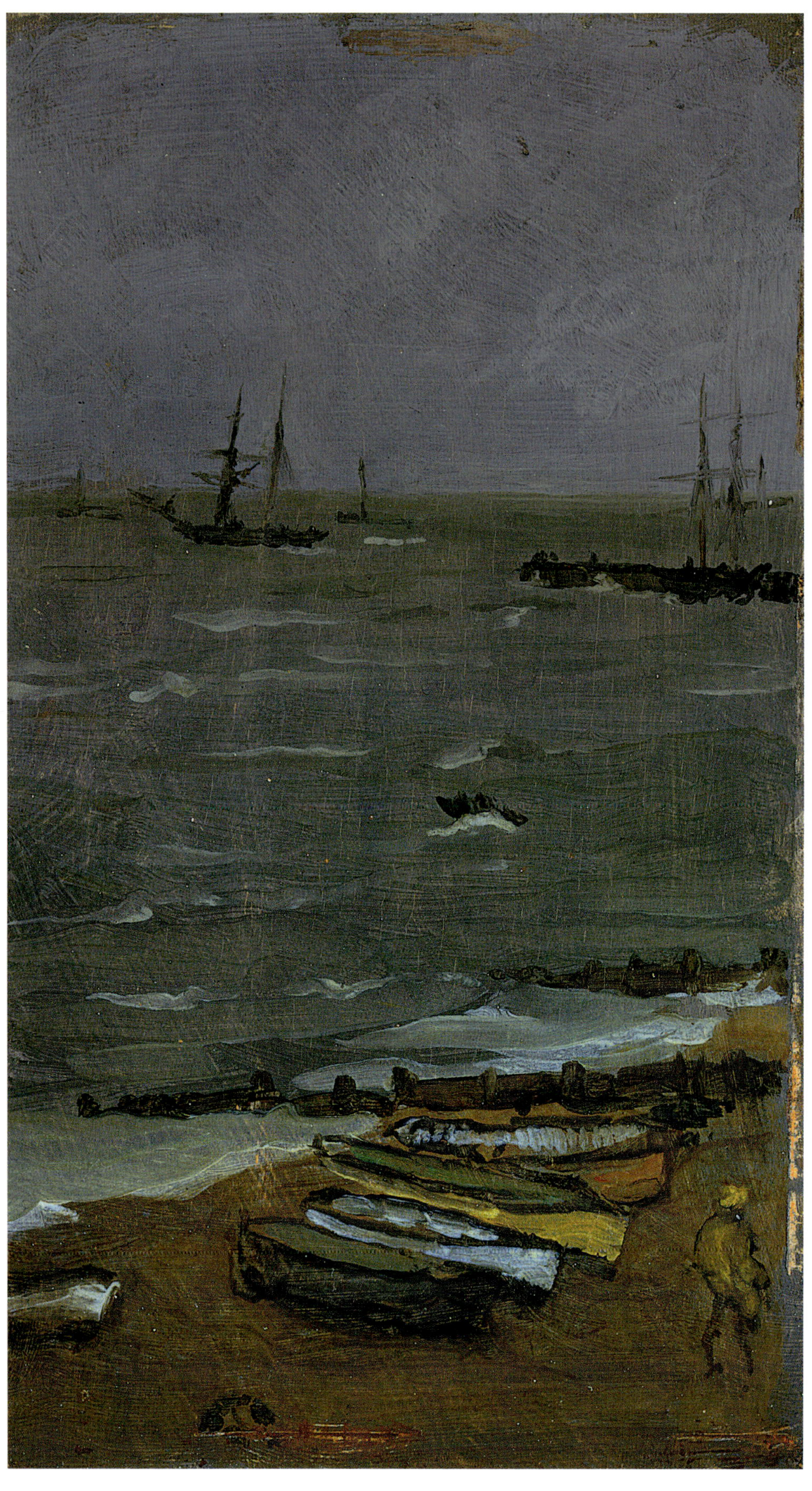

JAMES ABBOTT MCNEILL WHISTLER, *A Freshening Breeze*, *c.* 1883
Oil on panel, 23.5 x 13.7 cm
Terra Foundation for American Art, Chicago,
Daniel J. Terra Collection, 1992.152

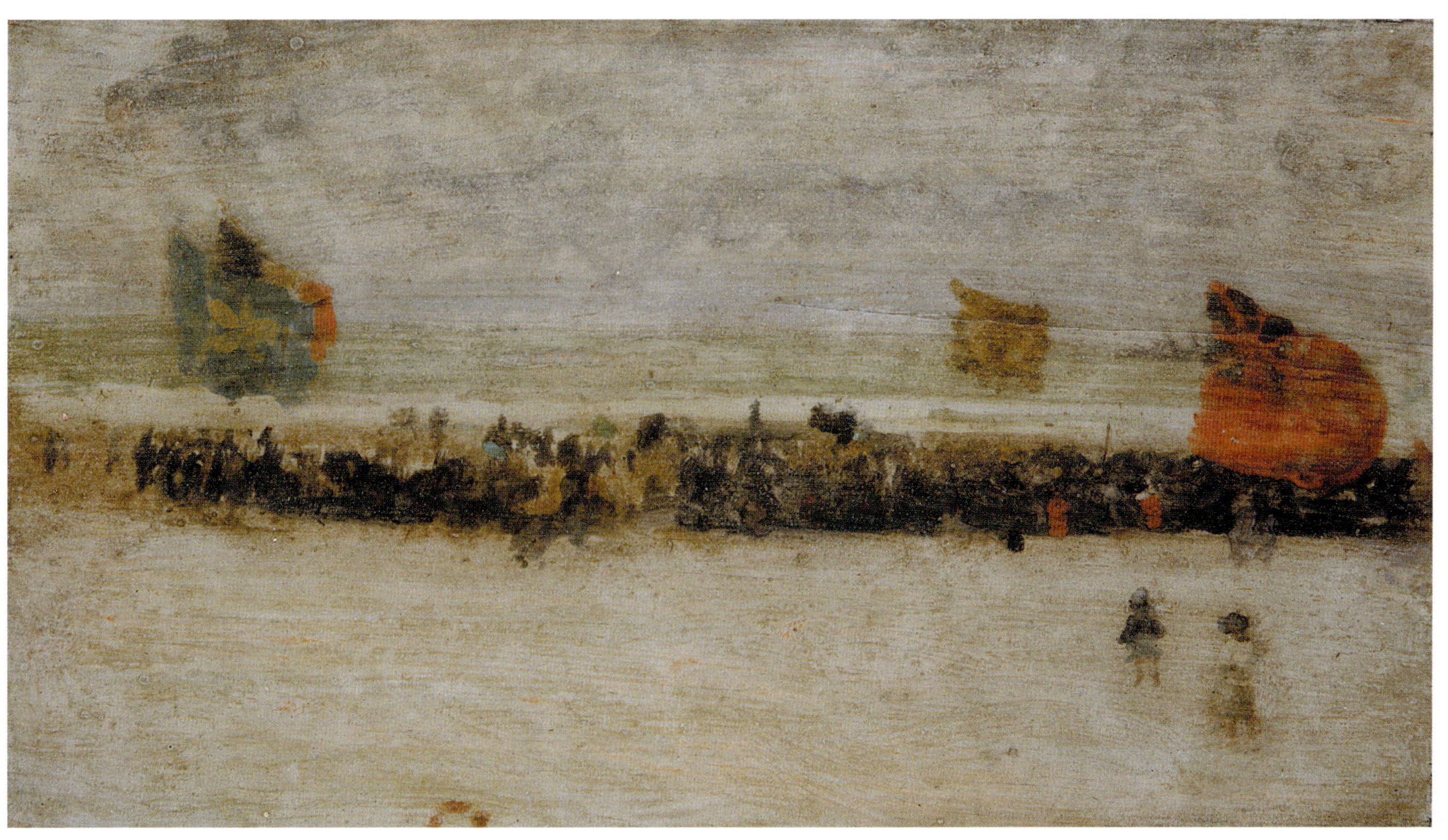

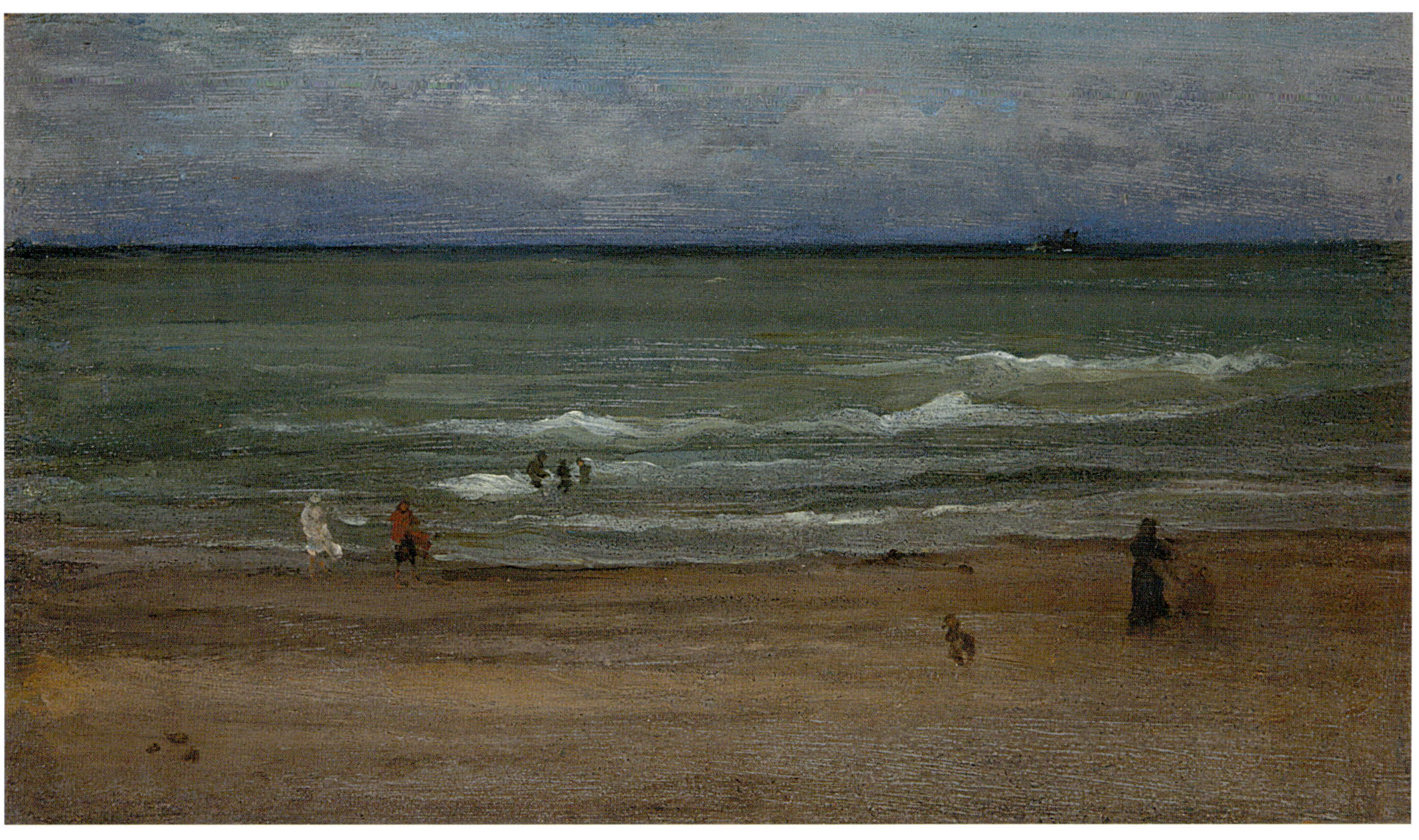

JAMES ABBOTT MCNEILL WHISTLER,
A Red Note: Fête on the Sands, Ostend, 1887
Oil on panel, 13.7 x 23.5 cm
Terra Foundation for American Art, Chicago,
Daniel J. Terra Collection, 1992.155

JAMES ABBOTT MCNEILL WHISTLER,
The Sea, Pourville, 1899
Oil on panel, 13.3 x 23.8 cm
Terra Foundation for American Art, Chicago,
Daniel J. Terra Collection, 1992.158

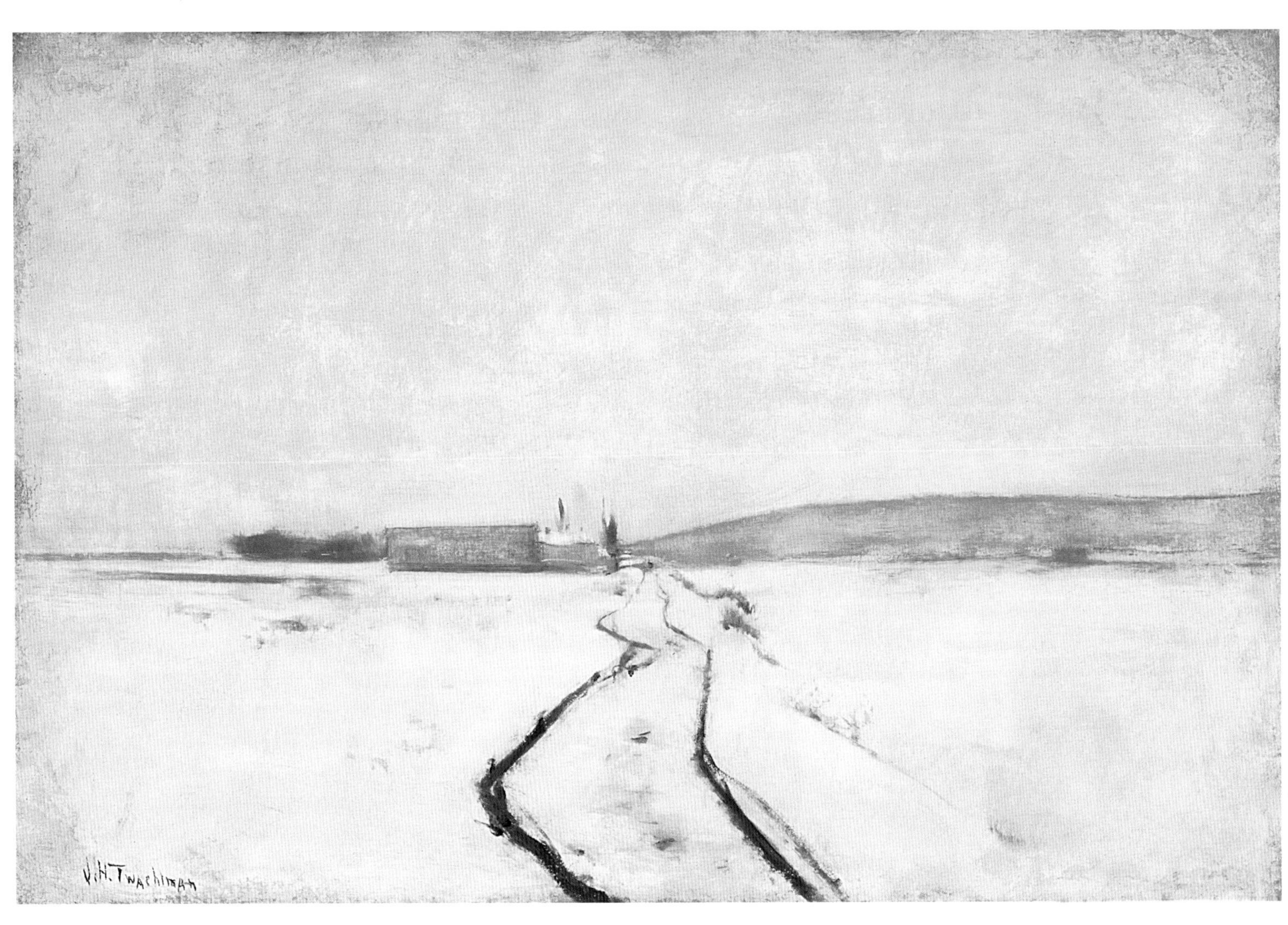

JOHN HENRY TWACHTMAN, *Along the River, Winter*, *c.* 1889
Oil on canvas, 38.4 x 55.2 cm
High Museum of Art, Atlanta, Georgia,
J.J. Haverty Collection, 49.28

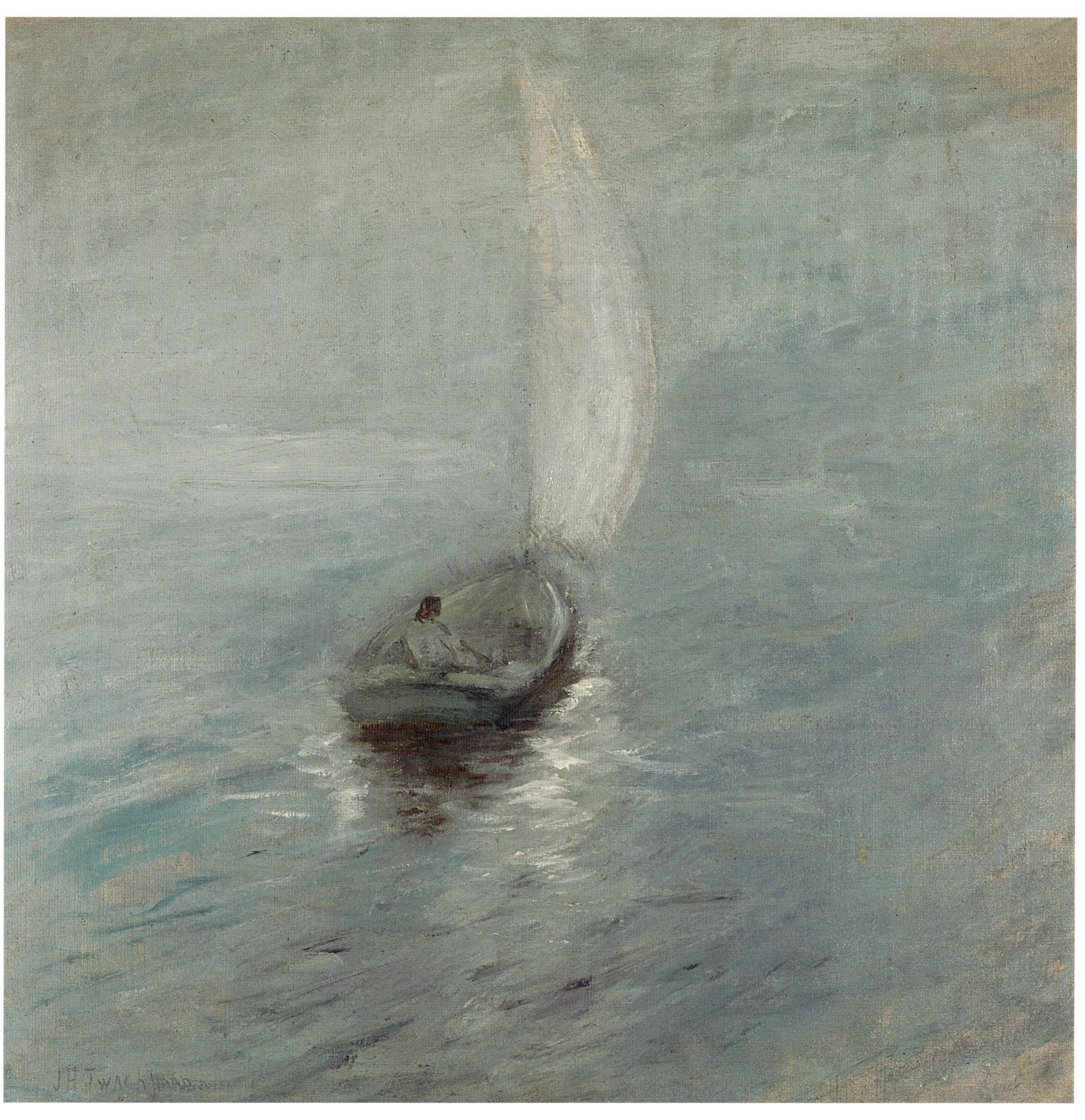

JOHN HENRY TWACHTMAN, *Sailing in the Mist*, 1890s
Oil on canvas, 76.7 x 76.5 cm
Pennsylvania Academy of the Fine Arts, Philadelphia,
Joseph E. Temple Fund, 1906.1

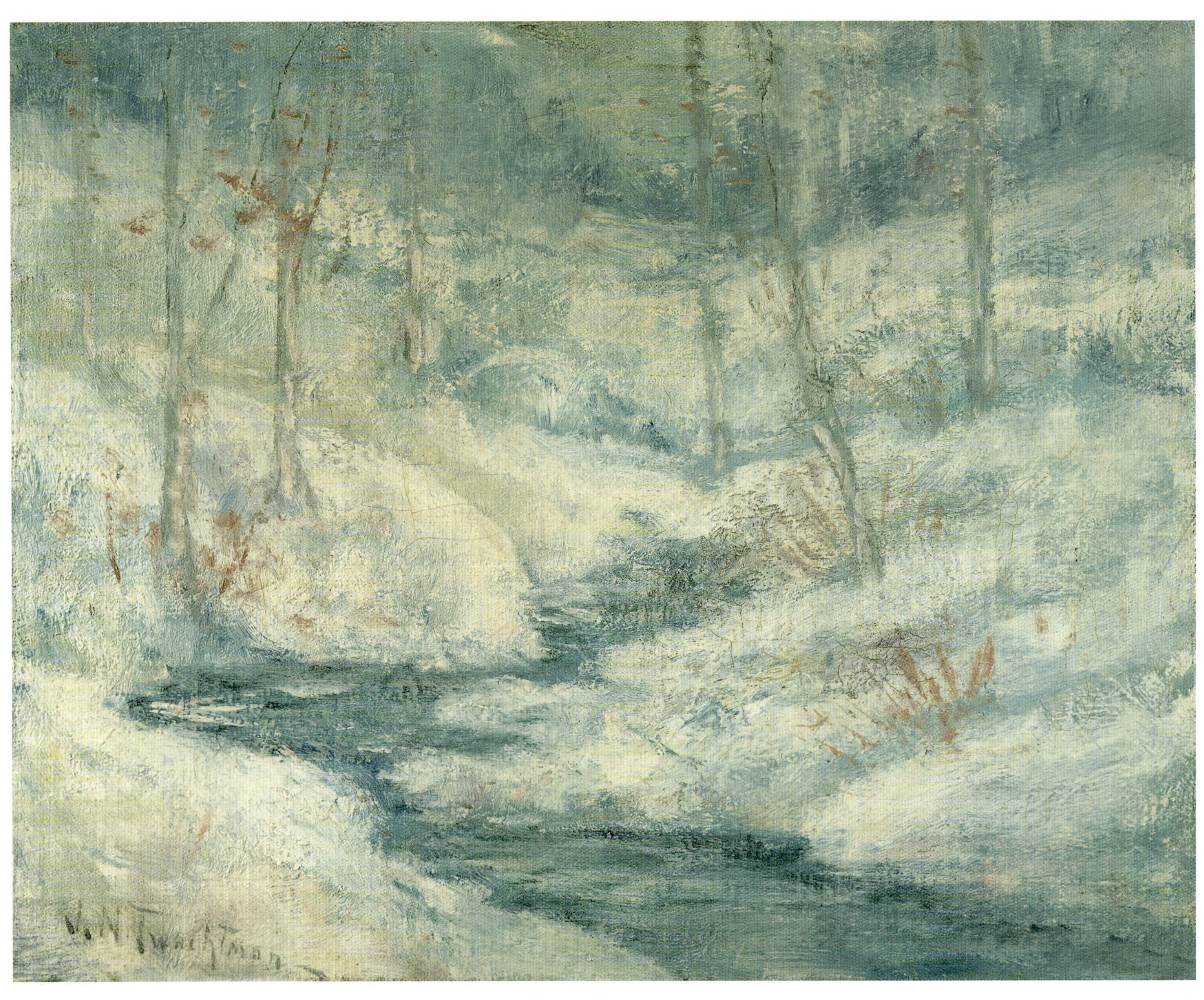

JOHN HENRY TWACHTMAN, *Snow Scene*, *c.* 1890–5
Oil on canvas, 40.6 x 50.8 cm
Carmen Thyssen-Bornemisza Collection,
on loan at the Museo Thyssen-Bornemisza, Madrid, CTB.1980.89

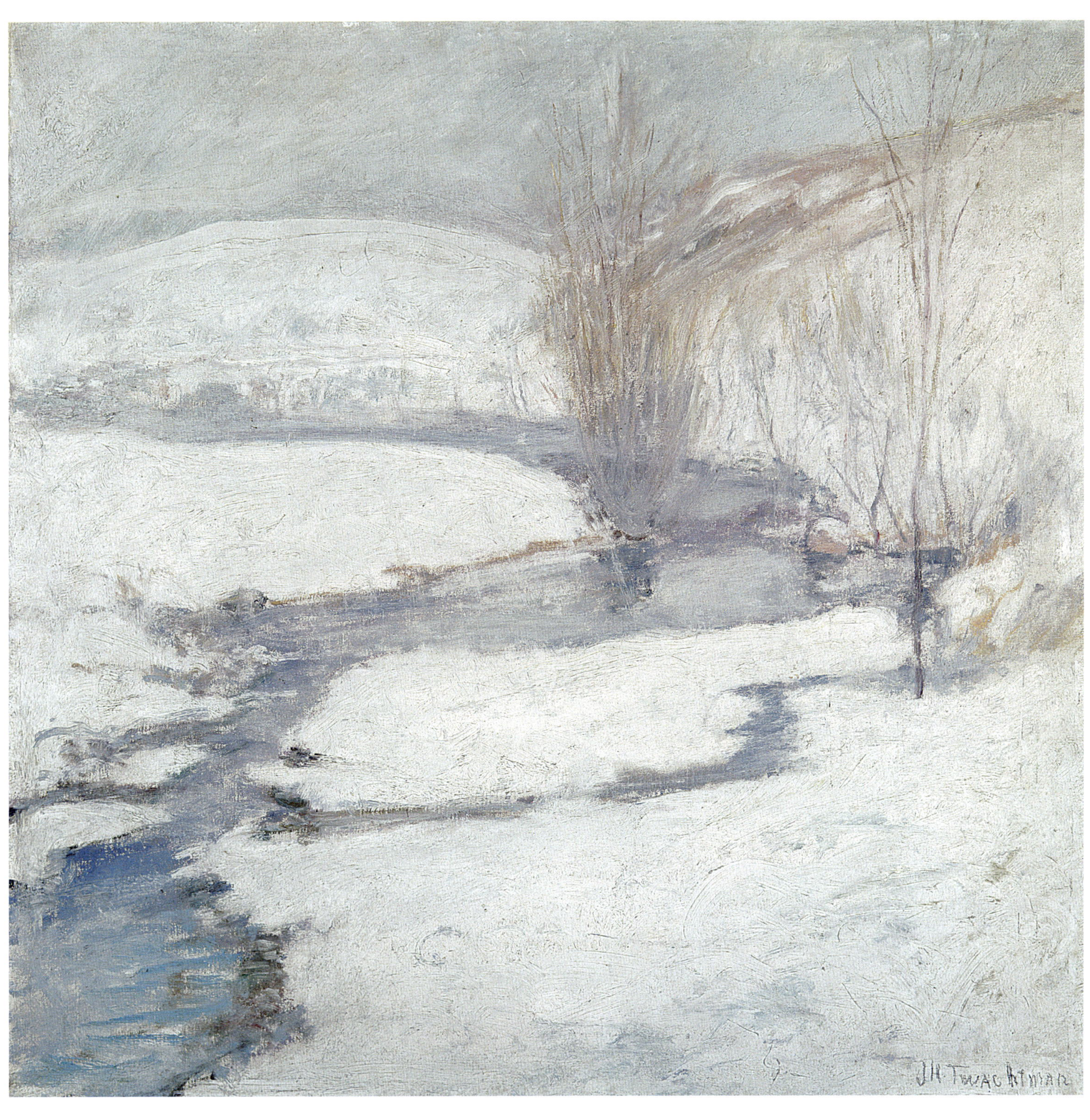

JOHN HENRY TWACHTMAN, *Winter Landscape*, 1890–1900
Oil on canvas, 76.5 x 76.5 cm
Terra Foundation for American Art, Chicago,
Daniel J. Terra Collection, 1992.136

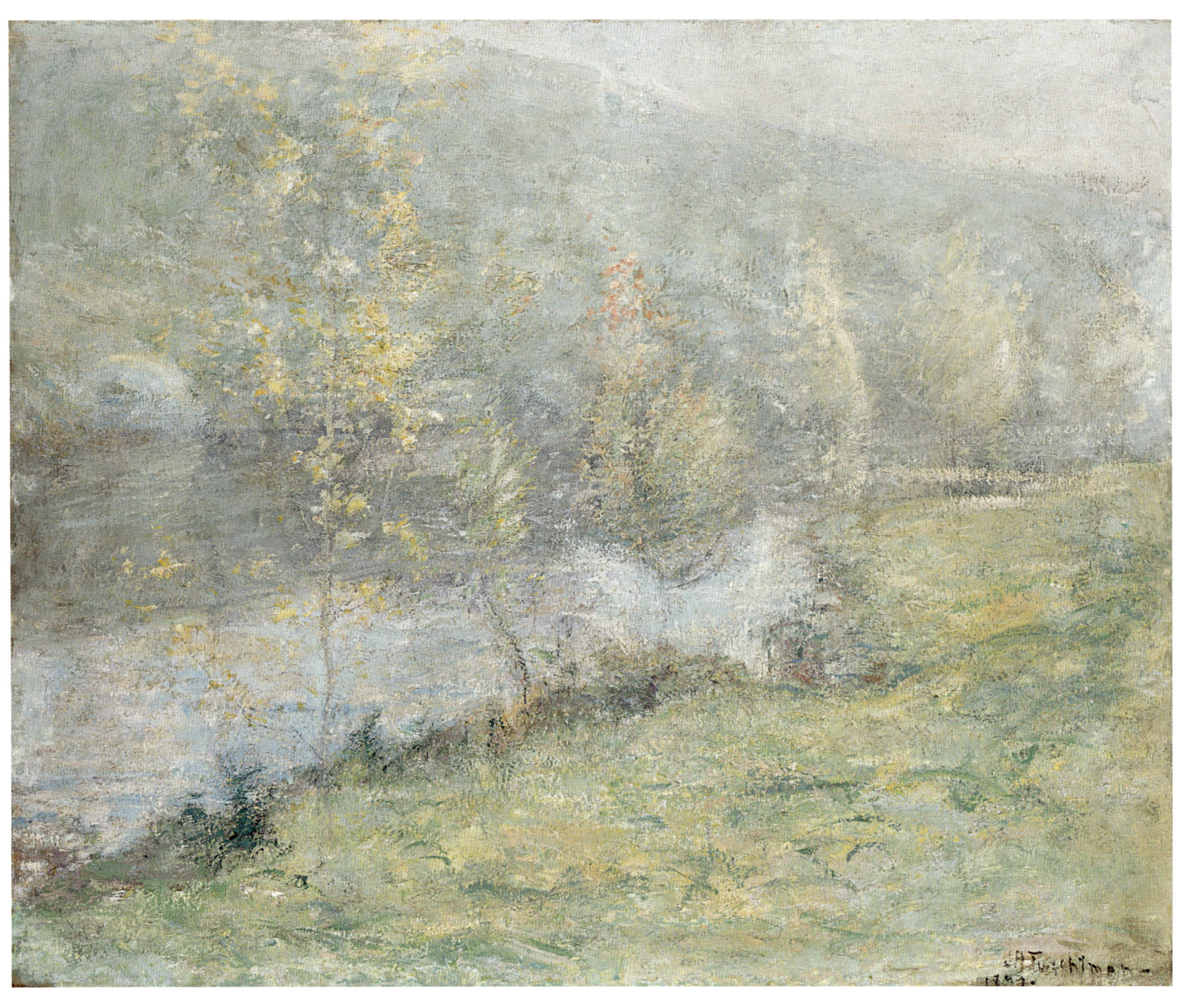

JOHN HENRY TWACHTMAN, *Misty May Morn*, 1899
Oil on canvas, 63.8 x 76.1 cm
Smithsonian American Art Museum, Washington D.C.,
Gift of John Gellatly, 1929.6.141

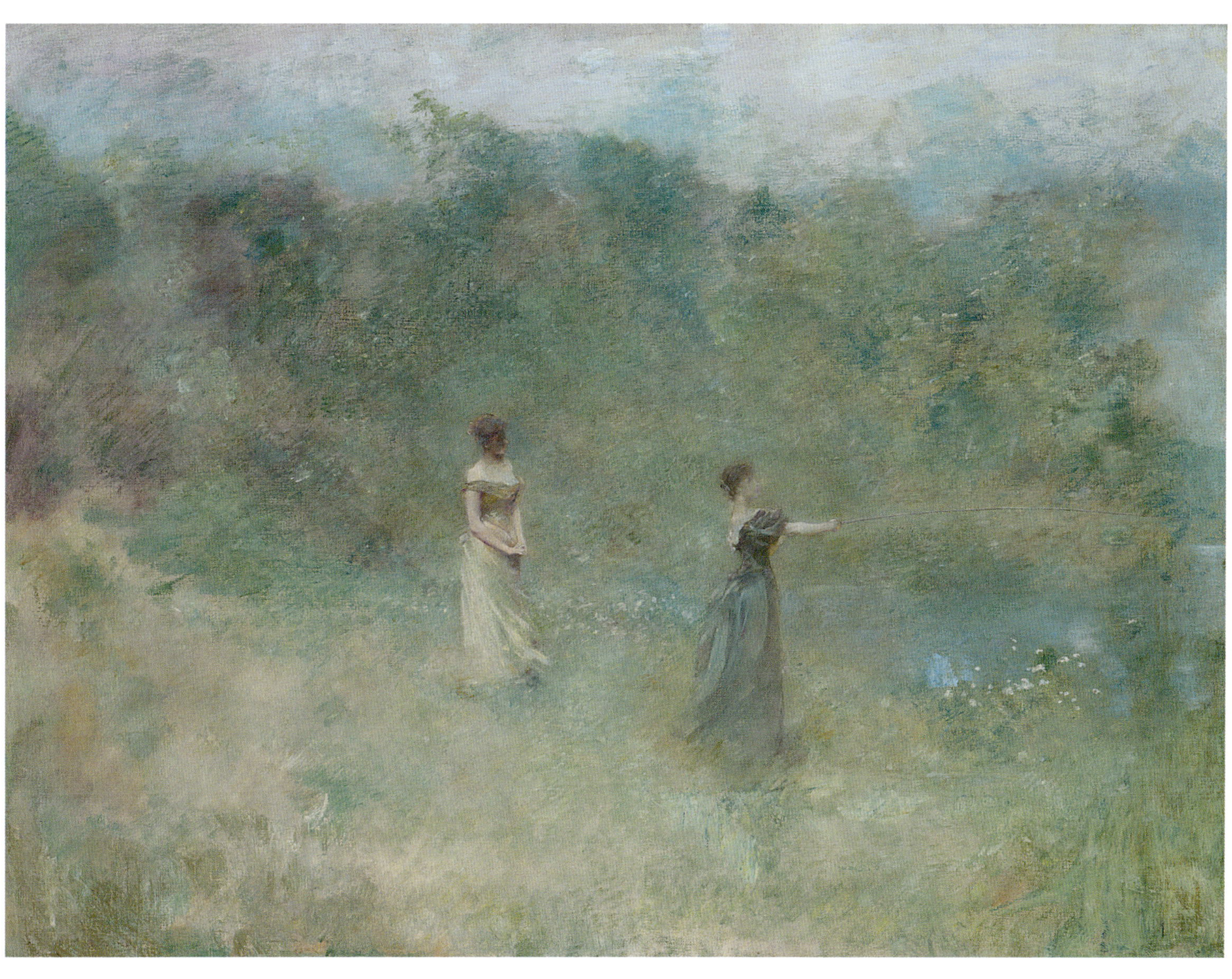

THOMAS WILMER DEWING, *Summer*, *c.* 1890
Oil on canvas, 107 x 137.8 cm
Smithsonian American Art Museum, Washington D.C.,
Gift of William T. Evans, 1909.7.21

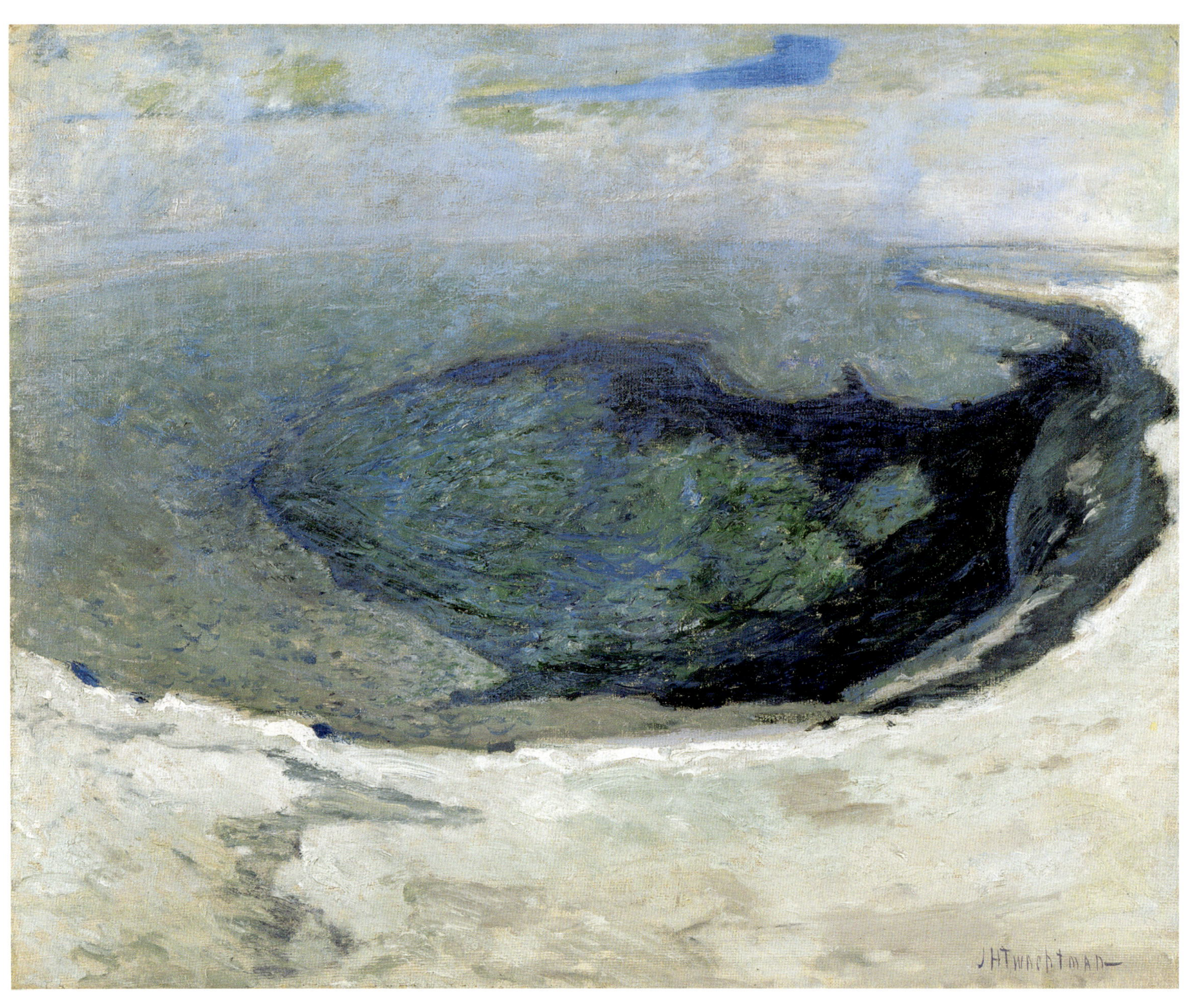

JOHN HENRY TWACHTMAN, *Emerald Pool, Yellowstone, c.* 1895
Oil on canvas, 64.1 x 76.8 cm
Wadsworth Atheneum Museum of Art, Hartford, Connecticut,
Bequest of George A. Gay, by exchange, and The Ella Gallup Sumner
and Mary Catlin Sumner Collection Fund, 1979.162
[Shown in Giverny and Edinburgh only]

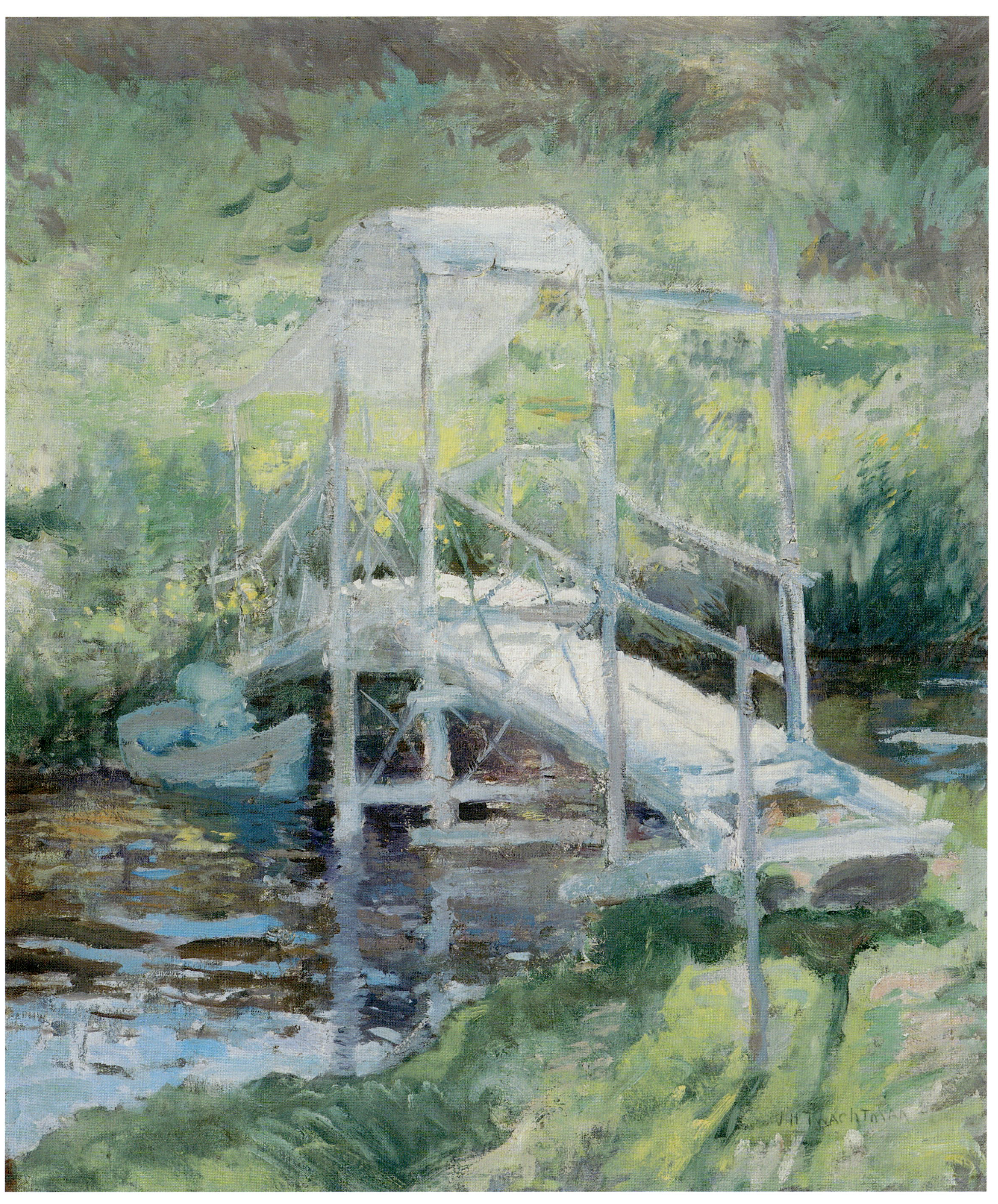

JOHN HENRY TWACHTMAN, *The White Bridge*, late 1890s
Oil on canvas, 76.8 x 63.8 cm
Memorial Art Gallery of the University of Rochester, New York,
Gift of Emily Sibley Watson, 16.9

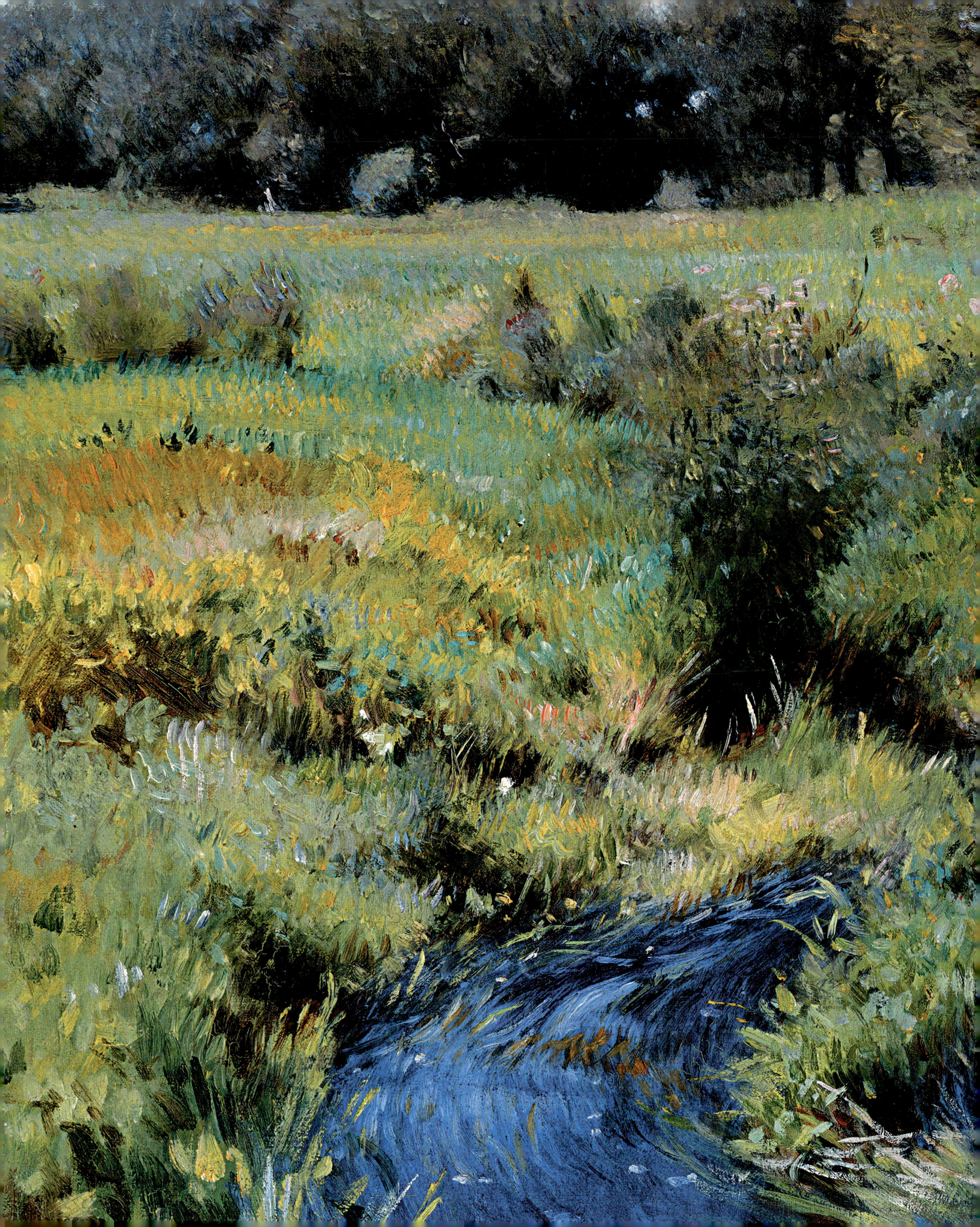

BIOGRAPHIES
CHRONOLOGY

DENNIS MILLER BUNKER, *The Pool, Medfield*, 1889, detail (see p.103)

Artist **Biographies**

Cecilia Beaux

(1855 Philadelphia, Pennsylvania – 1942 Gloucester, Massachusetts)

Beaux began attending classes at the Pennsylvania Academy of the Fine Arts, Philadelphia, in 1876 and first came to international attention in 1887 when her large canvas *Les derniers jours d'enfance (The Last Days of Infancy)* of 1883–5 (Pennsylvania Academy of the Fine Arts) was exhibited at the Paris Salon. In 1888, at the age of thirty-two, she travelled to Paris where she studied at the Académies Julian and Colarossi. Her academic training and precise technique never fully gave way to Impressionism, but two years in Europe brightened her palette and softened her paint application. In her later portraits, Beaux combined bright colours and complementary highlights with more traditional techniques of portrait-making, much like Sargent. In 1895 Beaux accepted a teaching position at the Pennsylvania Academy, the first woman to have such an appointment. Five years later, with a successful range of commissioned portraits, she settled in New York and began spending summers in Gloucester, Massachusetts where she moved in 1906.

Frank W. Benson

(1862 Salem, Massachusetts – 1951 Salem, Massachusetts)

Benson became a leading figure in the development of Impressionism in America. He studied at the School of the Museum of Fine Arts, Boston, between 1880 and 1883 where he met Tarbell who would have a great influence on his work. Benson travelled to Paris in 1883, enrolling at the Académie Julian and painting in Concarneau and London during the summer months. A few years after his return to the United States in 1885, he began teaching at his Alma Mater. His early work consisted of portraits and interior scenes as well as decorative murals, but by the end of the 1890s his style had shifted to the bright colours and sun-filled outdoor scenes for which he would become most famous. In late 1897, he became a founding member of the 'Ten American Painters', a group that rejected the strict exhibition policies at the Society of American Artists. Benson moved to Maine in 1901 where he continued to paint until the end of his life.

John Leslie Breck

(1860 Hong Kong – 1899 Boston, Massachusetts)

Born at sea to an American naval captain and his wife, Breck grew up in Boston before travelling first to Munich in 1877 and later to Paris in 1886 to complete his artistic training. In 1887 he accompanied a small group of American and Canadian painters to the village of Giverny where he painted *en plein air* and became friends with Monet and the Hoschedé sisters. This friendship may have inspired Breck to lighten his palette and depict hazy, atmospheric effects in his landscapes. When he exhibited these impressionist works in Boston in 1890, critics expressed surprise at his purple shadows and loose paint application, complaining that the young American had come under the influence of the French master. In 1891, his final summer in Giverny, Breck produced a series of sketches based directly on Monet's series of Haystacks (pp.84-5). Like many of the American impressionists, Breck responded to different artistic aesthetics, producing several moodier paintings towards the end of his life. He died in 1899 at the age of thirty-nine before obtaining recognition as a leading artist of his day.

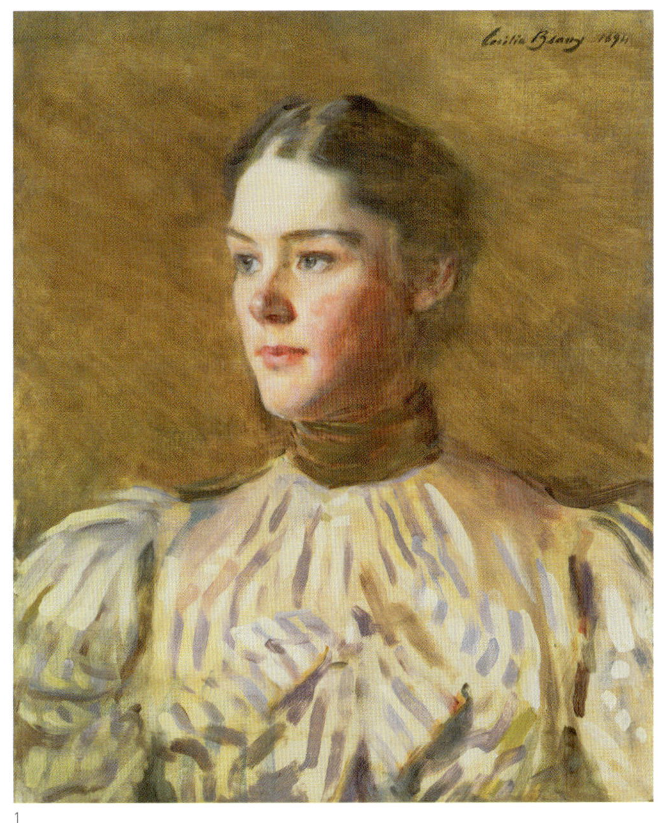

1

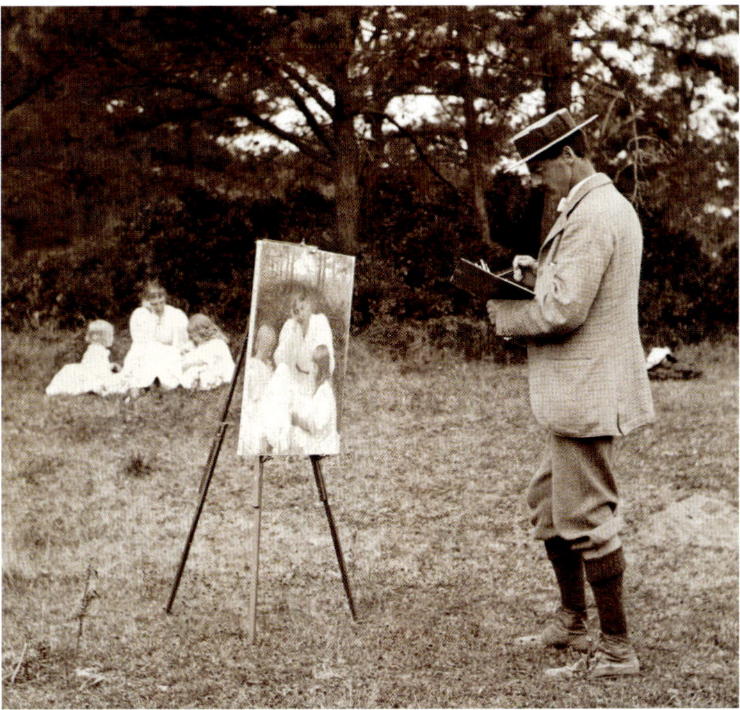

2

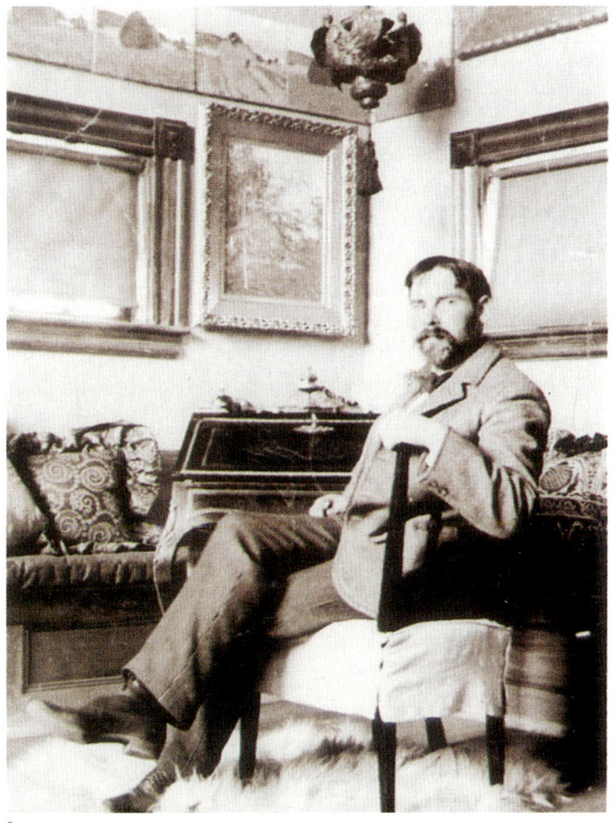

3

1. CECILIA BEAUX,
Self-Portrait, 1894
Oil on canvas, 63 × 50.8 cm
National Academy Museum,
New York, 67-P

2. Frank W. Benson painting
Plein Air, 1893, unidentified photographer
Benson Family Manuscript Collection,
Phillips Library, Peabody Essex Museum,
Salem, Massachusetts

3. *John Leslie Breck in his studio*,
undated, unidentified photographer
Breck Family Archives, courtesy of
Jeffrey Brown, Brown-Corbin Fine Art

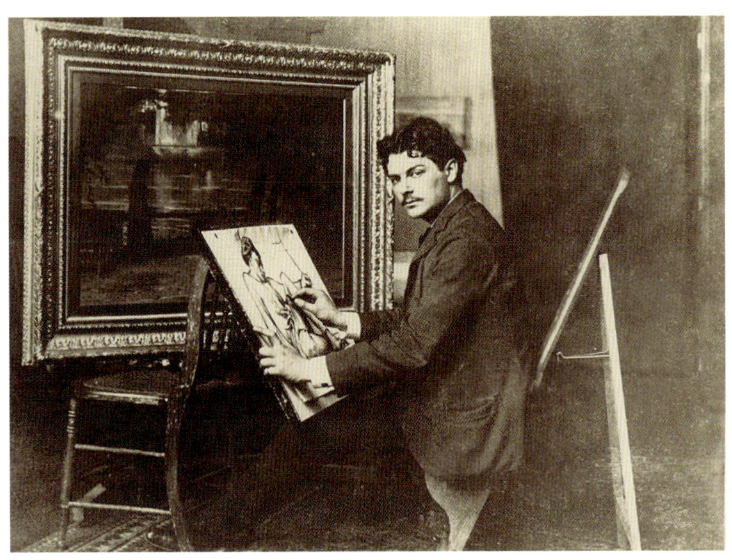

4

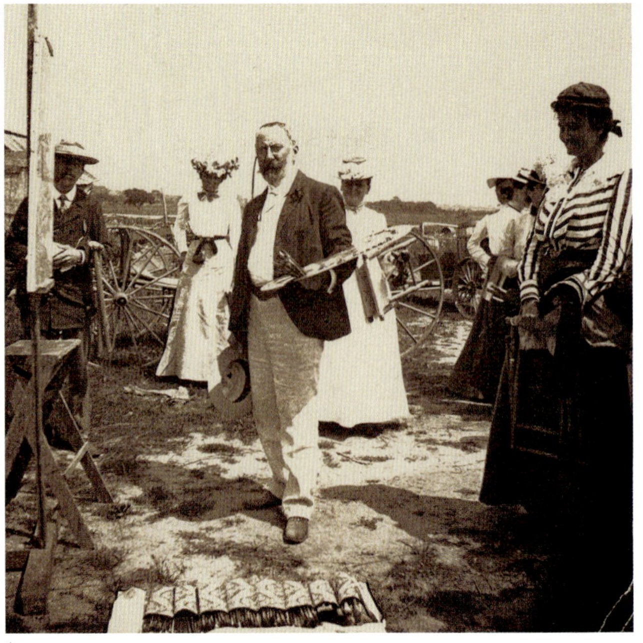

6

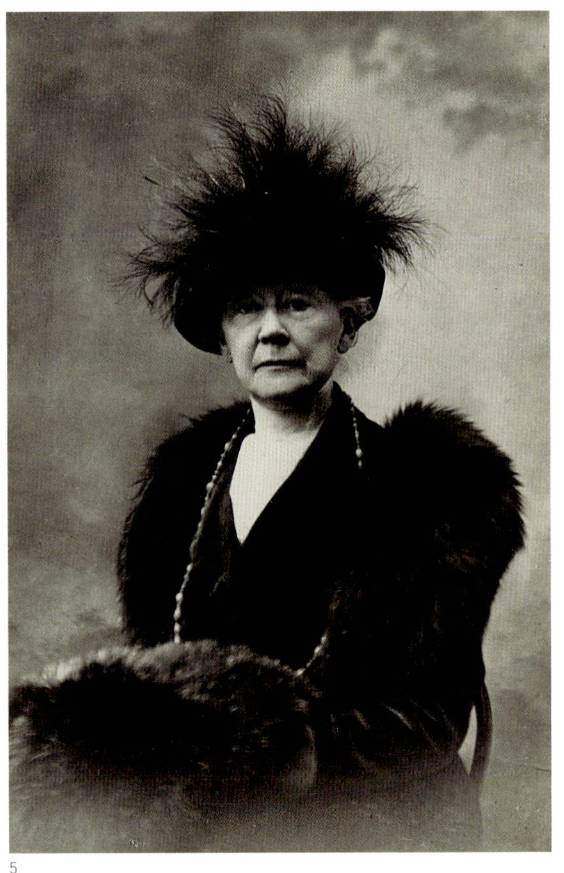

5

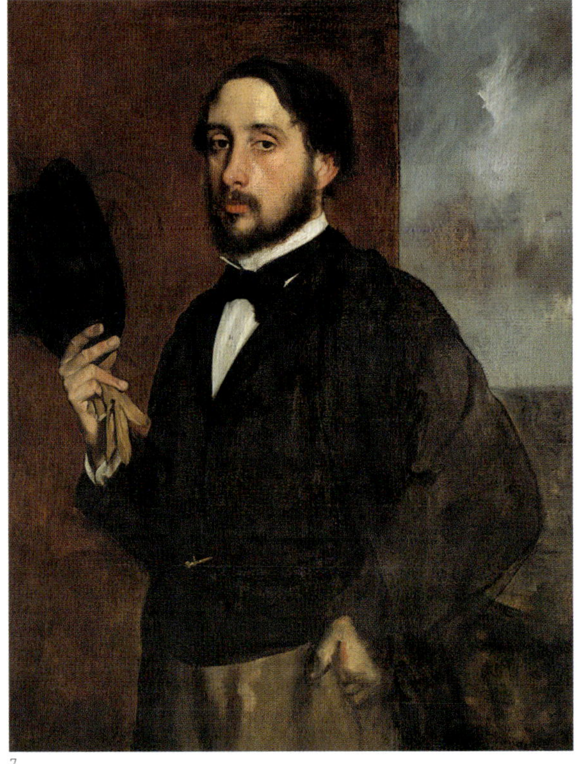

7

4. Dennis Miller Bunker in his studio, between 1884 and 1890
Berry-Hill Galleries, photographer
Dennis Miller Bunker papers
Archives of American Art, Smithsonian Institution, Washington D.C.

5. Mary Cassatt, 1914
Unidentified photographer
Frederick A. Sweet research material on Mary Cassatt and James A. McNeill Whistler, Archives of American Art, Smithsonian Institution, Washington D.C.

6. William Merritt Chase, *c.* 1900
Unidentified photographer
Rockwell Kent papers, Archives of American Art, Smithsonian Institution, Washington D.C.

7. EDGAR DEGAS,
Self-Portrait, *c.* 1862
Oil on canvas, 92 × 69 cm
Museu Calouste Gulbenkian, Lisbon, inv. 2307

Dennis Miller Bunker

(1861 New York – 1890 Boston, Massachusetts)

A native of New York, Bunker studied at the National Academy of Design and the Art Students League, working with Chase. In 1882, he travelled to Paris and enrolled at the Ecole des Beaux-Arts and studied with Jean-Léon Gérôme. During the summers, Bunker painted outdoors in Brittany and Normandy. Gradually he began to introduce into his art brighter colours and looser painting techniques, inspired by the impressionists. After his return to the United States in 1885, Bunker moved to Boston and began teaching at the Cowles Art School. He met Sargent in late 1887 through Isabella Stewart Gardner, a well-known patron of the arts, and spent the following summer painting with Sargent in the English countryside. Bunker did not wholeheartedly embrace the techniques and colours of Impressionism until 1889, while working in rural Massachusetts, and he always reserved a more traditional palette and paint application for commissioned portraits and other figurative work. His death in 1890, shortly after his marriage, cut short a promising career.

Mary Cassatt

(1844 Allegheny City, Pennsylvania – 1926 Mesnil-Theribus)

After attending classes at the Pennsylvania Academy of the Fine Arts in Philadelphia, Cassatt moved to Paris in 1866 and studied with Jean-Léon Gérôme, although, as a woman, she was not permitted to attend the Ecole des Beaux-Arts. In 1868, she exhibited her first painting at the Paris Salon where she would continue to submit work in the following years. In 1879, encouraged by her friend Degas, Cassatt participated in the fourth impressionist exhibition, and continued to exhibit with the group in 1880, 1881 and 1886, the only American artist to take part in these exhibitions. By the 1890s, Cassatt had become famous for her paintings of women and children and excelled at pastel and printmaking. She produced a mural for the Chicago World's Columbian Exposition in 1892, and though she enjoyed the new format, it was not successful. Cassatt remained in France for the rest of her life, where she exibited her paintings and prints widely and received the French Legion of Honour. She played a key role in promoting French Impressionism in America.

William Merritt Chase

(1849 Williamsburg, Indiana – 1916 New York)

Famous during his lifetime as an award-winning painter, influential teacher and founder of numerous art societies, Chase played a significant role in the development of Impressionism among American artists. His early training, however, did not make him a likely candidate for the bright, *plein-air* pictures he would produce after 1890. Indeed, he enjoyed a classical artistic education in New York and, between 1872 and 1877, at the Royal Academy in Munich, where he mastered the dark, painterly manner taught at the school. Upon his return to New York, Chase established himself as a teacher and practising artist. His elaborate studio, decorated with Old Master pictures and props acquired during his European travels, set a new standard for the professional American artist. By the 1880s, Chase began adopting lighter colours, modern subjects and cropped compositions. His pictures of public parks in New York and Brooklyn attracted attention in the press. In 1891 Chase opened a summer school for painting out of doors in Shinnecock on Long Island. In 1896, he opened the Chase School of Art in New York, which became the New York School of Art two years later. After the death of his fellow artist Twachtman, Chase replaced him as a member of the 'Ten American Painters'.

Edgar Degas

(1834 Paris – 1917 Paris)

Born into a wealthy banking family, Degas studied briefly at the Ecole des Beaux-Arts in Paris under Louis Lamothe, a pupil of Ingres. Degas's mother was an American from New Orleans, and he visited the city in the autumn of 1872 with his brother René. He was introduced to the impressionist circle through his friendship with Manet, whom he met while copying paintings at the Louvre. In 1868 he joined Manet, Monet, Renoir, Sisley and others at their regular meetings at the Café Guérbois in Paris. He participated in seven of the eight impressionist exhibitions but, like Cassatt, whom he invited to exhibit with the group in 1879, he regarded himself an 'independent' artist, rather than an impressionist. Between 1869 and 1895 he produced in various media several series of images of working women, including washerwomen, milliners, café performers and ballerinas. He was fascinated by the body in motion, an interest expressed above all in his sculptures, drawings and paintings of racehorses and dancers. A gifted printmaker and pastellist, in his later career he experimented with a series of women washing and drying themselves.

Thomas Wilmer Dewing

(1851 Boston, Massachusetts – 1938 New York)

Best known for his dream-like depictions of women in quiet indoor spaces or nebulous outdoor worlds, Dewing created a unique aesthetic. He trained in Boston and Paris, where he became a student at the Académie Julian as early as 1870. In Europe, he found inspiration in the art of Whistler and in Japanese prints. In 1877, he returned to Boston and began teaching at the School of the Museum of Fine Arts. He moved to New York in late 1880, joined the staff at the Art Students League, and later married fellow painter Maria Richards Oakey. Dewing exhibited regularly in Boston and New York and was recognised for his delicate colouring, muted palette and soft, decorative compositions. In 1897 he joined the 'Ten American Painters', a group that chose to break away from the Society of American Artists. Though his art differed greatly from the bright impressionistic pictures of its other members, such as Benson, Hassam and Tarbell, his presence demonstrated the variety of visual responses to modernist artistic trends that existed in the American art world at the turn of the nineteenth century.

Childe Hassam

(1859 Dorchester, Massachusetts – 1935 East Hampton, New York)

Born in Massachusetts, Hassam worked as an illustrator and commercial draughtsman in Boston from an early age. He had his first solo exhibition of watercolours in 1882 at the age of twenty-four. The following year, he made a study trip to Europe, producing watercolours throughout the journey. Back in Boston, he painted city views with dark, muted colours to emphasise rain, snow or specific light effects. Between 1886 and 1889 Hassam settled in France with his wife where he enrolled at the Académie Julian and gradually adopted a brighter palette and a softer, sketchier technique, similar to that of the impressionists. Moving to New York in late 1889, Hassam became known for urban and coastal scenes of upper-middle-class leisure, painted in a bright impressionist style. Throughout his long life, he spent many summers on the Isles of Shoals near New Hampshire and Maine, becoming a close friend of Celia Thaxter, poet and patron of the arts. In late 1897, he resigned from the Society of American Artists along with nine colleagues, forming the group known as the 'Ten American Painters'. He continued to paint and exhibit on both sides of the Atlantic until his death in 1935.

Edouard Manet

(1832 Paris – 1883 Paris)

Manet was an important precursor of Impressionism, but never participated in the impressionist exhibitions. After twice failing the competition to enter naval college in 1848, he was encouraged by his family to follow an artistic vocation and joined the studio of Thomas Couture. In 1863 and 1865 Manet challenged the traditional tenets of the French academy with his paintings *Le Déjeuner sur l'Herbe* and *Olympia* (both Musée d'Orsay, Paris), both of which are broadly painted and rework a classical theme in a contemporary setting. In 1866 he met Frédéric Bazille, Cézanne, Monet, Renoir and the naturalist writer Emile Zola, whom he invited to regular meetings at the Café Guérbois in Paris. In 1868, through Henri Fantin-Latour, he met Morisot, who posed for his painting *The Balcony* (Musée d'Orsay, Paris), strongly influenced by the art of Goya and Velázquez. Morisot, who married Manet's brother Eugène, benefited from his guidance, but later influenced his developing style by encouraging him to paint out of doors.

Claude Monet

(1840 Paris – 1926 Giverny)

Born in Paris, Monet spent his youth in Le Havre where he showed an early talent for caricature and where Eugène Boudin initiated him into the practice of *plein-air* painting. In 1862 Monet joined the studio of Charles Gleyre and met Bazille, Renoir and Sisley. At his first attempt, in 1865, he was admitted to the Salon. To evade the Franco-Prussian war in 1870, he travelled to London where he had the opportunity to admire the works of Turner and Constable. From 1871 to 1878 he lived in Argenteuil, but then moved to Vétheuil, Poissy and finally, in 1883, to Giverny, where he remained until his death. At the first impressionist exhibition, in 1874, he showed the famous painting *Impression – Sunrise* of 1872 (see fig.1). He travelled abroad frequently during the 1880s, including trips to London where he visited Whistler and Sargent. At his home in Giverny, he planned his garden, the creation of which would last more than twenty years, from 1883 to 1904. In 1891 he exhibited fifteen versions of his series of Haystacks at the Durand-Ruel Gallery in Paris. These paintings would inspire several of the young American artists working in the village of Giverny. The following year he presented a series of Poplars at the same gallery, and began a series of views of Rouen Cathedral. By the 1910s the water-lily pond had become his only motif. In 1915 he began work on his famous water-lily cycle, *Les Grandes Décorations*, which he donated to the French State in 1922.

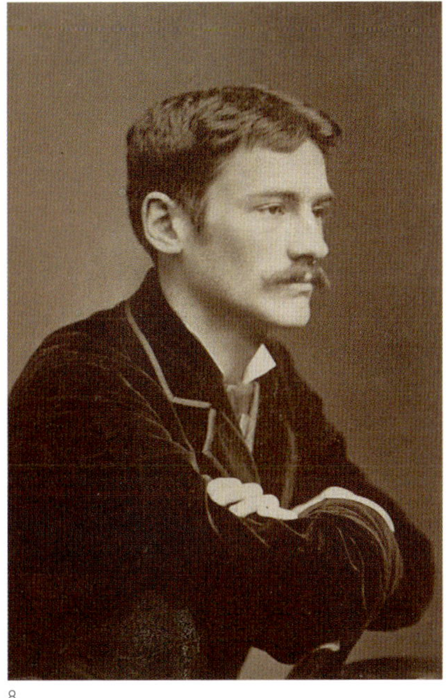

8

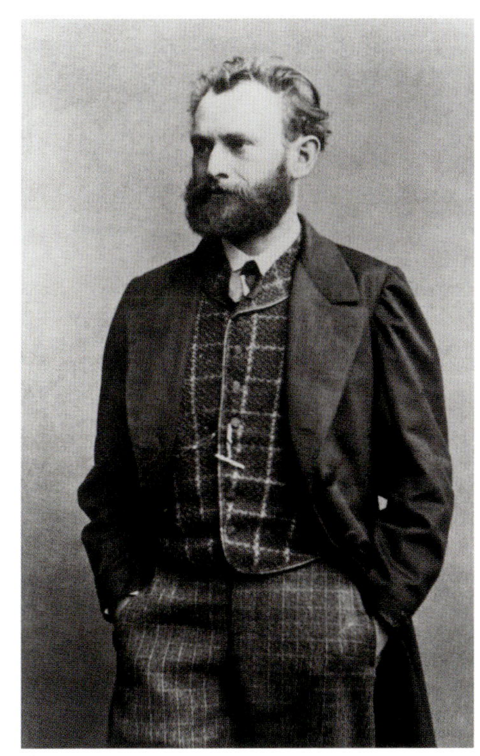

10

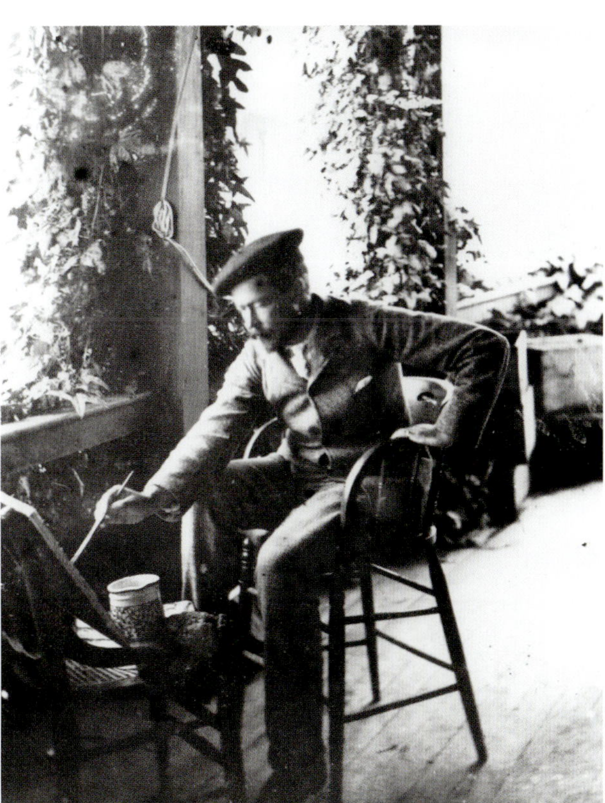

9

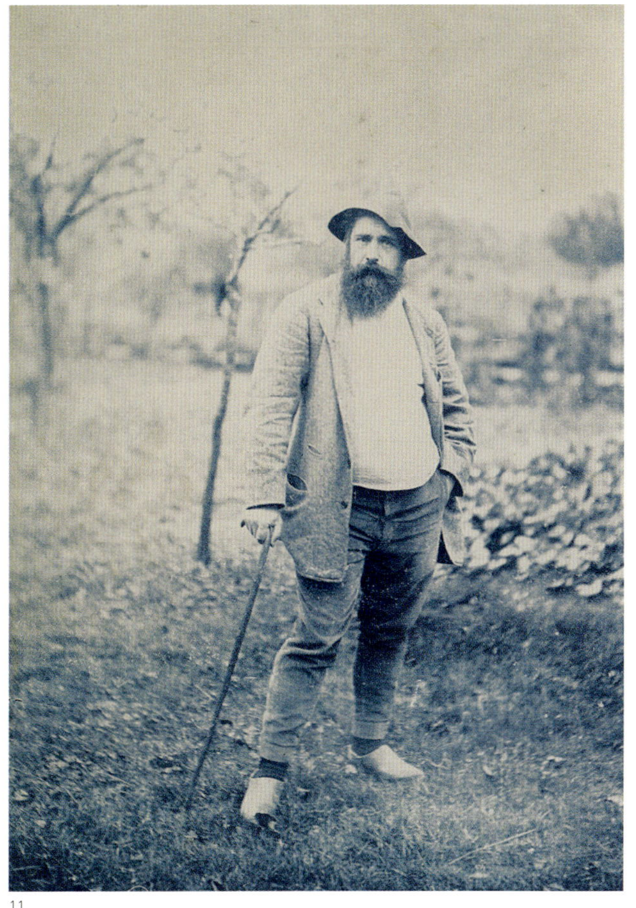

11

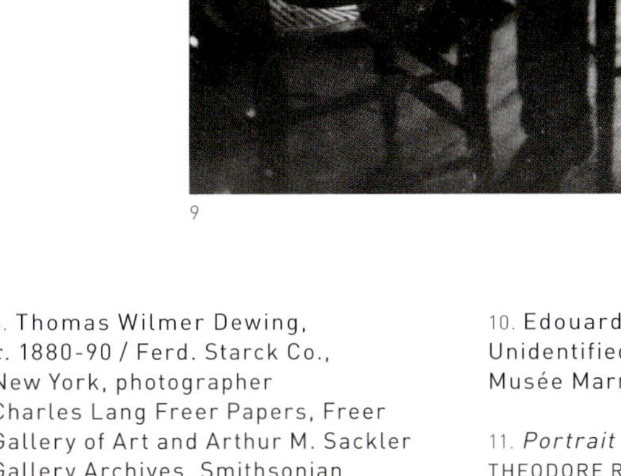

8. Thomas Wilmer Dewing, *c.* 1880-90 / Ferd. Starck Co., New York, photographer Charles Lang Freer Papers, Freer Gallery of Art and Arthur M. Sackler Gallery Archives, Smithsonian Institution, Washington D.C., Gift of the Estate of Charles Lang Freer

9. Childe Hassam painting on porch of Celia Thaxter's cottage, 1880-1910 / Karl Thaxter, attributed Portsmouth Athenaeum Archives, New Hampshire, P21.095

10. Edouard Manet
Unidentified photographer
Musée Marmottan Monet, Paris

11. *Portrait of Monet*, *c.* 1888–90,
THEODORE ROBINSON
Cyanotype, 24 × 16.8 cm
Terra Foundation for American Art, Chicago, Gift of Mr. Ira Spanierman, C1985.1.6

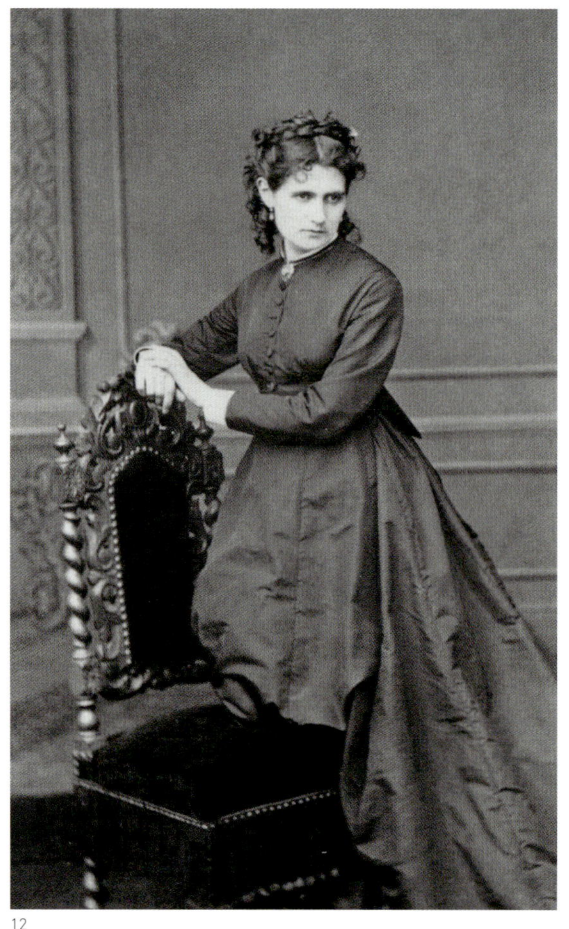

12

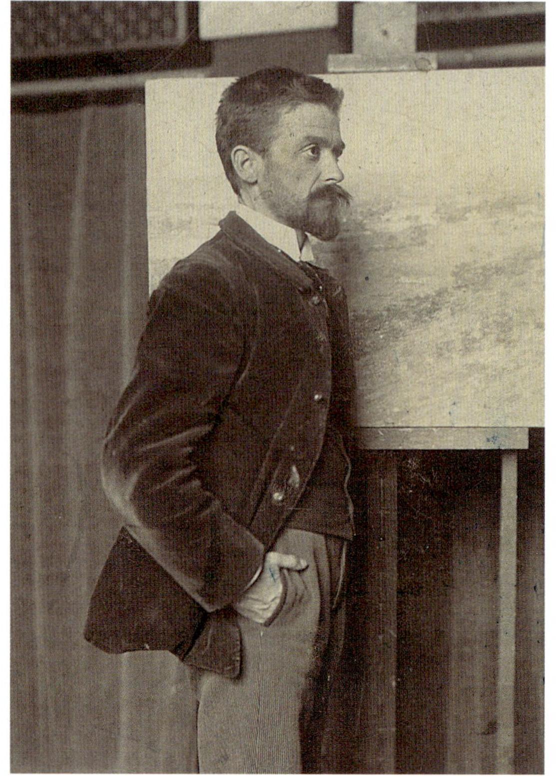

14

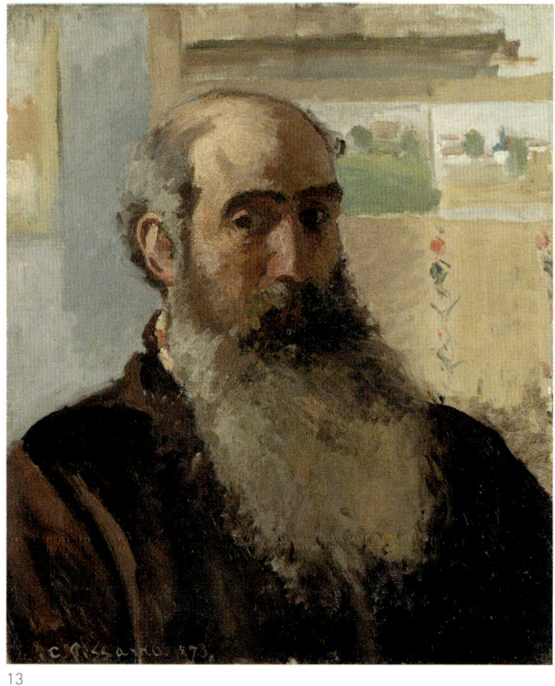

13

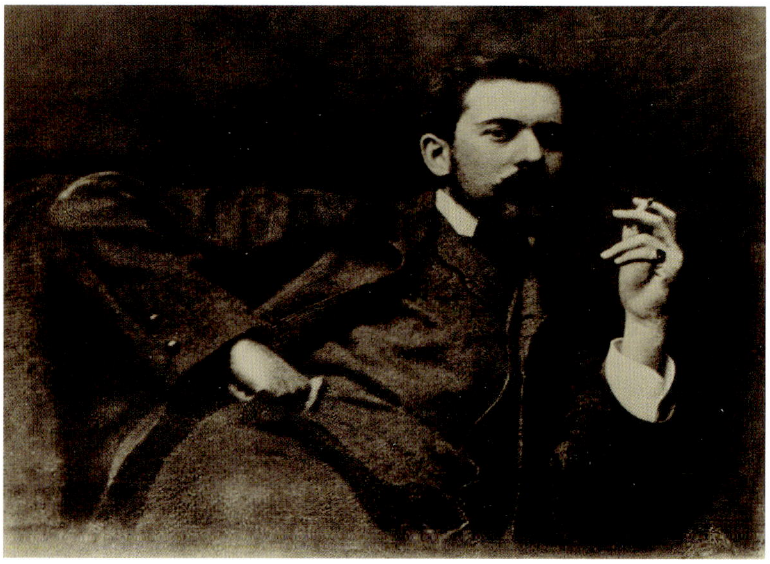

15

12. Berthe Morisot, 20 February 1869
Pierre Petit photographer
Private collection,
Archives Charmet

13. CAMILLE PISSARRO,
Self-Portrait, 1873
Oil on canvas, 55.5 × 46 cm
Musée d'Orsay, Paris, RF 2837

14. Theodore Robinson, *c.* 1882
Unidentified photographer
Macbeth Gallery records, Archives of American Art, Smithsonian Institution, Washington D.C.

15. John Singer Sargent, *c.* 1880
Unidentified photographer
R.L.Ormond material relating to John Singer Sargent, Archives of American Art, Smithsonian Institution, Washington D.C.

Berthe Morisot

(1841 Bourges – 1895 Paris)

Morisot took drawing classes in 1857 and later joined the studio of Camille Corot, who encouraged her to paint out of doors. She was admitted to the Salon in 1864 and exhibited her work there regularly. In 1868 she posed for Manet's *The Balcony* (Musée d'Orsay, Paris) and became one of his favourite models. In 1874 Morisot married Manet's brother, Eugène. From 1874 to 1886 she showed her work in the impressionist exhibitions, with the exception of the 1879 event, which was held shortly before the birth of her daughter Julie. At the third impressionist exhibition, in 1877, Morisot showed *The Cheval-Glass* (p.61), which attracted the attention of the critics. Between 1880 and 1884 she spent her summer's in Bougival. She visited Nice for the first time in 1881 and, four years later, travelled to Belgium and Holland. She also visited Monet in Giverny. In 1891 she bought the Château de Mesnil in Juziers with her husband, who died a year later. She held her first solo exhibition in 1892. In 1896, a year after Morisot's death, her friends the poet Stéphane Mallarmé, Degas, Monet and Renoir organised a posthumous exhibition in her memory at the Durand-Ruel Gallery.

Camille Pissarro

(1830 Charlotte Amalie, St Thomas, Danish Virgin Islands – 1903 Paris)

Pissarro was born in the Caribbean, where his father, a Jewish merchant originally from Bordeaux, had emigrated in 1824. In 1842 he left for Paris to study for two years before returning home to run the family business. He returned to Paris in 1855, where he discovered the paintings of Corot, Courbet and Delacroix at the Exposition Universelle. On Corot's advice, he began to paint out of doors. He attended the free academies at 5 Rue Cadet and the Académie Suisse on Quai des Orfèvres, where he befriended Cézanne and Monet. He lived in Pontoise from 1866 to 1882, working alongside Cézanne and Armand Guillaumin at Auvers-sur-Oise in 1873. Between 1874 and 1886 he participated in all eight impressionist exhibitions – the only member of the group to do so. He also encouraged younger artists such as Gauguin. His first solo exhibition was held in May 1883 at the Durand-Ruel Gallery. In 1886 he experimented with Seurat's divisionist technique but abandoned it in the early 1890s. At the invitation of American artist Lilla Cabot Perry, in May 1895 he met several American artists and collectors in Paris. During the last ten years of his life, he travelled a great deal in Normandy, Belgium and Amsterdam, and regularly visited his son Lucien in London.

Theodore Robinson

(1852 Irasburg, Vermont – 1896 New York)

Growing up in Vermont and Wisconsin, Robinson studied briefly in Chicago before arriving in New York in 1874 to enrol in the National Academy of Design and the Art Students League. Two years later he sailed for Paris where he worked with Carolus-Duran and Jean-Leon Gérôme at the Ecole des Beaux-Arts. He exhibited naturalistic landscapes and genre paintings at the Paris Salon in 1877 and returned to America in 1879. To earn a living, Robinson worked with a group of young artists, under the direction of John La Farge, on architectural mural decorations. It was not until a subsequent trip to Paris in the mid-1880s that Robinson, under the influence of Impressionism, would gradually adopt a brighter palette, flamboyant brushwork and an interest in capturing the fleeting moment. He probably visited Giverny for the first time in 1885 and continued to paint in the village until 1892, becoming friends with Monet. He exhibited his Giverny paintings in America, attracting attention and earning awards. Perhaps following the French master's advice to paint his own country, Robinson devoted himself to outdoor scenes of rural and coastal New England. He died prematurely at the age of forty-three.

John Singer Sargent

(1856 Florence – 1925 London)

A cosmopolitan artist known for his portraits, Sargent was born in Italy to American parents and spent his life in Europe. He entered the Ecole des Beaux-Arts in Paris in 1874, working in the studio of Carolus-Duran, who favoured a direct painting approach with little emphasis on careful under-drawing. Sargent's natural talents and fluent French allowed him to move freely in artistic circles, and he soon gained the attention of the Parisian art world. In 1877 he exhibited for the first time at the Paris Salon where he would continue to show work almost annually for the rest of his career. He also exhibited frequently at the Royal Academy in London, earning praise and moving to the city in 1885 before settling there more permanently in 1886. Sargent experimented with Impressionism in the mid-1880s when he was a close acquaintance of Monet, whom he painted in Giverny (see p.69). His art inspired several younger artists such as Beaux, Bunker and Chase. In the late 1890s and throughout the early twentieth century, Sargent focused on ambitious mural projects in Boston. He continued to earn honours and receive important portrait commissions, becoming known as one of the most important American painters of the nineteenth century.

Edmund C. Tarbell

(1862 West Groton, Massachusetts – 1938 New Castle, New Hampshire)

An American impressionist artist and member of the 'Ten American Painters', Tarbell enjoyed a long career. He trained as a lithographer before entering the School of the Museum of Fine Arts in Boston in 1879 and the Académie Julian in Paris in 1883. During his three-year sojourn in Europe, Tarbell visited Belgium, Holland, Germany and Italy and made acquaintances with several American artists abroad. Returning to Boston he began teaching at his Alma Mater, where he would inspire a new generation of artists until 1912. In the 1890s, Tarbell adopted bright colours and visible brushwork for his highly impressionistic representations of elegantly dressed women in outdoor settings. These paintings attracted so much attention when he exhibited them in the United States and abroad that younger Boston artists who worked under his influence were soon called 'Tarbellites'. By 1900 Tarbell had turned his attention to quiet, darker interior scenes where solitary female figures are absorbed in thought. These moody canvases seem unrelated to his cheerful outdoor pictures, but, in fact, the genteel women depicted are often the same, reflecting two sides of an upper-class society.

John Henry Twachtman

(1853 Cincinnati, Ohio – 1902 Gloucester, Massachusetts)

At a young age Twachtman studied drawing and painting in his native Cincinnati. By 1874 he was enrolled in classes with Frank Duveneck, an influential American painter who encouraged his students to paint from the world around them. Twachtman followed his teacher to Munich where he studied at the Royal Academy between 1875 and 1878, meeting fellow student Chase. It was here that he learned the rich, dark manner associated with the school. Twachtman pursued his artistic training in New York at the Arts Students League and then in Paris at the Académie Julian. When he returned to the United States in 1885, he began painting in a unique style that combined influences from Impressionism, Japanese art and the Nocturnes of Whistler. In 1889, Twachtman purchased a farm in Greenwich, Connecticut, where he produced snow-filled landscapes and quiet, family scenes for the rest of his life. Though he earned the respect of his fellow artists, his unusual, haunting pictures never brought him critical or financial success. He was one of the original 'Ten American Painters'.

James Abbott McNeill Whistler

(1834 Lowell, Massachusetts – 1903 London)

Influential and controversial, Whistler cultivated a strong artistic personality that set him apart throughout his long career.
A true expatriate, Whistler spent little time in the United States, preferring to live in Paris and London. He first arrived in Paris in 1855, making friends with French realist artists such as Henri Fantin-Latour and Alphonse Legros. Achieving greater success in London, Whistler moved there in 1859. During the following decade he produced experimental landscapes known as Nocturnes and figurative works known as 'symphonies' or 'harmonies' painted in subdued, almost monochromatic colours. These works were not at first understood by critics and artists, but during the artist's lifetime, they would become increasingly important. During the 1880s, he earned international acclaim and promoted his art throughout Europe and in the United States, attracting a wide following among younger American and British artists. He moved back to Paris in the 1890s, finally achieving approval from the French government in 1891 when it purchased his *Arrangement in Grey and Black, no. 1* (p.148). Though Whistler never exhibited with the impressionists, his paintings, prints and writings were admired by many of the group, including his friend Monet.

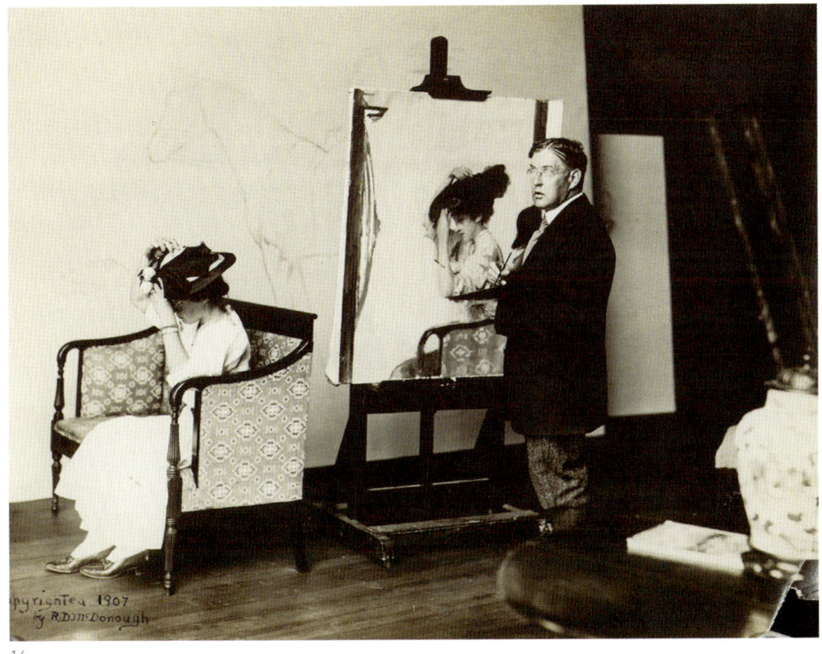

16

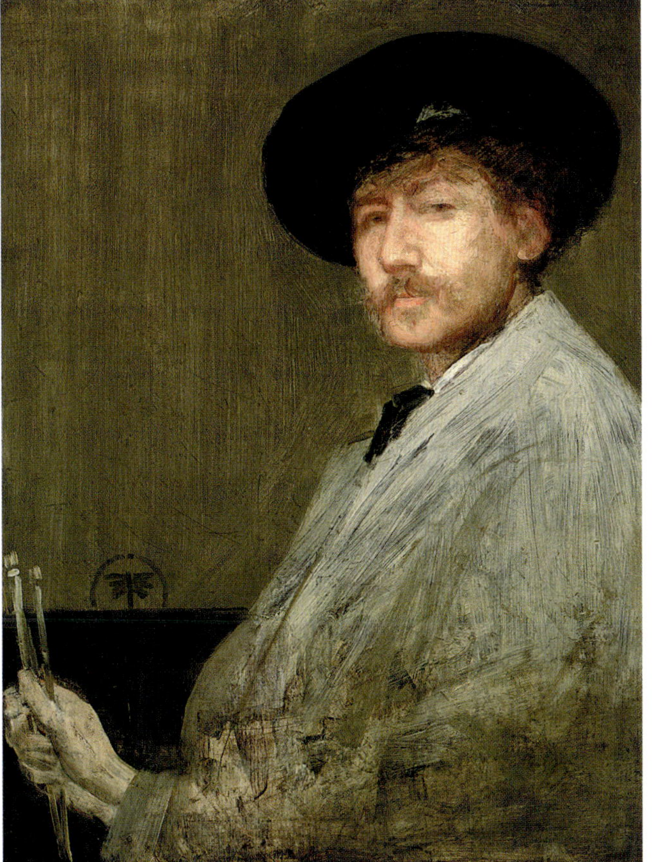

18

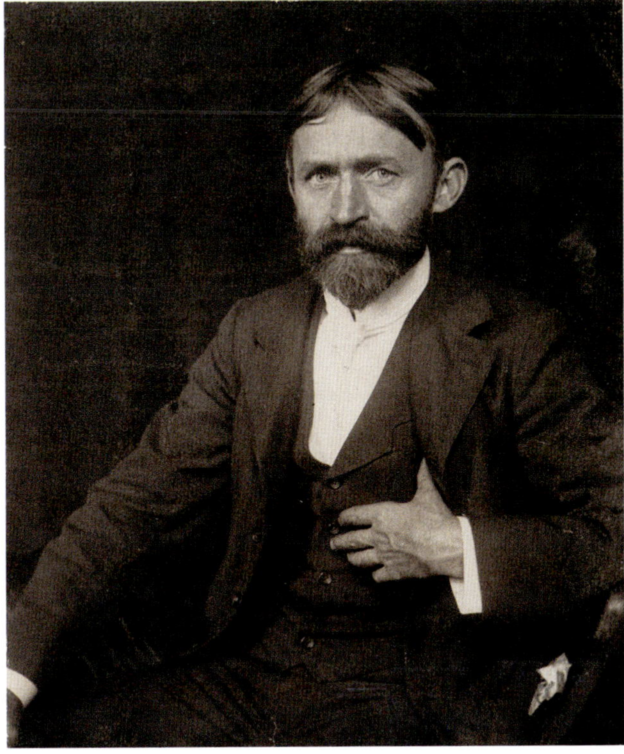

17

16. Edmund C. Tarbell at work on
Girl Putting on Her Hat, 1907
R.D.McDonough, photographer
Edmund Charles Tarbell papers, Archives of American Art, Smithsonian Institution, Washington D.C.

17. John Henry Twachtman, *c.* 1900
Gertrude Käsebier, photographer
Macbeth Gallery records, Archives of American Art, Smithsonian Institution, Washington D.C.

18. JAMES ABBOTT MCNEILL WHISTLER
Arrangement in Grey: Portrait of the Painter, *c.* 1872
Oil on canvas, 74.9 × 53.3 cm
Detroit Institute of Arts, Bequest of Henry Glover Stevens in memory of Ellen P. Stevens and Mary M. Stevens, 34.27

Chronology of American Impressionism **1874–1900**

Katherine M. Bourguignon, Laura Valette and Hadrien Viraben

1874

Thirty artists exhibit together in Paris at what will become known as the first impressionist exhibition. They include Paul Cézanne, Edgar Degas, Armand Guillaumin, Claude Monet, Berthe Morisot, Camille Pissarro, Auguste Renoir and Alfred Sisley. No Americans participate.

Mary Cassatt exhibits a painting at the Paris Salon, attracting Degas's notice. John Singer Sargent enters the studio of Carolus-Duran.

In New York, Theodore Robinson meets Winslow Homer and studies at the National Academy of Design.

James Abbott McNeill Whistler holds his first solo exhibition in London.

1875

In Paris, Cassatt exhibits at the Salon.

Sargent enrols at the Académie Julian. Thomas Wilmer Dewing also enrols, returning to this school where he was a student between 1870 and 1873.

John Henry Twachtman and Frank Duveneck arrive in Munich to study at the Royal Academy. They join William Merritt Chase who is already a student there.

The Art Students League is founded in New York.

1876

The second impressionist exhibition opens in Paris with nineteen artists.

Cassatt sends two portraits to the Paris Salon. It is the last time she participates.

Robinson enters the studio of Carolus-Duran where he meets Sargent.

Sargent meets Monet and Paul-César Helleu in April at the Gallery Durand-Ruel in Paris before travelling to the United States for the summer.

In Philadelphia, at the Centennial Exhibition, Chase wins a medal of honour for *Keying Up – The Court Jester* (Pennsylvania Academy of hte Fine Arts, Philadelphia), 1875.

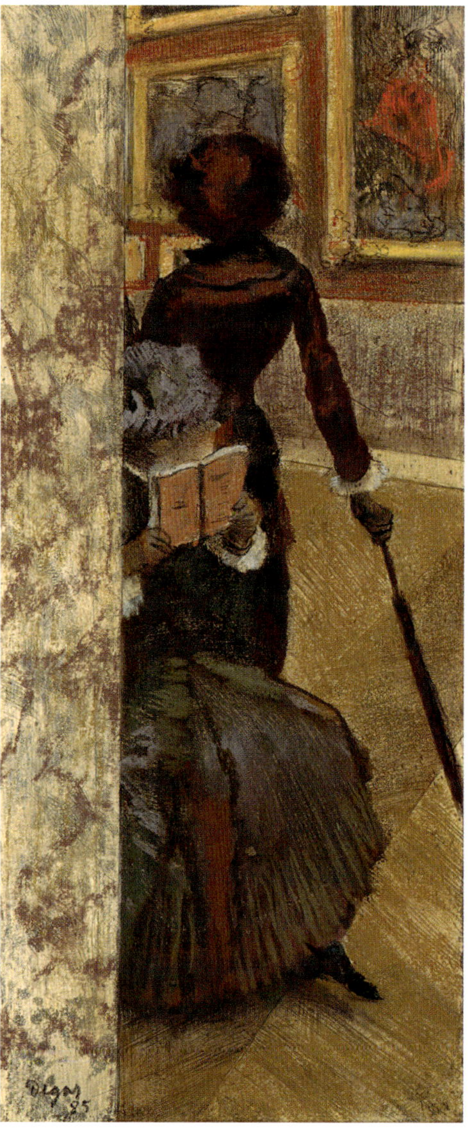

EDGAR DEGAS,
Mary Cassatt in the Painting Gallery of the Louvre, 1879–80
Pastel, over etching, aquatint, drypoint, and crayon électrique on tan wove paper, 30.5 × 12.7 cm
The Art Institute of Chicago, Bequest of Kate L. Brewster, 1949.515

1877

The third impressionist exhibition opens in Paris with eighteen artists.

When Cassatt's pictures are rejected for the Paris Salon, Degas invites her to exhibit with the impressionists in future shows.

Robinson and Sargent, both based in France, exhibit paintings at the Paris Salon. During this year, Robinson works in the artists' colony in Grez-sur-Loing and Sargent travels to Cancale in Brittany.

Chase, Twachtman and Duveneck travel to Venice.

In London, John Ruskin criticises Whistler's pictures, on view at the Grosvenor Gallery, and the artist sues for libel.

In New York, the avant-garde Society of American Artists is formed.

Dewing returns from Paris and settles in Boston.

1878

Sargent exhibits *En route pour la pêche* (*Setting Out to Fish*) of 1878 (see fig.2) at the Paris Salon and sends a similar work entitled *Fishing for Oysters at Cancale* (Museum of Fine Arts, Boston) to the first exhibition of the Society of American Artists in New York.

Sargent and Cassatt participate in the Exposition Universelle in Paris. One of Cassatt's paintings, however, is rejected by the jury.

In London, Whistler's suit against Ruskin goes to trial, and while the verdict is in his favour, it is a financial and critical disaster for him. Whistler publishes a pamphlet about the ordeal.

Chase returns from Europe and begins teaching at the Art Students League in New York.

1879

The fourth impressionist exhibition opens in Paris with fourteen artists including Cassatt, the first American. She contributes twelve pictures. Cézanne, Morisot, Renoir and Sisley do not participate.

Degas, Cassatt and Pissarro discuss the creation of a journal of prints to be entitled *Le Jour et la nuit* (Day and Night). It is never published.

Sargent wins an honourable mention at the Paris Salon.

Whistler declares bankruptcy in London and destroys several paintings to prevent them from being seized. He travels to Venice where he will work for more than a year.

Robinson travels to Italy where he meets Whistler before returning to the United States.

Twachtman moves to New York.

Edouard Manet receives attention among American critics when his *The Execution of Emperor Maximilian* of 1868–9 (Kunsthalle Mannheim) is exhibited in New York and Boston.

1880

The fifth impressionist exhibition in Paris includes works by Gustave Caillebotte, Cassatt, Degas, Paul Gauguin, Morisot and Pissarro. Cézanne, Monet, Renoir and Sisley do not participate.

Foreign artists are separated from French artists for the first time at the Salon. Robinson and Sargent participate. Monet exhibits in the Salon for the first time in ten years (and the last time).

Twachtman travels to Venice to teach with Duveneck where he meets Whistler.

In New York, Denis Miller Bunker participates for the first time in the annual exhibition at the National Academy of Design.

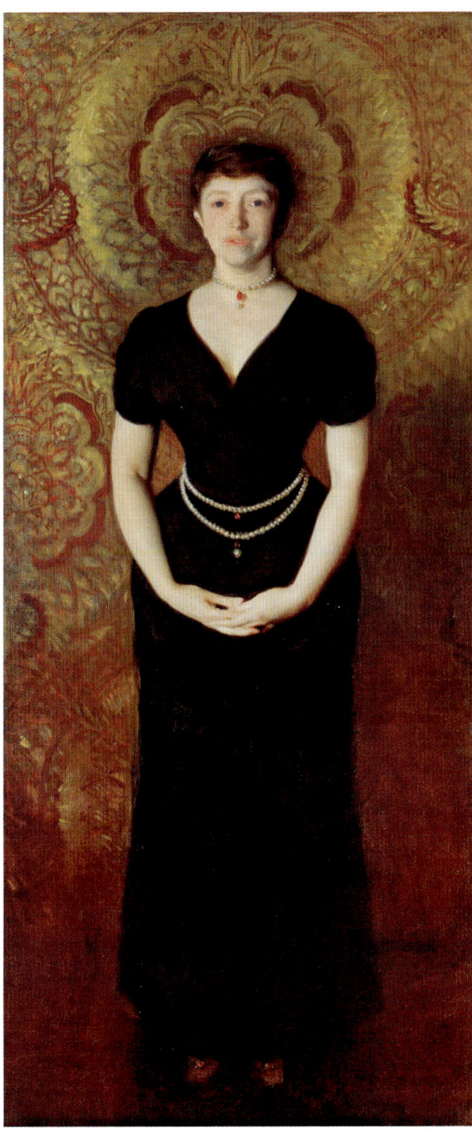

JOHN SINGER SARGENT,
Isabella Stewart Gardner (1840-1924), 1888
Oil on canvas, 190 × 80 cm
Isabella Stewart Gardner Museum,
Boston, P30w1

Dewing is elected to the Society of American Artists.

Frank W. Benson and Edmund C. Tarbell are students at the School of the Museum of Fine Arts in Boston.

1881

The sixth impressionist exhibition is held in Paris with thirteen artists. Cassatt, Degas, Morisot and Pissarro participate. Monet, Renoir and Sisley do not.

Chase wins an honourable mention at the Paris Salon. He travels in Europe where he meets Sargent and visits Cassatt.

The dealer Paul Durand-Ruel begins to purchase works by Cassatt who in turn acquires pictures by Degas, Monet and Pissarro for her brother, Alexander.

Sargent meets Whistler in Venice. Sargent and Monet exhibit at the Cercle des Arts libéraux.

Whistler's portrait of his mother, *Arrangement in Grey and Black, no.1* of 1871 (p.148) is displayed at the Pennsylvania Academy of the Fine Arts.

1882

The seventh impressionist exhibition is sponsored by Morisot and her husband, Eugène Manet. Cassatt and Degas do not participate. Monet and Renoir return.

Chase, Sargent and Whistler exhibit at the Paris Salon. It is Whistler's first participation since 1867.

Bunker studies at the Ecole des Beaux-Arts.

In London, Sargent exhibits at the Royal Academy. He and Whistler both hold exhibitions at the Grosvenor Gallery. Robinson returns to the United States.

1883

Chase, Sargent and Whistler participate in the Paris Salon. Whistler's

Arrangement in Grey and Black, no. 1 (p.148), earns a third-class medal.

In Paris, Tarbell and Twachtman enrol at the Académie Julian. Benson, Bunker, Chase, Dewing and Hassam travel individually in Europe. Durand-Ruel holds solo exhibitions of Monet and Pissarro. Whistler exhibits at the Georges Petit Gallery.

Monet settles in Giverny.

Alexander Cassatt commissions Whistler to paint a portrait of his wife. When Mary Cassatt visits Whistler's studio in London to see the portrait in progress, she writes 'as young Sargent said to Mother this afternoon, it is a good thing to have a portrait by Whistler in the family' (Mathews 1984, p.172).

The Glaspalast in Munich holds an exhibition of American art.

French impressionist art is exhibited for the first time in the United States at the *Foreign Exhibition* in Boston and in the Pedestal Fund Art Loan Exhibition in New York.

1884

Sargent, Twachtman and Whistler exhibit at the Paris Salon.

Robinson returns to France where he lives for the next eight years in Paris, Barbizon, Grez-sur-Loing and Giverny.

In Paris, Sargent meets the writer Henry James. Through the poet Stéphane Mallarmé, Morisot and Monet become closer friends.

Sargent exhibits at the Royal Academy in London. Whistler is elected member of the Society of British Artists.

Chase, Sargent and Whistler participate in the first exhibition of Les XX, a group of artists that is formed the previous year in Brussels.

Hassam settles in Boston after his marriage.

1885

In Paris, Sargent and Whistler exhibit at the Salon. Sargent and Monet exhibit at the Georges Petit Gallery.

Morisot begins to host weekly gatherings at her home for artists and writers including Degas, Mallarmé, Monet and Renoir.

In London, Whistler gives his 'Ten O'Clock' lecture several times during the year. He and Chase decide to paint each other's portraits. Whistler dislikes Chase's likeness of him, calling it a 'monstrous lampoon'.

Twachtman travels in Holland and Italy.

Robinson arrives in Giverny with a letter of introduction to Monet. Sargent visits separately, spending time with Monet.

Bunker wins an award for a painting submitted to the National Academy of Design and is elected to the Society of American Artists. He works as a teacher in Boston where his solo exhibition opens at the J. Eastman Chase Gallery.

Benson returns to the United States.

1886

The eighth and final impressionist exhibition includes seventeen artists. Cassatt exhibits six paintings (including *Children Playing on the Beach* of 1884, p.57 and *Young Girl at a Window* of about 1883–4, p.55) and helps to finance the exhibition along with Degas and Morisot.

Sargent, Tarbell and Whistler exhibit at the Paris Salon.

At the Ecole des Beaux-Arts in Paris, students are unhappy with the growing enrolment of foreign art students (including Americans).

Hassam arrives in Paris and enrols at the Académie Julian.

Sargent occupies Whistler's former studio in London and summers in the countryside. He meets Isabella Stewart Gardner, American patron of the arts and philanthropist (p.145).

Whistler is elected President of the Society of British Painters.

Monet sends ten works to the annual exhibition of Les XX in Brussels. Cassatt declines an invitation to participate.

In New York, Durand-Ruel organises a major exhibition of French art, primarily works by the impressionists. Cassatt is the only American included.

Twachtman returns to the United States after three years in France, settles in Connecticut, and exhibits at the J. Eastman Chase Gallery in Boston.

After three years in Europe, Tarbell begins teaching at the School of the Museum of Fine Arts in Boston.

1887

Both Sargent and Whistler are absent from the Paris Salon this year. Hassam exhibits *Une Averse – Rue Bonaparte* of 1887 (p.88). Cecilia Beaux and Robinson also participate.

Sargent and Auguste Rodin visit Monet in Giverny. Robinson and John Leslie Breck rent houses in the village with several American artists.

Monet travels to London and exhibits with the Royal Society of British Artists, thanks to Whistler.

In New York, Durand-Ruel stages another exhibition and holds an auction of French impressionist art.

Tarbell is elected to the Society of American Art and Dewing is made an associate of the National Academy of Design.

Sargent arrives in Boston where he meets Bunker through Gardner.

1888

Hassam exhibits *Le Jour du Grand Prix* of 1887 (p.89) at the Paris Salon. Sargent and Whistler both participate.

Monet introduces Whistler to Mallarmé who translates the 'Ten O'Clock' lecture into French.

Beaux travels to France, Italy, Belgium and Holland. In Paris the following year she enrols at the Académies Julian and Colarossi.

Bunker travels to the United Kingdom to spend the summer painting with Sargent. Monet visits Sargent in London.

Whistler sends works to the annual exhibition of Les XX in Brussels.

The St Botolph Club in Boston organises a solo exhibition of Sargent. This arts club will be a champion of Impressionism throughout the 1890s.

Durand-Ruel opens a gallery on Fifth Avenue in New York.

1889

Beaux, Hassam and Robinson exhibit at the Paris Salon. Sargent serves on the jury.

At the Exposition Universelle, American art receives praise, but critics comment on the strong French influence. Beaux, Benson, Chase (silver medal), Dewing (silver medal), Hassam (bronze medal), Robinson, Sargent (grand prix) and Tarbell all exhibit. Whistler decides to exhibit in the British pavilion after a disagreement with the American committee. Sargent and Monet visit the exhibition together.

Sargent receives the Legion of Honour.

Cassatt participates in an exhibition of 'peintres-graveurs' at the Durand-Ruel Gallery in Paris.

Sargent visits Monet in Giverny. Robinson and Breck are working in the village.

Dewing and Hassam are in New York. Twachtman chooses to live in rural Connecticut. Benson and Tarbell are teaching at the School of the Museum of Fine Arts in Boston.

1890

The Société Nationale des Beaux-Arts begins holding a second official Salon on the Champ de Mars, which favours newer styles and is more inclusive of foreign artists. Hassam, Robinson and Whistler participate in the traditional Salon while Sargent exhibits in the new one.

Cassatt and Morisot visit a large exhibition of Japanese prints held at the Ecole des Beaux-Arts. Cassatt encourages Morisot to exhibit with the Woman's Art Club in New York.

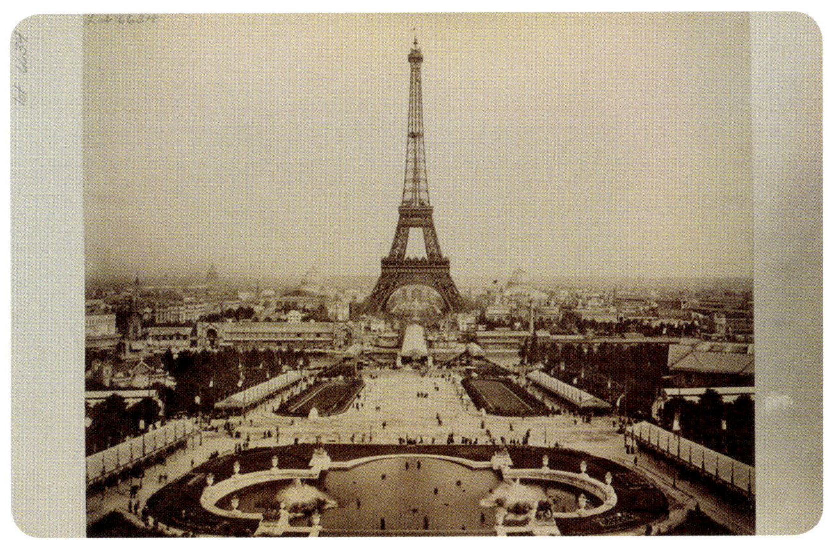

Eiffel Tower and Champ de Mars seen from Trocadéro Palace, Paris Exposition Universelle, 1889, unidentified photographer
Library of Congress, Washington D.C.

Monet purchases the house he has rented since 1883 in Giverny. Robinson and Breck are still living in the village.

Pissarro travels to London with his son Lucien and Maximilien Luce.

In Boston the St Botolph Club exhibits impressionist works by Breck, Bunker and Sargent. Bunker is married in October and dies in late December.

In New York, the American impressionists begin to garner attention: Tarbell wins a prize at the National Academy of Design. Robinson wins a prize for *Winter Landscape* of 1889 (p.77) at the Society of American Artists, where Hassam is elected a member.

1891

Sargent and Whistler participate in the Salon of the Société Nationale des Beaux-Arts.

In Paris, Durand-Ruel exhibits a series of Haystacks by Monet. His gallery also organises an exhibition of prints by French artists (thus excluding foreigners like Cassatt and Pissarro) and holds an exhibition of paintings by American artists, including works by Hassam and Twachtman.

The French Government purchases Whistler's *Arrangement in Grey and Black, no. 1* (p.148).

Monet's paintings can be seen in New York at the Durand-Ruel Gallery and in Boston at the J. Eastman Chase Gallery.

Chase begins the first of twelve consecutive years teaching summer classes in Shinnecock Hills on Long Island. Hassam begins to paint every summer in Appledore on the Isles of Shoals.

1892

Sargent and Whistler participate in the Salon of the Société Nationale des Beaux-Arts. Whistler receives the Legion of Honour and moves to Paris.

Dewing and Whistler each win gold medals at the International Exposition in Munich.

In Giverny, Monet marries Alice Hoschedé just days before Theodore Earl Butler marries Suzanne Hoschedé (Robinson attends both ceremonies before moving back to the United States).

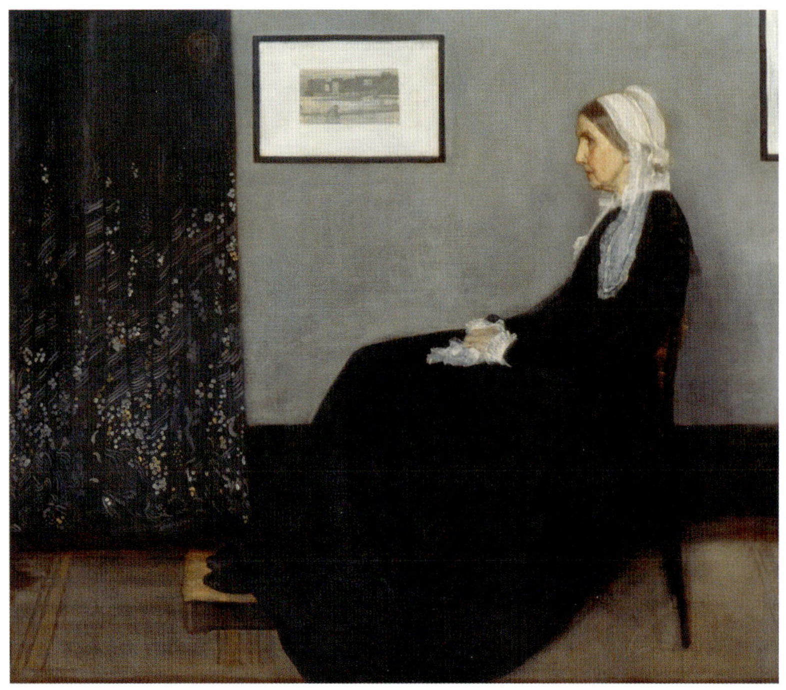

JAMES ABBOTT MCNEILL WHISTLER, *Arrangement in Grey and Black, no. 1*, or *Portrait of the Artist's Mother*, 1871
Oil on canvas, 144.3 × 163 cm. Musée d'Orsay, Paris, RF 699

In Brussels, Cassatt exhibits her colour prints with Les XX.

Monet has a solo exhibition at the St Botolph Club in Boston. Morisot has a solo exhibition at Boussod, Valadon et Cie in Paris.

Robinson returns to the United States and receives an award from the Society of American Artists in New York.

1893

In Paris, Durand-Ruel organises a large exhibition of Cassatt.

Monet buys land adjacent to his Giverny property and begins work on the water-lily pond. Morisot visits.

Sargent accepts a commission to paint murals for the Boston Public Library.

At the World's Columbian Exposition in Chicago, Beaux, Cassatt, Chase, Dewing, Hassam, Robinson, Sargent, Tarbell, Twachtman and Whistler all participate. Cassatt's mural is not well received. Hassam earns medals for oil painting and watercolour, exhibiting *Une Averse – Rue Bonaparte* of 1887 (p.88) and *Le Jour du Grand Prix* of 1887 (p.89) both works had already appeared at the Paris Salon).

Dewing exhibits seven paintings, including a portrait of Chase. Robinson exhibits several Giverny works, including *Winter Landscape* of 1889 (p.77). Tarbell exhibits three pictures including *In the Orchard* of 1891 (p.111). Whistler earns a gold medal.

Twachtman and Weir are included in an exhibition with works by Monet and Albert Besnard at the American Art Galleries in New York.

1894

Sargent and Whistler participate in the Salon of the Société Nationale des Beaux-Arts.

Cassatt acquires a chateau in Mesnil-Theribus, north-west of Paris, where she will live until her death in 1926. Pissarro begins working on colour aquatints with her.

Dewing arrives in Europe for a year, working occasionally with Whistler in London.

Sargent is elected an associate of the Royal Academy.

Hassam is named a member of the Munich Secession (Verein Bildender Kunstler Munchens) founded in 1892.

Beaux, Chase and Sargent exhibit at the National Academy of Design in New York.

1895

Dewing exhibits three paintings at the Salon of the Société Nationale des Beaux-Arts.

CHILDE HASSAM, *Columbian Exposition, Chicago*, 1892
Gouache 'en grisaille' over graphite on tan wove paper, 27 × 35.6 cm
Terra Foundation for American Art, Chicago, Daniel J. Terra Collection, 1992.38

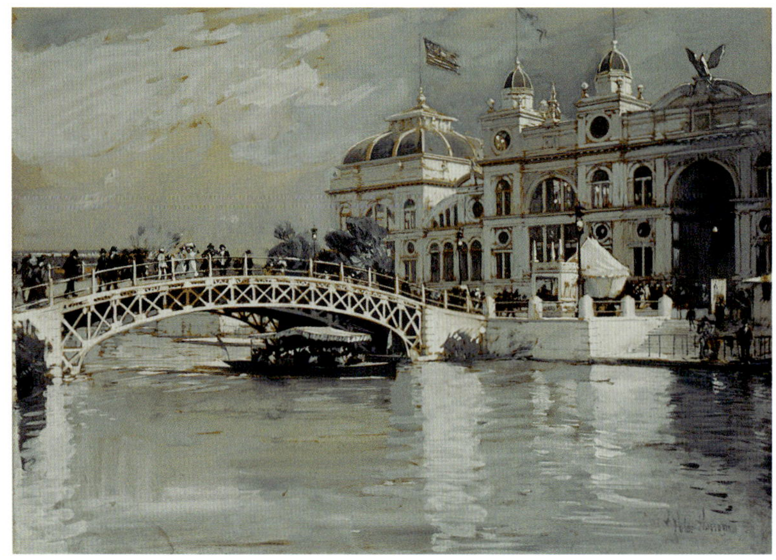

Through Lilla Cabot Perry, Pissarro meets several American artists, including John La Farge.

Morisot dies.

In New York, Cassatt has her first solo exhibition in the United States at the Durand-Ruel Gallery. Robinson has his first solo exhibition at the Macbeth Gallery.

Beaux teaches at the Pennsylvania Academy of the Fine Arts.

Twachtman visits Yellowstone Park. Hassam travels to Cuba.

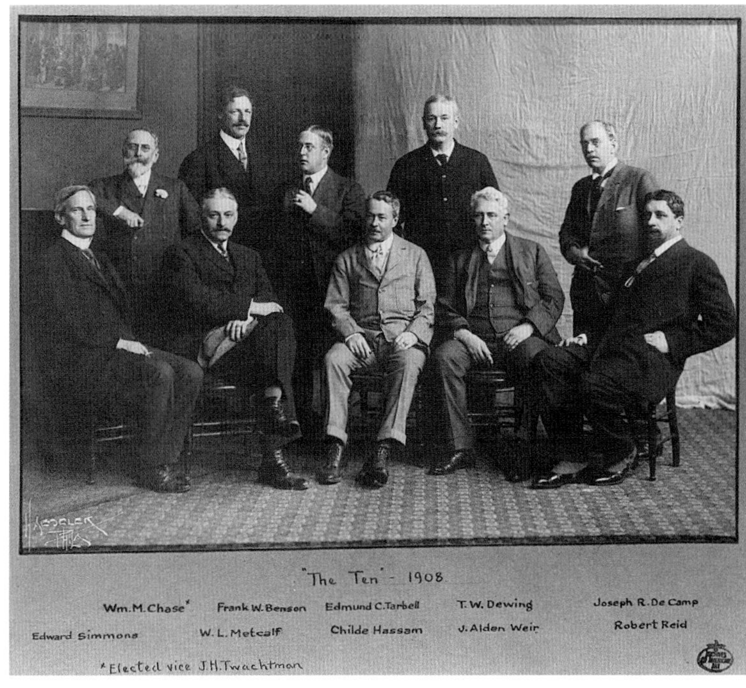

'The Ten', 1908, unidentified photographer. Macbeth Gallery records, Archives of American Art, Smithsonian Institution, Washington D.C.

1896

Beaux exhibits *Sita and Sarita* of 1893–4 (p.113) at the Salon of the Société Nationale des Beaux-Arts. Cassatt visits but writes that she is no longer interested in this kind of exhibition.

Beaux meets Monet and Perry in Giverny.

Sargent lends his studio to Whistler in London.

Chase spends six months in Europe, teaching a class in Madrid. Back in New York he opens the Chase School of Art.

Hassam has a solo exhibition at the St Botolph Club in Boston and exhibits 205 pictures at the American Art Association Gallery in New York.

Robinson dies.

1897

Hassam and Whistler participate in the Salon of the Société Nationale des Beaux-Arts.

Sargent is elected to the Royal Academy in London and the National Academy of Design in New York. He travels to Italy.

Pissarro is in London.

Ten artists resign from the Society of American Artists and become known as 'The Ten' or the 'Ten American Painters'. The group's members are Benson, Dewing, Joseph Rodefer De Camp, Hassam, Willard Leroy Metcalf, Robert Reid, Edward E. Simmons, Tarbell, Twachtman and J. Alden Weir. Chase joins the group a few years later. Despite differences in their art, critics associate the group with Impressionism. They exhibit together almost annually until 1919.

Beaux has solo exhibitions at the St Botolph Club in Boston and the American Art Galleries in New York.

1898

Hassam and Sargent participate in the Salon of the Société Nationale des Beaux-Arts.

Artist's model Carmen Rossi opens an art school in Paris where Whistler teaches. He and Sargent attend the opening of Monet's exhibition at the Georges Petit Gallery.

Sargent chairs the hanging committee of the Royal Academy. He exhibits with the Vienna Secession, a group that formed the previous year.

Cassatt travels to the United States for the first time in twenty years, exhibiting in New York and Boston.

The Ten American Painters hold their first exhibition at the Durand-Ruel Gallery in New York.

The Chase School becomes the New York School of Art. Hassam and Twachtman teach at the Art Students League.

Dewing has a solo exhibition at the St Botolph Club in Boston.

1899

Monet begins to paint the Japanese bridge and water-lily pond in his garden in Giverny and travels to London.

The Cincinnati Art Museum purchases *Pont Royal, Paris*, of 1897 by Hassam, his first painting to enter a museum collection.

Breck dies in Boston.

In Paris, Chase serves on the jury for the selection of American paintings to be included in the Exposition Universelle.

1900

American artists make an important showing at the Exposition Universelle in Paris. They include Beaux (gold medal), Benson (silver medal for *The Sisters* of 1899, p.118), Chase (gold medal), Hassam (silver medal), Robinson, Sargent, Tarbell and Whistler (who exhibits with the Americans). Sargent and Whistler are praised as leading expatriate artists, and both earn awards.

Bibliography

Anderson 1991
Benedict Anderson, *Imagined Communities; Reflections on the Origin and Spread of Nationalism*, revised and expanded edition, London, 1991

Atlanta 1999
Lisa N. Peters (ed.), *John Henry Twachtman: An American Impressionist*, exh. cat., High Museum of Art, Atlanta, 1999

Atlanta and Detroit 2003–4
Linda Merrill *et al.*, *After Whistler: The Artist and his Influence on American Painting*, exh. cat., High Museum of Art, Atlanta; Detroit Institute of Arts, 2003–4

Atlanta, Tacoma and Philadelphia 2007–8
Sylvia Yount (ed.), *Cecilia Beaux: American Figure Painter*, exh. cat., High Museum of Art, Atlanta; Tacoma Art Museum; Pennsylvania Academy of the Fine Arts, Philadelphia, 2007–8

Baltimore, Columbus, Worcester *et al.* 1973
Sona Johnston, *Theodore Robinson, 1852–1896*, exh. cat., The Baltimore Museum of Art; The Columbus Gallery of Fine Arts, Ohio; Worcester Art Museum; Joslyn Art Museum, Omaha; Munson-Williams-Proctor Institute, Utica, 1973

Baltimore, Phoenix and Hartford 2004
Sona Johnston, *In Monet's Light: Theodore Robinson at Giverny*, exh. cat., Baltimore Museum of Art; Phoenix Art Museum, Arizona; Wadsworth Atheneum Museum of Art, Hartford, Connecticut, 2004

Bedford 1994
Faith Bedford, *Frank W. Benson: American Impressionist*, New York, 1994

Benfey 1997
Christopher Benfey, *Degas in New Orleans: Encounters in the Creole World of Kate Chopin and George Washington Cable*, Berkley and Los Angeles, 1997

Berson 1996
Ruth Berson (ed.), *The New Painting: Impressionism 1874–1883: documentation*, 2 vols, San Francisco and Washington D.C., 1996

Boston, Chicago and Denver 1994–5
Erica E. Hirshler, *Dennis Miller Bunker: American Impressionist*, exh. cat., Museum of Fine Arts, Boston; Terra Museum of American Art, Chicago; Denver Art Museum, Denver, 1994–5

Boyle 1974
Richard J. Boyle, *American Impressionism*, Boston, 1974

Breeskin 1970
Adelyn Dohme Breeskin, *Mary Cassatt: A Catalogue Raisonné of the Oils, Pastels, Watercolors, and Drawings*, Washington D.C., 1970

Brooklyn, Chicago and Houston 2000
Barbara Dayer Gallati, *William Merritt Chase: Modern American Landscapes, 1886–1890*, exh. cat., Brooklyn Museum; The Art Institute of Chicago; The Museum of Fine Arts, Houston, 2000

Brooklyn, Washington and Detroit, 1996–7
Susan A. Hobbs (ed.), *The Art of Thomas Wilmer Dewing: Beauty Reconfigured*, exh. cat., Brooklyn Museum; National Museum of American Art, Washington D.C., Detroit Institute of Arts, 1996–7

Brownell 1879
William C. Brownell, 'Whistler in Painting and Etching', *Scribner's Monthly*, vol.18, no.4, August 1879, pp.481–96

Buckley 2001
Laurene Buckley, *Edmund C. Tarbell: Poet of Domesticity*, New York, 2001

Burns 1996
Sarah Burns, *Inventing the Modern Artist: Art and Culture in Gilded Age America*, New Haven and London, 1996

Burns and Davis 2009
Sarah Burns and John Davis, *American Art to 1900: A Documentary History*, Berkeley and Los Angeles, 2009

Burty 1878
Philippe Burty, *L'Eau Forte en 1878: Trente Eaux-Fortes Originales et Inédites par trente des artistes les plus distingués*, Paris, 1878

Charteris 1927
Evan Charteris, *John Sargent*, London, 1927

Chicago, Boston and Washington 1998–9
Judith A. Barter (ed.) *Mary Cassatt: Modern Woman*, exh. cat., The Art Institute of Chicago; Museum of Fine Arts, Boston; National Gallery of Art, Washington D.C., 1998–9

Child 1884
Theodore Child, 'Joseph de Nittis', *The Art Amateur*, vol.11, no.6, November 1884, p.123

Child 1887
Theodore Child, 'The Paris Salon of 1887', *The Art Amateur*, vol.16, no.6, May 1887, p.126

Clark 1924
Eliot Clark, *John Twachtman*, New York, 1924

Coffin 1889
William A. Coffin, 'The Fine Arts at the Paris Exposition', *Nation*, no.1268, 17 October 1889, p.311

Cousinié 2013
Frédéric Cousinié (ed.), *L'impressionnisme: du plein air au territoire*, Rouen, 2013

Cox 1889
Kenyon Cox, 'William Merritt Chase, Painter', *Harper's New Monthly Magazine*, vol.78, March 1889, pp.549–57

Crowninshield 1883
Frederic D. Crowninshield 'What Should the American Artist Paint?', *The American Architect and Building News*, 10 November 1883, p.223

De Fourcaud 1890
L. De Fourcaud, 'Les Artistes Américains', *L'art dans les Deux Mondes*, no.3, 6 December 1890, pp.23–4

De Kay 1891
Charles De Kay, 'Mr. Chase and Central Park', *Harper's Weekly*, 2 May 1891, pp.327–8

Downes 1892
William Howe Downes, 'Impressionism in Painting', *New England Magazine*, vol.12, no.5, July 1892, pp.600–3

Downes 1893
William Howe Downes, 'New England Art at the World's Fair', *New England Magazine*, vol.8, no.3, May 1893, pp.352–77

Dublin 2008
Janet McClean (ed.), *Impressionist Interiors*, exh. cat., National Gallery of Ireland, Dublin, 2008

Edinburgh 2003
Ann Dumas, *Degas and the Italians in Paris*, exh. cat., National Galleries of Scotland, Edinburgh, 2003

Edinburgh and Madrid 2010–11
Clare A.P. Willsdon, *Impressionist Gardens*, exh. cat.,

National Galleries of Scotland, Edinburgh; Museo Thyssen-Bornemisza, Madrid, 2010–11

Eiland 1996
William U. Eiland (ed.), *Crosscurrents in American Impressionism at the Turn of the Century*, Athens, GA, 1996

Fink 1990
Lois Marie Fink, *American Art at the Nineteenth-Century Paris Salons*, Cambridge, 1990

Fisher 2000
Paul Fisher, *Artful Itineraries: European Art and American Careers in High Culture, 1865–1920*, New York and London, 2000

Fowle 2006
Frances Fowle (ed.) *Monet and French Landscape: Vétheuil and Normandy*, Edinburgh, 2006

Frankfurt 2008
Ingrid Pfeiffer and Max Hollein, *Women Impressionists*, exh. cat., Schirn Kunsthalle, Frankfurt, 2008

Gallati 1995
Barbara Dayer Gallati, *William Merritt Chase*, New York, 1995

Garland 1899
Hamlin Garland, 'Theodore Robinson', *Brush and Pencil*, vol.4, no.6, September 1899, pp.285–6

Garland 1960
Hamlin Garland, *Crumbling Idols: Twelve Essays on Art Dealing Chiefly with Literature, Painting and the Drama* [1894], Cambridge, MA, 1960

Gellner 1983
Ernst Gellner, *Nations and Nationalism*, London, 1983

Gerdts 1984
William H. Gerdts, *American Impressionism*, New York, London and Paris, 1984 (reprinted 2001)

Gerdts 1993
William H. Gerdts, *Monet's Giverny: An Impressionist Colony*, New York, 1993

Gerdts 1994
William H. Gerdts, *Impressionist New York*, New York, 1994

Gimpel 1966
René Gimpel, *Diary of an Art Dealer*, New York, 1966

Giverny and Bordeaux 2008
Vanessa Lecomte (ed.), *Portrait of a Lady*, exh. cat., Musée d'Art Américain, Giverny; Musée des Beaux-Arts de Bordeaux, 2008

Giverny and San Diego 2007
Katherine M. Bourguignon (ed.), *Giverny impressionniste: une colonie d'artistes 1885–1915 / Impressionist Giverny: A Colony of Artists, 1885–1915*, exh. cat., Musée d'Art Américain, Giverny; San Diego Museum of Art, San Diego, 2007

Greenwich 2005
Susan G. Larkin, *American Impressionism: The Beauty of Work*, exh. cat., Bruce Museum of Arts and Sciences, Greenwich, CT, 2005

Greta 1891
Greta, 'Art in Boston', *The Art Amateur*, vol.24, May 1891, p.141

Hamel 1889
Maurice Hamel, 'Les écoles étrangères', *Gazette des Beaux-Arts*, no.31, series 3, vol.2, October 1889, p.368–88

Hamilton 1886
Luther Hamilton, 'The Work of the Paris Impressionists in New York', *The Cosmopolitan*, June 1886, p.240

Hartmann 1894
Sadakichi Hartmann, 'A Lecture on American Art', *The Art Critic*, vol.1, no.3, March 1894, pp.41–9

Helmreich 2003
Anne L. Helmreich, 'John Singer Sargent and the Conditions of Modernism in England 1887', *Victorian Studies*, vol.45, no.3, Spring 2003, pp.433–55

Herbert 1979
Robert Herbert, 'Method and Meaning in Monet', *Art in America*, vol.67, no.5, September 1979, pp.96–108

Hitchcock 1886
J. Ripley W. Hitchcock, 'French Impressionism', *Christian Union*, 22 April 1886, p.8

Hoopes 1972
Donelson F. Hoopes, *The American Impressionists*, New York, 1972

Igra 1999
Caroline Igra, 'Spatial Engineer and Social Recorder: Giuseppe de Nittis and the development of 19th-century cityscape imagery', *Van Gogh Museum Journal*, 1999, pp.94–103

'The Impressionists. II' 1886
'The Impressionists. II', *Mail and Express* (New York), 17 April 1886, p.5

Lausanne 2002
William Hauptman, *L'impressionisme américain, 1880–1915*, exh. cat., Fondation de l'Hermitage, Lausanne, 2002

Lavery 1940
John Lavery, *The Life of a Painter*, London, 1940

Leja 2000
Michael Leja, 'Monet's Modernity in New York in 1886', *American Art Journal*, vol.14, no.1, Spring 2000, pp.50–79

Lejeune 1879
L. Lejeune, 'The Impressionist School of Painting', *Lippincott's Magazine of Popular Literature and Science*, December 1879, p.720

Lochnan 1998
Katharine Lochnan, *The Etchings of James McNeill Whistler*, Chicago, 1998

Lochnan 2003
Katharine Lochnan, 'Whistler and Monet: Impressionism and Britain', in *James McNeill Whistler in Context: Essays from the Whistler Centenary Symposium. University of Glasgow, 2003*, Washington D.C., 2003, pp.45–64

London 2005
Erica E. Hirshler, *Impressionism Abroad: Boston and French Painting*, exh. cat., Royal Academy of Arts, London, 2005

London, Amsterdam and Williamstown 2001
Richard Brettell, *Impression, Painting Quickly in France, 1860–1890*, exh. cat., The National Gallery, London; Van Gogh Museum, Amsterdam; Sterling and Francine Clark Art Institute, Williamstown, MA, 2001

London, Boston and New York 2006
Kathleen Adler, Erica E. Hirshler and H. Barbara Weinberg, *Americans in Paris 1860–1900*, exh. cat., The National Gallery, London; Museum of Fine Arts, Boston; Metropolitan Museum of Art, New York, 2006

London, Paris and Washington 1994
Richard Dorment and Margaret F. MacDonald, *James McNeill Whistler*, exh. cat., Tate Gallery, London; Musée d'Orsay, Paris; National Gallery of Art, Washington D.C., 1994

Low 1908
Will H. Low, *A Chronicle of Friendships 1873–1900*, New York, 1908

Manchester, Wilmington and Chicago 2001
Susan Strickler (ed.), *Impressionism Transformed: The Paintings of Edmund C.*

Tarbell, exh. cat., Currier Gallery of Art, Manchester, NH; Delaware Art Museum, Wilmington; Terra Museum of American Art, Chicago, 2001

Mathews 1984
Nancy Mowll Mathews (ed.), *Cassatt and her Circle: Selected Letters*, New York, 1984

Mathews 1994
Nancy Mowll Mathews, *Mary Cassatt: A Life*, New York, 1994

Meixner 1982
Laura L. Meixner, *An International Episode: Millet, Monet and their North American Counterparts*, Memphis, 1982

Millet 1891
F. D. Millet, 'What are Americans Doing in Art?', *The Century Illustrated*, vol.43, 1891, pp.46–9

Montpellier and Grenoble 2007
L'Impressionnismes, de France et d'Amérique, exh. cat., Musée Fabre, Montpellier; Musée de Grenoble, 2007

Morris 2005
Edward Morris, *French Art in Nineteenth-Century Britain*, New Haven and London, 2005

New York 1903
Catalog of the Work of the Late John H. Twachtman, exh. cat., American Art Galleries, New York, 1903

New York 1986
Warren Adelson *et al.*, *Sargent at Broadway: The Impressionist Years*, exh. cat. Adelson Galleries, New York, 1986

New York 1989
Faith Andrews *et al.*, *Frank W. Benson: A Retrospective*, exh. cat., Berry-Hill Galleries, New York, 1989

New York 1991
Ulrich W. Hiesinger, *Impressionism in America: The Ten American Painters*, exh. cat., Jordan-Volpe Gallery, New York, 1991

New York 1994
Ulrich W. Hiesinger, *Childe Hassam: American Impressionist*, exh. cat., Jordan-Volpe Gallery, New York, 1994

New York 2000
H. Barbara Weinberg and Susan G. Larkin, *American Impressionists Abroad and at Home*, exh. cat., Metropolitan Museum of Art, New York, 2000

New York 2003
Warren Adelson *et al.*, *Sargent's Women*, exh. cat., Adelson Galleries, New York, 2003

New York 2004a
H. Barbara Weinberg, *Childe Hassam: American Impressionist*, exh. cat., Metropolitan Museum of Art, New York, 2004

New York 2004b
Bruce Weber and Sarah Kate Gillespie, *Chase Inside and Out: The Aesthetic Interiors of William Merritt Chase*, exh. cat., Berry-Hill Galleries, New York, 2004

New York 2006
Lisa N. Peters, *John Twachtman (1853–1902), A 'Painter's Painter'*, exh. cat., Spanierman Gallery, New York, 2006

New York 2010
Elaine Kilmurray, *Sargent and Impressionism*, exh. cat., Adelson Galleries, New York, 2010

New York and Chicago 1987
Patricia Hills, *John Singer Sargent*, exh. cat., Whitney Museum of American Art, New York; The Art Institute of Chicago, 1987

New York, Fort Worth, Denver and Los Angeles 1994–5
H. Barbara Weinberg, Doreen Bolger and David Park Curry, *American Impressionism and Realism: The Painting of Modern Life, 1885–1915*, exh. cat., Metropolitan Museum of Art, New York; Amon Carter Museum, Fort Worth; Denver Art Museum; Los Angeles County Museum of Art, 1994–5

Ormond and Kilmurray 2006
Richard Ormond and Elaine Kilmurray, *John Singer Sargent: Figures and Landscapes 1874–1882* (*Complete Paintings*, vol.IV), New Haven and London, 2006

Ormond and Kilmurray 2010
Richard Ormond and Elaine Kilmurray, *John Singer Sargent: Figures and Landscapes, 1883–1899* (*Complete Paintings*, vol.V), New Haven and London, 2010

Montclair and Paris 1999–2001
Diane Fischer (ed.), *Paris 1900: The 'American School' at the Universal Exposition*, exh. cat., Montclair Art Museum; Musée Carnavalet, Paris, 1999–2001

Pisano 2006
Ronald G. Pisano, *The Complete Catalogue of Known and Documented Work by William Merritt Chase (1849–1916)*, vols 1–4, New Haven and London, 2006

Philadelphia, Norfolk and Memphis 1989
Annette Blaugrund (ed.), *Paris 1889: American Artists at the Universal Exposition*, exh. cat., Pennsylvania Academy of the Fine Arts, Philadelphia; Chrysler Museum, Norfolk; Memphis Brooks Museum of Art, TN, 1989

Poe 1846
Edgar Allan Poe, 'The Philosophy of Composition', 1846, www.vahidnab.com/philocompo.pdf

Pollock 1988
Griselda Pollock, *Vision and Difference: Femininity, Feminism and the Histories of Art*, London 1988

Prettejohn 1998
Elizabeth Prettejohn, *Interpreting Sargent*, London, 1998

Pyne 1996
Kathleen Pyne, *Art and the Higher Life: Painting and Evolutionary Thought in Late Nineteenth-Century America*, Austin, 1996

Quilter 1887
Harry Quilter, 'The Royal Academy', *Spectator*, vol.60, 30 April 1887, p.591

Reff 1976
Theodore Reff, *Degas: The Artist's Mind*, London, 1976

Rewald 1946
John Rewald, *The History of Impressionism*, New York, 1946

Robins 2007
Anna Gruetzner Robins, *A Fragile Modernism: Whistler and his Impressionist Followers*, New Haven and London, 2007

Robins 2008
Anna Gruetzner Robins, *Walter Sickert: The Complete Writings on Art*, Oxford, 2008

Salem 2000
Faith Bedford et al., *The Art of Frank W. Benson, American Impressionist*, exh. cat., Peabody Essex Museum, Salem, 2000

San Francisco and Washington 1986
Charles S. Moffett (ed), *The New Painting: Impressionism 1874–1883: an exhibition*, exh. cat., 2 vols, The Fine Arts Museums of San Francisco; National Gallery of Art, Washington D.C., 1986

Seattle and Los Angeles 1980
William J. Gerdts, *American Impressionism*, exh. cat., Henry Art Gallery, University of Washington, Seattle; Frederick S. Wright Gallery, University of California at Los Angeles, 1980

'The Society of American Artists' Exhibition' 1892
'The Fine Arts: The Society of American Artists' Exhibition', *The Critic*, 7 May 1892, p.270

Strahan 1879
Edward Strahan, 'The Art Gallery', *The Art Amateur; A Monthly Journal Devoted to Art in the Household*, 1879, p.4

Toronto, Paris and London 2004
Katharine Lochnan (ed.), *Turner, Whistler, Monet*, Art Gallery of Ontario, Toronto; Galeries Nationales du Grand Palais, Paris; Tate Britain, London, 2004

Van Rensselaer 1883
Marina Griswold Van Rensselaer, 'A French Critic on Current French Art', *The American Architect and Building News*, vol.14, 20 October 1883, p.184

Van Rensselaer 1886
Marina Griswold Van Rensselaer, 'Pictures of the Season in New York', *American Architect and Building News*, vol.20, 21 August 1886, p.86

Washington 1993
Carolyn Kinder Carr *et al.*, *Revisiting the White City: American Art at the 1893 World's Fair*, exh. cat., National Museum of American Art and National Portrait Gallery, Smithsonian Institution, Washington D.C., 1993

Washington and Chicago 1987
D. Scott Atkinson and Nikolai Cikovsky, *William Merritt Chase: Summers at Shinnecock 1891–1902*, exh. cat., National Gallery of Art, Washington D.C.; Terra Museum of American Art, Chicago, 1987

Washington and Greensburg 1995
Tara Leigh Tappert, *Cecilia Beaux and the Art of Portraiture*, exh. cat., National Portrait Gallery, Washington D.C.; Westmoreland Museum of Art, Greensburg, PA, 1995

Washington, Houston and London 2009
Sarah Cash (ed.), *Sargent and the Sea*, exh. cat., Corcoran Gallery of Art, Washington D.C.; Museum of Fine Arts, Houston; Royal Academy of Arts, London, 2009

Washington, London and Boston 1999
Elaine Kilmurray and Richard Ormond (eds), *John Singer Sargent*, exh. cat., National Gallery of Art, Washington D.C.; Tate Gallery, London; Museum of Fine Arts, Boston, 1999

Weinberg 1991
H. Barbara Weinberg, *The Lure of Paris: Nineteenth-Century American Painters and their French Teachers*, New York, 1991

Wildenstein 1974–91
Daniel Wildenstein, *Claude Monet: biographie et catalogue raisonné*, 5 vols, Lausanne and Paris, 1974–91

Williamstown 1997
Marc Simpson *et al.*, *Uncanny Spectacle: The Public Career of the Young John Singer Sargent*, exh. cat., Sterling and Francine Clark Art Institute, Williamstown, MA, 1997

INDEX OF PEOPLE

The numbers in italic refer to illustrations.

EDMUND C. TARBELL, *In the Orchard*, 1891, detail (see p.111)

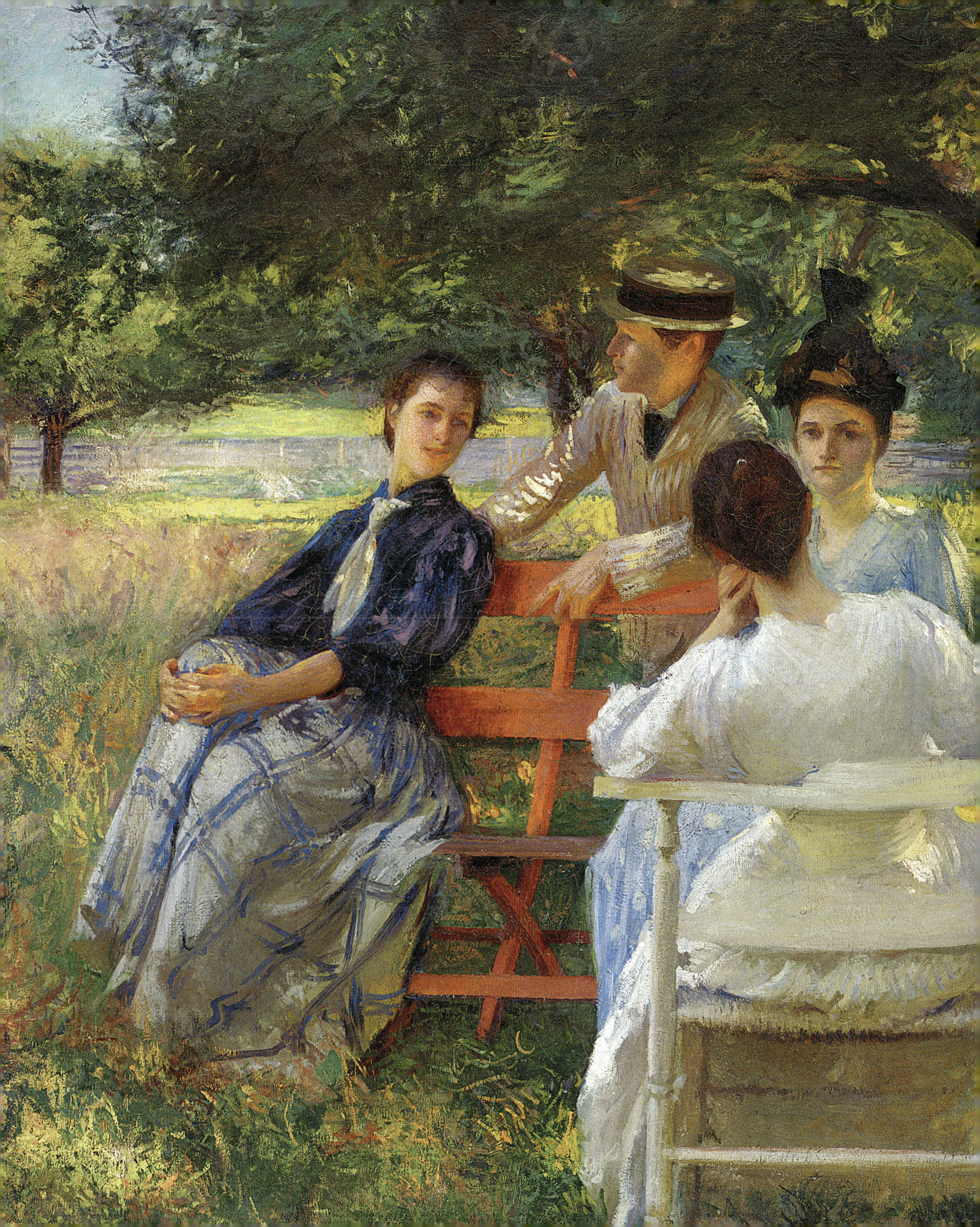

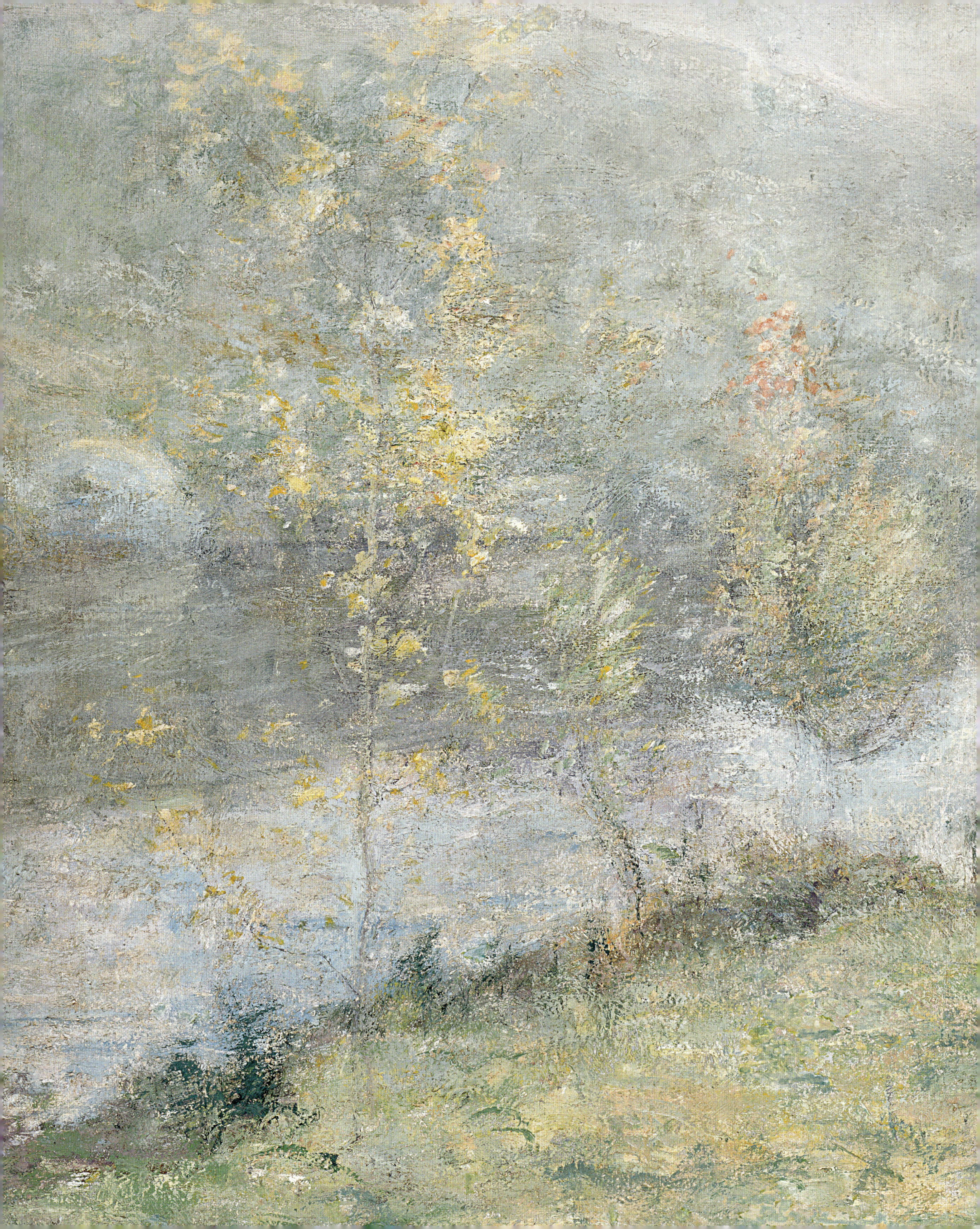

PHOTOGRAPHIC CREDITS

Every effort has been made to contact the copyright holder. If notified the publisher will be pleased to rectify any errors or ommissions at the earliest opportunity.

Atlanta, Gorgia
High Museum of Art: p.124

Bilbao
Museo de Bellas Artes de Bilbao: p.58

Boston, Mass.
Museum of Fine Arts, 2014: p.68, p.103, p.132 (detail)
Isabella Stewart Gardner Museum: p.39 (fig.12)

Brooklyn
Brooklyn Museum: p.104

Chicago
Terra Foundation for American Art: cover, p.31 (fig.8), p.40 (fig.13), p.44, p.51 (detail), p.59, p 63, p.64, p.65, p.67, p.73, p.77, p.78-81, p.83, p. 84-5, p.88, p.97, p.98, p.101, p.108, p.111, p.114, p.118, p.122, p.123, p.127, p.139 (11), p.148, p.157 (detail)
The Art Institute of Chicago: p.27 (fig.4), p.30 (fig.7), p.31 (fig.9), p.42 (fig.15), p.144

Edinburgh
National Galleries of Scotland / Photo: A. Reeve: p.12 (detail), p.72, p.82, p.112

Hartford, Connecticut
Wadsworth Atheneum Museum of Art / Art Resource, NY/Scala, Florence, 2014: p.130

Indianapolis
Indianapolis Museum of Art: p.119

Lisbon
Calouste Gulbenkian Foundation M.C.G. / Photo: Catarina Gomes Ferreira: p.48 (detail), p.74 & p.136 (7)

London
Tate, 2014: p.14 (detail), p.22 (detail), p.23, p.69, p.121

The Bridgeman Art Library: p.66, p.135 (1), p.139 (10), p.140 (12), p.143 (18), p.145

Madrid
Museo Thyssen-Bornemisza / Photo: Hélène Desplechin: p.61, p.106, p.115, / Photo: José Loren: p.56, p.76
Carmen Thyssen-Bornemisza Collection, on loan at the Museo Thyssen-Bornemisza / Photo: Hélène Desplechin: p.36 (detail), p.37, p.96, / Photo: José Loren: p.126

Milwaukee, Wisconsin
Milwaukee Art Museum / Photo: John R. Glembin: p.90 (detail), p.110

Montpellier
Musée Fabre de Montpellier Agglomération / Photo: Frédéric Jaulmes: p.52

New Britain, Connecticut
New Britain Museum of American Art: p.89

New York
Owen Yost Collection: p.41 (fig.14)
The Metropolitan Museum of Art, Dist. RMN-Grand Palais / image of the MMA: p.43 (fig.16), p.71, p.87

Northampton, Massachusetts
Smith College Museum of Art: p.99

Paris
RMN-Grand Palais (musée d'Orsay) / Photo: René-Gabriel Ojéda: p.62, p.113, / Photo: Hervé Lewandowski: p.29 (fig.6), p.140 (13), / Photo: Jean Schormans: p.148
Petit Palais / Photo: Roger-Viollet : p.53
RMN-Grand Palais / rights reserved: p.24 (fig.1)

Philadelphia
Pennsylvania Academy of the Fine Arts: p.40, p.100, p.125
Philadelphia Museum of Art: p.26 (fig.3), p.70

Portsmouth, New Hampshire
Portsmouth Athenaeum Archives: p.139 (9)

Providence
Museum of Art, Rhode Island School of Design / Photo: Erik Gould: p.32 (fig.10), p.45 (fig.17), p.75, p.117

Rochester, New York
Memorial Art Gallery of the University of Rochester: p.131

Salem, Massachusetts
Peabody Essex Museum: p.135 (2)

Toledo, Ohio
Photography Incorporated, Toledo: p.2 (detail), p.109

Tulsa, Oklahoma
Gilcrease Museum: p.120

Washington
Archives of American Art, Smithsonian Institution: p.136 (4, 5 & 6), p.140 (14 & 15), p.143 (16 & 17), p.149
Corcoran Gallery of Art: p.25 (fig.2), p.55
Freer Gallery of Art and Arthur M. Sackler Gallery Archives, Smithsonian Institution: p.139 (8)
House Collection, Dumbarton Oaks: p.60
Library of Congress: p.147
National Gallery of Art: p.45 (fig.18), p.57, p.102
Smithsonian American Art Museum: p.46 (fig.19), p.93 (detail), p.107, p.128, p.129, p. 157 (detail)

Water Mill, New York
Parrish Art Museum: p.95, p.105

Waterville, Maine
Colby College Museum of Art: p.94

All rights reserved: p.28 (fig.5), p.33 (fig.11), Courtesy of Jeffrey Brown, Brown Corbin Art p.135 (3)

JOHN HENRY TWACHTMAN, *Misty May Morn*, 1899, detail (see p.128)